Preface to Scripture

SOLOMON B. FREEHOF, D.D.

Preface to Scripture

NEW YORK

UNION OF AMERICAN HEBREW
CONGREGATIONS

Second Printing, 1957

COPYRIGHT, 1950, BY

UNION OF AMERICAN HEBREW CONGREGATIONS

PRINTED IN U. S. OF AMERICA

To
MY BELOVED
BROTHERS AND SISTERS

Editor's Introduction

WHAT," the reader may say, "another introduction to the Bible! There are so many of them." Yes, there are many introductions to the Bible, but very few from a Jewish point of view. What introduction to the Bible do we have which explains how the Masora was developed, the extraordinary technique devised by our forefathers for the meticulous preservation of the Bible text from generation to generation? Or which of the many introductions throws light on how our forefathers studied lovingly and interpreted and reinterpreted our Book of Books and used it as a basis for the creation of a whole literature—the Mishnah, the Talmud, and the Midrash?

Preface to Scripture by Dr. Solomon B. Freehof is planned, in the first place, to answer such questions. It is intended as a popular introduction to the Jewish Bible for the layman, and it will serve at the same time as a general introduction to our entire series of popular commentaries on the Bible initiated by the Commission on Jewish Education and published by the Union of American Hebrew Congregations.

This volume is divided into two books. Book One discusses such general questions as the intelligent reader will ask himself before reading the Bible. How was the Bible compiled? How was it preserved? How was it introduced into worship both Jewish and Christian? These and other significant questions are discussed by the author in an authoritative yet popular style.

Book Two, *Selections from Scripture*, constitutes a new experiment. For each of the books in the Bible the author gives a brief descriptive outline, stressing the significance of the main ideas of the book. Then follows a mosaic of verses which, although selected, is generally so constructed as to read consecutively. This is completed by a commentary on the verses chosen. It is hoped that the student will read these in the order mentioned and then return to the synopsis of verses. In that way he will get a clear concept of the message of each of the Biblical books. It is our further hope that by reading these mosaics of verses and such a chapter as "Treasures in the Bible," he will come tc feel the vital impact of the power of the Bible and will be stimulated to read it from time to time, using the Book of Books as our forefathers did, when in joy they studied the Song of Songs or in sorrow, the Book of Lamentations.

The book should be of help to youth and adult study groups and to our upper high school grades, who will find in the popular presentation in Book One, and especially in the "Selections" in Book Two, a genuine aid to an understanding of that work which constitutes the greatest contribution of the Jew to civilization.

EMANUEL GAMORAN

Acknowledgments

THE author acknowledges his great indebtedness to his colleagues, Drs. Bernard J. Bamberger, William H. Braude, and Barnett R. Brickner, for their editorial reading of the manuscript; to Dr. Emanuel Gamoran for his valuable criticisms and suggestions; to Mr. M. Myer Singer for the excellent format of the book; to Miss Sylvia Schiff for her careful reading of the typescript and the proofs; and to Miss Ruth Schulman and Mrs. Solomon B. Freehof for their great assistance in the preparation of the manuscript. He is grateful to the publishers listed below for permission to print quotations from their books, as follows:

JEWISH PUBLICATION SOCIETY, Philadelphia
    The Jewish version of *The Holy Scriptures.*

JOHNS HOPKINS UNIVERSITY PRESS, Baltimore
    Albright, William F., *Archeology and the Religion of Israel.*

HARPER AND BROTHERS, New York
    Kenyon, Sir Frederick, *The Bible and Archeology.*

AMERICAN TRACT SOCIETY, New York
    Robinson, George L., *The Bearing of Archeology on the Old Testament.*

SCRIBNER'S, New York
    The Encyclopedia of Religion and Ethics, edited by James Hastings, Vol IV, page 317. 1912.

                                                                S. B. F.

Introduction

INTRODUCTIONS to Scripture are a comparatively modern phenomenon. It is true that Don Isaac Abarbanel (at the end of the fifteenth century) wrote an introduction for each Biblical book to precede his commentary. But introductory books to the entire Scripture were relatively unknown in the past. Older Jewish scholars must have felt that the Bible speaks for itself. Actually the term "Introduction to the Bible" is a Christian term. The early Christian church needed such works because the Church was really introducing a book which was new to the Gentile world. Therefore, the Bible required general introductory explanation. In modern times, although the Bible had through many centuries become the best known and most deeply studied book in the world, a new need for introductions to the Bible arose. Modern critical study of the Bible arrived at entirely new datings for books in Scripture and a new concept of the ideas and the order of their development. The old mental picture of what the Bible contained was completely destroyed and a new one was created. Hence, the many modern introductions to Scripture (note: for a discussion of Scriptural introductions and the history of this type of writing, see Cornill, *Introduction to the Canonical Books*, pp. 3 ff.). These new introductions were, therefore, chiefly introductions to the literature of the Bible: the style, poetic and prose, as newly analyzed, and the dating of the various documents and their rearrangement into a new and modern literary history of Scripture.

Our purpose in writing an introduction to Scripture is different. We do, of course, need to include a study of modern critical analysis of Scripture and its findings as to Scriptural style and content and dating. But we have a much wider aim. This book is not written primarily for technical students of the Bible, but for the general reader, and indeed, also for those readers who have lost touch with Scripture and perhaps have never looked at a Bible except casually. Or if they have read the Bible to some extent, they have not read it deeply enough for the Bible to explain itself to them. The modern reader needs to be rewon to the enterprise of regular reading of Scripture. The philosophy and mood of Scripture must be made clear to him; its style clearly explained so that reading may become easy. The leading thoughts of the various parts of the Bible must be given clearly and, if possible, in the words of the Biblical authors themselves, so that the reader may recognize the ideas and their phrasing once he begins to study the Scriptural text. He should learn to appreciate the Bible and its place in civilization. He must be won again to a conviction of the worthwhileness of the enterprise of reading the Bible regularly.

Besides, there are many types of information which to a Jewish reader are especially significant. The modern Jewish reader should know how Jewish Massoretic science preserved the Bible text with such remarkable success; how the Bible became the parent of other great Jewish literatures, the Midrash and the Talmud, etc.; how the Bible was used in the synagogue and became a vital force in the development of Jewish worship. Therefore this book will deal with many subjects which have not been found generally in other Biblical introductions.

The entire book is divided into two parts of about equal length. The first part is a description and analysis of the Bible as a whole. The second part is an epitome (with commentary on parts of the Biblical text), book by book.

With regards to the title of the book, *Preface to Scripture*, the current Hebrew word for the Bible is *Mikro*, "The Reading," instead of the current English word *Scripture*, which means "Writing." If we used the correct Latinized translation of the Hebrew word *Mikro*, we would call the Bible "Lecture" (i.e., "The Reading"). So, for example, the fine modern Hebrew introduction to the Bible by Professor M. Segal of the Hebrew University is called *M'vo ha Mikro*, "Introduction to the Reading" (i.e., "Lecture" instead of "Scripture"). Yet the use of the usual English word *Scripture* (i.e., "The Writing") for Bible has plenty of warrant in Talmudic literature. Just as *Mikro* is used generally for the whole

Bible besides its specific usage for the Pentateuch, so *Kisvei Kodesh* and even *K'suvim* are used for the entire Bible in general, as well as specifically for the Hagiographa.

This book is part of a larger enterprise by the Commission on Jewish Education—a series of popular commentaries to the American English version of the entire Hebrew Bible. Of this larger task, the *Commentary on the Book of Psalms* has already been published, and the commentaries on a number of other books are approaching completion. May this great enterprise, of which *Preface to Scripture* is meant to be the introductory volume, continue to move toward completion and serve to win a new generation to the knowledge and love of the Book of books.

S. B. F.

Table of Contents

TABLE OF CONTENTS

PART TWO

SELECTIONS FROM SCRIPTURE

PART ONE

Preface to Scripture

CHAPTER I

The Book of Books

"SOME day I will read the Bible." Who has not expressed this wish every now and then? There is in the mind of most people a sense of unfulfilled obligation, of a task which has been neglected, an awareness of an opportunity for knowledge and moral help that has not been grasped. The Bible nags at the modern conscience.

Most people make two or three attempts to read the Bible but they fail to overcome certain initial difficulties and thus do not achieve the habit of regular study. At first glance the Bible seems to be an unattractive book. Its language, in any translation, is usually so old-fashioned that it takes some time before the reader can become accustomed to it. If the reader persists long enough to overcome the barrier of its old-fashioned style, he soon arrives at long, dull passages either of genealogies or of ancient laws which seem to be of interest only to the specialist. The magnificent passages are usually buried in great masses of dull material as a precious stone is often found imbedded in valueless mineral.

The Bible is not an easy book to read. Sometimes it demands a great deal of patience from him who would unearth its splendors. Older generations brought this patience and devotion to their reading of Scripture. They began with the conviction that it was the word of God and therefore deserved patient search and study. But modern people, who are less firm in their faith and are at the same time more impatient, do not have the will to persist in their reading until the difficulties are overcome and Scripture becomes for them a clear enlightenment and a constant joy as it was to their fathers. Former generations knew of the great value of Scripture because they read the Bible so much that the Bible itself revealed its treasures to them. But the modern reader, before he can be moved to exert the persistent effort required to become at home in Scripture, must first be convinced that Scripture is great enough to deserve his close attention and study.

It is difficult to give an adequate description of the influence which the Bible has exerted upon the life of the countless millions of individuals for whom it was the "Tree of Life." There is much to say, for there are many different ways in which Scripture has changed the life of humanity. It has aroused the minds and awakened the hearts of millions of people whose thoughts and feelings have never come to open literary expression. It has given them courage to endure, patience to wait, an understanding of the past, and hope for the future. It has renewed for them their allegiance to the enterprise of living. The great influence of Scripture has been written "on the tablets of the heart" of countless men, women and children. No one can read that magnificent record. But it is possible to describe at least the outward influence of Scripture, its influence on dramas which thousands have seen, its inspiration of books which millions have read, its influence on laws which nations have obeyed. These outward and visible things can be recalled to the mind of the reader.

In the year 1929, an archaeologist was digging in a pile of rubble at Ras Shamra on the northern coast of Phoenicia. He was fortunate to discover a large number of inscriptions in an ancient writing. When these inscriptions were deciphered, the scholarly world realized that an extraordinary find had been made. This hoard of inscriptions was the largest mass of ancient writing ever found in the near vicinity of Palestine. They were religious epics and ritual texts of the ancient Canaanitish religion and dated back thirty-two centuries, to the time of the Biblical patriarchs. These discoveries have thrown a new light on early Biblical history. They are now engaging the attention of many scholars who are working at translating and analyzing them, reconstructing from them the ancient Canaanitish religion and turning a new light upon the events described in the early Biblical history.

It is very strange that these vital records of the life and faith of people in one of the most important centers of civilization should have remained completely hidden for thirty-two hundred years. It is hard to realize that so large a portion of past history could have slept, hidden away from the eyes of man in a Rip Van Winkle sleep of thirty-two centuries. Yet actually such a complete historical disappearance is not at all unusual. It also happened in the case of the records of the Assyrian and Babylonian Empires. The Assyrian Empire was one of the mightiest military powers in the history of mankind. It was the heir of the great Babylonian civilization which had dominated the Near East for many centuries. This Assyrian-Babylonian Empire was the master of all the Near East for thousands of years. Its influence was immense in culture, religion, and government. Yet when Nineveh, the Assyrian capital, fell in the seventh pre-Christian century, most of the records of Assyria and Babylonia were buried in its ruins and remained buried for twenty-four hundred years. Until archaeologists discovered and deciphered the Assyrian and Babylonian records about a century ago, the world knew very little of this mighty empire except for a few references to it found in the Bible. The Persian Empire, which followed Assyria, was overthrown by Alexander the Great; his successors were overthrown by the Roman Empire. The world went through vast changes and the great Assyrian Empire was almost entirely forgotten until recent years.

The same is true of Assyria's great rival, Egypt. Its massive temples stood crumbling through the centuries. Their walls were covered with inscriptions, but the languages in which they were written were long forgotten. Egypt slept away the sun-drenched centuries, until about a hundred years ago, when the ancient writing was again deciphered and old Egypt awakened to life once more.

There are many such ancient empires which still remain asleep far away from the notice of living humanity. Their writings, their types of government, their legal systems might have had a valuable contribution to make to struggling humanity, but they disappeared and slept away their opportunity to influence the lives of men. It is in contrast with the strange disappearance of many great civilizations that we can appreciate the exceptional influence of the Bible upon the history of mankind.

The sacred writings of Israel, almost from the very moment that they were collected into a book, began to spread over the world. First through Greek-speaking Jews and then through Christians, the books were copied and passed from hand to hand and from language to language. They have never disappeared from the light of the sun. They have never passed from the notice of man. Babylonian and Assyrian astronomy and law, Egyptian ideals of life and the hereafter, the Canaanitish religious epics and rituals, the civilizations and the cultures of countless peoples vanished as a direct influence on the lives of struggling humanity. The Bible is therefore incomparable among the literatures of the ancient world at least in this regard—that it carried the influence of a noble religious culture as an uninterrupted transforming power through all the changes of human history for over twenty-two unbroken centuries. The legislation of the Biblical lawgiver, the ethical preachment of the prophets, and the songs of the Psalmist never disappeared from human notice and never ceased to influence the lives of men. The Bible is the steadiest and most continuous cultural influence in the history of human thought.

*   *   *

An American poet, G. E. Woodberry, speaking of the world influence of great books, said: "What holy cities are to nomadic tribes, great books are to the wandering soul of man. They are the Mecca of the mind." A book is written in a specific environment in the language of a specific nation by a human being of special temperament and individuality. It begins as a local, personal expression, but if the book is great it soon overleaps the national boundaries, the limits of the national language, and the specific characteristics of the individual author. When the book thus comes to be read in many languages by millions of people it becomes a bond among separate and often hostile nations. Though politics and economics and national pride may divide the peoples of these various lands, the books which they read in common are a bond of union tending to cancel the forces of national and racial division and creating a sense of fellowship. Because thoughtful people in the modern world have read in translation Russian and German plays, French and English novels, they share a world of ideals and understanding with each other and will never be completely separate. Great books are, as the poet said, a holy city of pilgrimage, a Mecca for the wandering tribes of men.

True as this is, that all great books tend to unite mankind, it is especially true of the Bible. The Bible exists in about eight hundred different languages and dialects. In far-off lands and isolated islands, where the great literature of Europe and America has never penetrated, people have read the Sacred Scriptures. The names of the Biblical characters, the story of their adventures, the words of Scriptures' prophets and the songs of its psalmists are known in almost all the languages of mankind. The Bible unites more people in a common spiritual and literary bond than any book ever written. There is hardly a tribe on earth or a little nation which has not read of the city of Jerusalem, that does not know the name of Moses and David. Every man has his own fatherland, but through the Bible little Palestine is the spiritual motherland of humanity. Aside from the doctrines of the Bible which teach the coming unity of all mankind and the equal dignity of every child of God regardless of race and color, the very fact that this vast variety of peoples has read the same book constitutes the greatest single spiritual bond in human history. The poet may well have said that the Book of books is the holy city, the Mecca of the mind of the separate tribes of mankind. Thus the Bible is not only the longest enduring, the most uninterrupted, but also the widest extending cultural influence in the history of man.

* * *

The fact that Scripture exists in over eight hundred languages means not only that it has a tendency to unify mankind, since this one great book is sacred to so many, but also that the Bible has become the mother of many literatures. Scores of tribes and nations never had a written language at all until the Bible was brought to them. In order to make the Bible available, their dialects were recorded for the first time; grammars were created for the first time, and many people saw human writing and printing for the first time when they looked upon the pages of Sacred Scripture. It was the Bible which created their written language.

A clear example of a literature created chiefly by the Bible comes from the fourth century of the present era. At that time the Germanic tribe of Goths was wandering over Europe and breaking into the Roman Empire. These Goths grew powerful in both the east and west of the Empire and their language was spoken not only in Europe but in northern Africa. Yet this barbaric people did not have a long history. Within a comparatively short time it was broken up into fragments; it was absorbed by other people, and its language rapidly disappeared. The Goths might well have been entirely forgotten except for a chance mention of their name among the names of other barbarians in the writings of some Roman historian. But the Bible happened to play a part in the history of these transient wanderers and won for them a permanent place in the history of literature. A Gothic Christian, Ulfilas, wanted to translate the Bible into Gothic. The Goths had a primitive alphabet, the "runes." This alphabet was insufficient to express the broad range of words and ideas in the Bible. Therefore, Ulfilas borrowed characters from the Greek alphabet and created an entirely new and usable method of writing. He then translated the Bible into the Gothic tongue.

This Gothic translation must have been copied many times and carried by the people on their wanderings. But as the people disappeared, the manuscripts disappeared, and all that is now left are some fragments of Ulfilas' Gothic translation of the Bible. In fact, this is the only Gothic literature remaining; perhaps that is all there ever was.

Yet this remnant of a Bible translation created long ago for a people now vanished has come to be of utmost importance in the modern science of comparative languages. Based upon the Gothic fragments, linguists have developed much of their theory of the ancient Germanic languages and their relationship to each other. Thus a Bible fragment not only introduced a wandering people to written literature but has preserved the memory of a vanished nation, and remains today an important monument in an important science.

It was not only among primitive and barbarian people that the Bible gave the language its first literary form, but even among the present-day people of Europe. The modern forms of their languages have in many cases come through Bible translation. The German language, for example, was spoken in many forms and dialects. There was no classic German in which the entire people could express itself. Its scholars wrote in Latin for the learned few. But when Martin Luther translated the Bible into German, he laid the foundation of the modern German language, creating new expressions, and choosing among dialects. Modern German literature, to a large extent, may be said to date from Luther's Bible translation.

This is equally true of the English language. English speech, wavering between Norman French and many dialects of Anglo-Saxon, burdened with irregular and chaotic spellings, received much of its modern form from the great Authorized Version of the Bible (The King James Version), which gave directions and standards and may be looked upon as the mother of the modern English language.

While a rich and a flexible language is an indispensable instrument for the creation of literature, it is far from sufficient. There first must be men and women who are eager to use the instrument, who feel impelled to attempt the difficult enterprise of literary creation. Perhaps the greatest service to literature which the Bible has performed is that it has awakened the hearts and minds of innumerable men and women and led them to literary expression. The Bible has been the vehicle of widespread education. The first schools were religious schools and the Bible was the text for instruction. Many colleges in our own country, for example, began as religious colleges, organized to meet the need for trained men to further the knowledge of the Bible among the people. But the greatest influence of the Bible in arousing literary creativeness is derived from the powerful combination of thought and style characteristic of Sacred Scripture. The Bible is unique among the great literatures of the world in the vivid simplicity with which it expresses its exalted ideas. The incomparable majesty of God, the inescapable impulse to moral nobility, the primacy of conscience, the dedication of a nation to exalted aims—some or all of these thoughts may have been expressed in other books in difficult and abstract language. The Bible uses the experiences of daily life, the sheep and the field, the farm and the trees, the hill and the still waters to voice the noblest ideals which man has yet grasped. Workmen and farmers, shepherds and merchants, humble men and women could grasp the exalted concepts of the Scripture. Were it not for Scripture's vivid simplicity, millions of men and women, who might never have attained to high levels of thought, have been stirred to meditate on profound thoughts and to understand exalted ideas. Scripture has raised the intellectual level of millions of men and has given them broader horizons.

Besides the profound simplicity of Scripture, which has brought great ideas within the reach of average men, the Bible has also a powerful emotional mood which has stirred their hearts to deep feeling and the hunger for self-expression. Any earnest reader of the Psalms could be stirred to emulation by the frank and vivid way in which the Psalmist poured out his inmost feelings. These ancient poets were echoed in innumerable lyric poems in all the languages and among all the people where the Psalms were read. Any reader of the Prophets who, like them, would have an impulse to public utterance, could not help learning from the powerful eloquence the art of bold and effective speech. Thus the Bible has stirred the imagination and awakened the creative impulse among men everywhere. It has not only provided the linguistic medium, but has given the emotional spur as well to much of world literature.

"The language of the Bible . . . has placed its indelible stamp upon our best writers from Bacon to Lincoln and even to the present day. Without it there would be no *Paradise Lost*, no *Samson Agonistes*, no *Pilgrim's Progress;* no Emerson or Thoreau, no negro spirituals, no Address at Gettysburg. Without it the words of Burke and Washington, Patrick Henry and Winston Churchill would miss alike their eloquence and their meaning. Without a knowledge of it the best of our literature remains obscure, and many of the characteristic features and qualities of our spoken language are threatened with extinction."– *The Bible and the Common Reader*, by Mary Ellen Chase, p. 9.

The dramas of Europe consisted for centuries of Biblical plays, such as the story of Creation and the story of Noah. As for the arts of painting and sculpture, if some vandal would be impelled to remove from the world's art galleries every painting and sculpture which has been inspired by a Biblical theme, we would be deprived of many of the works of Leonardo da Vinci, of Michelangelo, of Rembrandt and of a thousand others, and the world of art would be poor indeed. Or if there were expunged from the world's treasury of music all the oratorios, all the other religious music which has been inspired by Biblical themes, the world would lose half of its "voice of song."

The immense influence of the Bible has lain not only in the impulse which it has given to creative men: authors, artists and musicians, statesmen and founders of religions; it has taught the average man his speech. It has given vigor to every-day language and beauty to daily conversation. It would be difficult to count up how many phrases in our ordinary speech are derived from Biblical language. We speak of "my brother's keeper," or "a land of milk and honey." We say that a "man cannot live by bread alone." We describe the downfall of some proud person in the words, "how are the mighty fallen," or say, "pride goes before a fall." We describe a hairbreadth escape as "escaping by the skin of my teeth," or we say that we are glad that we are "in the land of the living." Or if we want to escape from an unpleasant circumstance, we wish that we had "the wings of a dove." We will describe a fruitful land by saying that "it blossoms as the rose." In all these instances and in innumerable others, we are using the language of Lawgiver, Prophet, and Psalmist. Our modern daily speech is enriched and beautified in more ways than we can ever trace by the speech of Scripture.

The influence of the Bible has been especially strong in creating historical movements. In Christianity, the Protestant Reformation gave a tremendous impulse to Bible reading. Men began to study the Bible intently and independently. They found in its texts not only personal guidance but new concepts of religion, new ideas for religious organizations. New religious denominations were founded upon Biblical ideas and even Biblical words.

The Bible was particularly influential in early American history. The Puritans derived their chief inspiration from Scripture. They lived in the Bible world. The Bible gave them names for their children. Palestine provided the names for the cities of New England. The laws of Moses were adopted in many of the Puritan settlements as the living law of the community. The Puritans in fact considered themselves children of Israel. The crossing of the Atlantic in flight from the tyrannies of Europe was to them the crossing of the Red Sea over which Israel fled from the tyranny of Pharaoh. This new land was the "promised land." And when the thirteen colonies began to organize for their independence, they frequently thought of this historic enterprise in Scriptural terms. Some even proposed as a coat of arms for the new nation a picture of Pharaoh drowning in the Red Sea and the motto: "Resistance to tyrants is obedience to God."

Beyond the literary, artistic, and political influence of Scripture is the influence of the ethical message which it conveys. Bible ethics created in brutal and barbarian cultures the beginnings of a social conscience and tamed the savagery of man. One need only contrast social service in the lands where the Bible has been a continuous influence with social service in those cities in Asia and Africa where the Bible has never penetrated. There the homeless sleep on the streets with none to give them shelter. The blind grope around in darkness with none to lead them. The sick and the lame have no help or healing. In the lands of Bible influence, the social conscience has grasped every instrumentality of science to fulfill the Biblical commands to shelter the poor and the homeless and to help the sick and the fatherless. Western science has been our instrument for social decency, but the impulse and the sense of responsibility come from Scripture.

A library of books would be needed to contain an adequate description of the influence of the Bible in all the many centuries during which it has reached the hearts and minds of men. Such books would contain the record of all the languages which found their first or their modern literary form through Bible translations. They would attempt to enumerate how many poets, painters, and musicians have done their greatest work when dealing with Biblical themes; which of the world's greatest art treasures are on Biblical ideas; how many poets writing on other themes have been aroused to their literary creativeness by the example of the dynamic self-expression of the Biblical writers. They would also tell how many organizations, religious and political, have been inspired by Biblical example; and finally, and this is truly incalculable, they would have to include the number of lives which have been consoled in their sorrows, encouraged in their tasks, and given a new impulse towards human comradeship or a new mission in public service through the reading of Scripture. The very sketching of such a list, questions which can never be fully answered, is sufficient to indicate that no literature ever recorded has touched so many lives, has ever created such artistic splendor, has ever evoked such moral grandeur as have Israel's Sacred Writings, the world's Book of books.

CHAPTER II

How the Bible Grew

STRUCTURE AND CANON

WHENEVER we wish to refer to the location of a passage in the Bible, we give its chapter and verse. Yet, if it would be possible for us, by some miracle, to speak with one of the great scholars of Talmudic times, and if we were to say that a certain Bible passage is in a certain verse and chapter, that great scholar would actually not know what we meant. No Bible that he would have ever seen would have been divided into chapters, nor would the sections have been divided into numbered verses. The division of the Bible into chapters and numbered verses seems so natural to us that we are surprised to learn that the division of chapters and verses was entirely unknown in Talmudic times, and in fact came into our Bible no earlier than the sixteenth century, and, furthermore, from Christian sources. Then how did they, in ancient times, divide Scripture so as to be able to refer to it and to its separate passages? What was the structure of the Bible in those days, and how much of their ancient structure is still used?

Scripture was first divided into its three main parts, the Torah, the Prophets, and the Holy Writings (Hagiographa). This major division is already referred to in the second century before the Christian era. The author of [the Prologue of] the Book of Sirach, which is very much like our Biblical Book of Proverbs, but which, as will be explained, is not now part of our Bible, says in his introduction that: "he had given himself to the reading of the law and the prophets and the other books of our fathers." Clearly, he already had before him three divisions of the Bible as we have today. However, since he refers to the third part of the Bible rather vaguely as "the other books of the fathers," it would appear that in his time this third part was not yet as definitely organized and fixed as to its contents as were the other two parts to which he refers specifically and definitely as the Law and the Prophets. It may well be, therefore, that the whole Bible, including this third part, was not yet completed in its present form.

This brings us to these questions: When was the Bible finished? How was it decided which books were to be included and which books omitted? The Talmudic literature records a great deal of discussion about certain individual books of the Bible, questioning whether they should be included or, as they said, "hidden away." We know that there are many books which might well have been included but which for some reason or other were "hidden away."

Fortunately for our knowledge of the history and literature of the past, many of the books which the ancient authorities had decided to put away were not entirely lost, as they might easily have been. They were preserved in Greek translation among the Jews in Alexandria, a great center of Jewish settlement and Greek culture around the beginning of the present era. These Jews also had a translation of our regular Biblical books, the translation known as the Septuagint, which means "the seventy," and refers to the fact that, according to tradition, seventy scholars collaborated in the work of translation. The Christian church, in its form of the Bible, preserves these books which were excluded from the Hebrew Bible. These books, together with the rest of the Bible, were translated from the Greek into Latin (the translation called the "Vulgate," which means the "common" or "popular" translation, from the Latin word *vulgus*, which means "a crowd" or "the people"). Therefore, to this day these "hidden away" books are part of the Roman Catholic Bible, and through the Christian church have been preserved for us.

The Protestant church in its early days was uncertain about including the Apocrypha (the "hidden" books). Some of the early Protestant churches did include it in the Bible, but in general it was excluded. Therefore the Protestant Old Testament is equivalent to our Hebrew Bible.

Among the books of the Apocrypha are the First and Second Books of the Maccabees, from which we get much of our knowledge of the struggle of the Maccabees against the Syrians, the Book of Sirach, which is a typical "wisdom" book (see Part Two, chapter VII), the Book of Judith, the Book of Tobit, the First and Second Books of Esdras (Ezra), and other books. Many of these books, it would seem, might well have been included in our regular Hebrew Bible, but for some reasons which cannot always be made clear with regard to every book, they were "hidden away." The Greek word for "hidden away" is still kept in the title for all these books, "The Apocrypha." These Apocrypha are sometimes referred to in Talmudic literature as the "S'phorim Chitsonim" (the "Outside Books").

It is clear, then, that the building up of our Bible involved a process of careful selection. There were a large number of books which could have been included but which were carefully and purposely excluded. How did those who collected our Scriptures proceed with their task? How did they decide which should be sacred books and which merely "hidden books" (Apocrypha)?

Those who arranged our Scriptures would sometimes object to the inclusion of a book on the ground that the book is inconsistent internally. For example, they objected to the Book of Koheleth on the ground that "its words contradicted each other." They raised the same objection also to the Book of Proverbs. But these objections were often raised by a few scholars against a book which the majority of scholars were inclined to include in Scripture. It was possible to explain away the various internal contradictions and also the contradictions against some statements in earlier books. Having explained away the contradictions, the book was admitted to the group of sacred books.

They had, of course, a more fundamental test as to whether or not a book was admissible. They would come to a decision as to whether certain debatable books were or were not written "by the Holy Spirit," that is to say, whether they were truly inspired books and hence belonged in Scripture (Tos. Yadaim II, 14). When, after debate, they decided that the book was written by the Holy Spirit, that is it was inspired, they included it in Scripture. Thus, for example, refuting the objections of some scholars that the Song of Songs, which seems to be a series of human love songs, was not written by the Holy Spirit, they decided that it indeed was so inspired and was "very holy" (m. Yadaim III, 5).

This test of whether a book was inspired by the Holy Spirit or not was the real measuring rod which the scholars used to decide whether a book should be admitted in the Bible or not. It was a practical test in spite of the apparent vagueness of the idea. It was practical because of a definite theory that they held. They believed, of course, that Moses was a prophet, and sometimes they even said that Abraham was a prophet. Therefore they believed that all the books which belong in the Bible were written by prophets who were inspired by the Holy Spirit. Since, they stated, the prophets Haggai, Zechariah and Malachi were the last of the prophets, and that after their time the direct prophetic inspiration by the Holy Spirit ceased, hence all the books which were clearly written after that time did not belong in Sacred Scripture. A book like the Book of Job, which modern scholarship would say was written more than a century after these last prophets, could nevertheless be included because the book is not dated and they believed that Job lived in very ancient times. They said, indeed, that the book was written by Moses the Prophet. Hence, being written by Moses who, being a prophet, was inspired by the Holy Spirit, the Book of Job belongs in Scripture. But a book like Ben Sirach, which, although judging by its contents alone could well be included in Scripture, dates itself as having been written in the Greek period after the age of prophecy, could not have been written by the Holy Spirit and had to be excluded. Hence, in general, we might say that all books which they knew to have been late in authorship they excluded. Other books which they debated were considered to have been written early enough to have been inspired, but they debated on other grounds, namely, as to whether their contents indicated their sacredness or whether their words were self-contradictory.

The early Christian church used a very convenient word to explain the admissibility or the inadmissibility of a book into Holy Scripture. It spoke of the "canon" of Scripture. The word "canon" means a "rod," a measuring rod. Thus modern scholars will speak of the ancient discussions as to the canonicity of a certain book, namely, its right to be admitted in the Bible. The Bible itself will be referred to as the Canon of Sacred Scripture– in other words, the books which come under the rule of admissibility. In a similar sense the term is extended to refer to those laws which are considered authentic in religious legislation. Hence church law is called "canon law." And in church history those clergymen who live in a cathedral house under the rule of the church law are called "canons."

There is no Hebrew word corresponding to the words *canon* and *canonical*, though, of course, the scholars who arranged the Bible had the idea or the thought of "canonical." They used a phrase which is meant to be its equivalent, but the phrase is a very strange one to us. They said frequently that "holy books defile the hands" (m. Yadaim III, 5), or, when they wanted to say that a certain book was not sacred, they would dismiss it with the statement that it did not defile the hands (*ibid.*).

It is a little difficult to explain how that phrase, "to defile the hands," came to mean what we now call "canonical." When hands were defiled through ritual impurities they required formal washing. The rabbis meant, therefore, that the touching of sacred books required washing of the hands. They had a general practice, or precedent, for the practice of washing the hands after touching sacred objects. For example, the high priest on the Day of Atonement, when he put on his various types of sacred garments, was required to wash his hands after handling them. This was a symbol of their sacredness. Applying it as a test for sacred books, they accomplished two purposes. First, they guaranteed against careless and irreverent handling. Second, they indicated that the books were so sacred that whoever touched them could not then proceed to touch ordinary profane objects without making a distinction by washing his hands. At all events, this was their phrase which is equivalent to our modern phrase, "canonical." If a book were sacred, it required a ritual washing of the hands after one touched it and before one touched any other object.

The Tosefta (an early Talmudic book parallel to the Mishnah) uses the phrase "to defile the hands" in the following quotation: "The blank margins of books and the books of the heretical sects do not defile the hands. The books of Ben Sirach and all the books that were written after them do not defile the hands" (Tosefta Yadaim II, 13). This passage indicates that the phrase "to defile the hands" describes the sacredness of a Biblical book. It also indicates that the date of a book's composition was a test of its admissibility into the Bible.

* * *

As to the time when the various parts of the Bible were put together and declared sacred, that is a subject of disagreement among modern scholars. The modern critical discussion of the growth of the Bible begins with the rise of the early documents called *E* and *J*, etc. (see Part One, chapter VI). It is sufficient for our purpose if we begin, not with the composition of the books themselves, but with the completed books and ask when they were put together with other books to form our present Bible.

In the Book of Nehemiah, chapters 8-10, we are told that all the people gathered to hear the reading of the Torah by Ezra the Scribe and accepted it in solemn covenant and signed their names as an evidence of the covenant. While certain modern scholars deny that the book which Ezra read in the presence of the people was the whole Torah, most traditional opinion says that it was, and therefore we may say that the "canon" of the Torah was completed at or near the time of Ezra, that is in the fifth century of the pre-Christian era. As for the canon of the Prophets, it is possible to date that with a fair amount of exactitude. The Book of Daniel, which is prophetic in nature (see Part Two, chapter IX) might well have been included among the Prophets. The fact that it was not so included would indicate that the prophetic canon had already been completed by the time this book was written. An analysis of the prophecies in the last part of Daniel makes it possible to date this book at about 166 B.C.E., just before Judas Maccabeus cleansed the temple of its defilement. Therefore most scholars agree that the prophetic canon was completed before the writing of the Book of Daniel, about 165 B.C.E. The last of the Prophets, Malachi, ends with this sentence, "Remember the law of Moses, My servant, which I commanded unto him in Horeb for all Israel, before I will send you Elijah the Prophet," etc. This sentence seems to be a reference to the canonizing of all the Prophets together with the Torah since this sentence, referring to both, seems to be a closing sentence for both parts of Scripture.

As for the third part of the Bible, the Hagiographa, beginning with Psalms and ending with Chronicles, since Sirach, in the middle of the second pre-Christian century, refers to them in rather vague terms as "others who have followed their steps" (i.e., "who have followed" the Law and the Prophets), it may well be assumed that in his day there was already a collection of these other books, but that this collection was not yet formally accepted as part of Holy Scripture. Since there was still discussion about some of the books in the time of Rabbi Akiba in the second century of the present era, it may be that this third part of the Bible was not definitely fixed and accepted as a whole until that late date.

As for the order of the separate books within these three divisions, there was no longer any doubt concerning the order of the books in the Torah after the time of Ezra and Nehemiah, but there was some disagreement as to the order of the books in the Prophets and the Hagiographa. For example, the Talmud (b. Baba Bathra 14b) quotes an earlier source which gives the order of the Prophets differently from the order that we have in our present Hebrew Bible. The three major prophets are given in the order Jeremiah, Ezekiel and Isaiah, whereas our present order is Isaiah, Jeremiah and Ezekiel.

The order of the Hagiographa which the Talmud gives is considerably different from ours. It begins with Ruth, Psalms, Job, Proverbs, Ecclesiastes, Song of Songs, Lamentations, Daniel, Esther, Ezra, and Chronicles, whereas our order is Psalms, Proverbs, Job, Song of Songs, Ruth, Lamentations, Ecclesiastes, Esther, Daniel, Ezra, and Chronicles. There is a still greater variation in the ancient Greek translation of the Bible, a variation which breaks over the borders of the three main divisions of Scripture. Ruth is not in the Hagiographa but among the earlier prophets following the Book of Judges, since Ruth was deemed to have been written in the days of the judges. Chronicles follows Kings since it was deemed to be the completion of the history in the Books of Kings. Lamentations is also not in the Hagiographa, but follows Jeremiah, since he was said to have been its author. Daniel, who was considered a prophet, follows Ezekiel. Furthermore, as has been mentioned above, the Apocrypha are included in the Greek Bible. Also the Prophets are the third division in the Greek Bible. Our present Christian English Bible follows the same order as the Greek translation. This accounts for its difference from our Hebrew Bible as to the order of the books. The only difference between the Protestant English Bible and the Greek and Catholic Bibles as to contents is that the Apocrypha is omitted from the former.

*   *   *

Within the books themselves there are certain subdivisions, especially in the Torah. In the Torah scroll used in the synagogue, the Five Books are separated from each other by four blank lines. Within each book there are certain paragraphs varying in length. They are of two types, those paragraphs which end in an open line and those paragraphs which end in a closed space, that is in which the new paragraph begins after some space on the same line. There are two hundred and ninety-eight of the open paragraphs and three hundred and seventy-nine of the closed paragraphs. The Masora, the system of statistics which guards the text from any change (see Part One, chapter III), counts these paragraphs carefully for each book. Thus the Masora at the end of Genesis says, "The open paragraphs in Genesis are forty-three and the closed paragraphs are forty-eight."

Beyond these there are no marks or divisions except for the "Taggin," the little decorative strokes on the tops of certain letters. There are no vowels or musical accents or punctuation marks in the Torah. Any use of punctuation in the Torah scroll makes it unfit for use in the synagogue service.

In the printed Pentateuchs there are other divisions. Since the Torah is read through in the synagogue once every year, it is divided into fifty-four portions, called *Sedras* (the Spanish-Portuguese Jews call them Parashiyos). In leap years all the fifty-four portions are needed, but in ordinary years certain of the weekly portions are combined so that two of them are read on one Sabbath. The custom of reading the Bible through every year in the synagogue originated in Babylon, but in Palestine the custom was to read it through in three years. Hence there are divisions (called *S'dorim*), generally one hundred fifty-four, dividing the Torah for a three-year reading. Each one of the Sedras of the annual cycle of Torah reading (according to the Babylonian and our present custom) has its own name, taken usually from the important word in the first sentence of the portion. Thus, the first portion is called *B'reshis*, the same name as the entire book ("In the beginning"). The second portion is called "Noah" (Genesis 6:9). The third weekly portion goes by the name of *Lech L'cho*, which means "Go thou," since its opening sentence reads: "And God said to Abraham, 'Go thou from thy land.' "

Since in all Orthodox congregations seven people are called up to the Torah on the Sabbath, the weekly portion is subdivided into seven parts in the printed Bible and marked second, third, etc.

This naming of each weekly portion gives the Jewish calendar a certain advantage of convenience. While the Jewish calendar has no name for the days of the week (except for the Sabbath, and Friday, which is called "the eve of the Sabbath"), it has, however, names for the various weeks, which no other calendar has. In an old-fashioned Hebrew letter, the date may be given either by the day of the month as in English letters, or the week itself may be identified. Thus a letter may be dated "the second day of the week of Noah," or "the third day of the week of 'Go Thou.'"

As far as verses are concerned, the Talmudic literature refers constantly to them. But we have no way of knowing to what extent those verses were the same as what we call "verses" in our present Bible. The natural division would be to call every sentence a verse, but it happens that some of the verses in our present Bible are half-sentences and some contain more than one sentence. The Talmudic authorities themselves were uncertain about verse division since it is difficult to know where a sentence, especially a long sentence, should be divided. Thus the Talmud (b. Kiddushin 30b) in discussing the number of verses found in the Torah says, "we are not expert in the matter of verse division."

Of course in the poetic books, where the poetic structure would indicate the end of a line, it is generally easy to divide the text into sentences, but in the prose books of the Bible it is often difficult. Hence we cannot tell to what extent their verses and our verses coincide. Certainly they did not number the verses as we number them now. Obviously, verses could not be numbered unless the text were first divided into chapters so that one would know where to begin numbering and where to end; as for chapters, they did not have them either in ancient times.

The chapters, and therefore the numbered verses in each chapter, designations which are characteristic of all modern Bibles, came into the Hebrew Bible from Christian sources. In the Middle Ages the Church forced upon the Jews of Europe the task of public disputations with Christian clergy as to the relative merits of Judaism and Christianity. The disputations were, of course, based largely on the Bible, the Christians claiming that many passages in the Old Testament prophesied the events of the New Testament.

This the Jewish scholars denied. In these disputations it was frequently necessary to refer to specific verses, and it became convenient to refer to the verses in such a way that the Christian clergy should know which verse was meant. Of course the Jewish disputant also had to be able to find, quickly, the verse to which the Christian disputant referred. Now the Vulgate, the Latin Bible, which was chiefly used in these disputations, had been divided into chapters and verses as early as the fourteenth century. Clearly then the Jewish scholars were compelled to have a similar division in order not to be at a disadvantage in referring to Biblical passages. The Christians not only had the convenience of having their Bible divided into chapters and verses, they also had concordances of Scripture, books in which all the verses of Scripture were arranged alphabetically by their important words and their location given according to chapter and verse. There was a concordance of the Vulgate which was written in 1244. With the use of this concordance any Christian disputant could look up a certain word and refer to all the places in the Bible where that word was found. Therefore a Jewish scholar, Isaac Nathan, of Arles, in southern France, wrote in 1437-45 a Hebrew concordance, and in this concordance, of course, he referred to the passages by chapter and numbered verse. This was the first use of chapter and numbered verse in Hebrew Biblical literature. From there it passed into the Hebrew Bibles, and all Hebrew Bibles today are marked by chapter and verse.

ChAPTER III

How the Bible Was Preserved

MANUSCRIPT AND MASORA

THE art of printing revolutionized the world of books. First of all, it made books plentiful. It was possible now to save the laborious task of copying every letter by hand. Once the book was set up in type, thousands of copies could be run off the presses. Books naturally became cheaper. Hundreds of thousands of people could borrow or own books, and the joys and the advantages of reading, instead of being the privilege of the chosen few, became the privilege and the birthright of millions.

Printing made another great change in the world of books. Books became not only plentiful and therefore cheap, they also became much more exact than they had ever been before. It is not very often that we come across an error in a printed book nowadays. When we do we are always surprised. Of course, during the hand-work stage of the making of a modern book, when the type is set up either by hand (foundry type) or, in the faster way, by machine (linotype, intertype, or monotype) which has a keyboard similar to a typewriter, errors can occur. But books are rarely printed just as they are first set up. Proof sheets are made and these are carefully proofread and the errors are indicated. Of course, even the proofreading is not a mechanical process but depends upon human beings who are always liable to error. But after a book has been proofread a number of times by different people, most of the printing errors are discovered, and after all the corrections are made, the book is printed. If the proofreading is exact, as it is most of the time, every one of the thousands of copies which are printed are all correct. No possible error can creep in. One can rely almost completely on the correctness of the text in a printed book.

But a written book, a manuscript, is all handwork. The scribe either takes down the dictation of the author or copies it from the author's manuscript. Manuscripts in the past were not as clear as modern manuscripts are because they were not typewritten but handwritten. The author himself may have made many mistakes when he wrote his book, as his hand worked fast trying to keep up with his mind. He may have corrected certain words and forgotten, as authors frequently do, to cross out the words which he meant to supplant. The scribe would therefore find both phrases, the original wrong one and the new right one, and often would copy both. Or the author could have made a mistake in numbering certain pages and thus one large section would come in the wrong place and would make no sense to the reader. There are many such errors that could creep into the author's manuscript.

The scribe, too, is prone to error, and the larger the manuscript the more opportunity for mistakes there are. It is of interest to all readers of ancient books to know of the types of mistakes which not only can easily occur but have occurred time and time again in ancient manuscripts. One frequent error may be called the error of sight. The scribe's eyes were misled as he glanced at the manuscript which he was copying. This frequently happened when two lines, one after another, had the same word in them. The scribe, meaning to look at line six, saw the same word in line seven and copied line seven instead of line six. Then, often, if he realized his mistake after he had copied line seven, he would write in line six after line seven so that the line would not be lost. This created even greater confusion for the reader and the next scribe.

Another error, besides the error of sight, is the error of memory. In many books there are passages which resemble each other. These passages may occur in different parts of the book. If the book happened to be a well-known one which had been frequently read and studied, the scribe as he looked at the passage before him would perhaps remember automatically the later or the earlier passage which resembled the one at hand, and his memory would dictate to him instead of his eyes the similar passage which, while indeed similar, was different from the correct one before him.

There is another error which is frequently found in ancient manuscripts which may be described as an error of intellect. Many of the old manuscripts, to save space and labor, were abbreviated.

Words were written in a shortened form. Sometimes an abbreviation of three or four letters would take the place of three or four words. The scribe would wish to write out the abbreviated word in full but he would confuse the abbreviation with another and write out a wrong sentence entirely. This has been the source of trouble in many manuscripts.

Sometimes a scribe who was very intelligent would create difficulties precisely because he was intelligent. He would be copying a difficult passage whose meaning was not immediately clear. Understanding the meaning of the passage, he would frequently write in the margin a word or two to make this difficult passage clear. A later scribe, not knowing just why the words were in the margin, would think that this marginal explanation was a record of words which had been omitted from the text by mistake and so would embody these words into the text, although the words did not belong in the original text at all. This is a frequent source of error in ancient manuscripts. (See *Books in Manuscript* by Falconer Madan, London, 1920.)

Now, when we consider that ancient books were copied thousands of times, generation after generation, and that each scribe added error after error, and that the mistakes piled up and that some scribes, trying to correct the errors, corrected them wrongly, thus piling up further mistakes, we can understand why most of the ancient manuscript books have come down to us with many of their passages so corrupted by scribal errors as to be virtually unintelligible. In fact, one authority on manuscripts (Madan, *op. cit.*, p. 48) says: "Yet all who know human nature, or who have studied paleography [the science of old manuscripts] will acknowledge that the probability against two consecutive leaves being correctly transcribed is about a hundred to one!"

If this be the case, then the Bible ought to be the most incorrect of all the texts we have. It is certainly one of the oldest texts in existence. Even the critical scholars who prefer to set the date of Biblical texts late place some documents of the Bible as early as the ninth pre-Christian century, which is twenty-seven hundred years ago. Other parts of the Bible are, of course, less ancient, but all of them have been subjected to copying by countless scribes for many centuries, all over the world. And what would seem to aggravate the situation is not only the fact that the Bible is old and therefore has been often copied, but that it certainly has been read by more people than any other manuscript which comes down to us from antiquity. According to the Law, every head of a household was in duty bound to have a copy of the Torah written for him. While this law was not strictly followed, nevertheless vast numbers were written. Every synagogue possessed many scrolls of the Law. More copies must have been made of the Bible in any one period than of any other manuscript. The opportunities for error are thus almost beyond calculation. Judging by all this, the Bible text should be more spoiled through scribal error than all other texts which have come down to us from the past.

Of course, there is no doubt that there are very many verses in Scripture which have been transmitted to us in incorrect form due to the typical scribal errors which we have described above. Certain words that should be separated have been run together. Other words that should be run together in one word are separated. Certain sentences have been misplaced from one column to another. There are some words and sentences in the Bible of which the most careful scholarship can hardly make sense, and our translations of such passages into modern languages are really only guesses. The ancient scholars were well aware of the fact that the text of the Bible had in many cases been incorrectly transmitted. They frequently record two types of reading, suggesting that the word be read differently than it is written. They often say that we must conjecture or theorize that the word must be read differently than it is found in the text. The Midrash says in one passage that certain of the sections in Scripture are not in their proper order (Midrash Tehillim III, 1).

There is a whole branch of modern study of the Bible which devotes itself to the attempt to correct the present texts and to find the original reading (the textual or the "lower" criticism). This science of text correction, like the general study of ancient manuscripts (paleography), has developed a definite scientific method. One of its essential principles is to rely upon the oldest manuscripts. The presumption is, and it is largely correct, that since each recopying of a manuscript incurs the danger of scribal errors, the older the manuscript the shorter the chain of recopying which preceded it, and therefore the more likely the manuscript is (leaving out other factors) to be a correct one.

Since this is so, one would imagine that the correction of scribal errors in the Bible text would be easier than the correction of other manuscripts. One could well assume that very ancient Hebrew manuscripts of the Bible are in existence. The Bible was used in synagogues centuries before the present era. The Five Books of Moses, the selections from the Prophets read in the synagogue, obviously must have existed in many copies centuries before the destruction of the Second Temple. Hence one could conclude, since the Bible was copied so early and in such large numbers, that many ancient copies would still be available to which more recent copies could be compared and corrected.

Strangely enough, this is not the case. There are almost no ancient copies in existence. The oldest fragment (second century) is on papyrus (the Nash Papyrus) and that contains only the Ten Commandments from Deuteronomy. There is a Pentateuch manuscript in Damascus which is said to go back to the third century, but the claim is doubted.

In the summer of 1947 a Bedouin found, in a cave near the Dead Sea, about eleven Hebrew manuscripts. One of these is a manuscript of the Book of Isaiah. There is a similarity between the writing and spelling of the manuscripts and that of the Nash fragment. Some scholars believe that these newly-found manuscripts are as old as the Maccabean period (second pre-Christian century). If this is so, then this newly-found manuscript of Isaiah is the oldest Scriptural manuscript known. But some scholars doubt that the manuscripts are anywhere near as old as that.

The British Museum has a large fragment from Genesis 25:20 to Deuteronomy 1:35, and this fragment dates from the ninth century. There is a manuscript of the Prophets in Leningrad, dated 916 of the present era. The oldest complete Bible in existence is also in Leningrad and is dated 1009. None of the copies referred to by the Masoretes in the eighth century, which they used to help fix the text, and none of the copies referred to by medieval scholars like Kimchi (twelfth century) is in existence today.

The reason for this strange fact, doubly strange because the books were deemed sacred, is that when a scroll became unfit for synagogue reading because of age and the fading of certain letters, it had to be put away or buried. Innumerable manuscripts were buried in the cemeteries, usually in the graves of righteous men,

Thus the older manuscripts were consciously disposed of, and therefore the best technique which modern scholars could have used in correcting the text of the Bible is not possible. Since the earliest dated complete Bible in existence today is 1009, one might say that at least eight centuries of manuscripts have disappeared.

Yet, granting that there are many cases in which the Bible text as we have it is not the original, and that we have no ancient manuscripts to guide us, the Bible is still one of the best, if not the very best preserved document which comes to us out of antiquity. There are fewer errors in it, and a far greater proportion of manifestly correct and original texts. Evidently the Bible, although subjected to more copying and therefore to more potential corruption than any other manuscript, had the advantage of certain factors which preserved it from corruption.

First of all, there is, and always has been, a stronger motive for preserving the correctness of Scripture than the natural motive for preserving the correctness of any other literature. Other books were carefully copied because of the general professional pride of the scribe or out of respect for the writer or for the importance of material, if it were legal material and legal practice were based upon it. All these motives which tended to protect other literature applied with much greater force to Scripture. The Scriptures were not merely literature whose contents and author were respected; Scripture was understood to be the word of God and therefore to be wholly reverenced. In fact, the scribe, when he copied the Five Books of Moses on a scroll for the synagogue reading, had consciously and worshipfully to sanctify the names of God which he was writing down. If he did not have this consciously sacred intent as he wrote down the names of God, the book would be unfit for public reading and would not be permitted to be used in the synagogue. In other words, scribes were constantly aware that they were writing not just a book but the word of God. Furthermore, besides being the word of God, the Bible, especially the Pentateuch, was unique as a law book. It was not only a record of laws but it was the foundation of a great elaboration into a vast, legal literature. Every word in the Torah, even a letter or a reading or an accent, could be the basis for later laws. Since Torah is the word of God, the slightest change in a phrase was deemed to be infinitely significant. Hence the scribes were scrupulously careful.

How the mood of sacred devotion on the part of the scribe and the feeling of the immense importance of every word or letter of Sacred Scripture would tend to preserve the text can be seen from the following account in the Talmud (b. Sota, 20a) of a conversation between Rabbi Meir, a young scribe, and Rabbi Ishmael, the great rabbi of the second Christian century. Rabbi Meir tells: "When I came to Rabbi Ishmael, he said to me, 'My son, what is thine occupation?' and I replied, 'I am a scribe.' Said he to me, 'My son, be very careful, for thy work is the work of heaven. Shouldst thou omit one letter or put in one superfluous letter, thou couldst destroy the entire world.'"

Of course, this was no guarantee against errors. It was a protection against carelessness but no sure guarantee that errors could not creep in. They were bound to appear, as they do in all manuscripts written by scribes. But because of the reverence and verbal importance of Scriptures, very much more care was exercised and therefore fewer errors occurred in Scriptures than in other documents.

Yet, although errors by scribes were inevitable, it is a fact and an almost unbelievable fact that after a certain date (eighth century) there was built up an absolute guarantee against any further change or error in the Biblical text. A system was developed whereby one could be sure that no more errors could ever creep into the text by scribal copying. This system was so successful that in spite of the fact that from the period of its highest development there were almost eight more centuries of scribal copying of Scripture all over the world, hardly a single error remained undetected to corrupt later manuscripts.

This astounding result was achieved by a technical branch of Jewish tradition called the "Masora." The word is variously translated. Some translate it to mean "tradition" (that which is handed down) and take it to refer to the handing down from scribe to scribe of certain protective rules and records as to the Scriptural text. Some translate the word *Masora* to mean "bands" or "chains," as if Scripture were, from then on, by means of the Masora, tied up and prevented from running off on the path of error.

The nature and achievement of this remarkable science which guarantees the preservation of the Scriptural text will be best appreciated if we first indicate a simple way in which the scholars of the Masora (the Masoretes) helped preserve the words of Scripture and prevent any of them from disappearing through scribal error. At the end of the Book of Genesis the Masoretic note reads as follows:

The total verses of the Book of Genesis are 1,534, and half of them is the verse "and by the sword thou shalt live." The weekly portions are twelve in number; the sections are forty-three; the chapters are fifty; the paragraphs whose last lines are open to the end of the column are thirty-four, and those which are closed [the new paragraph beginning on the same line on which the preceding paragraph closed] number forty-eight.

Concerning this note, it is enough for us to observe that the total number of verses are given and a record made as to which one is the middle verse of the book. While it is true that no one is going to sit down and count the number of verses, still the exact number exists as a check. If any verse dropped out through scribal error and then another manuscript showed up containing one more verse and a dispute arose as to whether the extra verse belonged there or not, the count would certainly have been a perfect check. Thus every book of the Bible has a Masoretic note which gives the number of verses, the middle verse and the number of sections. Therefore, there is always a check against any verses dropping out, or for that matter against any verse being smuggled in. The technique of counting the number of letters in the Biblical book is an ancient one. The Talmud (b. Kiddushin 30a) says that it goes back to the time of the disciples of Ezra (fifth century before the present era).

This counting of verses was only a minor part of the work of the Masorete scholars. While the count of verses and the indication of the middle verse in every book was a guarantee against any verses dropping out or others creeping in, it was equally important to guard against changes in the text itself. The counting of verses would not guarantee against other scribal errors such as the changing of words or of the order of words. To guard against such errors the Masoretes began to record every recognizable characteristic of the Biblical text. If from ancient times certain variations in the text appeared, all these variations were carefully preserved. There was not a peculiarity, there was not an unusual punctuation, there was not a variation from the pronunciation of a word from one place and its pronunciation in another that was not carefully recorded.

All this material was systematized in many ways and recorded in so many different cross-reference tables and lists that any type of scribal error could be quickly detected. It will be of interest to notice the types of variations and even minute eccentricities of the text which the Masoretes carefully recorded. Most of the Masoretic notes are recorded in what is known as the Rabbinic Bible, that is to say, the Bible published with the more popular rabbinic commentaries surrounding the text. These Masoretic notes in the Rabbinic Bible are found in various places on the page, some of them being centered around the initial words of the section written in tiny letters, generally to form some sort of a decoration. This is known as the "Initial Masora." Then there is the Masora on the inner column, called the "Inner Masora"; then fuller notes at the bottom of the column, called the "Outer Masora"; and then often rather elaborate notes at the end of a section called the "Terminal Masora." A fairly clear idea of the contents of the Masora will be obtained if we give an example from each type.

The Initial Masora, printed as a decoration around the opening letter of the Book of Genesis, rests on the fact that in all manuscripts the word *B'reshis*, which means "In the Beginning," the opening word of Scripture, begins with a large *B*. This Initial Masora calls the attention of the scribe to the fact that this large *B*, beginning the book of Genesis, to which the note is appended, is not the only extra large letter in Scripture. For some reason there are extra large letters all over Scripture, sometimes in the middle of a chapter and sometimes even in the middle of a word. Which are these extra large letters? How can they be remembered by the scribe so as to guard against the error of omitting them and thus changing the recorded text even in this slight manner? To answer these questions, this initial note lists all the large letters and rearranges them alphabetically, according to the Hebrew alphabet, so they can be easily memorized or recorded. The note, therefore, begins as follows:

The *B* of *B'reshis* ["In the Beginning"] is large and is one of the large letters which are as follows: the *A* of *Adam* in the names of Adam and Seth in Chronicles I:1; the *B* of *B'reshis* here; the *G* [Gimel] of the word *vehisgaloch* ["and he shall shave"] in Leviticus 13:33; the *D* of *Echod* ["The Lord is One"] – Deuteronomy 6:4 . . .

and so through all the alphabet, collecting all the extra large letters in the entire Scripture and recording them.

A similar Initial Masora surrounds the opening word of the book of Leviticus. This opening word is *vayikro*, "and He called." It happens that in the transmitted text the letter *aleph*, which closes the word *vayikro*, is smaller than the normal size. This gives the Masora a chance to record all the extra small letters found all the way through the Scripture and to arrange them alphabetically.

Obviously, the Masoretic recording of the large and the small letters was for the purpose of instructing the scribe to be so careful in recording Scripture precisely as it is, even with all the eccentricities of the text, that not the slightest change would be made. Thus even certain inverted letters which by chance crept into the text are recorded and transmitted. The duty of the scribe was to record the text just as it is.

The Inner Masora is usually a brief note, generally dealing with the punctuation, or the grammatical form of the word, and recording how many times such forms of the word occur in Scripture. Usually these brief notes are elaborated by the Outer Masora. For example, in the opening verse of Genesis, the Inner Masora marks the word "God created" with the number three, which the Outer Masora explains as follows: "The phrase 'God created' occurs three times in Scripture," and it lists the three times. The word "the earth," which ends the verse, occurs in Scripture at the end of a verse three times and in each of the three times the next sentence begins with the words "and the earth." The Masora lists these three times in Scripture. Thus all through the Bible the occurrence of every important word is recorded, its peculiarities, its differences, its similarities. The text of Scripture is thus surrounded by thousands of checks and lists. It is virtually impossible for any error to remain undetected. Errors might have crept in, but they were soon detected and corrected.

How long this nearly perfect system of checks and listing of words was used we cannot tell. In the eighth century the science of Masora was well developed and had had its classic period. But undoubtedly Masoretic activity and certain of the lists are very old, and certain of the notes are too. The Talmud (b. Kiddushin 30a) says that the ancient scribes (in the time of Ezra in the fifth pre-Christian century) were called *Soferim* (which means not only "scribes" but also "enumerators") because they counted all the letters in the Torah and noted that letter *Vav* of the word *Gochon* (in Leviticus 11:42) is the middle letter of the entire Torah. It is interesting to observe that Philo, who lived in Alexandria at the beginning of the present era declared in his day: "And though many years have passed, I cannot tell the exact number, but more than two thousand, the Jews have never altered one word of what was written by Moses." (See article by Isadore Harris, *Jewish Quarterly Review, Old Series,* Vol. 1, page 128.) So too Josephus (*Against Apion*, 1, 8) said: "During so many ages as have elapsed, no one has been so bold as to add anything to the words of Scripture or to take anything therefrom."

These two statements, dating from the beginning of the present era, are sufficient to indicate that in the time of their authors there were already so many safeguards that they were confident that the text had been preserved unchanged for centuries. The various Masoretic safeguards accumulated gradually. Some (according to the Talmudic passages just quoted) may well have been begun in the time of Ezra, five centuries before the present era. Certainly from the time of the climax of Masoretic work in the seventh century (or eighth) the Scripture was adequately protected. The text was by then quite properly known as the Masoretic text, i.e., the text was safeguarded by the Masora.

There remained from the eighth century to the age of printing seven centuries of manuscript writing. The Bible in these seven centuries was copied by scribes all over the world countless thousands of times and yet we can be sure of Scripture of what cannot be said of any other document of antiquity, that during these long centuries it was completely protected against any permanent error. The Bible, because of the Masora, is the most carefully preserved text in all the world.

ChAPTER IV

The Bible in Worship

GREAT book finds its way into the minds of men. Its ideas may be difficult to grasp, and its language may be hard to read, and at first it may attract only a handful of readers. But one or two of its readers will rewrite the ideas into a more popular book, until step by step the difficult but important teachings of the original book will have reached many minds.

Thus, the high ethical ideals of the great Greek teachers, Socrates, Plato and Aristotle, were taught primarily in select schools to small groups of students. These teachings were intended for the upper classes, to train the future rulers of the community in the art of noble government. But later more popular philosophers summarized what seemed to them to be the best of the teachings of their great predecessors and taught them to ever-increasing circles. In fact, the Stoic philosophers became wandering preachers who travelled all over the Roman Empire, teaching to multitudes the choicest ethical ideals of their great philosophic predecessors. Thus do great ideas and books spread their influence through the world.

Yet even in this regard the Bible was different, from the very beginning. The prophets spoke indeed to kings and nobles, but their messages were directed chiefly to large gatherings of the people at popular festivals, in the temples, in the great cities, and in the villages. This fact explains the popular style of the prophetic speech and writings. Exalted ideas were expressed in such a vivid way, in such concrete words and in such telling metaphors, that the simple farmer and blacksmith could understand them. The ethical teachings of the Bible were from the very first universal not only in their meaning, but also in their human appeal. For the first time in the history of man's ethical growth the attempt was made to exalt an entire nation to the level of a sanctified and holy people.

The ethical standards of the Bible were intimately related to its exalted conception of God. The idea of a spiritual and universal God was never easy to grasp. It had happened occasionally among other peoples that the idea of one spiritual God was reached by some great philosophic minds. None of these scattered thinkers would ever have imagined that this exalted idea of one Omnipresent, purely spiritual God could be understood by the uneducated. The few, the very few philosophers held to their noble God-conception, but the masses were left to their familiar little idols, their comforting little rituals and handy spells and incantations. Yet in Israel, for the first time, the attempt was made to teach this delicate and difficult idea of the one universal God to every human being, even the humblest and the most simple-minded.

On this matter the prophets gave the people no rest. They denounced them repeatedly for their comfortable little idolatries wherein they were like all the rest of the people of the world. They insisted upon transforming their listeners into the one truly monotheistic people in all the earth. And that, too, is why the God-conception of the Bible is not presented theoretically on the purely philosophic level but is described in vivid, picturesque, and eloquent terms. The prophets and the lawgivers were successful. After the return from the Exile, idolatry vanished in Israel. For the first time the world saw a non-idolatrous people. What was once the rare thought of a few choice souls had become the conviction of an entire nation. Israel, all of it, could say, with whole-hearted understanding: "The Lord our God is One." It had become a nation of philosophers.

Thus in the early days, when the Bible was still in the making as a book and the lawgivers and the prophets still lived and talked, their teachings, although difficult to understand and to observe, were never confined to a chosen few. Later, when these great geniuses had ceased to appear and their words were recorded and collected into the Sacred Scripture, the Book itself took the place of the spoken word. The Bible became the intellectual and emotional property of the entire people.

* * *

How the Bible became "the inheritance of the congregation of Israel" is a remarkable chapter in the history of adult education. This great achievement was accomplished through the Synagogue, itself a unique spiritual organization. Before the days of the Synagogue, the worship of the gods among all settled nations was conducted by the members of a special priestly clan who knew the ritual and observed it in the temples in which they were the guardians and the sole officiants. Through the rites of sacrifice and incense and by the special priests the gods were worshipped. As for the people, whenever they were present at all they participated merely in the role of spectators.

But after Israel returned from its exile, it established a new institution, the like of which had never before been seen. It is true that it rebuilt the Temple in which, as in all other temples on earth, sacrificial ritual was carried on by the caste of priests. But, in addition, all over Palestine there soon grew up little meeting houses, synagogues in which God was worshipped without ritual sacrifices (which, of course, could be offered only in Jerusalem and at the Temple). In these synagogues all over the land people worshipped through song and through prayer. The Synagogue was the first non-priestly, pure spiritual institution of worship in human history. It was in the Synagogue that the great enterprise in adult education was carried out, that of bringing the Bible into the thought and feeling of the entire people.

The method whereby this was done was as original as it was successful. Very early in the history of the synagogue, the building which was devoted to worship contained also a school, the *Beis Ha-midrosh*, the house of study, in which people gathered for the study of the law and all its branches. The house of worship and the house of study were throughout the centuries in the same premises. But, in addition, the house of worship itself was primarily a school, and the ritual of worship was essentially a course of studies. This was not due to a gradual process of adding instructional material to a service composed of prayers and hymns. Characteristically enough, the material for study during worship was the original part of the ritual. It may well be said that the house of prayer, the synagogue itself, actually began as a house of study.

During the Babylonian exile, before the Synagogue was founded, the people gathered to hear the words and the prophecies of Ezekiel. We may presume, also, from the fact that the prophet Jeremiah sent letters to the community in Babylon, that his letters and prophecies were read to them in public. The exiles must have listened with fair regularity to the spoken and written words of the prophets. These gatherings were not meetings for worship but meetings for instruction and guidance. They could not have been for worship because the chief mode of worship which the people knew was the offering of sacrifices, and such offerings could only be made in the Temple on Mount Zion.

When the people returned they not only, as has been said, rebuilt the Temple for sacrificial worship, but they continued the custom of meeting for instruction and guidance which they had begun in Babylon. Thus, these meetings, which became the synagogues, actually began as places for adult instruction and therefore it is quite likely that the public readings from Scripture were perhaps the first regular element in the synagogue service.

Jewish tradition has long felt that the system of reading from Scripture in the synagogue is very ancient. The Talmud says that the custom of reading the Law on the Sabbath and holidays goes back to Moses himself (b. Megillah 32a). This indicates how old the institution was presumed to be. Certainly when the people returned from exile the custom soon became well established.

This reading was no mere formality or ritual. It was organized in such a way as to be genuine, creative study. As the classic Hebrew language gradually was supplanted by Aramaic, a kindred language, it was ordained that the Scripture be not only read to the people but also translated. The reading of the Prophets was translated three verses at a time and the reading of the Torah was translated verse by verse. The Torah was law, and important legal enactments might be based on any one verse of it. Therefore, it was studied more closely. Another difference between the reading of the Torah and that of the Prophets was the fact that not a single verse of the Torah was omitted from public reading. Each Sabbath's section began precisely where the preceding Sabbath section left off. This was not so with regard to the Prophets. On one Sabbath the prophetical reading might be from Isaiah, on another Sabbath from Ezekiel, and on another Sabbath from Zechariah. The readings from the Torah were thus consecutive while the readings from the Prophets were selective. The selection from the Prophets was made to fit the regular consecutive reading from the Torah. Either there was a similarity of phrasing or, more generally, a similarity of ideas between the two.

Thus, for the first Biblical reading from Genesis dealing with the Creation, the prophetical reading is Isaiah 42, beginning with the verse (5): "Thus saith the Lord God, He that created the heavens." The second section of the Torah, which tells the events of the Flood, has as its prophetical reading the selection from Isaiah 54 (beginning with verse 9) containing the words of God's promise to Israel, "for this is as the waters of Noah unto me." So, for example, the Torah portion beginning with Genesis 23, which tells of Abraham in his old age making provision for the family life of his son Isaac, has for its prophetic portion the first chapter of the First Book of Kings, which describes the aged King David making provision for the career of his son Solomon.

The readers were not specially trained professional readers as is the custom today. In the early days, the men who were called up to the Torah (seven men on Sabbath) not only recited the blessings before and after each section as they do today, but read the entire sections themselves to the congregation. Therefore, the congregation had actually to prepare as students for the Sabbath service. Indeed, later tradition records that each man was in duty bound to ready every week the weekly portion twice in Hebrew and once in the Aramaic translation (b. Berachos 8a).

Besides the public readings of Torah and Prophet in which the people themselves took part, and besides the translations, there were also regular explanatory discourses, the world's first regular sermons. These sermons were generally based upon a text in the portion of the Torah and upon another text in the portion from the Prophets. These texts were analyzed and interpreted, and their deeper implications were made clear. Sometimes the discourses were legal in nature, since the people needed guidance in the Law. They had the democratic privilege of understanding independently how the laws which governed them were derived from the word of God. Sometimes these legal discourses were mainly ethical, in order to inspire and edify. Fragments of these ancient sermons, developments of texts in Torah and Prophet, are preserved for us in shortened form in the great Midrashic literature.

The phenomenon of public Scripture reading, translation, and interpretation was unique in the history of religion and in the history of education. The sacred books of other faiths were the secret property and privilege of the priest. This was the first time that the sacred books of a faith were made available to all the people. In the history of education it was the first time that an attempt was made to arouse the mind of every adult to study, and to the acquisition of knowledge, intellectual and spiritual. It is not by chance that later Jewish tradition has called the synagogue a "schul," which means a "school."

Since the reading of Scripture was so original and important a part of the developing synagogue service, it was to be expected that when other parts of the service developed they, too, would be influenced by Scripture and would serve as means of further instruction of the contents of the Bible. Thus besides the Torah and the Prophets, the third part of Scripture, the Sacred Writings, played its part in the synagogue worship. The five "scrolls" were read at certain stated times of the year—The Song of Songs at Passover, Ruth, at Shovuos, etc. (see Part Two, chapter VIII). The most influential part of the Hagiographa was the Psalms. Some modern writers call the Book of Psalms the hymn book of the Second Temple. They mean that the Psalms were used chiefly as songs by the Levites to accompany the sacrificial worship in the Second Temple on Mount Zion. But it would be more nearly correct to say that the Psalms were the hymn book of the little synagogues scattered throughout the land. Most of the Psalms were essentially prayers. Those written in the singular were especially devotional and could also be understood as applying to the whole people. It well may be that the Psalms were among the first prayer elements in synagogue worship, as the public Scripture readings were its first instructional elements. To this very day more than fifty per cent of the traditional daily and Sabbath service is actually composed of whole psalms. Many of the other prayers are composed of verses from the Psalms and other parts of Scripture.

It is evident from the Biblical language and Biblical phrases found in most of the classic prayers that a conscious effort was made to search through Scripture for suitable ideas and phrases through which to voice prayerful aspirations. A clear example of this is in the Shofor Service of the New Year. The Shofor Service is intended to express three thoughts: first, that of God the King,

"Malchios"; second, God remembering the past, "Zichronos"; and third, the sounding of the trumpet of deliverance, "Shofros." In order to express these three ideas, the people were instructed to select verses from Scripture appropriate to the thought (m. Rosh Hashona IV, 6). Gradually these verses became fixed, but a reading of the traditional series of verses will indicate how one thought was searched for throughout Scripture. The following quotation is from the traditional prayer book for the first shofor thought, God the King. It will be noted how the idea of God's kingship was taken from all three parts of the Bible.

And it is said, 'He hath not beheld iniquity in Jacob . . . the Lord God is with him and the shout of the King is among them' [Numbers 23:21]. And it is said, 'And He was King of Jeshurun when all the heads of the people were gathered . . .' [Deuteronomy 33:5] and in thy holy words it is written: 'For sovereignty is the Lord's and He is Ruler over all the nations' [Psalm 22:27]. And it is said, 'the Lord reigneth, He is clothed with majesty' [Psalm 93:1]. 'Lift up your heads, O ye gates, that the King of Glory may come in . . .' [Psalm 24:7]. And by the hands of thy servants the Prophets it is written: 'The Lord shall be King over all the earth; in that day the Lord shall be One and His Name One' [Zechariah 14:9]. Hear O Israel . . . [Deut. 6:4].

Thus, in order to express the thought of God's sovereignty they found the most appropriate verses first in the Torah, then in the Holy Writings, and then in the Prophets, and concluded with the great verse from the Torah again.

Indeed, it was the Biblical verse from Deuteronomy (chapter 6), "Hear O Israel . . . and thou shalt love the Lord thy God," which became the focus for the development of the morning and evening prayers.

The prayers grew up around Scripture, and as the people prayed they were learning the Bible. They were well aware, in ancient times, that this universal adult education was exceptional and unprecedented. Josephus, living at the beginning of the present era, in his writings against a defamer of the Jews, points out the uniqueness of the fact that the law was taught to all of Israel.

The law-giver demonstrated the law to be the best and the most necessary instruction, permitting the people to leave off their other appointments and assemble together for hearing the law and learning it exactly, and this not once or twice or oftener, but every week, which all other legislators seem to have neglected. – Contra Apionem II, 18.

Thus was started a unique process of democratic education which made the Bible the first book of any kind which was part of the life of an entire people. When the Bible was carried over into Christianity, the habit of universal study was carried over with it, and therefore the Bible has never been a mere fetish to be kept and worshipped, but a book to be read and studied. The Bible quickly became the most widely read book in the world. The Arabian prophet Mohammed was right when he called the Jews and the Christians "the people of the Book." They were the people of the Book because from the very beginning of the Synagogue in Jewish worship the Bible has been "the Book of the people."

CHAPTER V

Ancient Bible Study

MIDRASH, MISHNAH, AND TALMUD

THE ancient study of the Bible grew like the development of a symphony. In a symphony, or in other elaborate musical constructions, a melody is sounded, then repeated with variations, and then the variations are elaborated, being transferred from one instrument to another. Finally, all the variations are woven together into one magnificent texture of inspiring sound. So in the ancient Biblical study the text of Scripture served as the theme or leading melody for an expanding structure of learning and literature built up of careful analysis, reconstruction, and variations, and the development culminated in the weaving of all of it together into the immense structure of the classic Jewish oral law.

The whole Midrashic literature and the entire Talmud are, in a definite sense, elaborate commentaries on Scripture. Almost all of the medieval Jewish literature took its origin from the Bible itself. When the old scholars wrote Jewish history, they began with Biblical history. The science of Hebrew grammar was of course based upon the Bible. Hebrew poetry was an outgrowth of Biblical poetry. Jewish philosophy was based upon an analysis and a reconstruction of Biblical ideas. All of the classic Jewish literature developed out of the Bible. The influence of the Bible upon general literature, drama, painting, and music was often indirect, but in Jewish literature it was direct and unmistakable. The Jewish classic literature is related to the Bible closely, as children are to a parent.

This was, of course, a predictable development. The Bible was the product of spiritual and literary genius, and was studied regularly in the *Beis Ha-midrosh* and through the public worship (see Part One, chapter IV). It was therefore a constant inspiration in the life of the people, week after week and day after day. It was bound to evoke original ideas and call forth further creativity.

In addition to the natural influence of a great literature inspiring further literature, the classic Jewish writers held to a certain theory about the Bible itself which made it inevitable that further literature should grow up around Scripture. This theory was based upon a conviction which was psychologically sound and artistically inspiring and may be described as the Doctrine of the Oral Law. The rabbis of the Midrash and the Talmud and all who in later generations followed their traditions believed that the visible text of the Bible was only part of the Law which God gave to Moses. They declared that when Moses was on Mount Sinai he received not one Law but actually two distinct Laws. One was the Written Law which we now have before us (*Torah she-bichsov,* "the law in writing"); in addition God gave him a vast body of Law which was not written down (*Torah she-b'alpe,* "the Torah by mouth"). This "Torah by mouth," the Oral Law, was not recorded by Moses and therefore had to be handed down by direct personal teaching from Moses to Joshua, from Joshua to the elders, from the elders to the prophets, etc., down to our day. Thus, besides the Written Law which carried the authenticity of its own words as they were read, there was also the invisible, unread but constantly taught Oral Law handed down from generation to generation. It was held that the Oral Law should never be written down, but should remain oral (b. Gittin 6ob). It was only in later generations, when the amount of known oral law was so large that it was impossible to keep it in the memory, that finally and reluctantly it was written down. The great post-Biblical books, the Midrash, the Mishnah, and the Talmud were, in the early stages of their development, actually carried in the mind by an astonishing effort of memory without full record, except perhaps some abbreviated notes of students.

This Oral Law was not merely handed down by teacher to pupil, for then it would never have developed. It would have been the same from Moses to Joshua all through the ages. Actually the law was constantly growing and endlessly developing. Yet they believed that even those additional and new ideas which were developed in each generation had authenticity as having been given by God to Moses on Mount Sinai. They declared that even any new teaching by an authorized scholar had previously been given by God to Moses (J. Peah II, 17a). The basis for this belief that the entire developing Oral Law was actually Mosaic was the conviction that the words of the written law meant very much more than what they actually meant in their simple definition. They believed that when Moses wrote the Law he embodied into it also, behind the words, as it were, or between the lines, the Oral Law. Therefore, if one would study the Written Law carefully enough, he would be able to discover or rediscover the Oral Law hidden in it. Thus, they insisted that there was no superfluous phrase or carelessly chosen word in the Torah. The very choice of one word rather than another, the very emphasis of phrases were made for a specific purpose, namely, to teach us certain elements of the Oral Law. It was necessary, therefore, to study the words of the Bible with meticulous care and thus derive from them the unwritten, unspoken law. This conviction they expressed in the statement, "turn its pages again and again and you will find everything in it."

This idea will not seem so strange if we translate it into modern phraseology. Whenever we study a profound book, we are convinced that the author expresses in it more than perhaps he is conscious of expressing. His whole personality goes into the book; not only his conscious purpose, but his unconscious mind. We may "read something into" a book from the very choice of phrases and emphasis of sentences; yet if we were to ask the author himself, he would not know whether he really meant that which we found in it. Yet he may well have meant more than he thought he meant, since he wrote his entire personality into the book. When, therefore, the ancient students of the Bible said that by careful analysis of the minutest phrasing in the Written Law they would find the Oral Law, given to Moses on Sinai, they meant the same as we would mean in declaring that certain unstated ideas were the unconscious intention of a modern author.

Because of this ancient theory that the Oral Law is hidden in the Written Law (although of course they would not say that Moses was unconscious of what he was doing), the Bible was given closer scrutiny and more loving attention than any book had ever received before or has since. The older scholars noted the most minute variations of phrase, and out of these they developed important laws and beautiful legends. An example of a Midrashic legend based upon close observation of a text variation, which must have escaped the attention of hundreds of generations of non-Jewish students of the Bible, is the legend about the stones upon which our father Jacob rested in the desert on the first night of his wanderings when he fled from Esau. The Bible says that when Jacob prepared himself for his night's repose, he gathered stones together as a sort of shield and pillow. The legend then declares that immediately the stones started to debate with each other. Each one insisted: Let it be upon me that this righteous man shall rest his head; let mine be the privilege. To still the quarrelling of the stones, the Lord merged them all into one large stone and in the morning Jacob took that newly merged stone and made of it an altar upon which he worshipped God. One can easily imagine how effectively some ancient preacher, speaking in a Palestinian synagogue, used this charming legend. He would say that all the hard stones, all the troubles and worries which we endure in nights of loneliness become ultimately the altar upon which we, purified by suffering, worship God. It is perhaps in reference to this legend that the medieval Hebrew poet said, "From the broken fragments of my heart I will build an altar unto Thee."

This legend, with its deeply spiritual implications, was simply created out of the Biblical text and, in a sense, was actually there as Oral Law. The ancient teachers noticed something in the text which millions of other readers might never have noticed. There is a slight variation in the written text of the Bible and this variation gave them their clue. It so happens that Scripture says that when Jacob composed himself for sleep: "And he took some of the *stones* and put them under his head"; when he awoke, Scripture says, he took the *stone* which lay under his head and made of it an altar. In any other book, not deemed to be inspired, a reader would say that this difference between *stones* and *stone* was merely carelessness on the part of the author; but in an inspired book, this too-simple explanation could not be applied. The rabbis held that this was a conscious variation in order to reveal to us the deeper meaning, the oral meaning, of Scripture.

A similar example is found in the same Biblical passage. The rabbis found particular significance in the details of the dream of Jacob in the desert. The angels whom he saw on the ladder were not just any angels but special groups of angels. In the first group

· 45 ·

were the angels that had accompanied him from home. These angels, who guarded him in his childhood were now leaving him and were ascending the ladder. But a new group of angels was descending to accompany him further on his journey. One can see how the ancient preacher would use this legend to point an enheartening moral. Jacob, the symbol of youth, is now going on the journey of life, henceforth to be self-reliant and adult. At first youth is always confused, and is apparently without any ideals to guide it. Now the sweetness of childhood is gone. The reliability of maturity has not yet come. But, though the protecting angels of home (the sweet lovableness of childhood) are gone, a new angelic company (new ideals) will come to carry him further on his journey.

This touching legend, rich in meaning, was derived from the fact that there is a curious order of the verbs in the story. Since angels are presumed to live in heaven, one would assume that the description of the angels traversing the ladder would read: "the angels of God descended and ascended the ladder." But the text happens to say, "they ascended and descended the ladder." First they went up and then they came down. In other words, those that ascended had already been on earth. They were the guardian angels of his home and childhood.

In order to illustrate how closely the ancient scholars studied Scripture to derive deeper meanings from its words, it might be helpful to quote this Bible section (Genesis 28:10) in which the two stories (that of the merged stones and the ministering angels) are found. The following are the chief Biblical texts and legends derived from them. For the convenience of the reader the text will be italicized and the legends found in it will be given as they follow each fragment of the text. The form of the legend is that given in the commentator Rashi.

And Jacob went out from Beer-sheba and went toward Haran. It would have been quite sufficient to say that Jacob went towards Haran. It seems unnecessary to preface it by saying: "He went forth from Beersheba" (where he lived). But this is mentioned for the purpose of telling us that when a righteous man leaves a place, his departure makes a deep impression, for when a righteous man lives in a city, he is its glory and its splendor, and when he goes forth from there, its glory departs and its splendor fades (from Midrash Rabba).

And he came upon the place. The same verb used here for "he came upon," also means to "entreat" or "to pray," thus teaching us that it was our father Jacob who instituted the regular evening prayers (b. Beracoth 26b).

And he placed them under his head. (The interpretation of this verse was given above and is found in the Talmud, b. Chullin, 91b.)

The angels ascended and descended. (The interpretation of this verse was given above and comes from Midrash Rabba.)

The God of Abraham and the God of Isaac. God's name is not generally united with that of a living man (for any man as long as he is alive might yet sin) and Isaac was still alive; but since Isaac was blind and confined to his home, the evil inclination had departed from him (Midrash Tanchuma).

The land upon which thou art lying, to thee will I give it and to thy seed. (Because he lay only upon a small bit of earth, the promise did not seem to be very great, and yet we know that God promised the descendants of Jacob all the land of Canaan.) Therefore the legend says the following: God rolled up the entire land of Israel under him (b. Chullin 91b).

It is evident that these legends are entirely different in origin from legends found in other literature. Most legends are of anonymous origin. They spring up in various ways as nature myths, or animal fables, or legends about historic persons. But these Midrashic legends were not an anonymous development of childlike stories. They were the product of keen minds, which made a careful study of every word of Scripture. They are works of art in which keen observation and careful analysis translate themselves into literary structures of beauty and meaning.

It was not only legendary material which was created by this careful scrutiny of every Biblical word and phrase. Of greater significance for the self-discipline of Jewish communities was the fact that the same method of study was used in the actual development of the laws which governed Jewish life. Most of these laws and practices are Oral Law, and they too were derived by the careful scrutiny of the Biblical text.

For example, the Mishnah (Sanhedrin 1, 6) seeks to prove that the smaller Sanhedrin (the ancient Palestinian Court of Appeals) should consist of twenty-three members. There was no difficulty about proving that the larger Sanhedrin (the Supreme Court) should consist of seventy-one members, since Scripture specifically tells Moses to gather seventy elders who should constitute the court; with Moses added to their number, they become seventy-one.

But how can it be proved that the smaller Sanhedrin must consist of twenty-three? This is done by a careful analysis of two verses, one in Numbers and one in Exodus. The verse in Numbers (14:27) reads: "How long must I bear with this evil congregation?" The verse in Exodus (23:2) reads: "Thou shalt not follow a multitude to do evil . . . to turn aside after a multitude." The reasoning then is as follows: A "congregation" consists of at least ten people (that is, the minimum quorum for a congregation for public prayers is ten). Now how do we know that a congregation quorum is ten? Because Moses said, "How long must I bear with this evil congregation?" He made this statement in reference to the twelve spies who came back with a report about Canaan. Two of the spies, Joshua and Caleb, brought back an optimistic report, but ten of the spies brought back an evil report. It was in reference to these ten that Moses said, "How long must I bear with this evil congregation?" Thus we know that a congregation is a minimum of ten.

Now we know that in the court there must be a possibility of a congregation, i. e., ten, to vote for acquittal and a congregation to vote for conviction. This we learn from the passage, "The congregation shall judge and the congregation shall deliver" (Numbers 35:24, 25). Hence this court must have a minimum of two congregations, which is twenty. Now Scripture says, "You shall not follow a multitude to do evil" (Exodus 23:2), which means that you shall not follow a mere majority in doing evil, that is, in convicting a man. There must be at least more than a majority of one; hence the court must be twenty-two. And since a court should not have an even number of judges, the smaller Sanhedrin must have twenty-three members.

One of the oldest post-Biblical legal works, the Mechilta, discusses the famous verse, "an eye for an eye" (Exodus 21:24, Lev. 24:20), and explains it to mean, as Jewish law has always taken it to mean, that he who destroys the eye of his neighbor must pay monetary damage, and that it does not mean, as some think it means, that his eye, too, be taken away. They prove it by the fact that the Book of Leviticus (24:21) mentions, in the same passage, the crime of wounding a man and the crime of wounding a beast. They argue that the fact that these two crimes are put together in one passage is, of course, not accidental, but that it is for the purpose of indicating a parallel between injuries inflicted upon beasts and injuries inflicted upon man. Now just as injuries inflicted upon beasts are to be made good by monetary damages, so the injuries inflicted upon man are to be made good likewise with monetary damages. Hence, "an eye for an eye" means that the legally adjudged value of an eye in money must be paid for such an injury (Mechilta ed. Lauterbach, Vol. III, p. 67).

* * *

The rabbis not only scrutinized each passage minutely, judging the special meaning of each word or phrase, but occasionally would sweep over the entire Bible, gathering passages from book after book in order to prove an ethical or spiritual idea. A justly famous passage in the Talmud (b. Maccos 23b-24a) discusses the question: which is the most essential of all the commandments? The rabbis enumerated six hundred and thirteen commandments, of which three hundred and sixty-five were negative commandments and two hundred and forty-eight were positive commandments. But they knew well that these manifold commandments were but the outward expression of fundamental spiritual principles. They therefore searched through entire Scripture in order to discover the essential principle underlying all the commandments in the law. The passage (abbreviated) is as follows:

Rabbi Simlai taught: six hundred and thirteen commandments were given to Moses, three hundred and sixty-five negative commandments corresponding to the number of days in the solar year, and two hundred and forty-eight commandments corresponding to the number of sinews in the human body. Rabbi Hamnuna said: on which text is this based? "Moses commanded us a Torah" (Deuteronomy 33:4). The word "Torah" by the numerical value of its letters is six hundred and eleven, and two commandments were directly uttered by God Himself, namely, "I am the Lord thy God," and "Thou shalt have no other gods," which brings the number to six hundred and thirteen. Then David came and based them [all the six hundred and thirteen commandments] upon eleven commandments as it is said, "A Psalm of David (Psalm 15); who shall dwell in thy tabernacle? He that walketh uprightly, he that doeth righteousness, he that speaketh the truth in his

heart, he who has no slander on his tongue," etc. . . . Then came Isaiah
and based them all upon six, as it is said (Isaiah 33:15), "He that walketh righteously and speaketh uprightly, he that despiseth the gain of
oppression, he that shaketh his hand from holding of bribes," etc. Then
came Micah and based all of them on three (Micah 6:8), as it is said,
"He hath told thee O man what is good, and what the Lord doth require of thee, only to do justly and to love mercy, and to walk humbly
with thy God." Then Isaiah returned and based them all on two (Isaiah
56:1), as it is said: "Thus saith the Lord, keep ye justice and do righteousness." Then came Amos and based them all on one (Amos 5:4),
as it is said: "Thus saith the Lord to the house of Israel: Seek ye Me
and live." But Rab Nachman, the son of Isaac, objected to that on the
ground that "Seek ye Me" might refer to all the Torah and all its commandments. Therefore we say that it was Habakkuk who came and
based all the commandments upon one, as it is said (Habakkuk 2:4):
"The righteous shall live by his faith."

Thus did these men, students and devotees of the Law, who built
and developed all the details of a vast legal system, indicate their
deep appreciation of the spiritual truth that all the discipline of
private life and all public order are based ultimately upon faith in
God and in His justice.

In this way the students of the Oral Law searched and studied
Scripture. They were confident that within its words lay a meaning
still deeper than even the magnificent words themselves. They
sought for God-given guidance beyond the text of even an inspired
written Law. In their search for the Oral Law they developed the
habits of keen observation, careful analysis and brilliant, creative
imagination. In this deep and creative way, reverent yet analytic,
by this study with mind and heart, they set the tone for centuries
of Biblical studies in Israel. Never was the Book of books studied
with such loving carefulness as it was among the descendants of its
authors who looked upon it as a living law in which God's word
still spoke to those who would listen and learn.

CHAPTER VI

Modern Bible Study

CRITICISM AND ARCHAEOLOGY

THE magnificent progress of science is the result of the scientific method of study. The scientist reveres only the facts. When he approaches a new problem he asks first of all: What are the facts, the actual facts that can be seen and tested? Then he decides which facts belong together in one related group. Next he asks: How can these related facts be explained? Which theory can unite these facts into one system? Can this theory be tested by further fact? If the theory stands up under the test of newly observed facts, it is finally established as a scientific principle or law.

The modern scientific spirit does not respect traditional ideas merely because they are old and have always been accepted. It avoids any opinions for or against older, inherited ideas. It is, therefore, properly skeptical and critical. It prefers to study each problem from the very beginning, with an open, critical mind.

This spirit of healthy doubt of old notions has swept away century-old ideas concerning astronomy, biology and medicine, and has created an entirely new body of knowledge. This scientific spirit moves on from field to field. It has turned to a study of history and literature. Books that have come down to us from antiquity, which have been revered for their very age as much as for their contents, are, in modern times, looked upon with a cold, critical eye by scholars. They are subject to the scientific critical attitude which asks about them: are the books as old as they claim to be? Are they a unity or a composite? Who really wrote them?

Thus, for example, the ancient works of Homer have been subjected in modern times to new study. All the doubts and hints as to their authenticity found in the writings of older authors in the past now have been patiently collected. The Homeric books themselves have been now scrupulously analyzed. Differences in grammar between one part and another, in vocabulary, in apparent background and in mood, have been carefully noted. With these facts modern scientific students have concluded that these ancient books are not a unit but are a composite of various documents.

Within the last hundred years this modern scientific desire to analyze traditional literature has been applied with greater enthusiasm to Sacred Scripture. While there have been scores of students working on the analyzing and subdividing of Homer or the old Hindu classics, there have been hundreds of scholars working on the analyzing of Scripture. Much more energy, much more enthusiasm, much more international scientific scholarship has gone into the analysis of Sacred Scripture than of any other of the great works bequeathed to us by antiquity.

There is a specific reason for the widespread scientific scrutiny of Scripture. There is a stronger motivation to analyze the Bible than there is to analyze any other traditional book. The analysis of Homer or of other such works grew out of the simple scientific desire to search out the truth. This motive was, of course, also involved in the new examination of Scripture, but there was a much more urgent motive in addition. The Bible is more than an honored traditional book; it is Sacred Scripture. Its authority is looked upon as divine. Its words are the foundation of many great religions. The authority of governments has been based upon its texts. It has dominated life in many countries for many centuries. Therefore, the question of whether the Bible is what it claims to be is more than a question of scientific truth or falsehood. It is a question of human government, of the foundation of monarchies and democracies, and of the claims of many religions to authority and truth. All these motives have given to the new scientific study of Scripture an especial enthusiasm and devotion.

Of course, there is a danger in this very enthusiasm. Scientific analysis should be calm and willing to accept any result that the analysis may produce. The scientist must play no favorites between one hypothesis and another. He must revere only the facts. Wherever the facts lead him, there he must go. This calm balance can be easily maintained in the analysis of Homer. After all, no modern institutions would be endangered and no modern faiths shaken if it were proved that there never was such a person as Homer. But critical analysis of the Bible could easily result in an attack on existing institutions. Scientific critics of the Bible have been, of course, well aware of the fact, and some of them have been glad of it. It has rather pleased them to find contradictions or errors in the Bible. It is clear that much of the modern criticism of Scripture began with a presupposition of the unreliability of Scripture. A statement found in a pile of Assyrian records was often more readily accepted as a reliable fact than a statement written and preserved in Scripture. In other words, there has been in the new criticism of the Bible not only pure science but also some propaganda.

But, whatever the various motives have been, the result has been that hundreds of modern scholars have been searching Scripture with a critical, and generally, with a scientific scrutiny. It is an inspiring fact that so many modern minds, so many scientifically trained intellects have been devoting lifetimes of work to the study of the Bible. The results of such a tremendous concentration of study were bound to be great. An entirely new understanding of the history and meaning of Scripture has resulted. These new ideas have already affected the religious ideas of millions of people and have changed the philosophies of many religious institutions.

Hence the modern scientific study of the Bible deserves the respectful attention of all who are interested in the meaning and influence of Sacred Scripture. No modern man can read the Bible intelligently without knowing something of the new modern ideas. How were these ideas arrived at? What methods were used? Are these ideas correct? What influence will they have on the place of the Bible in the religious beliefs of tomorrow?

The most original part of the new Bible study is known as "Higher Criticism." This term is used in contrast to the term "Lower Criticism." Lower Criticism (the phrase is now old-fashioned and is rarely used) concerns itself merely with the correction of words and sentences in Scripture, whereas Higher Criticism deals with entire books and the sources of which they were composed. It is called Higher Criticism because it is more thoroughgoing, more basic; it is a criticism on a wholesale or a higher level.

Of course, the critical study of the Scripture is not entirely the invention of modern scholars. The Talmudic literature itself contains a considerable number of references which indicate that the ancient scholars more than fifteen centuries ago made certain comments about the Bible which might well be described as being of a critical nature. For example, in discussing a certain part of Scripture they say that "Here there is the wrong arrangement of the sections of the text" (j. Shovuos vi, 1); or frequently they will say that the order in which certain laws or events now appear in Scripture is not necessarily the order in which we must understand them actually to have occurred ("There is no order of precedence or lateness in the Torah," b. Pesachim 6b, etc.). The Midrash (Leviticus Rabba vi, 6) says that the Prophet Beeri (the father of Hosea) prophesied only two verses. These verses, being of course insufficient to be made into a separate book, were inserted into the Book of Isaiah, and are the verses 19 and 20 of chapter 8 of that book. The Talmud indicates that the authorship or the editorship of certain books was not by the personage whose name appears at the heading of the book. Thus, it says: "Joshua wrote his own book. Samuel wrote his book and the Books of Judges and Ruth. Jeremiah wrote his book and the Books of Kings and Lamentations. Hezekiah and his group wrote Isaiah, Proverbs, Song of Songs, and Ecclesiastes. The men of the Great Synagogue wrote Ezekiel; and the twelve Minor Prophets, Daniel and the scroll of Esther. Ezra wrote his book and the genealogy in the Book of Chronicles up to his own date" (b. Baba Bathra, 14b-15a). That does not mean, of course, that the Talmud did not believe that Amos, for example, was the author of the prophecies of Amos, but rather that the Biblical book itself, in the form in which they had it, and the other eleven minor prophets, were edited by the men of the Great Synagogue.

After Talmudic times there were certain scholars who expressed themselves in what we would call a critical, independent way with regard to Scripture. Best known among these is the great Spanish grammarian, poet, and traveller, Abraham Ibn Ezra (twelfth century). He said, basing his statement upon an earlier opinion, that Moses did not write the last chapter of Deuteronomy, which deals with the death of Moses. He seems furthermore to hint that certain verses in the Torah were later additions. In his commentary to Deuteronomy, chapter one, verse one, he refers to these verses and hints as to their later origin. (However, Friedlander in his essays on the writings of Ibn Ezra, pages 60 ff., denies that Ibn Ezra believed that any of the verses were later additions.) Ibn Ezra also believed that Samuel wrote only the first twenty-four chapters of the Book of Samuel, and that the latter part of Isaiah, beginning with chapter 40, was written during the Exile, and not by Isaiah, the author of the first thirty-nine chapters. (See Friedlander's *Essays*, p. 57.)

The great philosopher Baruch Spinoza (seventeenth century) was a pioneer in radical Bible criticism. He made reference to the radical hints of Ibn Ezra and found many contradictions in the Biblical books. He doubted that Moses was the author of the Pentateuch.

The real founder of what can truly be called Biblical Criticism was Jean Astruc, a French physician, who was a professor at the University of Paris in the eighteenth century. He was the first relatively modern scholar to notice that certain parts of the Biblical book of Genesis referred to God only as *Elohim* and that other parts referred to him as *Yahveh*. (Most modern scholars accept "Yahveh" as the correct pronunciation of the four consonants *Y H V H*, which are traditionally read "Adonoi.") He gathered together the passages in Genesis which used the word *Elohim* and considered them to be an entirely different document from all the scattered passages that used the word *Yahveh*. This conclusion became the foundation of the basic theory in modern Biblical criticism, namely, the documentary theory. According to this theory there were two different documents in the Torah, the *E* document (which uses *Elohim* as the name of God) and the *J* document (which uses *Yahveh* as the name of God). How the modern scholars reconstructed these documents, fragment by fragment, from all over the Five Books of Moses, can be seen from the following list from Cornill's *Introduction to the Canonical Books of the Old Testament*, New York & London, 1907. It will be observed by even a quick glance at the list that small parts of verses are broken off from each other and assigned confidently to one document or the other. Thus, in Cornill, pages 43 ff., there is the following detailed analysis of the Torah into documents:

To *J* belong: Gen. 2:4b-4:26; v. 29; 6:1-8; 7:1-2, 3b, 4-5, 7, 10, 12, 16b, 17b, etc., etc.

Ex. 1:6, 7a plus, 8-10, 14a plus, 20b, 22 ?; 2:11-23a plus, etc., etc.
Numbers 10:29-32; 11:4-6; 10-13, 15, 31-35; 13:17ba, etc., etc.
To *E* belong: Gen. 15:1, 2b-3a, 5, 11, 12a plus, 13-14, 16, 20-22, etc., etc.
Ex. 1:11-12, 15-22, 2:1-10; 3; 4:17-18, etc., etc.
Num. 10:33, 35-36 ?; 11:1-3, 14, 16-17, etc., etc.

The scholars who took up the work of Astruc found that these two sources, *J* and *E,* are distinctly different from each other not only in the use of different names of God but also in general style and in thought. Then still later scholars discovered other documents. The Book of Deuteronomy was considered a separate document dating from a later time than *J* and *E*. Then a fourth document was worked out, the Priestly Code, known to scholars by the initial capital *P*. This Priestly Code was exilic and belonged to the time of Ezra. Later there was further dissection even of these documents, and an old document, the Book of the Covenant, was discovered in the Biblical book of Exodus, and a Holiness Code in Leviticus. The Higher Criticism did not depend entirely upon the internal evidences discovered by the careful analyses of the Biblical texts. Its conclusions were aided by studies of other ancient documents, mostly ancient Babylonian documents. Much use was made of the discoveries in the field of ethnology, on the ground that the ritual and customs of primitive people would throw light upon the ritual and customs of the early life of Israel. Especial use was made of the customs of Semitic tribes, particularly the life of Bedouins. Since the Bedouins preserved many primitive customs and were also Semites still resident in the Bible lands, their mode of life was considered to be closely analogous to the life of the patriarchs and the period described in the Biblical Book of Judges.

The climax of all these years of Biblical study came in the work of two German scholars, Graf and Wellhausen. The modern theory of the Biblical documents received its complete form through their work and is known today as the Graf-Wellhausen theory. The Graf-Wellhausen theory not only divides the Torah into these documents but attempts to arrange the documents in chronological sequence and thus to write the literary history of the growth of the Bible. The *J* document is the oldest and the *E* the next (the ninth to the eighth pre-Christian century); then follow *D*, a century or so later, and finally *P*, late in the sixth pre-Christian century. Successive editors in ancient times merged the various codes, changing them as they worked. Similar methods were applied by critical scholars to the other books of the Bible. (A clear, concise account of the development of Bible criticism and the Graf-Wellhausen theory is given by the late Isaac Landman in the *Universal Jewish Encyclopedia*, Vol. II, pp. 284-293.)

Considered purely as an analysis of documents, there would seem to be little in the Higher Criticism to which any open-minded student of Scripture could object, except, of course, Orthodox Jews or Christians who would naturally resent the irreverent handling and the rough dissection of an ancient, God-given document. But the Graf-Wellhausen theory is more than an analysis of documents. It goes further and it is this further step which is meeting with increasing objections even from many who are not old-fashioned in their attitude to Scripture.

On the basis of these documents assembled from the Scriptural text, Wellhausen particularly attempts to reconstruct the whole history of Israel and Judaism and arrives at conclusions which depreciate considerably the status of ancient Israel and its contribution to the religions of the world. In the first place, he says that in the earlier times which the Bible so vividly depicts, the times of the Patriarchs and Moses, there was no monotheism at all. The religion of the Israelites was virtually the same paganism as the religion of the Canaanites and other surrounding people. None of the more exalted portions of Scripture could have been recorded in those ancient days (about the time of the thirteenth or fourteenth pre-Christian century and earlier) because there was no knowledge of writing. The Prophets were the first to bring ethical monotheism to Israelitish paganism, and even this ethical splendor did not endure because the priests, the authors of the Priestly Code, who rewrote the Bible into a ritual document, soon made of Judaism a mere priestly organization.

Perhaps it would be helpful to give a dual picture of the history of Israel, contrasting the Bible's own view of it and the view that emerges from the Graf-Wellhausen theory. According to the Bible itself, monotheism and the history of Israel begin with our patriarchs, with Abraham, who recognized the True God in the midst of the world's paganism. This tradition was carried on by his descendants who were enslaved in Egypt. As the Twelve

Tribes of Israel, they were redeemed from Egypt by Moses, the first of the prophets and the great lawgiver. The laws of Moses were the practical expression of the ritual worship and the ethical obligations involved in the service of the One True God and, therefore, began with a great prelude, showing that God was the Creator and Father of all mankind. The people of Israel when they came to Canaan were corrupted from their loyalty to God by the influence of the Canaanites, and the prophets arose to bring them back to the true worship of God, emphasizing the duty to avoid idolatry and to stress the ethical law. After the fall of the First Temple and the Babylonian exile, the law was promulgated once more by Ezra, who strengthened its hold upon the entire people. By that time idolatry had completely disappeared among them; Moses and the Prophets had won their battle and Israel had become a people devoted to the Eternal God. The Jewish traditional view thus unites into one unbroken spiritual chain Moses, the Law, the people of Israel, and the Prophets. This view of an historically consistent faith is expressed in the ancient Blessing recited before the reading of the prophetical portion: "Praised be Thou, O God, who has chosen the Law and Moses, His servant and Israel, His people and the Prophets of truth and justice" (from Masseches Sofrim XIII, 7).

The Graf-Wellhausen theory completely rewrites this entire history. It denies the existence of the early monotheism of the patriarchs, and in fact monotheism, according to the theory, does not really appear until the time of the Prophets. The patriarchs are merely legendary and Moses himself is not more than half-legendary. It also denies that the legislation of the Torah was promulgated by Moses (about the fifteenth century before the present era) since it seems unbelievable that from such a legislative system the exalted ethical doctrine of the Prophets could ever emerge. It insists that the whole literary activity which went into the making of the Bible hardly began before the eighth pre-Christian century (i.e., six hundred years after Moses). At that time, under the influence of the prophets, the document E was developed in the northern kingdom and J in the southern kingdom, then the document D, until the post-exilic period, when the priestly code embodied the earlier material and rewrote it as a legalistic system, priestly influence thus destroying prophetism. In other words, the old monotheism of the patriarchs and Moses never actually existed. Those personalities are mere symbols. The true religion of Israel began with the Prophets and then was buried under the legislation of the early pre-exilic period.

One can understand how Dr. Schechter, in his essay, "Higher Criticism — Higher Anti-Semitism," felt moved to say these words:

> Our great claim to the gratitude of mankind is that we gave to the world the word of God, the Bible. . . . The Bible is our sole *raison d'etre*, and it is just this which the Higher Anti-Semitism is seeking to destroy, denying all our claims for the past, and leaving us without hope for the future. . . . The Bible is our patent of nobility granted to us by the Almighty God, and if we disown the Bible, leaving it to the tender mercies of a Wellhausen, Stade and Duhm, and other beautiful souls working away at diminishing the "nimbus of the Chosen People," the world will disown us.

While the indignation of Dr. Schechter is understandable, yet it would be hard to demonstrate that a conscious desire to deprecate the contribution of Israel motivated many of the higher critics, although this was the effect of much of their rewriting of Israelitish history. Perhaps it would be more correct to say that the Graf-Wellhausen picture of Israelitish history reveals the New Testament attitude. The New Testament in general despises the Law of Moses as a burden and a curse and a source of sin. Christian scholars who developed the modern critical theory, having been brought up on the New Testament idea that the Law is a curse and a source of evil, could not believe that the great Prophets could grow up under the influence of the "Law of Moses." Thus the critical scholar Duhm (see the quotation in Strachan's article in Hasting's *Encyclopedia*, Vol. IV, page 317) gives the typical viewpoint of the higher criticism on this matter. "The great Prophets are not the children of the Law but the inspired creators of the religion of Israel. Prophecy is the supreme initial fact which transcends explanation. The Levitical system which gave the death blow to prophecy in the post-exilic age could never have been its nursing mother in earlier times."

As much as the New Testament despises the old Law, so it reveres the Prophets. Jesus, it says, is the true spiritual climax of prophecy; but the Jews never appreciated their prophets. (Matthew

5:12: "For so they persecuted the Prophets which were before you.") In other words, although the Graf-Wellhausen theory of Jewish history was motivated chiefly by careful, scientific analysis, it was written chiefly by Protestant theologians who could not escape from the New Testament contempt for the Law and the New Testament conviction that the Israelites never appreciated the Prophets who really came into their own in the new religion.

Fortunately, this deprecation of earlier Jewish history has been abandoned by many recent scholars. New science, more exact knowledge, has given them a deeper insight. Since the days of Wellhausen, the science of Near East archaeology has greatly advanced. New and startling finds have been made in various places in Palestine and the surrounding country, and these finds have changed the minds of many students about the Wellhausen rewriting of the history of Israel and of Judaism. The first of these discoveries were not in the close proximity of Palestine but in Babylonia and Egypt. In 1872 the Babylonian legends of a great flood (the Gilgamish Epic) were deciphered. The tablets which tell the story go back to originals as old as two thousand years before the present era. In 1901 the legal code of the Babylonian King Hammurabi was discovered. These laws were generally dated at twenty-one hundred years before the present era. In 1887 a large number of clay tablets were discovered in Egypt. These tablets, known as the Tel El-Amarna Letters (after the village where they were found), were written in Babylonian by Egyptian governors in Palestine and vicinity, to Akhnaton, the Egyptian Pharaoh who lived in the fourteenth century B.C.E.

These and other discoveries in western Asia and Egypt threw new light upon the life described in the Bible. They showed that a highly developed civilization existed in Palestine at that early time when, according to the Graf-Wellhausen theory, the Israelites were still too primitive to develop legislation or even to have the art of writing. If the theory were still to be maintained in the light of these discoveries, it would be necessary to make the strange assumption that the laws of Hammurabi (in ways resembling those of the Bible) and the arts of civilization were known to the entire Near East *except* the Israelites, who mysteriously remained primitive!

Perhaps the most important finds were made between 1929 and

1939 at Ugarit (Ras Shamrah on the coast of northern Syria). A vast number of inscriptions there throw a new light on the Canaanitish religion of about 1400 years before the present era. From this site alone scholars have drawn new conclusions which tend to defend the reliability of Scripture against some of the attacks of the critical theory. In the first place, a Semitic alphabet was found with a vast amount of religious literature, indicating that the art of writing must have been well known and far spread many centuries earlier than the Graf-Wellhausen theory assumes. Hence, the nobler religious parts of Scripture could well have been written down as early as the days of Moses. Furthermore, the ritual detail (sacrifices, etc.) described in these new-found documents and dating from the thirteenth pre-Christian century so closely parallels the sacrificial ritual given in the Torah that it is no longer necessary to say, as the Wellhausen theory says, that these rituals are the products of a very late century (the sixth century, when the Priestly Code was written). The great archaeologists have expressed themselves quite strongly on this whole question.

There can be no doubt that archaeology has confirmed the substantial historicity of Old Testament tradition. Divergences from basic historical fact may nearly all be explained as due to the nature of oral tradition, to the vicissitudes of written transmission.

These divergences seldom result in serious modifications of the historical picture. (William F. Albright, *Archaeology and the Religion of Israel*, Johns Hopkins University, p. 176.)

These adaptations by Israel from Canaanite religion lay almost entirely in the domain of religious architecture, cultic symbolism and sacrificial practice, poetic language and temple music. But the God of Israel was so far superior to the gods of the pagans, both conceptually and ethically, that theological borrowing from Canaanite sources was scarcely thinkable. (*Ibid.*, p. 94.)

With regard to the critical theory that there was no true monotheism before the time of the prophets (9th century), Professor Albright says:

The cosmic monotheism of Solomon's Temple makes Mosaic monotheism a *sine qua non* for the comprehension of early Israelite religious history, since there is no suggestion in any of our sources that a paramount spiritual leader had arisen between Moses and David. (*Ibid.*, p. 155.)

In essentials, however, orthodox *Yahwism* remained the same from Moses to Ezra. From first to last ethical monotheism remained the heart of Israelite religion. (*Ibid.*, p. 175.)

The Mosaic tradition is so consistent, so well attested by different pentateuchal documents, and so congruent with our independent knowledge of the religious development of the Near East in the late second millennium B.C., that only hypercritical pseudo-rationalism can reject its essential historicity. (*Ibid.*, p. 96.)

It is at least the belief of the present writer that the progress of archaeological research will be found to constitute a steady march in the direction of establishing the essential trustworthiness of the Bible narrative, and of greatly increasing our intelligent comprehension of it, and thereby our appreciation of its spiritual message, which constitutes its real value for mankind. (Sir Frederic Kenyon, formerly Director of the British Museum, *The Bible and Archaeology*, p. 30.)

First, as most fundamental and perhaps most important of all, is the evidence as to the antiquity and wide dissemination of writing. Here the contribution of archaeology has been decisive and of far-reaching effect. Within the lifetime of the present writer [Professor Kenyon] classical scholars such as Grote could maintain that writing was unknown to the Greeks until the seventh century at the earliest, and Biblical scholars such as Wellhausen that it was unknown to the Hebrews (except in the form of carved inscriptions) until the ninth. All information (or what purported to be such) about earlier ages could at best be nothing but oral tradition. Such conclusions were then justifiable, for at that time there was no evidence of writing at an earlier date. Now there is overwhelming evidence from all quarters. (*Ibid.*, p. 263.)

And the following quotation from Professor George L. Robinson, in *The Bearing of Archaeology on the Old Testament*, p. 158:

As Professor Meek in the Preface of his Oberlin Lectures, *Hebrew Origins* (1936), frankly concedes:

"In these later days of Old Testament research, the old documentary hypothesis is being seriously questioned. I occasionally use the documentary symbols, *JEDP*, but in no instance have I used an argument that is dependent upon the documentary hypothesis" (p. viii).

Some of the wisest Old Testament critics are willing to concede even more; for example, the late Prof. A. R. S. Kennedy of the University of Edinburgh, in a Conference of Old Testament scholars (1934) said: "Though thirty years may be required to evaluate these Ras Shamra tablets properly, it looks as though by them we shall be required to antedate the Book of Leviticus a thousand years earlier than Criticism has allowed." French savants do not hesitate frankly to allow, that "Higher Criticism has received from these tablets a serious blow."

Thus it seems clear that the latest advance in the science of archaeology has outdated many of the conclusions of the classical Biblical critical theory. But this should not be surprising. Such outdating of scientific theories has occurred over and over again in all the long progress of science in every field. A scientific theory holds sway for a long time. It seems unshakable. Then new facts are discovered upon which an entirely different theory is based, supplanting the old. At first the enthusiasm for the new theory leads scholars to believe that the old must be swept away entirely. But later and more sober consideration leads to the conclusion that the old scientific theory, although now largely outdated, has left a residue of truth which is permanent.

So it undoubtedly will be with the Graf-Wellhausen theory. A tremendous amount of brilliant scholarship has gone into it. Scholars, working under the aegis of this hypothesis, have boldly dissected Biblical texts, changing verses at will, denying the dating which the Biblical narrative claims for itself, and rewriting the entire history of Israel in a fashion which no way resembled the original Scripture. These extremes have now been entirely overcome by new knowledge. At present the scholars in the new field of Near East archaeology are themselves inclined to be extreme in their statements with regard to the old theory. Some of them say that, "The props have been knocked out of Higher Criticism," or that "Higher Criticism has received a death-blow." Yet later thought will surely reveal that while the older critical theory has been considerably outdated, some of it remains as a permanent part of our knowledge of Scripture.

It will take a great deal of careful evaluation to decide just how much of the Graf-Wellhausen theory can still be maintained. It is fairly clear now what must be abandoned. What goes by the board is its sweeping rewriting of Jewish history, its allegation of widespread Israelitish paganism, its notion that the Prophets were only a passing glory, that Judaism soon petrified under the Priestly Code into a priestly formalism. We know now, scientifically, that that is not so or at least that it can no longer be proved to be so. The superiority of Biblical monotheism shines clearly from the earliest days of Israel as the Bible said it did.

Yet the great amount of ingenuity and scholarship which has gone into the Higher Criticism will remain valuable. Much of the analysis of the Torah into its various documents will stand. Perhaps Biblical critical theories of the future will go back to the standpoint of the pioneer of Biblical criticism, Jean Astruc, in the eighteenth century, the title of whose famous work means "the documents which Moses used in writing the Pentateuch." In other words, there were documents substantially as Biblical criticism has discovered, but these documents were very old and may have well been used (and why not by Moses?) in the writing of the Torah. This idea has some Talmudic precedent. In the Talmud (b. Gittin 60a) there is one opinion that the Torah was given to Moses all "sealed," that is, in one unit altogether. But another opinion is that it was given to him in separate scrolls and he united them into one.

It must not be concluded that archaeology has vindicated the Bible in all its details. The Bible, written by the hands of man, and as the Talmud says, "speaking in the language of man," contains many inconsistencies which cannot be harmonized, and its text has been in many cases corrupted by errors of the scribes. It is a human document and must be judged not only with reverence but with human understanding. What archaeology has vindicated is not the detailed facts of Scripture, but its larger background. Its general dating, the antiquity of its monotheism, are now reestablished. Archaeology has not proved that the Bible is always correct, but it has proved that it is essentially credible. Scholars will now no longer be as ready to doubt Scriptural verses or as eager to correct its texts to get rid of the slightest difficulty. The presumption is that the Bible is largely correct and deserves respectful and conservative study. The contribution of modern archaeology has won a new reverence for Sacred Scripture.

CHAPTER VII

The Bible and the Modern Reader

THE Bible is old, but it is still a best-seller. In an age in which people love novelty, and prefer the latest novel and drama, this ancient book, whose most popular English translation was made over three centuries ago, is still bought in larger numbers than any other book.

This does not mean that the Bible is read today as much as it once was read. It is still bought by the millions more than any other book, and it may even be read more than any modern book, but it is not read as regularly and as steadily as it was read in the past. The Bible is a much bought book but also a much neglected one.

The modern grandchildren of regular Bible readers are not Bible readers themselves. The reason for this lies partly in the modern temperament; it is not merely the modern love for novelty. People realize that although the Bible is very old it is worthy of being read. That is why almost every home has a Bible. The reason for the neglect of the Bible goes somewhat deeper into the modern mood.

The Bible is a difficult book. While there are many passages which are instantly recognizable as beautiful, these passages are scattered and are often imbedded in long, dull sections of text. Moreover the essential meaning of the Bible is a deep one. It cannot be instantly grasped. A person must read certain books in the Bible over and over again until "deep calleth unto deep," until the profound thought of the Bible reaches the deeper understanding of the reader. The Bible cannot be scanned; it must be studied. It cannot be studied once or twice; it has to be read over and over again. This is just the way in which earlier generations read the Bible.

Many new and interesting books are being published nowadays. A modern reader will read about twenty-five books a year. He cannot possibly read them more than once, or at most twice. Generations ago people had fewer books, and chief among them was the Bible. It was not read just once and then put aside forever. The Bible was a lifetime book. People read it over and over again until it became part of their lives and its language colored their daily speech. But modern people believe that we have not the leisure to make of any book a lifetime book. Very few of us read Shakespeare over and over again all through our lives. There are no lifetime books any more. Perhaps our reading is more varied than the reading of the past, but the reading of our fathers awakened much more meditation. Our reading is broader; theirs was deeper. Since the Bible needs deep reading to be understood, modern people set it aside for some later date, one which perhaps never comes.

Besides the fact that our crowded modern life and our restless mood makes it difficult for us to give the Bible the deep, meditative lifelong thought by which alone it can be properly understood, there are more positive reasons why many modern people consciously turn away from the Bible. A modern man will often say or feel that he has outgrown the Bible, that the Bible expresses ideas which he can no longer accept, and also that there is nothing in the Bible which he, as a modern man, particularly needs.

Which ideas are there in Scripture which a modern man thinks he has outgrown? First of all he will say that the Bible is unscientific. He believes, for example, that the very beginning of the Bible is all wrong, that its description of the creation of the world is contrary to the ideas of modern science, and that, therefore, since it starts out wrong, the entire book is out of date for the modern man.

But what difference should it make to the modern reader if an ancient book, which is primarily a spiritual guide, begins with a description which is not in accord with modern scientific ideas of astronomy? The answer, of course, is that the Bible claims to be inspired. If the Bible itself maintains that all its ideas are God's word, then an unscientific idea claiming to be God's word creates, for us, a real religious difficulty. It seems impossible then for a modern man to believe in modern science and also to believe in the God of the Bible. Some people make a choice between the two.

Some reject modern science, evolution, etc., and choose the Bible; but most people, if compelled to choose, stand by modern science and reject the Bible.

Clearly we must come to some decision as to what we mean when we say that the Bible is God's word. It would be too simple a solution of the difficulty to say that the Bible is not God speaking to man but man speaking to God; that it represents man's search for God rather than God's search for man. Such an explanation, while it contains considerable truth, would make the Bible entirely a human book and would solve all difficulties at once by ascribing all objectionable parts in Scripture to weakness in the men who uttered them. This would be solving the problem by refusing to face it. It would end the battle by running away from the battlefield. In trying to discover what revelation means, we must consider first of all what the Bible itself says.

The Bible does not definitely claim that all of its text is the word of God. However, it does make such a claim for the Torah, the Five Books of Moses. At the end of the prophecies of the last literary prophet, Malachi, we find a clear statement on the part of the prophet, or on the part of the editor of the prophetic writings, that the Five Books of Moses are to be considered divinely inspired. "Remember ye the law of Moses, My servant, which I commanded unto him in Horeb for all of Israel." (Malachi 3:22.) Also, in the books of the Prophets there are many prophecies in which the Prophet opens his address with the clear statement, "Thus saith the Lord." It is clear, therefore, that the Prophet did not consider that his statements to the people were merely his own ideas, but were thoughts put into his mind by God himself. "The Lord God hath spoken; who can but prophesy?" (Amos 3:8.) But the prophetic books also contain more than these prophecies. They also give us descriptions of many historical and biographical events. The prophets themselves nowhere claim that the history or the wording of these events constitute a divinely inspired text. Then, also, in the third part of Scripture, the Hagiographa, the Sacred Writings, there are many poems, psalms which are addressed by man to God and not by God to man, and semi-skeptical philosophy, as in Ecclesiastes, etc. The Bible nowhere claims that all this material constitutes a divinely inspired text.

It is true that later scholars in Talmudic times, when they had to decide, after long debate and many doubts, as to which books to include in Scripture and which books to exclude, decided that there was a measure of inspiration in all of the books which were included in the Bible (see Part One, chapter ii). They claimed, of course, a greater degree of inspiration for the Pentateuch, the Torah, than for the other two parts of Scripture, the Prophets and the Holy Writings. They were convinced that the Torah was actually dictated by God to Moses, and so was directly inspired. The other two parts of the Bible were written by Prophets who received the inspiration of what they called "the holy spirit." In other words, the latter two parts of Scripture have a sort of secondary inspiration.

It is important, however, to notice that the Bible itself does not make this sweeping claim of complete inspiration for itself. The Torah, as has been said, is claimed by the Bible itself to have been inspired directly. The other two parts of Scripture are looked upon as containing, among other and human material, the word of God. The Biblical writers were aware that many of the psalms of self-expression, many of the unhappy doubts and questionings, many of the prosaic recordings of historical events, came from them and not from God. But they were confident that even in these later parts of the Bible God frequently spoke. To the Biblical authors, the inspiration of God is to be found throughout Scripture, though not necessarily everywhere in it. The positive opinion of the Bible about itself amounts to this: it is not merely that man searched for God but also that God searched for man. It is not merely that man was somehow inspired but that the Bible insists that truth was revealed. The essential thought of the Bible is that God, the Infinite, makes Himself known in our finite world, giving to transient and mortal man a revelation of His Omnipotence and of His will. God's revelation to man is the essential thought of the Bible. One may deny such revelation, but the denial cannot serve to help us to an understanding of Scripture. If one does not merely brush the entire Bible aside, one must acknowledge that the Bible itself declares that God enters into the life of mankind, reveals Himself, selects instruments for His purposes, and makes it possible for His purposes to be fulfilled.

This fundamental Biblical doctrine in no way contravenes modern ideas. If a modern man believes in God at all, and there is no sound reason why he should refuse to do so, he must admit that God the Infinite and the Omniscient finds it within His power to reveal Himself to the human mind, which is a fragment of Total Intelligence. The only question is, can the Bible, with its strangely unscientific ideas and its occasional repugnant incidents, be considered by modern man to be, as it claims to be, the revelation of God?

Great Jewish religious philosophers, Maimonides among them, said centuries ago that many of the phrases and expressions in the Bible are visions which people saw. When they say "God walked" or "God talked," these things are dreams or visions and not to be taken literally. The Talmud says that the Bible speaks in the language of man. These ideas should give us a guide as to how we should look upon the Bible.

God reveals himself through a human instrument and the instrument is imperfect. God speaks eternal truth, but we can grasp only a small and often a vague fragment of it. The human instrument of God's revelation slowly improves and the understanding of Infinite Truth becomes clearer and truer. Therefore, all Biblical thought must be studied as a growth of ideas. We must see how the thoughts in the Bible develop from age to age. God's eternal word was but imperfectly grasped by man in the early stages of his development. This is true of the entire Bible, the Torah as well as the Prophets and the Holy Writing. God's word came through the imperfect human instrument and was garbled in its transmission through the childlike spirit of earlier generations. Hence the imperfect ideas in science and morals, though spoken in the name of God, are only the more simple-minded man's concept of the divine revelation.

It is, therefore, immaterial that the astronomy given in the Book of Genesis is now outgrown. Even if the book were written today, in terms of the latest modern astronomy, as follows: God said: "Let a star come out of the heavens and pass by the sun and draw from it the material for the earth and the moon," this statement so closely in accord with our modern science might be outgrown in a few years and become quickly unscientific. The primitive science of the Book of Genesis is merely the clothing to the idea given in the distant past and is outgrown now just as our own science will seem primitive a hundred years from now.

We must disentangle the changeably mortal in the Biblical

revelations from the eternally divine. What the story of Genesis means to us is not that the Creation took place in accordance with a certain specific method there described and that the animals were created in a certain order; that was the mortal concept of creation. The divinely inspired idea is that God is the Source and Creator of all life, that man is created in His spiritual image and is therefore bound to strive to become more Godlike, that all men are descended from one Source of life and must therefore work toward brotherhood. This is the divine and the eternal message of Genesis.

This suggests what our attitude should be to some of the harsher passages in Scripture. For example, the children of Israel are told to exterminate the inhabitants of Canaan. To our modern conscience this seems cruel, not that our modern age is above such mass extermination. Our age has produced more wholesale, cold-blooded extermination than any in the past. Our objection is that such extermination is given in the Bible in the name of God.

Again we must understand that this is how men in those days understood the divine command. The divine mandate was essentially to destroy idolatry ("not the sinners but the sin"), so that Israel might become the first community in the world freed from the blindness and corruption of idol worship. Those who transmitted the divine command felt that the safest way to achieve it was to remove the corrupt Canaanites as a source of infection. It is to be noted that unlike modern mass-slaughter this was not for booty or bloodthirstiness. They were forbidden to take any booty from the defeated Canaanites. And, as a matter of fact, the extermination never took place. The Canaanites did remain and did corrupt the people with their idolatrous and immoral practices. In the early stages of its history, Israel took the divine command to conquer idolatry as meaning to destroy the idolators out of the land; but as the divine inspiration continued within it, the human instrument grew more receptive and the Revelation revealed itself more clearly in the words: "Thou shalt love thy neighbour as thyself," and "ye shall love the stranger for strangers were ye in the land of Egypt," and "My house shall be a house of prayer for all peoples." It was not a different God who gave these different commands but men in different stages of moral growth who understood God's will more clearly. When human beings in parts of the Bible withdraw from the sense of God's nearness and speak in terms of racist bitterness or group jealousy, then their writings are no better than writings that express such moods even in our day. The Book of Esther, although a late book, does not once contain the name of God, and in it we are told that as a certain group of Persians wanted to slaughter all the Jews, the Jews rose and with the help of Persian officials were revenged of their enemies. But wherever in the Bible the Spirit of God speaks clearly, His voice teaches men to arrive at the conviction, "Have we not all one Father, Has not one God created us all?"

It is therefore insufficient to say that the Bible is a human book and that it was written by men of religious genius, although indeed genius is a mysterious quality, and may come from mysterious sources of inspiration. The Bible by its own basic testimony is a book of revelation, and as such must be rejected or accepted. Our modern view of this revelation is not that the whole Bible, every word of it, is revelation. We believe that the Bible contains revelation. This revelation even at its best comes by way of the human mind and therefore is always marred by the imperfection of the instrument, yet even in its most imperfect expression it reveals the divine spark.

It is of no great significance to us that the astronomy of three thousand years ago is different from the astronomy of today, or that later writers describing reverently the lives of the ancient patriarchs in the blessed days before the flood imagined them to have lived six and seven and eight and nine hundred years. Since life itself was in their eyes a blessing, they considered those ancient men to have been richly blessed. It is not particularly significant that one source says that the animals came into the Ark two by two and another says that the animals came in by sevens, or that chronology of kings in one book of the Bible does not quite harmonize with the chronology in another.

These contradictions would be crucial if we would believe that every word in the entire Scripture is as God revealed it. But the Talmud long ago indicated that there are degrees of sanctity in the book. It says that some commandments came directly by the voice of God, and some through Moses. It says that the Divine Spirit of Revelation ceased with the Prophets Zechariah and Malachi. We say too that there are degrees of sanctity in Scripture. God's word emerges slowly into clear expression. God reveals Himself to man in all ages and at all times. "Day unto day uttereth speech" (Psalm 19). He speaks through the grandeur of nature. "The heavens declare the glory of God" (Psalm 19). He speaks in the moral conscience of man. "Thou shalt do no unrighteousness . . . thou shalt love thy neighbour as thyself. I am the Lord." To the religious geniuses who wrote the Bible, God's word was clear and unmistakable in nature, in the human conscience and in the history of nations. When the prophet said: "Thus saith the Lord," he had no doubt that he was but an instrument of the Eternal. "The Lord God hath spoken; who can but prophesy" (Amos 3:8).

This essential Biblical conviction is unaffected by the uncertainties, the confusions, or even the occasional evil of the human vehicle through which God made His revelation. The basic thought of Scripture is that God revealed Himself to man. The eternal Spirit spoke through man, who shares a fragment of His eternity; and man, sometimes clumsily, sometimes magnificently, sometimes with confused ethics, and sometimes with exalted morality, sought to voice in Scripture the eternal word.

*　　*　　*

It is, therefore, foolish to search in the Bible for those expressions or ideas which are not inspiring to us. They are there. Sometimes they do not inspire us because we do not understand them and sometimes indeed because man does not understand "what doth the Lord require." It is much more important to find in this great book of revelation what we need and what is vital to us. While the entire basic message of Scripture is of eternal value, each age differs from every other and must seek response for its especial needs in the word of God. There is in Scripture great healing for our modern hurt.

Many ancient thinkers found life senseless, meaningless—the product of chance or of blind, callous fate. Much of this feeling of helplessness in a world which "makes no sense" exists in the heart of modern man. Man today has endured many disappointments, has found many of his high hopes frustrated. He has witnessed war and mass slaughter and has found that science, in which he trusted with such childlike faith, has by its very discoveries helped bring the world to the edge of annihilation. There is a deep sense of futility and confusion in the modern world. Men ask despairingly, "What is it all about? What meaning is there to life?" The question springs from the growing conviction that life really has no meaning, that it is just a blind struggle which mercifully does not last too long. This fundamental pessimism, which was basic to ancient Greek thought, is now recapturing the frustrated mind of modern man.

The Bible's essential doctrine is that life has a deep meaning and a sure purpose. This purpose may be beyond us. We may be saddened that we fail to discern it as the suffering Biblical hero Job was saddened, but even he, in his despair did not doubt that the mysterious universe is mysterious only to us, but clear to its Creator and Guide. Life has a purpose because it was created with a purpose by an Infinite Intelligence.

The modern man has therefore a choice between two world attitudes, the pagan or the Biblical. He can either say, as he is inclined to say nowadays, that life makes no sense, or that it must make sense because there is a deeper meaning in it. Life must make sense or science is meaningless. One does not search for universal laws in a world which one believes is a product of chance and accident. The scientist searches nature with a faith which he cannot prove, namely, that behind all the evident confusion there surely is order and law. To the faith of science the Bible adds that the source of world law is the Universal Mind, the world's Creator. Whether we believe that life is senseless, or, as the Bible teaches, that it is meaningful, then, in either case, we will have to endure the world as it is in our time. We will not escape the world and its menace. We will have to bear our personal disappointments and pains. But if we believe that all this danger and pain is due to blind chance, then we are hopeless victims of universal accident. But if enduring, as all must do, we believe that there is a sense to be discovered, a purpose to be fulfilled, and an inherent order to be reestablished, we can then endure with patience and work with hope. The basic meaningfulness of life, written into it by God the Creator and to be rediscovered by man, His child, is an indispensable faith for the troubled soul of modern man.

* * *

The modern psychologist expends immense effort to discover the foibles and the individual complexes of each sick personality.

Medicine has discovered innumerable remedies for his individual diseases and protection against his pain. Yet in this age of individual psychology, mass movements have arisen which force unchangeable doctrines upon masses of men. The individual's own reactions are not considered relevant. He must obey and be disciplined. Entire nations, whole races, have in our day been declared to be sub-human, and all the techniques of modern science have been employed for their mass destruction.

In general, the modern state has grown mighty and the citizen has grown smaller. The sense of the unimportance of the individual is sweeping into all departments of modern life and thought. This is partly due to the modern machine production. Men have ceased to be skilled artisans making objects of individuality, but have become mechanical tenders of machines producing objects of unvarying similarity. It is partly due to the mass mediums of entertainment which teach everybody the same ideas and the same jests and the same songs at the same time. People are less inclined to live their own types of lives, to accept public duty as personal responsibility, to resist mass opinion with individual conviction. The time has come for a rediscovery of the human individual and the reevaluation of each separate personality.

The uniqueness of each individual is a cardinal teaching of Scripture. Although the Bible devotes its strongest admonitions to the people of Israel as a community, the ethics and status of Israel depend upon the conscience of the individual Israelite. The Bible begins with the creation of man as one person. The rabbis in the Talmud say that God could have created many individuals at one time, a whole species simultaneously, but He created man alone in order to indicate that each individual in each generation is a unique person, created in the image of God.

Life then is precious; we dare not destroy it. Life is unique; we dare not suppress it in anyone else. Each one has the potentiality of growth, of using and developing the God-spirit in him. For ourselves in our place in the world, for our fellow men in their places in the sunlight, the modern world needs to renew allegiance to the Bible teaching of the uniqueness of man endowed by his Creator with inalienable rights and the possibility of noble living.

* * *

The Bible has a specific significance for the world community of Israel. Israel is central in the Bible. The Bible itself would be incomprehensible without an understanding of what occurs in the world through Israel. In clear and unmistakable terms the Bible declares that Israel is a chosen people.

It is precisely this unique or chosen status of Israel which turns many modern Jews against the Bible. They feel impelled to insist that there is no basic difference between Israel as a community and other human communities. They object to the whole idea, first because of anti-Semitism. Those who harbor prejudice against Jews insist upon the fact that the Jews are "different" from other people and that this difference is deep-rooted and ineradicable. Hence the very concept of the difference of Jews from others is disliked and often bitterly attacked by Jews. Another motive for modern Jewish objections to the doctrine of Israel's uniqueness is motivated not by defense against the perverse anti-Semitic form of the doctrine, but by a Jewish feeling of liberalism. Many Jews look upon the idea of Israel as a "chosen people" as a sort of unjustified boasting, a proclamation of self-superiority.

The thought that Jews are in no way different from these people may seem justified to many modern Jews, but there is no doubt that it is anti-Biblical, at least as far as Israel as a group is concerned. The Bible cannot be understood without this teaching. Israel's uniqueness is at the very heart of Scripture. It is clear that modern Jews will not be rewon to Scripture until they come to terms with the idea of Israel's special place in history, the central idea of Holy Writ.

Whatever we think of Israel's status in present-day history, there can be no doubt as to Israel's uniqueness in the past. The great Biblical ideas which have so deeply influenced the world grew up in the land of Israel and among the people of Israel. This is simply a fact, yet it is a fact that is difficult to explain. By our ordinary human explanations we are unable to account for the emergence of these great doctrines. None of the stock historical explanations, such as the influence of environment, or the effect of racial impulse, can adequately explain why these group ideas arose in Palestine and among the people of Israel, and only there.

In attempting to explain the origin of the great Scriptural ideals, scientists have subjected the Bible to intense scrutiny. Its books have been analyzed and still more ancient documents have been discovered to be embodied in them. Its institutions have been traced step by step and arranged along the line of an evolutionary order. But the basic doctrines of Scripture still are of mysterious origin. Why should the idea of monotheism have arisen only in Israel and only there developed? None of the paganisms of other nations arrived at that idea in its purity as it is found in Scripture. None of the mighty empires in which we would expect to find great universal ideas harmonizing with their wide sway of earthly power ever produced the concept of the One and Only universal God. Yet among this little people, whose independence was short-lived, whose troubles were endless and whose dangers were constant, which was largely an agricultural people and saw little of the outer world, only there appeared the grand and complete doctrine of the Only God, the Father of all men. There is no explanation on ordinary material grounds. We can only say that God revealed Himself to Israel.

If then we are dealing with a unique historical event, the choice by God of one people out of all mankind to become His instrument for a universal purpose, then the rest of Israel's status in the Bible becomes clear. This people, chosen to be the first vehicle of revelation, burdened by this heavy task, denounced by its prophets for sins which would not have been noticed among other people, grew under this stern discipline to become a people different from all other peoples. Its conscience was stirred and trained as no social conscience elsewhere was stirred and trained.

Although the people of Israel were uncomfortable and frequently bitter when the Prophets kept denouncing them, they nevertheless remembered and preserved those very denunciations. There is no other people in antiquity whose historical records preserved the record of that people's weaknesses and sins. Other chronicles preserved the victories or the triumphs, or even the heroic and gallant defeats of the kings and nations. Only the Bible, preserved by the people of Israel itself, records for all the future the iniquities, the stubbornness, the weaknesses and the idolatries of Israel. Here was a people which, in spite of the sins which it shared with all humanity, was the first to become aware that these were sins.

A people which was the vehicle of God's mysterious Self-revelation, which under the impact of law and prophecy developed a unique ethical conscience, was inevitably looked upon as the instrument of a divine purpose "to open the blind eyes and to bring the prisoner from the dungeon." Although frequently in Scripture Israel is promised reward for loyalty to God and punishment for sin and unfaithfulness, the purpose of his entire existence was not merely to be happy himself, but to aid in the enlightenment of the world, in the ridding of it of idolatry and the bringing of it to the worship of the God of all.

Modern Jews have lived through a campaign of unparalleled vilification. The insults, the false charges, the contemptuous prejudices propagated from Nazi sources will long remain in the world atmosphere before they are dispelled by cleaner ideas. The worst effect of these insults is that they frequently enter within the spiritual fortress of the individual Jew. Individual Jews harbor within themselves an anti-Semitic fifth column. There is a tragic mood in modern Jews of dislike for other Jews, and what is psychologically even more harmful, a tragic self-mockery or self-pity, or, worse, Jewish self-hatred.

This at least can a modern Jew derive from the Bible, that whether or not he himself is a worthy descendant, he comes from a grand ancestry. It was through his people that the noblest ideas which the world possesses came into human consciousness. At least he has the dignity of a great memory, of a noble past.

The modern Jew need not hastily agree to anti-Semitic contempt and conclude that all the generations of Biblical ethical influence have forever faded from among the children of Israel. Is there not justification for the conclusion that the stern, moral training, the awakened conscience which the Prophets achieved among our fathers, has not yet been entirely dissipated, and that the sense of mercy and justice still lives among us today? We could well be still more merciful than we are and our sense of justice could be still nobler, but justice and mercy do live in us to a marked degree.

The Bible has imposed a world-task upon Israel. Part of it has been fulfilled. Half of the world, the world of Christianity and Mohammedanism, where the Bible influence has reached, has been cured of the confusion and corruption of idolatry. But another part of the task has not been fulfilled. Men have learned of the One and Only God, but have not yet drawn the conclusion of the one united humanity. They know well that "we all have One Father" but still "they deal treacherously one with another."

Does the unfulfilled half of the task of Bible-Israel constitute a mandate for modern Israel? Is it our task any more? Is there any way in which modern Jewish groups or individuals can help fulfill the promise first uttered to our father Abraham and repeated through Scripture, that all the families of the earth will find blessing through us? Modern Jews will yet have to decide whether they can be of especial blessing to the world. It seems that in one way or another we cannot quite escape the Biblical insistence that we are not commonplace. Anti-Semites insist that we are an especial curse to the world. We had better accept the teaching of Scripture that we are and can become a special blessing to the world. How we may bless, each man will decide for himself, and each Jewish community will seek its own way.

The modern Jew who studies Scripture may find that the Bible has changed his thinking and living. He will learn dignity and duty, and if he himself cannot quite see how he may fulfill any unique function in the world, he may nevertheless come to feel, as Scripture feels, that God has a purpose of His own through us and with us, and that it is God's intention that neither hatred on the part of others nor indifference on our part will ever avail to remove the eternal people from amongst the children of men. "I the Lord change not and ye children of Israel will not be consumed."

CHAPTER VIII

The Bible as Literature

A YOUNG writer learns first by imitation. He is impressed by the style of certain authors and consciously or half-unconsciously imitates them. But as he gradually acquires the literary art, his work resembles less and less the work of other authors and begins to express his own temperament. His writing becomes calm or tense, according to whether he is a calm or a tense person. It becomes clear or confused, according to the degree of the clarity of his own mind. The story which he writes rambles along or comes swiftly to its climax, according to whether he is leisurely in mood or dynamic. This is what the great French scholar of the eighteenth century meant when he said, "The style is the man himself." An analysis of an experienced author's style will therefore reveal the nature of the author's personality.

This is eminently true of the Bible. While the spiritual content of the Bible can be learned from an analysis of its various ideas, it is also revealed in the very style of Scripture. The message of Scripture cannot be fully grasped without an appreciation of the literary grandeur which brought its ideas into human life. It is a fortunate coincidence that the people of Israel, who wrote the Bible, possessed two great requisite characteristics: a profound spiritual awareness which made them susceptible to the revelation of God's presence in the world, and a magnificent literary power which clothed that message in such words as could reach across the continents and over the centuries.

Although the student of Scripture senses that the Bible is great literature, he does not usually stop to analyze and discover wherein its greatness lies. He is moved by its power but he cannot trace adequately the source of that power. It is questionable whether this can ever be adequately done, but at least it may be possible to describe the chief characteristics of the Biblical style and indicate a few of the methods whereby literary power was achieved.

In both the poetic and the prose parts of Scripture there are certain literary characteristics which stamp the writing of the Bible as great art. First of all, writing in the Bible is vivid. The author makes his thought shine in clear colors from the page. Except in some cases where the text has not come down to us in perfect condition, there is almost never any doubt of what the author wants to say. Many authors, although they may have definite ideas and deep feelings, somehow cannot make these ideas and feelings visible through the dark screen of language. The language of Scripture is not a curtain. It is sunlight.

The Bible style is also dynamic. Most writing, even when it is clear, creeps on at a slow pace. The Bible moves swiftly from idea to idea. Furthermore, the Bible phrases are quotable and memorable. Hundreds of Biblical phrases possess a proverb-like terseness. Five or six words thus carry a profound thought and record it on the memory. The authors of the various books of Scripture succeeded time and time again in expressing their ideas in phrases that engrave themselves "on the tablets of the heart."

These literary qualities of Scripture—its vividness, its dynamic motion, and its memorableness in phrasing—are quickly recognized. But it is not easy to analyze the ways that these artistic excellencies were achieved. The following suggestions indicate a few of the various ways in which the Bible attains its literary quality.

* * *

The Bible achieves its vividness by means of what might be called "picture language." It rarely resorts to abstract ideas or theoretical phrasing. Although the thoughts which it expresses are often profound and sometimes extremely delicate in their distinctions, the language is the visual language which is found in the simple eloquence of simple people. In this way, the great Biblical thoughts are brought right down to earth and poured into the vessel of objects that can be seen and handled. The Bible could almost be painted as well as it was written, so visual is it.

For example, the Prophet Jeremiah wishes to indicate that the people of Israel have turned away so long from God to many idolatries and have become so accustomed to the injustices of their daily life, that by now it seems hopeless for them ever to rid themselves of their sinfulness. Instead of speaking, as we would of a "deep-rooted habit of sin which cannot be easily discarded," the Prophet expresses the idea in an image that leaps immediately to the eye. He says: "Can the leopard change his spots, or the Ethiopian his skin?" (Jeremiah 13:23.) When he wants the people of Israel to be sobered by the realization of their inevitable national sorrow, he does not use the language that we would use and tell them to "face the future" and realize what trouble is in store. He makes a vivid picture of a woman undergoing the ritual of mourning and says: "Cut off thy hair and cast it away and take up a lamentation on the high hills." (Jeremiah 7:29.)

When the Prophet Isaiah desires to explain to the people that there can be no true worship of God without righteous action, that brutality and violence make all worship and ritual meaningless, he does not use words such as those we have just used, the abstract words "brutality" and "violence" and "worship" and "meaningless." He sees the people spreading out their hands in prayer and he explains why their prayers will be in vain. He says: "When ye spread forth your hands, I will hide Mine eyes from you. Your hands are full of blood." (Isaiah 1:15.) When Isaiah desires to describe the ideal future, when a righteous king will usher in a period of peace and when violence will disappear as a motive for human action, he does not speak as we would do, using the vague terms "era" and "violence" and "human cooperation." He says vividly and concretely: "The wolf shall dwell with the lamb and a little child shall lead them." (Isaiah 11:6.)

This vividness is found not only in the poetic books of the Bible; it is characteristic of the entire writing of Scripture, the prose as well as the poetry. When the Book of Leviticus, describing the blessings of obedience to God, and desiring to indicate that the joy of righteousness comes from the sense of God's presence, it does not say, as we would say, "the sense of God's presence," but says in a visual image: "I will set My tabernacle among you and I will walk among you and I will be your God, and ye shall be My people." (Lev. 26:11, 12.)

It is evident that many of the phrases which are used about God in Scripture, such as God "speaking" with human words, or "walking," or "stretching out His hand," are not to be explained as mere primitive ideas of God. It is the natural genius of Scripture to speak of the Infinite Spiritual God in language that is vivid to human beings. It was not that they were naive enough to think of God as having feet or hands; it was simply that God's presence was so real to them that they could not talk of Him in abstract terms, such as "the awareness of the Infinite Presence." They said, in warm awareness: "I will walk among you." They were artists. Thus there are thousands of Biblical sentences which a painter could put on canvas. It is this concreteness of visual images which makes the religion of the Bible so near and so alive.

Such picture language is very close to metaphor. A spiritual idea is compared to a physical fact. It is often unconscious metaphor. But the Bible is also full of conscious metaphor, apt and impressive. When the Prophet Isaiah wants to say that God will forgive the people their sins, that He will afford them an opportunity for repentance so that they may be righteous once more, he thinks of the contrast between sinfulness and righteousness in the metaphor of two brilliant colors, and he says: "Though your sins be as scarlet, they shall be as white as snow." (Isaiah 1:18.)

The Prophets seek to explain why a people chosen by God should yet be so sinful. Both Jeremiah and Isaiah use the same metaphor to explain this difficulty. It is a word picture that was familiar to the people of Palestine who worked in their vineyards, and who knew how important it is to have the proper stock for the vine, and who also found to their sorrow that often a good breed of vine somehow degenerates. So the Prophet Jeremiah says of Israel:

> Yet I had planted thee a noble vine,
> Wholly a right seed;
> How then art thou turned into the degenerate plant?
> — Jer. 2:21.

So too Isaiah uses the same metaphor: "For the vineyard of the Lord of hosts is the house of Israel." (Isa. 5:7.)

In a prose portion of the Bible, when the lawgiver desires to make clear to the people the punishments that will be theirs for their sinfulness, he makes use of a vivid agricultural metaphor.

Instead of saying that they will suffer drought and that nothing will grow and there will be sandstorms instead of rain, he says: "And thy heaven that is over thy head shall be brass and the earth that is under thee shall be iron. The Lord will make the rain of thy land powder and dust." (Deut. 28:23, 24.) When, in a similar passage in Leviticus, the author wants to say that part of God's punishment will be that the people will lose their inner confidence and become terror-stricken and nervous, he says that they will be terrified at the sound of a leaf rustling behind them in a wind and they will run away when no one drives them. But he says it much more vividly and pictorially than we moderns would express it. He says: "And the sound of a driven leaf shall chase them; and they shall flee as one fleeth from the sword; and they shall fall when none pursueth." (Lev. 26:36.) It is thus through concrete image and clear meaningful metaphors that the Bible achieves everywhere its brilliant vividness.

One cannot describe, except perhaps negatively, just how the Bible achieved its second literary quality, namely, its dynamic forward motion, which keeps the writing from bogging down. The Bible avoids long explanatory phrases, unnecessary adverbs and adjectives. Its style seems to be based chiefly upon nouns and verbs, the nouns for the picture and the verb for the action. Even in English and other modern languages, where the translation requires the addition of many words and which therefore is always an expansion of the terser Hebrew style, even there the succession of nouns and verbs and the swift sequence of images makes the Bible style move on rapidly without lagging. For example, Jacob's sons ask permission to take young Benjamin with them down to Egypt. Jacob resists their request. He recalls his old sorrow at the loss of his son Joseph and he fears that a similar loss will befall him with Benjamin. Then he would have no children left from his beloved wife Rachel. And if this would occur, life would lose all its joy for him. He would age rapidly and die. All this he expresses in the following, swift succession of phrases: "My son shall not go down with you; for his brother is dead and he only is left; if harm befall him by the way in which you go, then will ye bring down my gray hairs with sorrow to the grave." (Gen. 42:38.)

The Prophet Isaiah desires to enumerate the evils which exist in his beloved city of Jerusalem, how violence has taken the place of peacefulness, how the nobility has lost its sense of high station and responsibility and how justice is neglected and the judges are corrupt. He states all this in a dynamic succession of sharp, short phrases, giving the picture in a minimum of words.

> How is the faithful city
> Become a harlot!
> She that was full of justice,
> Righteousness lodged in her,
> But now murderers.
> Thy silver is become dross,
> Thy wine mixed with water.
> Thy princes are rebellious,
> And companions of thieves;
> Everyone loveth bribes,
> And followeth after rewards;
> They judge not the fatherless,
> Neither doth the cause of the
> widow come unto them. – Isa. 1:21-23.

The Prophet Amos, desiring to indicate that God's mandate to the prophet is one that cannot be ignored, that it startles the sleeping heart to alert attention, says it in this succession of phrases: "The lion hath roared, who will not fear? The Lord God hath spoken, who can but prophesy?" (Amos 3:8.)

Thus do the phrases in the Bible move swiftly. The style does not halt nor get lost in the swamps of verbiage. One phrase follows another quickly, and in each phrase the verb and the noun are prominent. The Book of Leviticus describes the reward that will come to the people of Israel for obedience to God's commandments. The reward is given as a happy, prosperous agricultural life in which one harvest is no sooner over than the next harvest begins. The land will have prosperity and security. Note the unbroken movement of the succession of phrases in this passage from Leviticus:

If ye walk in My statutes and keep My commandments, and do them, then will I give your rains in their season and the land shall yield her produce and the trees of the field shall yield their fruit. Your threshing shall reach unto the vintage and the vintage shall reach unto the sowing time. Ye shall eat your bread until you have enough, and dwell in your land safely. I will give peace in the land and ye shall lie down and none shall make you afraid. – Lev. 26:3-6.

The Hebrew originals in all these quotations have half as many separate words as do the modern translations, and yet even the translations reveal the ceaseless, forward motion characteristic of the dynamic Biblical style.

Because the Bible style is so vivid and so swift moving it is a joy to read, once the style is appreciated. But the Bible has still a third quality: it is memorable. It has remained in the minds of people to accompany them all through their lives. The Bible achieves this memorableness chiefly because of the terseness of its writing, which gives it the vividness and the dynamism we have mentioned above. The sentences are stripped of all superfluity, and therefore as simple yet brilliant phrases they write themselves on the memory. The Biblical phrases are often like popular proverbs which have travelled from father to son, from mother to daughter, for so many generations that the very erosion of time has rubbed away all unnecessary words. A proverb is like a sharply cut gem, bright and indestructible. This proverbial quality is found all through Scripture. That is why its phrases remain in the memory of men. Who can forget, once having heard them, the words of Ruth to Naomi: "Entreat me not to leave thee . . . Whither thou goest I will go; thy people will be my people and thy God my God." (Ruth 1:16.) Or the words of the blind Isaac when his son Jacob appears in the guise of his brother Esau: "The voice is the voice of Jacob but the hands are the hands of Esau." Or the phrase in Isaiah indicating in simple and unforgettable words the universal human tendency to evil: "We all like sheep did go astray." (Isaiah 53:6.)

Sometimes this proverb-like sharpness of phrase is aided, as are most popular proverbs, with an attractive similarity of sounds. As in Proverbs, where sound groups like "sticks and stones" and "kith and kin" make the phrases memorable, so there is the same sound similarity (assonance) throughout the Bible. Most of these are too difficult to translate into English, although sometimes the translator succeeds. For example, in the Book of Lamentations, the author says that God has increased the weeping and the mourning for the children of Israel. The Hebrew says God has increased for the daughter of Judah *Ta-ania va-ania*. These two synonyms, which sound so quotably and so musically alike, are translated with fair success as "He hath multiplied in the daughter of Judah mourning and moaning." (Lam. 2:5.) When Elijah the Prophet was in the wilderness and God spoke to him, and God was not in the. strong wind and not in the earthquake, but was in the "still small voice," the similarity of sound in "still small voice" is a successful translation both for sound and meaning of the Hebrew *kol d'momo dako*. (1 Kings 19:12.)

But many of the greatest examples of this enchanting similarity of sound have not yet been successfully rendered in English. In the fifth chapter of Isaiah, where the Prophet describes God's reproof of Israel, there is the verse, "he looked for justice but behold, violence." The Hebrew has a beautiful similarity in sound. The word for "justice" is *mishpot* and the word for "violence" is *mishpoch*. So too in the next sentence, "He looked for righteousness, but behold, a cry" (verse 7). The word for "righteousness" is *ts'doko* and the word for "a cry" is *ts'oko*. In the original therefore this sentence of Isaiah has a sharp impact, lacking in the translation. While these phrases and many others lose half their magic in translation, enough have been successfully translated to indicate that for their similarity of phrase and proverbial terseness, hundreds of Biblical verses are memorable in many languages.

A listing of some of the memorable phrases will be given in the next chapter. Here it is sufficient to indicate that these great characteristics of Biblical style are all the more remarkable when we realize that the Bible was written over many centuries and by many authors. While it is indeed a fact that not all of the Biblical books are equal in quality, nevertheless the style of the great books influenced all the later writing. There are of course dull portions in Scripture but there is no other literature in which the dull portions form so small a proportion. There is no literature anywhere which is so vivid because of its concreteness, so dynamic because of its reliance upon nouns and verbs and rapid phrases, and so memorable as almost to defy forgetfulness.

These qualities of literary excellence are found in almost every type of literature found in Scripture. It is not surprising that the poetic writings, such as the Psalms and the Proverbs, are vivid and memorable, but it is remarkable how much true art there is in the

THE BIBLE AS LITERATURE

prose portions. The prose narratives in Scripture move forward from incident to incident with hardly an aside or a delay, and the whole episode comes to quick conclusion. Note, for example, the story of Esau selling his birthright to Jacob. In this narrative not only is the whole action given—Esau coming from the field, asking for the red pottage (then follows the only aside explaining the name *Edom*, which means "red"), then feeling that the satisfaction of his hunger is more important than the keeping of the birthright, the sale and Esau's contempt for the birthright which he has just sold—all this is told in four or five quick sentences, a model of narration.

And Jacob sod (boiled) pottage; and Esau came in from the field, and he was faint. And Esau said to Jacob: "Let me swallow, I pray thee, some of this red, red pottage; for I am faint." Therefore was his name called Edom. And Jacob said: "Sell me first thy birthright." And Esau said: "Behold, I am at the point to die; and what profit shall the birthright do to me?" And Jacob said: "Swear to me first"; and he swore unto him; and he sold his birthright unto Jacob. And Jacob gave Esau bread and pottage of lentils; and he did eat and drink, and rose up, and went his way. So Esau despised his birthright. – Gen. 25:29-34.

Besides the swift succession of incidents which tell the whole story in these four or five sentences, note especially the rapid sequence of phrases so typical of the best of the dynamic Biblical style in the sentence: "And he did eat and drink and rose up and went his way."

As an example of the biographical style of Scripture, it is worth paying especial attention to the short biographies of kings written, one very much like the other, in the Biblical Book of Kings. Especially in the cases of the wicked kings, the authors of the books were eager to compress, and so managed to say a good deal in short compass. This is the biography of King Omri, the father of Ahab, who founded the capital of the northern kingdom, the city of Samaria:

In the thirty and first year of Asa king of Judah began Omri to reign over Israel, and reigned twelve years; six years reigned he in Tirzah. And he bought the hill Samaria of Shemer for two talents of silver; and he built on the hill, and called the name of the city which he built, after the name of Shemer, the owner of the hill, Samaria. And Omri did that which was evil in the sight of the Lord, and dealt wickedly above all that were before him. For he walked in all the way of Jeroboam the son of Nebat, and in his sins wherewith he made Israel to sin, to provoke the Lord, the God of Israel, with their vanities.

Now the rest of the acts of Omri which he did, and his might that he showed, are they not written in the book of the chronicles of the kings of Israel? And Omri slept with his fathers, and was buried in Samaria; and Ahab his son reigned in his stead. – 1 Kings 16:23-28.

Undoubtedly the "book of the chronicles of the kings of Israel" here referred to had many scrolls devoted to the doings of this King Omri, and many of the passages must have been dull indeed. The writer of our book selected all that he considered significant in this king's reign and compressed the whole history in eight verses.

There is a great amount of legal literature in the Bible, and even that somehow has a liveliness and a vividness exceptional to legal literature. Even law is often pictured in visible images and beautified by a glow of religious idealism. Note this passage of legal enactments from the famous holiness code, Leviticus, chapter 19:9-14:

And when ye reap the harvest of your land, thou shalt not wholly reap the corner of thy field, neither shalt thou gather the gleanings of thy harvest. And thou shalt not glean thy vineyard, neither shalt thou gather the fallen fruit of thy vineyard; thou shalt leave them for the poor and for the stranger: I am the Lord your God. Ye shall not steal; neither shall ye deal falsely, nor lie to one another. And ye shall not swear by My name falsely, so that thou profane the name of thy God: I am the Lord. Thou shalt not oppress thy neighbour, nor rob him; the wages of a hired servant shall not abide with thee all night until the morning. Thou shalt not curse the deaf, nor put a stumbling block before the blind, but thou shalt fear thy God: I am the Lord.

The poetry of the Bible occupies perhaps half of the entire volume of the book. There are poetic passages even in the Five Books of Moses and in the history books. The Prophets are almost entirely poetry and the Book of Psalms is all poetry, and so is the Book of Job.

Poetic writing may be described as a combination of imagery and rhythm. It is, therefore, a merger of the qualities of two other arts, painting and music. The dance is likewise a combination of the qualities of these two arts. Poetry, like the dance, must evoke visual images and also have a regular rhythm of utterance. Hebrew poetry has rhythm, the stress of a sequence of syllables, in many of its examples. But the outstanding poetic quality is not within the syllables but between the lines. There is a special relationship between the lines which is characteristic of Hebrew poetry. Usually it is written in two-line couplets, the meaning of the first line being definitely related to the meaning of the second line. Sometimes the second line is merely a reecho of the first line in different words. This type of parallelism is generally referred to as synonymous parallelism, both lines having the same meaning. This is the most frequent type of Hebrew poetry. A number of examples will indicate how the thought in the second line of each couplet is a reechoing of a thought in the first line. Thus Psalm 19 begins:

> The heavens declare the glory of God
> And the firmament showeth His handiwork.
>
> Day unto day uttereth speech,
> Night unto night revealeth knowledge.
>
> There is no speech, there are no words,
> Neither is their voice heard.

So too in Psalm 145:

> I will extol Thee My God O King
> And I will bless Thy name for ever and ever. . . .
>
> The Lord is gracious and full of compassion
> Slow to anger, and of great mercy.
>
> The Lord is good to all
> And His tender mercies are over all His works.

The thought is always reinforced in the second line and two by two the whole poem marches forward.

Very often the second line is not synonymous in thought with the first but is a contrast, an antithesis of the first. This is generally referred to as antithetical parallelism. Thus the 10th chapter of Proverbs begins:

> A wise son maketh a glad father
> But a foolish son is the grief of his mother.

> Treasures of wickedness profit nothing
> But righteousness delivereth from death. . . .

> He becometh poor that dealeth with a slack hand
> But the hand of the diligent maketh rich. . . .

> The memory of the righteous shall be for a blessing,
> But the name of the wicked shall rot.

Sometimes the second line of the couplet is neither a synonym nor an antithesis, neither the same, nor the opposite of the first line, but is merely an expansion of it. This type of couplet may well be called "the progressive parallelism." This is frequently found in the prophetic books. Thus, in Isaiah, chapter 5:

> Let me sing of my beloved
> A song of my beloved touching his vineyard.

> My beloved had a vineyard
> In a very fruitful hill.

> And he digged it and cleared it of stones
> And planted it with the choicest vine.

> And he built a tower in the midst of it
> And also hewed out a vat therein.

> And he looked that it should bring forth grapes
> And it brought forth wild grapes.

There are also certain poetic sections in Scripture in which the grouping is not two lines but three, and some even of four. But generally the couplet either of synonymous lines or two antithetical lines or a progression of two lines is the usual form of Biblical poetry.

Wherever the Bible is read, wherever one picks it up, one is likely to find powerful writing. Prose and poetry alike, narrative or history, mystic vision and even law tend to have the same magnificent characteristics, a vividness of style that makes the writing almost rise like a picture before the eye, a dynamic movement which carries the reader along from sentence to sentence, and a proverb-like phrasing which makes so much of the Bible unforgettable and beloved.

CHAPTER IX

Treasures in the Bible

SINCE the Bible is so vivid and terse in its diction, it is generally possible to find the greatest ideas of the Bible expressed in a single phrase or a single sentence. A choice therefore of great Bible sentences is, because of the vividness of Bible speech, more than a succession of quotable excerpts. It is a summary of exalted ideas and profound insights.

Scripture has been studied for so many centuries, particularly for the use of sermons, that many of its great verses have passed into public usage and therefore those phrases that are most meaningful are also the most familiar. Sometimes certain verses become familiar, not through sermons, but through general literature. An author will find a certain verse in Scripture which he considers eminently suitable as the summing up of the theme of a book which he is writing. He will use this Biblical verse or phrase as the title of the book. It is rather remarkable how many book titles are Biblical phrases. Thus the phrase, "The woman thou gavest me," was more familiar to the last generation as the title for Hall Caine's once popular novel than as the words of Adam in the Book of Genesis. Or in that generation, the phrase, "many waters" was well known as the title of a book by the popular novelist Margaret Deland rather than as a quotation from the last chapter of The Song of Songs, "Many waters cannot quench love." And in our time, "a lion in the street," was a widely known phrase three years ago as the title of Adria Locke Langley's novel about a demagogue-dictator rather than as a quotation from the Book of Proverbs. The words "the sun also rises" is known as the title of Ernest Hemingway's novel; but it comes from the first chapter of Ecclesiastes,

So the phrase "the days of our years" is more widely known as the title of Van Paassen's book than as a quotation from Psalm Ninety. And the words "the grapes of wrath" are known as the novel by John Steinbeck rather than as the quotation from Isaiah, by way of Julia Ward Howe's song, "The Battle Hymn of the Republic." The "valley of decision" was widely known as the title of Marcia Davenport's novel rather than a quotation from the Prophet Joel. So too the phrase "little foxes" and "the voice of the turtle" are known as the titles of plays rather than quotations from the Song of Songs, just as in the last generation "the silver cord" was widely known as the title of a drama than from its source in the Book of Ecclesiastes.

Many Biblical phrases are known simply because they have been current in daily speech. A man says he has escaped "by the skin of his teeth" without realizing that he is quoting the Book of Job. (For other Biblical phrases in current speech, see Part One, chapter 1.) But there are many which may be well known in one language because some author in that language gave them currency and yet not well known in another language. There are many which were current in past generations when the Bible was more widely read, and, although they are significant, have passed out of usage in contemporary speech and writing.

There are at least two ways in which these great and justly famous quotations can be given. They may either be classified according to subject matter or else given in sequence as they appear in book after book of the Bible. The value of classifying them according to subject matter under the heading "justice," "mercy," "creation," etc., is that they would thus be more usable for writers, but such is not the purpose of this chapter, which is to give those verses which stand out against the duller texture of the rest of the page as one reads. Citing them thus in sequence will give the impression which the Bible made in its more impressive passages on the generations which read the Bible through. One, of course, cannot be certain always which verse is the most important in a chapter or in a section. People vary in their spiritual needs and receptivity and a particular verse may be meaningful to one person and not to another. Except, therefore, for those verses which have become famous in literature or in current speech, a selection such as this is necessarily personal.

GENESIS

And God said: Let there be light, and there was light. –1:3.

And God blessed them, saying: Be fruitful and multiply. –1:22.

And God created man in His own image, in the image of God created He him. –1:27.

Then the Lord God formed man of the dust of the earth and breathed into his nostrils the breath of life, and man became a living soul. – 2:7.

And the Lord God said: It is not good that man should be alone. I will make him a helpmate for him. – 2:18.

And the man said: This is now bone of my bone and flesh of my flesh. She shall be called woman. – 2:23.

And he said: I know not. Am I my brother's keeper? – 4:9.

While the earth remaineth, seed time and harvest and cold and heat and summer and winter and day and night shall not cease. – 8:22.

Whoso sheddeth man's blood, by man shall his blood be shed, for in the image of God made He man. – 9:6.

Come, let us go down and there confound their language that they may not understand one another's speech. – 11:7.

And I will make thee a great nation and I will bless thee and make thy name great and be thou a blessing. And I will bless them that bless thee and him that curseth thee will I curse and in thee shall all of the families of the earth be blessed. – 12:2, 3.

And Abraham said to Lot, let there be no strife, I pray thee, between me and thee for we are brethren. Is not the whole land before thee? – 13:8, 9.

I will not take a thread nor a shoe-latchet nor aught that is thine lest thou shouldest say I have made Abraham rich. – 14:23.

I am the Lord Almighty. Walk before Me and be thou wholehearted. – 17:1.

And Abraham drew near and said: Wilt Thou indeed sweep away the righteous with the wicked? – 18:23.

Shall not the Judge of all the earth do justly? – 18:25.

Behold now I have taken upon me to speak unto the Lord who am but dust and ashes. – 18:27.

But his wife looked back from behind him and she became a pillar of salt. –19:26.

And he said: Lay not thy hand upon the lad, neither do thou any thing unto him; for now I know that thou art a God-fearing man, seeing thou hast not withheld thy son, thine only son, from Me. – 22:12.

And she said: Drink, my lord; and she hastened, and let down her pitcher upon her hand, and gave him drink. And when she had done giving him drink, she said: I will draw for thy camels also, until they have done drinking. – 25:18, 19.

And he said: Come in, thou blessed of the Lord; wherefore standest thou without?– 24:31.

And they called to Rebekah and said unto her, Wilt thou go with this man? And she said: I will go. – 24:58.

The voice is the voice of Jacob, but the hands are the hands of Esau. – 27:22.

And Jacob awakened out of his sleep and said: Surely God is in this place and I knew it not. – 28:16.

And Jacob vowed a vow saying: If God will keep me in this way that I go and will give me bread to eat and raiment to put on, so that I come back to my father's house in peace, then shall the Lord be my God. – 28:21.

This heap (of stone) is witness between me and thee this day. There-fore was the name of it called . . . Mizpah, for he said: The Lord watch between me and thee, when we are absent one from another. – 31:48, 49.

I am not worthy of all the mercies and of all the truth which thou hast shown unto Thy servant. – 32:11.

And he said: I will not let thee go unless thou bless me. – 32:37.

And the man asked him, saying: what seekest thou? And he said, I seek my brethren. – 37:15, 16.

Behold this dreamer cometh. – 37:19.

And Pharaoh said unto Joseph . . . I have heard say of thee, that when thou hearest a dream thou canst interpret it. And Joseph answered Pharaoh, saying: It is not in me; God will give Pharaoh an answer of peace. – 41:15, 16.

If harm befall him by the way in which he go, then will ye bring down my gray hairs with sorrow to the grave. – 42:38.

And Jacob said unto Pharaoh: Few and evil have been the days of the years of my life and they have not attained unto the days of the years of the life of my fathers. – 47:9.

And he blessed them that day saying: God made thee as Ephraim and Manasseh. – 48:20.

Unstable as water. – 49:4.

Cursed be their anger for it was fierce. – 49:7.

EXODUS

Now there arose a new king over Egypt who knew not Joseph. –1:8.

But the more they afflicted them, the more they multiplied, and the more they spread abroad. –1:12.

And behold the bush burned with fire and the bush was not consumed. – 3:2.

Put off thy shoes from off thy feet, for the place whereon thou standest is holy ground. – 3:5.

And God said unto Moses: I am that I am. Thus shalt thou say unto the children of Israel: I AM hath sent me unto you. – 3:14.

And Moses said unto the Lord: I am not a man of words . . . for I am slow of speech and of a slow tongue. – 4:10.

But they hearkened not unto Moses for impatience of spirit and for cruel bondage. – 6:9.

Then the magicians said unto Pharaoh: this is the finger of God. – 8:15.

Thus saith the Lord, the God of the Hebrews, Let My people go that they may serve Me. – 9:1.

And Moses said, We will go with our young and with our old, with our sons and with our daughters. –10:9.

And the Lord said unto Moses: why criest thou unto Me? Speak unto the children of Israel that they go forward. –14:15.

Who is like unto Thee, O Lord, among the mighty? Who is like unto Thee, glorious in holiness. –15:11.

And ye shall be unto Me a kingdom of priests and a holy nation. –19:6.

Thou shalt have no other gods before Me. Thou shalt not make unto thee a graven image. – 20:3, 4.

Honor thy father and thy mother. – 20:12.

And a stranger shalt thou not wrong, neither shalt thou oppress him, for ye were strangers in the land of Egypt. – 22:30.

And ye shall serve the Lord your God and He will bless thy bread and thy water. – 23:25.

And He said: Thou canst not see My face for no man shall see Me and live. – 33:20.

The Lord, the Lord God, merciful and gracious, long suffering and abundant in goodness and truth, keeping mercy unto the thousandth generation. – 34:6, 7.

Then the cloud covered the tent of meeting and the glory of the Lord filled the tabernacle. – 40:34.

LEVITICUS

Fire shall be kept burning upon the altar continually; it shall not go out. – 6:6.

That ye may put difference between the holy and the common and between the unclean and the clean. –10:10.

I am the Lord your God. After the doings of the land of Egypt wherein ye dwell, shall ye not do; and after the doings of the land of Canaan whither I bring you, shall ye not do. –18:3.

Ye shall therefore keep My statutes and Mine ordinances which if a man do he shall live by them. –18:5.

Ye shall be holy for I the Lord your God am holy. –19:2.

Thou shalt not curse the deaf nor put a stumbling block before the blind, but thou shalt fear thy God. Thou shalt not respect the person of the poor, nor favour the person of the mighty, but in righteousness shalt thou judge thy neighbour. Neither shalt thou stand idly by the blood of thy neighbour. I am the Lord. Thou shalt not hate thy brother in thy heart. Thou shalt not take vengeance nor bear any grudge against the children of thy people, but thou shalt love thy neighbour as thyself. I am the Lord. –19:14-18.

And proclaim liberty throughout the land unto all the inhabitants thereof. – 25:10.

NUMBERS

The Lord bless thee and keep thee . . . and give thee peace. – 6:24-27.

And Moses said unto him: Art thou jealous for my sake? Would that all the Lord's people were prophets, that the Lord would put His spirit upon them. –11:29.

The land through which we have passed to spy it out, is a land that eateth up the inhabitants thereof, and all the people that we saw in it are men of great stature . . . and we were in our own sight as grasshoppers. —13:32-33.

Would that we had died in the land of Egypt, or would that we had died in this wilderness. —14:2.

How long shall I bear with this evil congregation that keep murmuring against Me?—14:27.

How shall I curse whom God hath not cursed?—23:8.

There is no enchantment with Jacob, neither is there any divination with Israel. Now it is said of Jacob and of Israel: What hath God wrought?—23:23.

How goodly are thy tents O Jacob, thy dwellings O Israel?—24:5.

DEUTERONOMY

This is your wisdom and your understanding in the sight of the peoples. —4:6.

Thou shalt not take the name of the Lord thy God in vain. —5:11.

Hear O Israel, the Lord our God, the Lord is One. And thou shalt love the Lord thy God with all thy heart and with all thy soul and with all thy might. —6:4, 5.

My power and the might of my hand hath gotten me this wealth. —8:17.

Behold I set before you this day a blessing and a curse. —11:26.

Ye are the child of the Lord your God. —14:1.

If there be among you a needy man . . . thou shalt not harden thy heart nor shut thy hand from thy needy brother. —15:7.

The poor shall never cease out of the land. —15:11.

Justice, justice, shalt thou follow that thou mayest live; and inherit the land which the Lord thy God giveth thee. —16:20.

Thou shalt not remove thy neighbour's landmark which they of old time have set. —19:14.

What man is there that is fearful and faint-hearted? Let him go and return unto his house lest his brethren's heart melt as his heart. —20:8.

A stubborn and rebellious son that will not hearken to the voice of his father or the voice of his mother. —21:18.

Thou shalt not muzzle the ox when he treadeth the corn. —25:4.

Blessed shalt thou be in the city and blessed shalt thou be in the field.
– 28:3.

In the morning thou shalt say, would that it were evening, and at even
thou shalt say, would that it were morning, for the fear of thy heart
which thou shalt fear. – 28:67.

Neither with you only do I make this covenant and this oath . . . and
also with him that is not here with us today. – 29:13, 14.

For this commandment which I command thee this day is not too hard
for thee, neither is it far off, but the word is very nigh unto thee in
thy mouth and in thy heart that thou mayest do it. – 30:11, 14.

I have set before thee life and death, the blessing and the curse, therefore choose life. – 30:19.

And he was buried in the valley in the land of Moab . . . and no man
knoweth of his sepulchre unto this day. – 34:6.

And there hath not arisen a prophet since in Israel like unto Moses
whom the Lord knew face to face. – 34:10.

JOSHUA

Be strong and of good courage. –1:6.

From a very far country thy servants are come because of the name of
the Lord thy God. – 9:9.

And the people answered and said, far be it from us that we should
forsake the Lord to serve other gods. – 24:16.

And Joshua said unto the people, ye are witnesses against yourselves
that ye have chosen you the Lord to serve Him, and they said, we
are witnesses. –24:22.

JUDGES

Until thou didst arise, Deborah, a mother in Israel. – 5:7.

The stars in their courses fought against Sisera. – 5:20.

Wherewith shall I save Israel?
Behold my family is the poorest in Manasseh and I am the least of my
father's house. – 6:15.

The sword for the Lord and for Gideon. – 7:20.

Out of the eater came forth food,
And out of the strong came forth sweetness. –14:14.

If ye had not plowed with my heifer, ye had not found out my riddle.
–14:18.

With the jawbone of an ass have I smitten a thousand men. – 15:16.

The Philistines are upon thee, Samson. –16:14.

And Samson said, let me die with the Philistines. –16:30.

In those days there was no king in Israel; every man did that which
was right in his own eyes. – 21:25.

SAMUEL

For the Lord is a God of knowledge and by Him are actions weighed.
–1 Sam. 2:3.

Speak, Lord, for Thy servant heareth. –1 Sam. 3:9.

Is Saul also among the prophets?– 1 Sam. 10:11.

Behold, to obey is better than sacrifice, for rebellion is as the sin of
witchcraft. – 1 Sam. 15:22, 23.

For man looketh on the outward appearance but the Lord looketh on
the heart. – 1 Sam. 16:7.

Saul hath slain his thousands, and David his ten thousands. – 1 Sam. 18:7.

How are the mighty fallen. Tell it not in Gath. – 11 Sam. 1:19, 20.

Saul and Jonathan, the lovely and the pleasant, in their lives, even in
their death, they were not divided. – 11 Sam. 1:23.

Wonderful was thy love to me, passing the love of woman. – 11 Sam. 1:26.

And Nathan said unto David, thou art the man. – 11 Sam. 12:7.

But now he is dead, wherefore should I fast? Can I bring him back
again? I shall go to him, but he will not return to me. – 11 Sam. 12:23.

O Absalom, my son, my son, Absalom, would I had died for thee, O
Absalom, my son, my son. – 11 Sam. 19:1.

With the merciful Thou dost show Thyself merciful. – 11 Sam. 22:26.

The saying of David, the son of Jesse . . . the sweet singer of Israel.
– 11 Sam. 23:1.

KINGS

Now the days of David drew nigh that he should die and he charged
Solomon his son, saying, I go the way of all the earth; be thou strong
therefore and show thyself a man. – 1 Kings 2:1, 2.

Moreover concerning the stranger that is not of thy people Israel, . . . when he shall come and pray towards this house, hear Thou in heaven Thy dwelling place. – I Kings 8:41-43.

My father chastised you with whips but I will chastise you with scorpions. – I Kings 12:11.

When Ahab saw Elijah, Ahab said unto him, 'Is it thou, thou troubler of Israel?' and he answered: 'I have not troubled Israel, but thou and thy father's house in that ye have forsaken the commandments of the Lord.' – I Kings 18:17, 18.

The Lord He is God, the Lord He is God. – I Kings 18:39.

After the earthquake, a fire; but the Lord was not in the fire; and after the fire, a still small voice. – I Kings 19:12.

Say now unto her . . . what is to be done for thee? wouldest thou be spoken for to the king . . . ? And she answered: I dwell among my own people. – II Kings 4:13.

And Isaiah the prophet the son of Amoz came to him and said unto him: 'Thus saith the Lord: Set thy house in order for thou shalt die and not live.' – II Kings 20:1.

ISAIAH

Though your sins be as scarlet, they shall be as white as snow. – 1:18.

And they shall beat their swords into plowshares and their spears into pruning hooks. – 2:4.

But the Lord of hosts is exalted through justice and God the Holy One is sanctified through righteousness. – 5:16.

Woe unto them that call evil good and good evil, that change darkness into light and light into darkness. – 5:20.

Holy, holy, holy is the Lord of hosts, the whole earth is full of His glory. – 6:3.

And I heard the voice of the Lord saying, Whom shall I send? and who will go for us? Then I said, Here am I, send me. – 6:8, 9.

Bind up the testimony, seal the instruction among My disciples. – 8:16.

The people that walked in darkness have seen a great light. – 9:1.

The spirit of wisdom and understanding. The spirit of counsel and might. – 11:2.

And the wolf shall dwell with the lamb . . . and a little child shall lead them. – 11:6.

They shall not hurt nor destroy in all My holy mountain for the earth shall be full of the knowledge of the Lord as the waters cover the sea. – 11:9.

Watchman, what of the night? – 21:11.

He will swallow up death forever; and the Lord God will wipe away tears from off all faces. – 25:8.

The mind stayed on Thee, Thou keepest in perfect peace. – 26:3.

Woe to the crown of pride of the drunkards of Ephraim, and to the fading flower of his glorious beauty. – 28:1.

Comfort ye, comfort ye, My people, saith your God. – 40:1.

Even youths shall faint and be weary . . . but they that wait for the Lord shall renew their strength. – 40:30-31.

I the Lord have called thee in righteousness and have taken hold of thy hand and set thee for a covenant of the people for a light of the nations, to open the blind eyes. – 42:6, 7.

He is God that formed the earth and made it; He created it not a waste; He formed it to be inhabited. – 45:18.

I am He, I am the First, I also am the Last. – 48:12.

How beautiful upon the mountains are the feet of the messenger of good tidings. – 52:7.

We all like sheep did go astray. – 53:6.

For the mountains may depart and the hills be removed, but My kindness shall not depart from thee. – 54:10.

For My house shall be called a house of prayer for all peoples. – 56:7.

Is such the fast that I have chosen . . . is it to bow down his head as a bulrush . . . is not this the fast that I have chosen, to loose the fetters of wickedness? – 58:5, 6.

Arise, shine, for thy light is coming. – 60:1.

The heaven is My throne and the earth is My footstool. – 66:1.

JEREMIAH

Go, and cry in the ears of Jerusalem, saying: Thus saith the Lord:
I remember for thee the affection of thy youth,
The love of thine espousals;
How thou wentest after Me in the wilderness,
In the land that was not sown. – 2:2.

As a cage is full of birds, so are their houses full of deceit. – 5:27.

They have healed also the hurt of My people lightly, saying, Peace, peace, when there is no peace. – 6:14.

Is there no balm in Gilead?
Is there no physician there?
Oh that my head were waters,
And mine eyes a fountain of tears,
That I might weep day and night
For the slain of the daughter of my people! – 8:22-23.

Let not the wise man glory in his wisdom. Let not the rich man glory in his riches. But let him that glorieth, glory in this, that he understandeth and knoweth Me. – 9:22, 23.

Woe is me for my hurt! But I said, this is but a sickness and I must bear it. –10:19.

Give glory to the Lord your God before it grow dark and before your feet stumble upon the mountains of twilight. – 13:16.

Can the Ethiopian change his skin, or the leopard his spots? – 13:23.

Woe is me, my mother, that thou hast borne me, a man of strife and a man of contention to the whole earth. – 15:10.

A voice is heard in Ramah, . . .
Rachel weeping for her children;
She refuseth to be comforted for her children,
Because they are not. – 31:15.

. . . I was shamed, yea, even confounded,
Because I did bear the reproach of my youth. – 31:19.

I will put My law in their inward parts and in their heart will I write it; and I will be their God and they shall be My people. – 31:33.

EZEKIEL

The fathers have eaten sour grapes and the children's teeth are set on edge. –18:3.

Have I any pleasure at all that the wicked should die? saith the Lord God; and not rather that he should return from his ways, and live? –18:23.

Cast away from you all your transgressions . . . and make you a new heart and a new spirit; for why will ye die O house of Israel? –18:31.

And He said to me, Son of man, can these bones live? – 37:3.

And He said unto me: Prophesy unto the breath . . . and say to the breath . . . : Come from the four winds O breath and breathe upon these slain that they may live. – 37:9.

THE MINOR PROPHETS

And I will betroth thee unto Me forever. I will betroth thee unto Me in righteousness and in justice . . . and thou shalt know the Lord. – Hosea 2:21,22.

When Israel was a child, then I loved him, and out of Egypt I called My son. – Hosea 11:1.

Return, O Israel, unto the Lord thy God, for thou hast stumbled in thine iniquity. – Hosea 14:2.

I shall be as the dew unto Israel. He shall blossom as the lily and cast forth his roots as Lebanon. – Hosea 14:6.

Your old men shall dream dreams; your young men shall see visions. – Joel 3:1.

Multitudes, multitudes in the valley of decision. – Joel 4:14.

The lion hath roared. Who will not fear? The Lord God hath spoken. Who can but prophesy? – Amos 3:8.

Let justice well up as waters and righteousness as a mighty stream. – Amos 5:24.

I am a Hebrew and I fear the Lord, the God of heaven Who hath made the sea and the dry land. – Jonah 1:9.

But they shall sit every man under his vine and under his fig-tree and none shall make them afraid. – Micah 4:4.

It hath been told thee O man what is good, and what the Lord doth require of thee: only to do justly and to love mercy and to walk humbly with thy God. – Micah 6:8.

For the stone shall cry out of the wall, and the beam out of the timber shall answer it. – Habakkuk 2:11.

But the Lord is in His holy temple, let all the earth keep silence before Him. – Habakkuk 2:20.

Mine is the silver, and Mine the gold, saith the Lord of hosts. The glory of this latter house shall be greater than that of the former, saith the Lord of hosts; and in this place will I give peace, saith the Lord of hosts. – Haggai 2:8-9.

Not by might nor by power but by My spirit saith the Lord of hosts. – Zechariah 4:6.

A son honoureth a father and a servant his master. If then I be a father, where is my honour? And if I be a master, where is my fear? – Malachi 1:6.

From the rising of the sun even unto the going down of the same, My name is great among the nations, and in every place offerings are presented unto My name. – Malachi 1:11.

For the priest's lips should keep knowledge and they should seek the law at his mouth for he is the messenger of the Lord of hosts. – Malachi 2:7.

Have we not all one father? Hath not one God created us? Why do we deal treacherously every man against his brother? – Malachi 2:10.

Behold I will send you Elijah the prophet, and he shall turn the heart of the fathers to the children and the heart of the children to their fathers. – Malachi 3:23, 24.

PSALMS

Why are the nations in an uproar? (In the Authorized Version: "Why do the heathens rage?") – 2:1.

Out of the mouths of babes and sucklings hast Thou founded strength. – 8:3.

When I behold Thy heavens, the work of Thy fingers . . . what is man, that Thou art mindful of him? – 8:4-5.

The fool hath said in his heart: there is no God. – 14:1.

The lines are fallen unto me in pleasant places, yea I have a goodly heritage. – 16:6.

The heavens declare the glory of God. – 19:1.

Let the words of my mouth and the meditation of my heart be acceptable before Thee. – 19:15.

The Lord is my shepherd; I shall not want. – 23:1.

Yea, though I walk through the valley of the shadow of death, I will fear no evil. – 23:4.

Lift up your heads, O ye gates, and be ye lifted up, ye everlasting doors, that the King of glory may come in. – 24:7.

The Lord is my light and my salvation. Whom shall I fear? – 27:1.

Wait for the Lord; be strong and let thy heart take courage. – 27:14.

Fret not thyself because of evil-doers. – 37:1.

Happy is he that considereth the poor. The Lord will deliver him in the day of evil. – 41:2.

As the hart panteth after the water brooks,
So panteth my soul after Thee, O God. – 42:2.

Deep calleth unto deep. – 42:8.

God is our refuge and our strength, a very present help in trouble. – 46:2.

Only for God doth my soul wait in stillness. – 62:2.

Whom have I in heaven but Thee? And beside Thee I desire none on earth. – 73:25.

In the midst of the judges, He judgeth. – 82:1.

How lovely are Thy tabernacles, O Lord of hosts. – 84:2.

Lord, Thou hast been our dwelling place in all generations. – 90:1.

For a thousand years in Thy sight are but as yesterday when it is past. – 90:4.

We bring our years to an end as a tale that is told. – 90:9.

Thou shalt not be afraid of the terror by night nor of the arrow that flieth by day. – 91:5.

The righteous shall flourish like the palm tree. – 92:13.

O sing unto the Lord a new song. – 96:1.

I shall not die but live and declare the works of the Lord. – 118:17.

The stone which the builders rejected. – 118:22.

I will lift up mine eyes unto the mountains, from whence shall my help come? –121:1.

Except the Lord build the house, they labour in vain that build it. –127:1.

Out of the depths have I called Thee, O Lord. –130:1.

Behold, how good and how pleasant it is for brethren to dwell together in unity. – 133:1.

By the waters of Babylon, there we sat down, yea, we wept. – 137:1.

If I take the wings of the morning and dwell in the uttermost parts of the sea. – 139:9.

Even the darkness is not too dark for thee but the night shineth as the day. – 139:12.

Thou openest Thy hand and satisfiest every living thing with favour. – 145:16.

PROVERBS

Hear my son, the instruction of thy father, and forsake not the teaching of thy mother. – 1:8.

Let not kindness and truth forsake thee . . . write them on the table of thy heart. – 3:3.

Go to the ant, thou sluggard; consider her ways and be wise. – 6:6.

The fear of the Lord is the beginning of wisdom. – 9:10.

The memory of the righteous shall be for a blessing; but the name of the wicked shall rot. –10:7.

Hope deferred maketh the heart sick. –13:12.

Righteousness exalteth a nation, but sin is a reproach to any people. –14:34.

A merry heart maketh a cheerful countenance. –15:13.

Pride goeth before destruction, and a haughty spirit before a fall. –16:18.

Better is a dry morsel and quietness therewith than a house full of feasting with strife. –17:1.

Wine is a mocker, strong drink is riotous. – 20:1.

Boast not thyself of tomorrow; for thou knowest not what a day may bring forth. – 27:1.

The refining pot is for silver, and the furnace for gold, and a man is tried by his praise. – 27:21.

The wicked flee when no man pursueth. – 28:1.

Grace is deceitful and beauty is vain, but a woman that feareth the Lord, she shall be praised. – 31:30.

JOB

The Lord gave and the Lord hath taken away, blessed be the name of the Lord. –1:21.

Shall mortal man be just before God? – 4:17.

But man is born unto trouble as the sparks fly upward. – 5:7.

Happy is the man whom God correcteth; despise thou not the chastening of the Almighty. – 5:17.

Is my strength the strength of stones? Or is my flesh of brass? – 6:12.

Canst thou find out the deep things of God? – 11:7.

Though He slay me yet will I trust in Him. – 13:15.

Man that is born of woman is of few days and full of trouble. – 14:1.

O earth, cover thou not my blood, and let my cry have no resting-place. – 16:18.

I know that my Redeemer liveth. – 19:25.

Who is this that darkeneth counsel by words without knowledge? – 38:1.

THE FIVE SCROLLS

I am a rose of Sharon, a lily of the valleys. – Song of Songs 2:1.

For lo the winter is past, the rain is over and gone, the flowers appear on the earth, the time of singing is come, and the voice of the turtle is heard in our land. – Song of Songs 2:11, 12.

For love is strong as death; jealousy is cruel as the grave . . . many waters cannot quench love. – Song of Songs 8:6, 7.

Entreat me not to leave thee . . . for whither thou goest, I will go, . . . thy people shall be my people and thy God my God. – Ruth 1:16.

I am the man that hath seen affliction. – Lamentations 3:1.

It is good for a man that he bear the yoke in his youth. – Lamentations 3:27.

Renew our days as of old. – Lamentations 5:21.

Vanity of vanities, all is vanity. – Ecclesiastes 1:2.

There is nothing new under the sun. – Ecclesiastes 1:9.

For in much wisdom is much vexation;
And he that increaseth knowledge increaseth sorrow. – Ecclesiastes 1:18.

A good name is better than precious oil; and the day of death than the day of one's birth. – Ecclesiastes 7:1.

A living dog is better than a dead lion. – Ecclesiastes 9:4.

The race is not to the swift, nor the battle to the strong. – Ecclesiastes 9:11.

Cast thy bread upon the waters, for thou shalt find it after many days. – Ecclesiastes 11:1.

And the dust returneth to the earth as it was and the spirit returneth unto God Who gave it. – Ecclesiastes 12:7.

Who knoweth whether thou art not come to royal estate for such a time as this. – Esther 4:14.

DANIEL, EZRA, NEHEMIAH, CHRONICLES

Thou art weighed in the balance and art found wanting. – Daniel 5:27.

The Ancient of days. – Daniel 7:22.

And many of them that sleep in the dust of the earth shall awake. – Daniel 12:2.

Happy is he that waiteth. – Daniel 8:12.

But we ourselves together will build unto the Lord. – Ezra 4:3.

Why should not my countenance be sad when the city . . . lieth waste? – Nehemiah 2:3.

Then all Israel gathered themselves to David unto Hebron saying, Behold, we are thy bone and thy flesh. – 1 Chronicles 11:1.

Touch not Mine anointed ones, and do My prophets no harm. – 1 Chronicles 16:22.

O Lord there is none like Thee . . . and who is like Thy people Israel, a nation one in the earth. – 1 Chronicles 17:20, 21.

Thine O Lord is the greatness and the power and the glory, and the victory and the majesty . . . Thine is the kingdom. – 1 Chronicles 29:11.

Questions and Bibliography

QUESTIONS I

1. The author indicates the great ethical influence of the Bible in the field of social service. What has been its influence in the following spheres of ethical activity: (a) relationships between men as individuals; (b) family relationships; (c) relationships between societies?
2. Give examples of the influence of the Bible on: (a) the language, and (b) the subject-matter of literature, painting, and music.

BIBLIOGRAPHY I

GOLDMAN, SOLOMON, *The Book of Books*, chap. I, Harper. 1948.

PFEIFFER, R. H., *Introduction to the Old Testament*, chap. II, Harper. 1941.

QUESTIONS II

1. What were the standards used to determine the admissibility of books into the Bible? By these standards, how do you account for the admission of the Book of Esther? For the admission of the Song of Songs?
2. Explain how and when the present numbering of the chapters and verses of the Bible came into existence.
3. Is it possible that many books written since the canonization of the Bible can be considered divinely inspired and hence worthy of inclusion in the Bible?

BIBLIOGRAPHY II

PFEIFFER, R. H., *ibid.*, Part I, chap. IV.

GOLDMAN, SOLOMON, *ibid.*, chap. III.

LOFTHOUSE, W. F., *The Making of the Old Testament*, London. 1915.

MARGOLIS, M. L., *The Hebrew Scriptures in the Making*, Phila. 1922.

QUESTIONS III

1. How can we account for the fact that the Bible text has come down to us with a minimum of alterations or errors?
2. How do we account for the fact that there are no ancient (before 1000 C.E.) copies of the Bible in existence?
3. What is Masora? Explain the difference between an Initial Masora and an Inner Masora.

BIBLIOGRAPHY III

ROBINSON, H. W., *The Bible in Its Ancient and English Versions*, Oxford University Press. 1941.

QUESTIONS IV

1. How was the knowledge of the Bible spread among the people?
2. The modern synagogue is frequently accused of failing to hold the interest of its membership. Do you think that a reemphasis as "beis ha-midrosh" might be a solution?
   Discuss the value of increasing the educational element of the service as well.
3. Comment on the author's statement that the prophetic speech and writings are in a popular style. Support your answer with suitable quotations.

BIBLIOGRAPHY IV

FREEHOF, SOLOMON B., *The Small Sanctuary*, U.A.H.C. 1942.

———, The Jewish Prayerbook, U.A.H.C.

QUESTIONS V

1. Explain the relationship between the Oral and the Written Law. Compare the two methods.

2. Modern Liberal Judaism holds that much of the old Oral Law is no longer applicable. Should, therefore, new laws be deduced from Scripture and substituted for those no longer meaningful?

BIBLIOGRAPHY V

MOORE, G. F., *Judaism*, Vol. I, Harvard University Press. 1927.

MIELZINER, M., *Introduction to the Talmud*, Part I, chap. 13, Bloch Publishing Co. 1902.

The following translations of source material is available:
The Mishnah, Herbert Danby, Oxford. 1933.
The Midrash, Soncino Press.
Pentateuch with Rashi's Commentary, A. M. Silbermann.
The Pentateuch and Haftorahs, J. H. Hertz, Soncino Press. 1938.
The Soncino Chumash, The Rev. Dr. A. Cohen (Ed.), Soncino Press. 1947.
See particularly the commentaries.

QUESTIONS VI

1. Who was the leader of modern Biblical Criticism? What were the major conclusions of his work?
2. On the basis of recent discoveries in the field of Near East Archaeology, what seems to be the attitude of many modern Biblical scholars with regard to the earlier conclusions of "Higher Criticism"?

BIBLIOGRAPHY VI

ADAMS, J. McKEE, *Ancient Records and the Bible*, Broadman. 1946.

ALBRIGHT, WILLIAM F., *Archeology and the Religion of Israel*, Johns Hopkins Press. 1942.

BARTON, GEORGE A., *Archaeology and the Bible*, American Sunday School Union. Revised 1937.

FINEGAN, JACK, *Light from the Ancient Past*, Princeton. 1946.

KENYON, SIR FREDERIC, *The Bible and Archeology*, Harper and Bros.

QUESTIONS VII

1. Summarize the author's thought with regard to the Bible as a Book of Revelation, and indicate his conclusions concerning the historical portions.

2. What is the answer of the Bible to the pessimism of modern man?
3. The author indicates the widespread neglect of the Bible in present times. In the light, therefore, of your answer to question 2, discuss the importance for our times of a more profound study of the Bible.
4. How are we to understand the concepts of Israel as the "Chosen People," and "the Mission of Israel"? Do you agree with the author? Give reasons.

BIBLIOGRAPHY VII

STEINBERG, MILTON, *Basic Judaism*, Harcourt, Brace & Co. 1947.

COHON, SAMUEL S., *Judaism—A Way of Life*, Union of American Hebrew Congregations. 1948.

KAPLAN, MORDECAI M., *The Meaning of God in Modern Jewish Religion*, Behrman. 1937.

MILLIKAN, R. A., *Evolution in Science and Religion*, Yale University Press. 1927.

QUESTIONS VIII

1. What are some of the reasons for the literary excellence of the Bible? Give examples.
2. What are the most common forms of Biblical poetry? Give examples.

BIBLIOGRAPHY VIII

PFEIFFER, R. H., *ibid.*, Part I, chap. II.

GOLDMAN, SOLOMON, *ibid.*, chap. VI.

DRIVER, S. R., *An Introduction to the Literature of the Old Testament*, chap. VII, Scribner's. 1906.

QUESTIONS IX

1. It is possible that some of your favorite verses are excluded from the author's selection. Point out such verses and give your reasons for feeling that they should be included in such a selection of key phrases.

PART TWO

Selections from Scripture

CHAPTER I

The Torah

GENESIS, EXODUS

IN ACCORDANCE with a tradition going back to the second century before the beginning of the present era, the Bible was divided into three parts, each part representing a different type of sacred literature. These three divisions were the Law, the Prophets, and the Holy Writings. The first division, the Law, consists of what was called "The Five Books of Moses," since Moses was deemed to be its author. This first division of Scripture is called simply "The Torah," meaning "The Law," although the term *Torah* also has a larger meaning. The word "Torah" is occasionally used for the entire Bible and in a more inclusive way is used for the entire body of Hebrew law based upon the Torah, both the written law, the Torah itself, and the oral or unwritten law, which became the Mishnah and the Talmud. When in Jewish life the phrase was used "to study Torah" it meant to study not only the Bible but also Mishnah and Talmud and all the other literature derived from it. But the specific use of the word "Torah" is for the first five books of Scripture. To this the Prophet Malachi refers (3:22): "Remember the Torah of Moses, My servant." Also, since there are five books in it, namely, Genesis, Exodus, Leviticus, Numbers, and Deuteronomy, it is sometimes called "The Five Fifths of the Torah" (*Chamisho Chumshei Torah*), or popularly, simply *Chumosh*, which means "the fifth."

The names "Genesis," "Exodus," etc., are of Greek origin. Many of the Greek names of Biblical books come from the Greek translation of the Bible (the Septuagint, which was completed before the beginning of the present era). Since this Greek translation was the first, many of the names which it gives to the Biblical books were kept in the later translations and so have come down to us. These names of Greek origin describe the contents of each of the five books. Thus "Genesis" means "the beginning"; "Exodus," "the departure" (from Egypt); "Leviticus," "the priestly or levite law"; and "Deuteronomy," "the repetition of the Law."

The Hebrew name for each book of the Torah is not meant to describe the contents but is usually the important word in the first sentence of the book. Thus Genesis is called *B'reshis*, which means "In the beginning." The Hebrew word which begins the Book of Exodus is *Sh'mos* which means "Names," from the opening sentence "These are the names." Leviticus is *Vayikro* which means "and He called," from the opening sentence "And He called unto Moses." Numbers is *Bamidbor*, which means "in the wilderness," the opening sentence being "And the Lord spoke unto Moses in the wilderness of Sinai." Deuteronomy is *D'vorim*, which means "words" from the opening sentence, "These are the words which Moses spoke."

There are also ancient Hebrew names for some of the five books which, like the Greek names, refer not to an opening word but to the contents. Thus Leviticus is called *Toras Kohanim* (the Law of the Priests), Numbers is called *Chomesh ha-p'kudim* (the Fifth Part of the Torah which deals with the numbered), and Deuteronomy is called *Mishne Torah* (the Repetition of the Law).

Modern critical study has made a new division of the Biblical books, declaring that these five books are not a unit in themselves, but that the Book of Joshua must be counted with them. Thus there is a unit of six books. The reason for this new combination by modern scholars is that the sixth book, Joshua, continues the narrative which begins in the first five. The first five books speak of God's choice of Israel and His promise to bring them to the land of Canaan. The Book of Deuteronomy, the last of the five, ends with the death of Moses before Israel enters the Promised Land, with the plan begun in the first five books not yet completed. It comes to completion in the sixth book, the Book of Joshua, in which the land is conquered and divided among the tribes. Furthermore, critical scholars see in the Book of Joshua some of the same original documents which they have traced in the first five books as the sources out of which these books were composed. Hence, since the Book of Joshua completes the thought of the first five books by showing the fulfillment of God's promise by giving Israel the land of Canaan, and since the same original documents found in the first five books are continued in it, modern critical scholars say the real unit of study should be the first six books. Therefore, instead of the ancient Greek term *Pentateuch*, which means "five scrolls" and is the translation of the traditional Hebrew phrase, "the five books of the Torah" (*chamisho chumshei Torah*), they coin a new word, *Hexateuch*, which means, of course, "the six scrolls." However, none of the oldest traditions know of any such combinations and all of them, Jewish and Christian, consider the first five books as a unit different from the other books of the Bible. It is advisable to follow this almost unanimous and unbroken tradition and study the five books, namely, the Torah, together.

The critical study of Scripture has devoted its greatest attention to the five books of the Torah, including the sixth book, Joshua. It is in these books that Biblical scholars have discovered what they consider to be the original documents out of which the present books were composed. Having carefully dissected the Torah into its component layers, Biblical critics then proceeded to date these various documents so as to fix an order of origin for the Torah and its various parts. Thus they have come to the conclusion that the Torah is not as old as it claims to be, not as old in fact by a thousand years. Whereas tradition fixes the entire Torah as having been written by Moses in approximately the fourteenth pre-Christian century, they say that the bulk of the Book of Leviticus was written in the exile in Babylon in the sixth century and the entire Torah put together in the time of Ezra, in the fifth pre-Christian century.

While it is of interest to all students of the Bible to understand the methods and the purpose of Biblical critical study, and to have a general judgment as to its present validity in the light of new scientific discoveries, especially in archaeology, these conclusions of the Bible critics are not essential to the average reader's understanding of the Torah. (For a full discussion of Biblical criticism and the effect of modern archaeology upon its theories, see Part One, chapter VI.) One can understand the Torah quite well without this radical analysis; for, after all, even if one would grant that the critics are right in their late dating of the Torah and that, as they say the Torah was not written in the fourteenth pre-Christian century by Moses, but was put together by Ezra in the fourth pre-Christian century, a thousand years later, even so the book is by now at least twenty-three hundred years old, and for this vast stretch of time was looked upon as a unit, studied as a unit, and has actually been a unit. The book then, even by the most radical opinion, is extremely ancient and has been for twenty centuries, a long time indeed, of profound and world-wide influence as a single book.

It is correct to say that the Torah is by far the most influential book in the whole history of Judaism. It is not the most influential Biblical book for Christianity, but it is for Judaism. Christianity, under the influence of Paul of Tarsus, who made of a Jewish sect a world religion, considered the Torah the least important part of the Bible. In fact, Christianity tended to scorn it as actually a harmful part of the old tradition, for the law, according to St. Paul, being, as he believed, impossible of fulfillment, only created in man the sense of disobedience and sin. To Christianity, the Prophets were much more important, since Jesus of Nazareth was deemed by it to be the greatest of prophets and his career was considered to have been predicted by the Prophets. He is looked upon as the fulfillment of Hebrew prophecy. Next to the Prophets, the most influential book in the Bible was the Psalms. It was the spiritual textbook of the early church.

While in Judaism both the Prophets and the Psalms were of immense importance and of profound influence, their importance and influence did not compare with that of the Torah. For the Torah was law, and Israel was governed in its daily life by the law of Moses. It was upon the Torah that the vast Talmudic literature, as well as all the later legal literature, was based. The whole Talmud may be looked upon as a commentary and an expansion of the five books of Moses. Just as the Constitution of the United States was studied word for word, and legal decisions, greatly affecting American life, were often based upon single phrases in it, and a vast literature of legal opinions in the Federal courts grew out of the few pages of the Constitution, in that sense almost exactly the Torah was the Constitution of Jewish life. Every phrase of it was studied and the legal decisions which governed Jewish life depended upon its words and phrases. The Psalms and the Prophets were inspiration; the Torah was strict law, actually governing the day by day life of the community and of the individual life of Israel. Thus it has been for countless centuries; and if the book be merely twenty-four hundred years old, as the critics say, instead of thirty-four hundred years old, as tradition says, it is still the most influential and enduring book of living law that the world has ever known.

We will, therefore, study the Torah as a unit. We will see that while the Torah is primarily law, it is not merely law. It is law based upon an idea, a clearly enunciated philosophy of history. It is this philosophy, the framework of Jewish law, into which the entire Torah legislation is fitted. It constitutes one of the basic attitudes of Judaism and when rightly understood is far from being in contradiction to the doctrines of the Prophets, as many recent scholars have repeatedly insisted. The reason and the purpose of the law is in harmony with the essential reason and purpose of Prophecy.

The framework, or what may be called the philosophy of the Torah, begins by implication, in the very first chapters of the Book of Genesis, the first book of the Torah. This book begins with God's creation of the entire earth, indicating as does the very first of the literary prophets, Amos, that God is the Creator and Father of all men whose happiness and whose spiritual growth are His loving concern. Because mankind was corrupted early, God chose one family of mankind for His special training to fulfill His aim for mankind. The Torah proceeds to describe the choice of this one small branch of mankind, the special covenant which God made with the people of Israel, and the responsibility which He imposed upon them to avoid all idol worship and to worship Him alone. In order to purify them and to train them for His service as His kingdom of priests and a holy people, He imposed upon them the discipline of many laws, the innumerable laws found in the Torah. In return for their obedience and their consequent development in His service He would shield them and guard them and give them the Promised Land of Canaan. The prophetic message is identical with this doctrine. The Prophets rebuke Israel for its sins of idolatry and disobedience, and in the climax of prophecy, in the Second Isaiah, remind Israel of its world-wide task to bring light to those who walk in darkness, to be God's servant to the peoples of the earth. In other words, what is foreshadowed in the grand prologue of Genesis is continued in the mighty epilogue of the Prophets. Genesis begins: God created heaven and earth and is the Maker and Father of all mankind; the prophets remind us, "have we not all one Father, has not one God created us all?" and the prophetic message ends with the fulfillment of Genesis, "in that day the Lord shall be One and His name shall be One."

The Torah, therefore, may be briefly described as the opening unit of Scripture in which God, the Creator of man, chooses the people of Israel as His servant, entering into a covenant with them that if they obey the laws which He gives through His servant Moses, He will give them the Promised Land and they will become His priests and His sacred people for the blessing of all the children of men.

GENESIS

The Book of Genesis, although it is the first book of the Torah, the Law, contains almost no law at all. It is entirely prologue and setting. It begins with the story of the creation of the heavens and earth, of the plants and all living things, and then proceeds to the early history of mankind, descendant from Adam and Eve. Yet the Book of Genesis was not intended to be a history of mankind. None of the books of the Bible, even the obviously historical books, is merely history. The historical books are selections of historical facts, chosen for a specific purpose.

The earlier part of the book, especially the story of the Flood, resembles the legendary material about the beginnings of the world which were current in the Near East in ancient times. Undoubtedly these ancient narratives were looked upon by the author of Genesis as exact descriptions of actual events. The main reason for recording them as well as the genealogies and histories in the early part of Genesis is to indicate God's selection for His purpose of the people of Israel. Hence, while at first all the descendants of Adam are named, certain branches are merely mentioned and then ignored; only a certain branch is continued until, of all mankind, the story comes down to Abraham, the patriarch who first turned aside from idol worship and devoted his love and his life to the One True God. Then, of the children of Abraham (while Ishmael, the elder son, is mentioned), the story continues with Isaac; while stories about Isaac's elder son, Esau, are mentioned, the main narrative continues with Jacob, later called Israel, the father of the twelve tribes of Israel. The story of Genesis, therefore, beginning as wide as all the world and all mankind, increasingly concentrates its attention upon the patriarchs, the ancestors of Israel. The book, therefore, is essentially the prelude to the story of Israel's selection, prefigured in the story of the patriarchs. It ends with the last of the patriarchs, Jacob, and his twelve sons, preparing for the first of Israel's great trials by going down to Egypt.

Just as the Book of Genesis does not aim to be a history of mankind, so it does not intend to be a book of science. The description of the creation of heaven and earth, of the various species of animals, was not intended to be what we would call a scientific picture of how the world of nature came into being; not that it does not describe how the authors of Genesis actually believed the world did come into being. That was truly their belief, and it is understandable that that belief has long been outgrown as many other such beliefs have been outgrown and as, undoubtedly, many of our present scientific theories of the origin of the world will be outgrown. Just now we happen to believe in the theory that the earth and the other planets were dragged out of the sun by some passing, wandering star. This latest scientific theory of the origin of our solar system has recently supplanted another belief, and undoubtedly still other beliefs will take its place. But in general it is beside the point to judge the description of the origin of the earth found in Genesis by the description to which now we give allegiance, not merely because theory follows theory on these vast matters, none of which can actually be proved, but for the simpler reason that scientific description was not their real intention any more than mere history was their intention. As their concept of history was used selectively to indicate the growth of the chosen people, so their concept of science was used illustratively to indicate their faith that God was the Creator and the Father of all. Both history and science in Genesis are only instruments and background to carry out the essential theme that God the Creator decided to teach and to discipline one people so that through them His aims and purposes for all mankind might some day be fulfilled.

* * *

In studying the Bible text we will not give a detailed analysis. Such a detailed analysis, verse by verse and chapter by chapter, belongs to special commentaries which deal with the entire texts of each book. Our aim in a general introduction to Scripture is to give a broad view of the contents of each Biblical book. Therefore, we will deal with each book in virtually the same manner, providing first a general descriptive introduction, as has just been given, then following it as we now will do with a selection of verses from the book which, when read consecutively, will give a survey of the book. Then will follow a commentary on these verses to explain the unusual phrases and the unfamiliar words. It is hoped that these introductory synopses and commentaries will provide the reader with a correct impression of the general content and mood of each Biblical book, and that with this preparation he will be able to proceed with the study of each book in its entirety.

SYNOPSIS OF TEXT

A.   In the beginning God created the heaven and the earth. Now the earth was unformed and void, and darkness was upon the face of the deep; and the spirit of God hovered over the face of the waters. And God said: 'Let there be light.' And there was light . . . and God said: 'Let us make man in our image, after our likeness; and let them have dominion over the fish of the sea, and over the fowl of the air, and over the cattle, and over all the earth, and over every creeping thing that creepeth upon the earth.' And God created man in His own image, in the image of God created He him; male and female created He them. . . . Then the Lord God formed man of the dust of the ground, and breathed into his nostrils the breath of life; and man became a living soul. . . .

This is the book of the generations of Adam. In the day that God created man, in the likeness of God made He him; . . . Adam begot a son; and called his name Seth. . . . And all the days that Adam lived were nine hundred and thirty years; and he died. . . . And Seth lived after he begot Enosh eight hundred and seven years, and begot sons and daughters. – 1: 1-3, 26-27; 2: 7; 5: 1, 3.

B.   These are the generations of Noah. Noah was in his generations a man righteous and whole-hearted; Noah walked with God.

And Noah begot three sons, Shem, Ham, and Japheth. And the earth was corrupt before God, and . . . was filled with violence.

And God said unto Noah: 'The end of all flesh is come before Me; for the earth is filled with violence through them; and, behold, I will destroy them with the earth. . . . And I, behold, I do bring the flood of waters upon the earth, to destroy all flesh, wherein is the breath of life, from under heaven; every thing that is in the earth shall perish. But I will establish My covenant with thee; and thou shalt come into the ark, thou, and thy sons, and thy wife, and thy sons' wives with thee.' . . .

And God spoke unto Noah, and to his sons with him, saying: 'As for Me, behold, I establish My covenant with you, and with your seed after you; . . . neither shall all flesh be cut off any more by the waters of the flood; neither shall there any more be a flood to destroy the earth.' – 6:9-12, 13, 17, 18; 9:8, 9, 11.

C.   Now the Lord said unto Abram: 'Get thee out of thy country, and from thy kindred, and from thy father's house, unto the land that I will show thee. And I will make of thee a great nation, and I will bless them that bless thee, and him that curseth thee will I curse; and in thee shall all the families of the earth be blessed.' . . .

And He said unto him: 'I am the Lord that brought thee out of Ur of the Chaldees, to give thee this land to inherit it.' . . . In that day the Lord made a covenant with Abram, saying: 'Unto thy seed have I given this land, from the river of Egypt unto the great river, the river Euphrates; . . .'

And it came to pass after these things, that God did prove Abraham, and said unto him: 'Abraham'; and he said: 'Here am I.' And He said: 'Take now thy son, thine only son, whom thou lovest, even Isaac, and get thee into the land of Moriah; and offer him there for a burnt-offering upon one of the mountains which I will tell thee of.' . . . And the angel of the Lord called unto him out of heaven, and said: 'Abraham, Abraham.' And he said: 'Here am I.' And he said: 'Lay not thy hand upon the lad, neither do thou any thing unto him; for now I know that thou are a God-fearing man, seeing thou hast not withheld thy son, thine only son, from Me.' . . . and said: 'By Myself have I sworn, saith the Lord, because thou hast done this thing, and hast not withheld thy son, thine only son, that in blessing I will bless thee, and in multiplying I will multiply thy seed as the stars of the heaven, and as the sand which is upon the seashore; and thy seed shall possess the gate of his enemies; and in thy seed shall all the nations of the earth be blessed; because thou hast hearkened to My voice.'–12:1-3; 15:7, 18; 22:1, 2, 11, 12, 16-18.

D.   And these are the generations of Isaac, Abraham's son: Abraham begot Isaac. And Isaac was forty years old when he took Rebekah, the daughter of Bethuel the Aramean, of Paddan-aram, the sister of Laban the Aramean, to be his wife. . . . And when her days to be delivered were fulfilled, behold, there were twins in her womb. And the first came forth ruddy, all over like a hairy mantle; and they called his name Esau. And after that came forth his brother, and his hand had hold on Esau's heel; and his name was called Jacob. And Isaac was threescore years old when she bore them. . . .

And Isaac called Jacob, and blessed him, and charged him and said unto him: 'Thou shalt not take a wife of the daughters of Canaan. Arise, go to Paddan-aram, to the house of Bethuel thy mother's father; and take thee a wife from thence of the daughters of Laban thy mother's brother. And God Almighty bless thee, and make thee fruitful, and multiply thee, that thou mayest be a congregation of peoples; and give thee the blessing of Abraham, to thee, and to thy seed with thee; that thou mayest inherit the land of thy sojournings, which God gave unto Abraham.'– 25:19,20,24-26; 28:1-4.

E.   And Jacob went out from Beer-sheba, and went toward Haran. And he lighted upon the place, and tarried there all night, because the sun was set; and he took one of the stones of the place, and put it under his head, and lay down in that place to sleep. And he dreamed and behold a ladder set up on the earth, and the top of it reached to heaven; and behold the angels of God ascending and descending on it. And, behold, the Lord stood beside him, and said: 'I am the Lord, the God of Abraham thy father, and the God of Isaac. The land whereon thou liest, to thee will I give it, and to thy seed. And thy seed shall be as the dust of the earth, and thou shalt spread abroad to the west, and to the east, and to the north, and to the south. And in thee and in thy seed shall all the families of the earth be blessed. . . .'

And God appeared unto Jacob again, when he came from Paddan-Aram, and blessed him. And God said unto him: 'Thy name is Jacob; thy name shall not be called any more Jacob, but Israel shall be thy name'; and He called his name Israel. And God said unto him: 'I am God Almighty. Be fruitful and multiply; a nation and a company of nations shall be of thee, and kings shall come out of thy loins; and the land which I gave unto Abraham and Isaac, to thee I will give it, and to thy seed after thee will I give the land.'—28:10-14; 35:9-12.

F.   And Jacob dwelt in the land of his father's sojournings, in the land of Canaan. These are the generations of Jacob. Joseph, being seventeen years old, was feeding the flock with his brethren, being still a lad, even with the sons of Bilhah, and with the sons of Zilpah, his father's wives; and Joseph brought evil report of them unto their father. Now Israel loved Joseph more than all his children, because he was the son of his old age; and he made him a coat of many colors. And when his brethren saw that their father loved him more than all his brethren, they hated him, and could not speak peaceably unto him. . . .

And Joseph was brought down to Egypt; and Potiphar, an officer of Pharaoh's, the captain of the guard, an Egyptian, bought him of the hand of the Ishmaelites, that had brought him down thither. And the Lord was with Joseph, and he was a prosperous man; and he was in the house of his master, the Egyptian. And his master saw that the Lord was with him, and that the Lord made all that he did to prosper in his hand. And Joseph found favour in his sight, and he ministered unto him. . . .

And it came to pass at the end of two full years, that Pharaoh dreamed: and, behold, he stood by the river. . . . Then Pharaoh sent and called Joseph, and they brought him hastily out of the dungeon. And he shaved himself, and changed his raiment, and came in unto Pharaoh. And Pharaoh said unto Joseph: 'I have dreamed a dream, And there is none that can interpret it; and I have heard say of thee, that when thou hearest a dream thou canst interpret it.' And Joseph answered Pharaoh, saying: 'It is not in me; God will give Pharaoh an answer of peace.' . . . And Pharaoh said unto Joseph, 'Forasmuch as God hath shown thee all this, there is none so discreet and wise as thou. Thou shalt be over my house, and according unto thy word shall all my people be ruled; only in the throne will I be greater than thou.' And Pharaoh said unto Joseph: 'See, I have set thee over all the land of Egypt.'— 37: 1-4; 39: 1-4a, 14-16, 39-41.

G.   And Israel took his journey with all that he had, and came to Beer-sheba, and offered sacrifices unto the God of his father Isaac. And God spoke unto Israel in the visions of the night, and said: 'Jacob, Jacob.' And he said: 'Here am I.' And He said: 'I am God, the God of thy father; fear not to go down into Egypt; for I will there make of thee a great nation. I will go down with thee into Egypt; and I will also surely bring thee up again; and Joseph shall put his hand upon thine eyes.' And Jacob rose up from Beer-sheba; and the sons of Israel carried Jacob their father, and their little ones, and their wives, in the wagons which Pharaoh had sent to carry him. And they took their cattle, and their goods, which they had gotten in the land of Canaan, and came into Egypt, Jacob, and all his seed with him; his sons, and his sons' sons with him, his daughters, and his sons' daughters, and all his seed brought he with him into Egypt. — 46: 1-7.

H.   And Jacob called unto his sons, and said: 'Gather yourselves together, that I may tell you that which shall befall you in the end of days.

 Assemble yourselves, and hear, ye sons of Jacob;
 And hearken unto Israel your father. . . .'

And Joseph dwelt in Egypt, he and his father's house; and Joseph lived a hundred and ten years. And Joseph saw Ephraim's children of the third generation; the children also of Machir the son of Manasseh were born upon Joseph's knees. And Joseph said unto his brethren: 'I die; but God will surely remember you, and bring you up out of this land unto the land which He swore to Abraham, to Isaac, and to Jacob.' And Joseph took an oath of the children of Israel saying: 'God will surely remember you, and ye shall carry up my bones from hence.' So Joseph died, being a hundred and ten years old. And they embalmed him, and he was put in a coffin in Egypt. — 49: 1-2; 50: 22-26.

COMMENTARY

A.   The prelude and background of the entire Scripture is in these opening chapters. All man is in the image of God. All men are His children. A great rabbi, Ben Azzai (Sifra to Kedoshin 89b), said that the verse "This is the book of the generations of Adam" is an even more basic principle of ethics than "Thou shalt love thy neighbour as thyself." The Mishnah (Sanhedrin IV,5) says that although God could have created an entire species of man, He purposely created one man and one woman so that no group or race could claim to be better than another, being all descendants of the same ancestors. The brotherhood of man, their common childhood to God, is an essential principle of the entire Bible. As to the genealogy, see Book Two, page 51.

B.   Man became corrupt and needed to be restored to nobility. God's method was to select a small remnant of mankind which managed to survive the universal corruption and make this remnant the source of human regeneration. Therefore He chose Noah and his family, and with Noah, after the Flood, God made a covenant that life on earth will never be destroyed again. All human beings are therefore children of Noah, according to Scriptural genealogy, since the other branches descended of Adam have disappeared. It is a principle of later Jewish law that all human beings who abandon idolatry and establish justice and live a moral life are called "children of Noah," half-proselytes of Israel, and have their portion in the world to come. These "children of Noah" are not required to obey all the manifold commandments ordained for the severer disciplining of Israel. It is sufficient if they obey the "seven commandments of the children of Noah" (morality, justice, non-worship of idols, etc.); then they are righteous in the sight of God.

C.   There follows another period of corruption, the Tower of Babel, etc. And God continues His process of selecting one group to carry out and to teach His word. God now selects Abraham and makes a covenant with him. While God promises him, as the reward for his obedience, prosperity and spiritual blessing, He makes it clear and repeats it in succeeding covenants that Abraham's work will be to bring blessing to mankind. "In thee shall all the families of the earth be blessed." Abraham is tested by his willingness to give up his only son, a sacrifice which in the end is not exacted from him. Again, thereafter, the covenant is renewed: his children will prosper and multiply, and again the purpose of it will be ultimately: "in thy seed shall all the nations of the earth be blessed."

D.   From now on, the Bible is on its main road. It tells the story of the training and the dedication of the descendants of Abraham, the first patriarch. Thus we are told of the life of Isaac and his blessing to his son Jacob.

E.   Now Jacob goes on his own career. The first night of his lonely journey he sees in a dream the ladder ascending heavenward, and hears God repeat the promise which He made to Abraham and Isaac. He hears the promise of the blessing to his descendants and now for the third time, repeated to the third patriarch, "in thee and in thy seed shall all the families of the earth be blessed."

Thus is the main theme of Scripture definitely expounded, and the rest of its narrative is the story of the rise and fall, the nobility and the corruption and the spiritual recovery of this family, descendant of the patriarchs, to whom the land of Canaan is promised and the task of world blessing assigned forever.

F.   The story of Genesis here begins to turn towards the Book of Exodus and the slavery of Egypt. The coming serfdom casts its shadow before it. We read how Jacob's son Joseph, hated by his brothers, is sold into slavery to be a herald, as it were, of his brothers who will yet come after him to that land. He becomes viceroy of Egypt, preparing the way for the coming of the rest of the family.

G.   Jacob and his family come now to Egypt, and going down there he seems to have a foreboding of the four centuries of slavery; but he receives God's assurance: "I will go down with thee into Egypt and I also will surely bring thee out again."

H.   Jacob, the last of the patriarchs, dies in Egypt. He dies with words of blessing for his sons, gathered around his bedside. Then Joseph dies and in dying repeats the promise that God will surely remember them and bring them up out of Egypt. Thus ends the story of the patriarchs, chosen from all the children of men to become the progenitors of the chosen people.

EXODUS

GENERAL OUTLINE

The Book of Genesis, although it begins with the story of the creation of the world and the beginning of all mankind, is essentially the story of the life of certain selected individuals—of Noah, in whom all of mankind receives a new beginning, and then of the three patriarchs, Abraham, Isaac and Jacob, the ancestors of Israel. The Book of Exodus, while it speaks of the life of certain individuals, some of them great, such as Moses and Aaron, is not primarily the story of individuals but the story of a people. It is the beginning of the history of Israel. Genesis is primarily biography; Exodus is essentially history.

Modern critical scholars have devoted a great amount of attention to the Book of Exodus. They have found in it not only the usual original documents which they find in the rest of the early part of the Bible, namely the documents called *J* and *E* and *D* and *P*, but they also find a document that may be older than any of them, one called the Book of the Covenant, an ancient booklet of laws (Exodus 20:22 to 23:33). Others find also a smaller Book of the Covenant in chapter 34:17-26. From these two old books of laws and from fragments of the documents mentioned above, the critical theory declares that Exodus was, by successive editors, gradually put together, the final editing taking place after the Exile.

But the general reader is concerned chiefly with the book as it is today. As it is today, it has been for at least twenty-four centuries. In whatever order and from whatever materials the book was put together, it has been together long enough to be considered a unit, a mansion built with architectural skill and for a specific purpose. We are interested in the mansion of Scripture, in the harmony of its architecture, and not so much in the various quarries in which its stones were found.

There is, then, a definite plan, an architectural unity in the Book of Exodus. It begins with Israel's enslavement in Egypt. God recalls the covenant which He made with the fathers and selects Moses to lead Israel out of Egypt towards the land which He promised to give to Abraham and his descendants. But as He made a covenant with the fathers, so must He renew the covenant with their descendants. Therefore, the journey to the Promised Land is by way of Mount Sinai, where God enters into His covenant with Israel, with the entire people, that they may be to Him "a kingdom of priests and a holy people." As Abraham left his father's house, abandoning the idolatries which were all around him, so Israel was to abandon idolatry forever: "Thou shalt have no other god beside Me." To carry out its part of the covenant, Israel must take upon itself the discipline of laws and commandments, the laws expressing either ethical relationships to their fellow men or obedience to God with whom they are now united in agreement. They can become aware of God's Presence among them now that they accept His commandments. Therefore He orders them to build a tabernacle "that I may dwell in their midst."

But, being human, they sin; they commit the sin of the golden calf. They fall into the corruption of idolatry as they will yet time and time again in the future, and Moses, the greatest of the prophets, rebukes them but also pleads for them. After they are punished, the covenant must be renewed at once. Certain of the formal laws are therefore now repeated. The building of the tabernacle is resumed and the Book of Exodus ends with God's radiance filling the tabernacles of Israel.

SYNOPSIS OF TEXT

A.   Now there arose a new king over Egypt, who knew not Joseph. And he said unto his people: 'Behold, the people of the children of Israel are too many and too mighty for us; come, let us deal wisely with them, lest they multiply, and it come to pass, that when there befalleth us any war, they also join themselves unto our enemies, and fight against us, and get them up out of the land.' Therefore they did set over them task-masters to afflict them with their burdens. And they built for Pharaoh store-cities, Pithom and Raamses. But the more they afflicted them, the more they multiplied and the more they spread abroad. And they were adread because of the children of Israel. . . .

And it came to pass in the course of those many days that the king of Egypt died; and the children of Israel sighed by reason of the bondage, and they cried, and their cry came up unto God by reason of the bondage. And God heard their groaning, and God remembered His covenant with Abraham, with Isaac, and with Jacob. —1:8-12; 2:23-24.

B.   And Moses said: 'I will turn aside now, and see this great sight, why the bush is not burnt.' And when the Lord saw that he turned aside to see, God called unto him out of the midst of the bush and said: 'Moses, Moses.' And he said: 'Here am I.' And He said: 'Draw not nigh hither; put off thy shoes from off thy feet, for the place whereon thou standest is holy ground.' Moreover He said: 'I am the God of thy father, the God of Abraham, the God of Isaac, and the God of Jacob.' . . . Go, and gather the elders of Israel together, and say unto them: The Lord, the God of your fathers, the God of Abraham, of Isaac, and of Jacob, hath appeared unto me, saying: I have surely remembered you, and seen that which is done to you in Egypt. And I have said: I will bring you up out of the affliction of Egypt unto the land of the Canaanite. . . .

And God spoke unto Moses, and said unto him: 'I am the Lord; And I appeared unto Abraham, unto Isaac, and unto Jacob, as God Almighty, but by My name I made Me not known to them. And I have also established My covenant with them, to give them the land of Canaan, the land of their sojournings, wherein they sojourned. And moreover I have heard the groaning of the children of Israel, whom the Egyptians keep in bondage; and I have remembered My covenant. Wherefore say unto the children of Israel: I am the Lord, and I will bring you out from under the burdens of the Egyptians, and I will deliver you from their bondage, and I will redeem you with an outstretched arm, and with great judgments; and I will take you to Me for a people, and I will be to you a God; . . .'—3:3-6a, 16-17a; 6:2-7a.

C.   And Moses and Aaron went in unto Pharaoh, and said unto him: 'Thus saith the Lord, the God of the Hebrews: How long wilt thou refuse to humble thyself before Me? Let My people go, that they may serve Me. Else, if thou refuse to let My people go, behold, tomorrow will I bring locusts into thy border; . . .' And Moses and Aaron were brought again unto Pharaoh; and he said unto them: 'Go, serve the Lord your God; but who are they that shall go?' And Moses said: 'We will go with our young and with our old, with our sons and with our daughters, with our flocks and with our herds we will go; for we must hold a feast unto the Lord.'

And the children of Israel journeyed from Rameses to Succoth, about six hundred thousand men on foot, beside children. . . . And they baked unleavened cakes of the dough which they brought forth out of Egypt, for it was not leavened; because they were thrust out of Egypt, and could not tarry, neither had they prepared for themselves any victual. Now the time that the children of Israel dwelt in Egypt was four hundred and thirty years. And it came to pass at the end of four hundred and thirty years, even the selfsame day it came to pass, that all the hosts of the Lord went out from the land of Egypt. It was a night of watching unto the Lord for bringing them out from the land of Egypt; this same night is a night of watching unto the Lord for all the children of Israel throughout their generations.

Then sang Moses and the children of Israel this song unto the Lord, and spoke, saying:

> I will sing unto the Lord, for He is highly exalted;
> The horse and his rider hath He thrown into the sea.
> The Lord is my strength and song,
> And He is become my salvation;
> This is my God, and I will glorify Him;
> My father's God, and I will exalt Him.
> Who is like unto Thee, O Lord, among the mighty?
> Who is like unto Thee, glorious in holiness,
> Fearful in praises, doing wonders?
> The Lord shall reign for ever and ever.
>
> —10:3-4, 8, 9; 12:37, 39-42; 15:1, 2, 11, 18.

D.   And the Lord spoke unto Moses and Aaron in the land of Egypt, saying: 'This month shall be unto you the beginning of months; it shall be the first month of the year to you. Speak ye unto all the congregation of Israel, saying: In the tenth day of this month they shall take to them every man a lamb, according to their fathers' houses, a lamb for a household; . . . And ye shall let nothing of it remain until the morning; but that which remaineth of it until the morning ye shall burn with fire. . . .'

And the Lord spoke unto Moses, saying: 'Sanctify unto Me all the first-born, whatsoever openeth the womb among the children of Israel, both of man and of beast, it is Mine.'

And Moses said unto the people: 'Remember this day, in which ye came out from Egypt, out of the house of bondage; for by strength of hand the Lord brought you out from this place; there shall no leavened bread be eaten. This day ye go forth in the month Abib. And it shall be when the Lord shall bring thee into the land of the Canaanite, and the Hittite, and the Amorite, and the Hivite, and the Jebusite, which He swore unto thy fathers to give thee, a land flowing with milk and honey, that thou shalt keep this service in this month. Seven days thou shalt eat unleavened bread, and in the seventh day shall be a feast to the Lord. . . .' – 12:1-3, 10, 13:1-6.

E.   In the third month after the children of Israel were gone forth out of the land of Egypt, the same day came they into the wilderness of Sinai. And when they were departed from Rephidim, and were come to the wilderness of Sinai, they encamped in the wilderness; and there Israel encamped before the mount. And Moses went up unto God, and the Lord called unto him out of the mountain, saying: 'Thus shalt thou say to the house of Jacob, and tell the children of Israel: Ye have seen what I did unto the Egyptians, and how I bore you on eagles' wings, and brought you unto Myself. Now therefore, if ye will hearken unto My voice indeed, and keep My covenant, then ye shall be Mine own treasure from among all peoples; for all the earth is Mine; and ye shall be unto Me a kingdom of priests, and a holy nation. These are the words which thou shalt speak unto the children of Israel.' . . .

And God spoke all these words, saying:

I am the Lord thy God, who brought thee out of the land of Egypt, out of the house of bondage.

Thou shalt have no other gods before Me. Thou shalt not make unto thee a graven image, nor any manner of likeness, of any thing that is in heaven above, or that is in the earth beneath, or that is in the water under the earth; thou shalt not bow down unto them, nor serve them; . . .

Now these are the ordinances which thou shalt set before them.

If thou buy a Hebrew servant, six years he shall serve; and in the seventh he shall go out free for nothing. . . .

He that smiteth a man, so that he dieth, shall surely be put to death.

And if a man lie not in wait, but God cause it to come to hand; then I will appoint thee a place whither he may flee. . . .

And if a man smite his bondman, or his bondwoman, with a rod, and he die under his hand, he shall surely be punished.

And if men strive together, and hurt a woman with child, so that her fruit depart, and yet no harm follow, he shall be surely fined, according as the woman's husband shall lay upon him; and he shall pay as the judges determine. —19:1-6; 20:1-5a; 21:1-2, 12, 13, 20-22.

F.   And the Lord spoke unto Moses, saying: 'Speak unto the children of Israel, that they take for Me an offering; of every man whose heart maketh him willing ye shall take My offering. And this is the offering which ye shall take of them: gold, and silver, and brass; and blue, and purple, and scarlet, and fine linen, and goats' hair; . . .'

And bring thou near unto thee Aaron thy brother, and his sons with him, from among the children of Israel, that they may minister unto Me in the priest's office, even Aaron, Nadab and Abihu, Eleazar and Ithamar, Aaron's sons. . . .

And I will sanctify the tent of meeting, and the altar; Aaron also and his sons will I sanctify, to minister to Me in the priest's office. And I will dwell among the children of Israel, and will be their God. And they shall know that I am the Lord their God, that brought them forth out of the land of Egypt, that I may dwell among them. I am the Lord their God. – 25:1-4; 28:1; 29:44-46.

G.   And when the people saw that Moses delayed to come down from the mount, the people gathered themselves together unto Aaron, and said unto him: 'Up, make us a god who shall go before us; for as for this Moses, the man that brought us up out of the land of Egypt, we know not what is become of him.' . . .
And all the people broke off the golden rings which were in their ears, and brought them unto Aaron. And he received it at their

hand, and fashioned it with a graving tool, and made it a molten calf; and they said: 'This is thy god, O Israel, which brought thee up out of the land of Egypt.' . . .

And the Lord spoke unto Moses: 'Go, get thee down; for the people, that thou broughtest up out of the land of Egypt, have dealt corruptly; . . .'

And Moses besought the Lord his God, and said: 'Lord, why doth Thy wrath wax hot against Thy people, that Thou hast brought forth out of the land of Egypt with great power and with a mighty hand? . . . Remember Abraham, Isaac, and Israel, Thy servants, to whom Thou didst swear by Thine own self, and saidst unto them: I will multiply your seed as the stars of heaven, and all this land that I have spoken of will I give unto your seed, and they shall inherit it for ever.' And the Lord repented of the evil which He said He would do unto His people. – 32: 1, 3, 4, 7, 11, 13, 14.

H.   And the Lord said unto Moses: 'Hew thee two tables of stone like unto the first; and I will write upon the tables the words that were on the first tables, which thou didst break. And be ready by the morning, and come up in the morning unto mount Sinai, and present thyself there to Me on the top of the mount. . . .' And the Lord passed by before him, and proclaimed: 'The Lord, the Lord, God, merciful and gracious, long-suffering, and abundant in goodness and truth, keeping mercy unto the thousandth generation, forgiving iniquity and transgression and sin; . . .' 'Observe thou that which I am commanding thee this day; behold, I am driving out before thee the Amorite, and the Canaanite, and the Hittite, . . . Take heed to thyself, lest thou make a covenant with the inhabitants of the land whither thou goest, lest they be for a snare in the midst of thee. But ye shall break down their altars, and dash in pieces their pillars, and ye shall cut down their Asherim. For thou shalt bow down to no other god; . . .'

And Moses assembled all the congregation of the children of Israel, and said unto them: 'These are the words which the Lord hath commanded, that ye should do them. Six days shall work be done, but on the seventh day there shall be to you a holy day, a sabbath of solemn rest to the Lord; . . .'

And Moses called Bezalel and Oholiab, and every wise-hearted man, in whose heart the Lord had put wisdom, even every one whose heart stirred him up to come unto the work to do it. And they received of Moses all the offering, which the children of Israel had brought for the work of the service of the sanctuary, wherewith to make it. And they brought yet unto him freewill-offerings every morning. . . .

And he reared up the court round about the tabernacle and the altar, and set up the screen of the gate of the court. So Moses finished the work.

Then the cloud covered the tent of meeting, and the glory of the Lord filled the tabernacle. . . . For the cloud of the Lord was upon the tabernacle by day, and there was fire therein by night, in the sight of all the house of Israel, throughout all their journeys.
— 34:1, 2, 6, 7a, 11-14a; 35:1-2a; 36:2, 3; 40:33, 34, 38.

COMMENTARY

A.   The enslavement begins, this section ending with Israel's prayer to God, and God remembering His covenant with Abraham, Isaac and Jacob.

B.   God summons Moses, reminds him of His promise to the patriarchs, "I have remembered My covenant," and tells him that He will redeem them, "and I will take you unto Me for a people and I will be to you a God."

C.   God sends Moses to Pharaoh, and it is announced that Pharaoh and the Egyptians must be punished with the ten plagues before Israel is allowed to leave Egypt.

The song of triumph at the crossing of the Red Sea praises the might of God who overthrows the tyrant and rescues the oppressed.

D.   The laws in Exodus, as frequently in the other books of the Torah, are not given merely as a list of laws, as a code which is published by itself, but are interwoven into the story of Israel. Thus, as Israel goes out of Egypt and is commanded to eat the first paschal lamb, the laws of the Passover are given. Later, when a systematic list of laws is given, this law will be repeated in its proper place in the list of the festivals. That is why many laws are often repeated in Scripture. They are first mentioned in the historical circumstances in which they were first proclaimed and then later repeated in a systematic list.

E.   Their journey is directed towards Mount Sinai where they hear God proclaim the Ten Commandments. Then follows a series of detailed laws which may be deemed to be an elaboration of the Ten Commandments. Critical scholars identify this part of the law book as the Book of the Covenant, a separate and an ancient legal code.

F.   Now that Israel has taken upon itself the discipline of the covenant and the discipline of the laws, God tells them to build a sanctuary and He will dwell in their midst.

G.   But the children of Israel, impatient at the delayed absence of Moses on the mountain, have already lost their newly rediscovered faith of the patriarchs and make an idol, the golden calf, which they worship. Thus they have already broken the new covenant and have turned astray to idol worship. Moses denounces them but pleads with God not to destroy them, presuming to remind God of His promises in the past.

H.   They are forgiven but the covenant must now be renewed. Moses hews out two new tablets of stone in place of the original two which he, in anger, had broken. God makes them promise never to worship idols again. Some of the earlier laws are now repeated. The tabernacle is now built and in the presence of the people who are reconfirmed in their bond with God: "The glory of the Lord filled the tabernacle." . . . "in the sight of all the house of Israel throughout all their journeys."

Chapter II

The Torah

Leviticus, Numbers, Deuteronomy

T̲HE Book of Leviticus is the shortest book in the Pentateuch, and is the best organized of all five. The critical scholars look upon this book largely as a unit, declaring it all to be from the Priestly Code (the source *P*). Leviticus is almost entirely composed of legislation, thus is not an intermingling of narratives and laws as are Exodus and Numbers, nor is it a blending of oratory and legislation as is Deuteronomy, nor a long succession of varied events, as is Genesis. It has only two or three incidental narratives bound up with its laws. Moreover, its laws differ from those in Numbers, Exodus, and Deuteronomy in that they do not cover so great a variety. They all are either ritual laws, dealing with the holy sacrifices in the holy tabernacle, or laws dealing with personal holiness. The old Hebrew name for the book was *Toras Kohanim*, "the law of the priests," a name which is more or less preserved in the Greek and Latin name for the book, Leviticus, which means "the laws of the Levites" (or priests).

The section from chapter 17-26 is described by certain modern scholars as a special code dealing with personal holiness rather than with sacrifices in the holy tabernacle and is therefore called "The Holiness Code."

While the laws of sacrifices and the ritual in the tabernacle and the Temple would seem to be of little interest to the many generations who lived after the destruction of the Temple, where this ritual was observed, nevertheless this book has been held in particular reverence among Jews all through the centuries. Children beginning their education always started their study of Scripture with the Book of Leviticus, the reason being the one given in the

Midrash (Leviticus Rabba VII, 3) that those who are pure should come and study the book of purity.

In the general order of the Torah as it is constructed, Leviticus follows as a logical sequence to the Book of Exodus. The Book of Exodus ends with the setting up of the sacred tabernacle in the wilderness and with the words, "And the glory of the Lord filled the Tabernacle, etc." Hence, with the radiance of God in the midst of Israel in their sanctuary, it was appropriate now that the ritual of devotion in the tabernacle should be described and that these sacred rites should be followed with laws of personal sanctity: "Ye shall be holy for I, the Lord, your God am holy."

SYNOPSIS OF TEXT

A.   And the Lord called unto Moses, and spoke unto him out of the tent of meeting, saying: Speak unto the children of Israel, and say unto them:

When any man of you bringeth an offering unto the Lord, ye shall bring your offering of the cattle, even of the herd or of the flock.

If his offering be a burnt-offering of the herd, he shall offer it a male without blemish; he shall bring it to the door of the tent of meeting, that he may be accepted before the Lord. –1: 1-3.

B.   And the Lord spoke unto Moses, saying: 'Take Aaron and his sons with him, and the garments, and the anointing oil . . .'

And Moses did as the Lord commanded him; and the congregation was assembled at the door of the tent of meeting. And Moses said unto the congregation: 'This is the thing which the Lord hath commanded to be done.' And Moses brought Aaron and his sons, and washed them with water. And he put upon him the tunic, and girded him with the girdle, and clothed him with the robe, and put the ephod upon him, and he girded him with the skilfully woven band of the ephod, and bound it unto him therewith. And he placed the breastplate upon him; and in the breastplate he put the Urim and the Thummim. And he set the mitre upon his head; and upon the mitre, in front, did he set the golden plate, the holy crown; as the Lord commanded Moses. . . .

And the Lord spoke unto Aaron, saying: 'Drink no wine nor

strong drink, thou, nor thy sons with thee, when ye go into the tent of meeting, that ye die not; it shall be a statute for ever throughout your generations. And that ye may put difference between the holy and the common, and between the unclean and the clean; and that ye may teach the children of Israel all the statutes which the Lord hath spoken unto them by the hand of Moses.'– 8: 1-2b, 4-9; 10:8-11.

C.   And the Lord spoke unto Moses and to Aaron, saying unto them: Speak unto the children of Israel, saying:

These are the living things which ye may eat among all the beasts that are on the earth. Whatsoever parteth the hoof, and is wholly cloven-footed, and cheweth the cud, among the beasts, that may ye eat.

These may ye eat of all that are in the waters: whatsoever hath fins and scales in the waters, in the seas, and in the rivers, them may ye eat. . . .

This is the law of the beast, and of the fowl, and of every living creature that moveth in the waters, and of every creature that swarmeth upon the earth; to make a difference between the unclean and the clean, and between the living thing that may be eaten and the living thing that may not be eaten.

And the Lord spoke unto Moses and unto Aaron, saying:

When a man shall have in the skin of his flesh a rising, or a scab, or a bright spot, and it become in the skin of his flesh the plague of leprosy, then he shall be brought unto Aaron the priest, or unto one of his sons the priests. . . . then the priest shall shut up him that hath the plague seven days.

Thus shall ye separate the children of Israel from their uncleanness; that they die not in their uncleanness, when they defile My tabernacle that is in the midst of them. –11:1-3, 9, 46-47; 13:1-2, 4b; 15:31.

D.   And the Lord said unto Moses: 'Speak unto Aaron thy brother, that he come not at all times into the holy place within the veil, before the ark-cover which is upon the ark; that he die not; for I appear in the cloud upon the ark-cover. Herewith shall Aaron come into the holy place: with a young bullock for a sin-offering, and a ram for a burnt-offering. He shall put on the holy linen tunic, and he shall have the linen breeches upon his flesh, and shall be girded with the linen girdle, and with the linen mitre shall he be attired; they are the holy garments; and he shall bathe his flesh in water, and put them on. . . .'

'And he shall make atonement for the holy place, because of the uncleannesses of the children of Israel, and because of their transgressions, even all their sins; and so shall he do for the tent of meeting, that dwelleth with them in the midst of their uncleannesses. . . .'

'And it shall be a statute for ever unto you: in the seventh month, on the tenth day of the month, ye shall afflict your souls, and shall do no manner of work, the home-born, or the stranger that sojourneth among you. For on this day shall atonement be made for you, to cleanse you; from all your sins shall ye be clean before the Lord. It is a sabbath of solemn rest unto you, and ye shall afflict your souls; it is a statute for ever. And the priest, who shall be anointed and who shall be consecrated to be priest in his father's stead, shall make the atonement, and shall put on the linen garments, even the holy garments. And he shall make atonement for the most holy place, and he shall make atonement for the tent of meeting and for the altar; and he shall make atonement for the priests and for all the people of the assembly. And this shall be an everlasting statute unto you, to make atonement for the children of Israel because of all their sins once in the year.' And he did as the Lord commanded Moses. –16: 2-4, 16, 29-34.

E.   And the Lord spoke unto Moses, saying: Speak unto the children of Israel, and say unto them:

I am the Lord your God. After the doings of the land of Egypt, wherein ye dwelt, shall ye not do; and after the doings of the land of Canaan, whither I bring you, shall ye not do; neither shall ye walk in their statutes. Mine ordinances shall ye do, and My statutes shall ye keep, to walk therein: I am the Lord your God. Ye shall therefore keep My statutes, and Mine ordinances, which if a man do, he shall live by them: I am the Lord.

None of you shall approach to any that is near of kin to him, to uncover their nakedness: I am the Lord.

And the Lord spoke unto Moses, saying: Speak unto all the congregation of the children of Israel, and say unto them:

Ye shall be holy; for I the Lord your God am holy. Ye shall fear every man his mother, and his father and ye shall keep my Sabbaths: I am the Lord your God. Turn ye not unto the idols, nor make to yourselves molten gods: I am the Lord your God. . . .

Ye shall do no unrighteousness in judgment; thou shalt not respect the person of the poor, nor favour the person of the mighty; but in righteousness shalt thou judge thy neighbour.

Thou shalt not take vengeance nor bear a grudge against the children of thy people but thou shalt love thy neighbour as thyself: I am the Lord.

Moreover, thou shalt say to the children of Israel:

Whosoever he be of the children of Israel, or of the strangers that sojourn in Israel, that giveth of his seed unto Molech, he shall surely be put to death; the people of the land shall stone him with stones. And the soul that turneth unto the ghosts, and unto the familiar spirits, to go astray after them, I will even set My face against that soul, and will cut him off from among his people. . . . And ye shall not walk in the customs of the nation, which I am casting out before you; for they did all these things, and therefore I abhorred them. But I have said unto you: 'Ye shall inherit their land, and I will give it unto you to possess it, a land flowing with milk and honey.' . . . And ye shall be holy unto Me; for I the Lord am holy, and have set you apart from the peoples, that ye should be Mine. –18:1-6; 19:1-4, 15, 18; 20:2, 6, 23, 24, 26.

F.   And the Lord spoke unto Moses in mount Sinai, saying: Speak unto the children of Israel, and say unto them:

When ye come into the land which I give you, then shall the land keep a sabbath unto the Lord. Six years thou shalt sow thy field, and six years thou shalt prune thy vineyard, and gather in the produce thereof. But in the seventh year shall be a sabbath of solemn rest for the land, a sabbath unto the Lord; thou shalt neither sow thy field, nor prune thy vineyard. . . .

And thou shalt number seven sabbaths of years unto thee, seven times seven years; and there shall be unto thee the days of seven sabbaths of years, even forty and nine years. Then shalt thou make proclamation with the blast of the horn on the tenth day of the seventh month; in the day of atonement shall ye make proclamation with the horn throughout all your land. And ye shall hallow the fiftieth year, and proclaim liberty throughout the land unto all the inhabitants thereof; it shall be a jubilee unto you; and ye shall return every man unto his possession, and ye shall return every man unto his family. – 25:1-4, 8-10.

G.   If you walk in My statutes, and keep My commandments, and do them; then I will give your rains in their season, and the land shall yield her produce, and the trees of the field shall yield their fruit. And your threshing shall reach unto the vintage, and the vintage shall reach unto the sowing time; and ye shall eat your bread until ye have enough, and dwell in your land safely. And I will give peace in the land, and ye shall lie down, and none shall make you afraid; . . .

But if ye will not hearken unto Me, and will not do all these commandments; and if ye shall reject My statutes, and if your soul abhor Mine ordinances, so that ye will not do all My commandments, but break My covenant; I also will do this unto you: I will appoint terror over you, even consumption and fever, that shall make the eyes to fail, and the soul to languish; and ye shall sow your seed in vain, for your enemies shall eat it. . . . And I will break the pride of your power; and I will make your heaven as iron, and your earth as brass. And your strength shall be spent in vain; for your land shall not yield her produce, neither shall the trees of the land yield their fruit.

These are the commandments, which the Lord commanded Moses for the children of Israel in mount Sinai. – 26:3-6b, 14-16, 19, 20; 27:34.

COMMENTARY

A.   The various classes of offerings, mandatory and voluntary, which should be brought in the tabernacle and later in the permanent Temple which took its place are discussed. Thus, burnt offerings, meal, peace, and sin offerings, etc., are enumerated.

B.   The ceremony of induction of Aaron and his sons, the anointing of them with oil, the special sacrifices of induction and the sacred garments is described. The special function of the priests to guard holy things, to distinguish between the holy and the profane, and to be the teachers of the people "that ye may teach the children of Israel all the statutes which the Lord had spoken unto them by the hand of Moses" (Leviticus 10:11) is stressed. This function of the priest as teacher and guide as described here by Moses, whom tradition reveres as the first of the Prophets, is repeated by Malachi, the last of the Prophets. "For the priest's lips should keep knowledge and they should seek the law at his mouth for he is the messenger of the Lord of hosts" (Malachi 2:7).

C.   Part of the personal holiness which all the children of Israel must observe is the abstention from foods which are considered unclean, and the careful quarantining of those with unclean diseases till they are cured. These laws of special sanctity, which in some similar form were observed only by the priesthood among other peoples, are here to be observed not merely by one class or clan but by an entire people which is to be now for the first time in human religious history a "kingdom of priests." Since God was in their midst, since the whole people was to be aware of God's presence, it was ordered that they conduct themselves as priests do in a sanctuary. "Thus shall ye separate the children of Israel from their uncleanness that they die not in their uncleanness when they defile My tabernacle which is in the midst of them" (Leviticus 15:31).

D.   Chapter 16 deals with the special ritual for the Day of Atonement, the various sacrifices and the various confessions. This ritual was greatly dramatized in the permanent Temple in Jerusalem. It is described in great detail in the Mishnah (*Tractate Yoma*) and it became a permanent part, written in prose and poetry, in the traditional afternoon service for the Day of Atonement in all the synagogues of Israel (the *Seder Avoda*).

E.   The section of the book which deals with purity in personal life and in family life constitutes what modern scholars call "The Holiness Code." It describes the degrees of relationship forbidden to marriage. It speaks of the sacred duty of reverence to parents, of turning away from idolatry, of overcoming all hatred and loving one's neighbor as oneself. This group of laws is characterized by the frequent explanatory phrase, "I am the Lord your God." In other words, it is the duty of every man to emulate to the extent of his human power, the holiness of God: "and ye shall be holy unto Me for I the Lord am holy" (Leviticus 20:26).

F.   As the week of work must be sanctified by one day of rest, and of devotion to spiritual thoughts, so must the land have its sacred Sabbath, and every seventh year the land must rest. After seven times seven years, the Jubilee will be proclaimed. "Jubilee" is from the Hebrew word *Yovel* used in Scripture describing this day, and means a ram's horn which is blown as proclamation of the beginning of the year, when, by the coming of the Jubilee year, all who are enslaved go free and all return to their families and their possessions. "Proclaim liberty throughout the land unto all the inhabitants thereof" (Leviticus 8:10). This is the verse which has been inscribed on the American Liberty Bell.

G.   As is the case in a number of places in the Torah where the laws involved with the covenant with God are described, they are here concluded with a statement of curses which will be incurred if they are violated, and blessings which will be received if they are fulfilled. All these laws were given, according to the Torah, in the second year of the Exodus, when Israel had not yet left Mount Sinai. And so the book of Leviticus ends with the words: "These are the commandments which the Lord commanded Moses for the children of Israel in mount Sinai."

NUMBERS

GENERAL OUTLINE

The Book of Numbers (in Hebrew, *Bamidbor*) is so named (in English through the Latin and the Greek title) because of the fact that the book begins with a census, a numbering of the children of Israel. This name corresponds with the older Talmudic name of the book, *Chomesh ha-pekudim*, "the fifth part" (of the Torah) dealing with those numbered. Of the four books of the Torah from Exodus to Deuteronomy which deal with the early history of the people of Israel, this book covers the longest span of time. The Book of Exodus deals with the last period of the slavery and one year of freedom; the Book of Leviticus is understood to have been given while the people were still near Mount Sinai; the Book of

Deuteronomy covers only the time needed for the three final speeches of Moses; whereas the Book of Numbers, beginning in the second year of the exodus, while Israel still remained at Mount Sinai, continues on to the end of the forty years of wandering in the wilderness. It covers a span of thirty-eight years. These thirty-eight years were eventful. There were a number of rebellions and abortive rebellions. There were periods of great privations and of special deliverances. Battles were fought with various people, and part of the lands on the eastern side of the Jordan were conquered for later settlement. The death of Miriam and the death of Aaron occurred in this period, and Moses at the end of his great career was left alone (except for his disciple Joshua) with the people whom he had delivered and had led so long.

The book therefore is full of action and is also rich in description of character. The burdens of Moses, his occasional impatience, his deep-rooted modesty, his anger at the people and his pleading in their behalf to God, are all vividly portrayed. We are with him through trials, rebellions, and battles, and with his last loneliness on the east side of the Jordan in the plains of Moab. More of the spiritual grandeur of him who is revered by tradition as first and greatest of the Prophets is seen in the Book of Numbers than in any other book of the Torah.

Also the character of the people just emerging from slavery is vividly described. They too had a heavy burden to bear. After centuries of serfdom they had to endure forty years of desert privation, with the Promised Land still unattained. It was not to be expected that such dire tribulations of body and spirit should be endured by ex-slaves and their children with calmness of mind. So they frequently complained and occasionally rebelled. What is remarkable is that the unpleasant story of their weakness and their rebellions and their evil doing should have been so carefully preserved by them and their descendants. Historical records of other peoples preserve the triumphs and the victories and the glories of the nations whose records they are. This is the one great historical record in which a people has preserved the story of its own weakness and its own sins. It has made this record of its sins part of its Sacred Scripture and has studied it reverently. This mood of open national confession makes the Bible one of the most sincere, one of the most touchingly human books preserved from antiquity. This record of

frank confession of weakness is preserved not only in this book
of the wanderings in the desert, but its events are frequently referred to in the Prophets and also in the Book of Psalms (see
Psalm 106).

A.   And the Lord spoke unto Moses in the wilderness of Sinai,
in the tent of meeting, on the first day of the second month, in the
second year after they were come out of the land of Egypt, saying:
'Take ye the sum of all the congregation of the children of Israel,
by their families, by their fathers' houses, according to the number
of names, every male, by their polls; . . .' And all those that were
numbered of the children of Israel by their fathers' houses, from
twenty years old and upward, all that were able to go forth to war
in Israel; even all those that were numbered were six hundred thousand and three thousand and five hundred and fifty. But the Levites
after the tribe of their fathers were not numbered among them.

And the Lord spoke unto Moses and unto Aaron, saying: 'The
children of Israel shall pitch (their tents) by their fathers' houses;
every man with his own standard, according to the ensigns; a good
way off shall they pitch round about the tent of meeting. Now
those that pitch on the east side toward the sunrising shall be they
of the standard of the camp of Judah, according to their hosts; the
prince of the children of Judah being Nahshon the son of Ammina-
dab, . . . and those that pitch next unto him shall be the tribe of
Issachar; the prince of the children of Issachar being Nethanel the
son of Zuar, . . .'

Then the tent of meeting, with the camp of the Levites, shall set
forward in the midst of the camps; as they encamp, so shall they
set forward, every man in his place, by their standards. And the
Lord spoke unto Moses, saying: 'Bring the tribe of Levi near and
set them before Aaron the priest, that they may minister unto him,
and they shall keep his charge, and the charge of the whole congregation before the tent of meeting, to do the service of the tabernacle. . . .'

And the Lord spoke unto Moses, saying: 'Command the children
of Israel, that they put out of the camp every leper, and every one
that hath an issue, and whosoever is unclean by the dead; both male

and female shall ye put out, without the camp shall ye put them; that they defile not their camp, in the midst whereof I dwell.'

And the Lord spoke unto Moses, saying: 'Speak unto Aaron and unto his sons, saying: On this wise ye shall bless the children of Israel; ye shall say unto them:

The Lord bless thee, and keep thee;

The Lord make His face to shine upon thee, and be gracious unto thee;

The Lord lift up His countenance upon thee, and give thee peace.

So shall they put My name upon the children of Israel, and I will bless them.'

And on the day that the tabernacle was reared up the cloud covered the tabernacle, even the tent of the testimony; and at even there was upon the tabernacle as it were the appearance of fire, until morning. And whenever the cloud was taken up from over the Tent, then after that the children of Israel journeyed; and in the place where the cloud abode, there the children of Israel encamped. At the commandment of the Lord the children of Israel journeyed, and at the commandment of the Lord they encamped: as long as the cloud abode upon the tabernacle they remained encamped. – 1: 1-2, 45-47; 2: 1-3, 5; 3: 5-7; 5: 1-3; 6: 22-27; 9: 15, 17, 18.

B. And the mixed multitude that was among them fell a lusting; and the children of Israel also wept on their part, and said: 'Would that we were given flesh to eat! We remember the fish, which we were wont to eat in Egypt for nought; the cucumbers, and the melons, and the leeks, and the onions, and the garlic; but now our soul is dried away; there is nothing at all; we have nought save this manna to look to.' . . . And Moses said unto the Lord: 'Wherefore hast Thou dealt ill with Thy servant? and wherefore have I not found favour in Thy sight, that Thou layest the burden of all this people upon me? . . . I am not able to bear all this people myself alone, because it is too heavy for me. . . .'

And the Lord said unto Moses: 'Gather unto Me seventy men of the elders of Israel, whom thou knowest to be the elders of the people, and officers over them; and bring them unto the tent of meeting, that they may stand there with thee. . . .' And the Lord came down in the cloud, and spoke unto him, and took of the spirit that was upon him, and put it upon the seventy elders; and it came to pass, that, when the spirit rested upon them, they prophesied, but they did so no more. . . . And there ran a young man, and told Moses, and said: 'Eldad and Medad are prophesying in the camp.' . . . And Moses said unto him: 'Art thou jealous for my sake? Would that all the Lord's people were prophets, that the Lord would put His spirit upon them!' –11:4-6, 11, 14, 16, 25, 27, 29.

C.   And the Lord spoke unto Moses, saying: 'Send thou men, that they may spy out the land of Canaan, which I give unto the children of Israel; of every tribe of their fathers shall ye send a man, every one a prince among them.' . . . And they returned from spying out the land at the end of forty days. . . . And they told him, and said: 'We came unto the land whither thou sentest us, and surely it floweth with milk and honey; and this is the fruit of it. Howbeit the people that dwell in the land are fierce, and the cities are fortified, and very great; and moreover we saw the children of Anak there.'

And all the congregation lifted up their voice, and cried; and the people wept that night. And all the children of Israel murmured against Moses and against Aaron; and the whole congregation said unto them: 'Would that we had died in the land of Egypt; or would we had died in this wilderness! And wherefore doth the Lord bring us unto this land, to fall by the sword? Our wives and our little ones will be a prey; were it not better for us to return into Egypt?' And they said one to another: 'Let us make a captain, and let us return unto Egypt.'

And the Lord spoke unto Moses and unto Aaron, saying: 'How long shall I bear with this evil congregation, that keep murmuring against Me? I have heard the murmurings of the children of Israel, which they keep murmuring against Me. Say unto them: As I live, saith the Lord, surely as ye have spoken in Mine ears, so will I do to you: your carcasses shall fall in this wilderness, and all that were numbered of you, according to your whole number, from twenty years old and upward, ye that have murmured against Me; . . .'

Now Korah, the son of Izhar, the son of Kohath, the son of Levi, with Dathan and Abiram, took men; . . . and they assembled themselves together against Moses and against Aaron, and said unto them: 'Ye take too much upon you, seeing all the congregation are holy, every one of them, and the Lord is among them; wherefore then lift ye up yourselves above the assembly of the Lord?'—13:1-2, 25, 27, 28; 14:1-4, 26-29; 16:1, 3.

D.   And the children of Israel, even the whole congregation, came into the wilderness of Zin in the first month; and the people abode in Kadesh; and Miriam died there, and was buried there. . . . And Moses did as the Lord commanded; and they went up into mount Hor in the sight of all the congregation. And Moses stripped Aaron of his garments, and put them upon Eleazar his son; and Aaron died there in the top of the mount; and Moses and Eleazar came down from the mount. And when all the congregation saw that Aaron was dead, they wept for Aaron thirty days, even all the house of Israel.

And Balak the son of Zippor saw all that Israel had done to the Amorites. And Moab was sore afraid of the people, because they were many; and Moab was overcome with dread because of the children of Israel. . . . And he sent messengers unto Balaam the son of Beor, to Pethor, which is by the River, to the land of the children of his people to call him, saying: 'Behold, there is a people come out from Egypt; behold, they cover the face of the earth, and they abide over against me. Come now therefore, I pray thee, curse me this people; for they are too mighty for me; peradventure I shall prevail, that we may smite them, and that I may drive them out of the land; for I know that he whom thou blessest is blessed, and he whom thou cursest is cursed.'

And the Lord put a word in Balaam's mouth, and said: 'Return unto Balak, and thus thou shalt speak.' . . .

How shall I curse, whom God hath not cursed?

And how shall I execrate, whom the Lord hath not execrated? . . .

How goodly are thy tents, O Jacob,

Thy dwellings, O Israel! . . .

Blessed be every one that blesseth thee,

And cursed be every one that curseth thee. — 20:1, 27-29; 22:2-3, 5, 6; 23:5, 8; 24:5, 9b.

E.   Now the children of Reuben and the children of Gad had a very great multitude of cattle; and when they saw the land of Jazer, and the land of Gilead, that, behold, the place was a place for cattle, the children of Gad and the children of Reuben came and spoke unto Moses, and to Eleazar the priest, and unto the princes of the congregation, saying: . . . And they said: 'If we have found favour in thy sight, let this land be given unto thy servants for a possession; bring us not over the Jordan.' . . .

And Moses said unto them: 'If ye will do this thing: if ye will arm yourselves to go before the Lord to the war, . . . and the land be subdued before the Lord, and ye return afterward; then ye shall be clear before the Lord, and before Israel, and this land shall be unto you for a possession before the Lord. . . .'

These are the stages of the children of Israel, by which they went forth out of the land of Egypt by their hosts under the hand of Moses and Aaron. And Moses wrote their goings forth, stage by stage, by the commandment of the Lord; and these are their stages at their goings forth.

And the Lord spoke unto Moses in the plains of Moab by the Jordan at Jericho, saying: 'Speak unto the children of Israel, and say unto them: When ye pass over the Jordan into the land of Canaan, then ye shall drive out all the inhabitants of the land from before you, and destroy all their figured stones, and destroy all their molten images, and demolish all their high places. . . .'

These are the commandments and the ordinances, which the Lord commanded by the hand of Moses unto the children of Israel in the plains of Moab by the Jordan at Jericho. – 32: 1, 2, 5, 20, 22; 33: 1, 2, 50-52; 36: 13.

COMMENTARY

A.   The numbering of the people is described, with the regular order of the encampments around the tabernacle which was in the center. This is an appropriate beginning for the Book of Numbers, since it will describe thirty-eight years of wandering, of encamping and breaking camp, of taking down and setting up the tabernacle. Hence the function of the Levite in dismantling the tabernacle and setting it up again at every encampment is also included. And therefore mention is made of the special function of the priest in blessing the people: "May the Lord bless thee and keep thee."

B.   The various complaints of the people—their longing to return to Egypt which now seems safer and more comfortable than the desert—are told. Since the burden of leading the people became heavy on Moses because of their complainings, God tells him to select seventy elders who likewise will receive the inspiration of the Divine Spirit and will prophesy. Thus inspired they are able to assist Moses with his tasks.

C.   The sending of the spies to Canaan and the pessimistic report of the majority of the spies as to the powerful people who will have to be conquered is related. The people, hearing this report, are panic-stricken. Because of their cowardly fear, God ordains that this slave generation shall die in the wilderness. The wandering must now continue till forty years are passed and a new and a free-born generation can enter the Promised Land.

The rebellion of Korah and its sudden ending occur here also.

D.   The death of Miriam, and then the death of Aaron open this section. The people approach the country east of the Jordan and the king of Moab, Balak, calls upon the pagan prophet Balaam to curse Israel. He comes to curse but remains to bless, and the word of his blessing now begins every morning's service in the worship of Israel: "How goodly are thy tents, O Jacob" (Numbers 24:5). This pagan prophet reechoes the promise which God made to the first patriarch, Abraham: "Blessed be every one that blesseth thee, and cursed be every one that curseth thee" (Numbers 24:9).

E.   When the land east of the Jordan is conquered, two of the tribes, Reuben and Gad, want to settle there, but Moses makes them promise that they will cross the Jordan when the time comes to help conquer the land, and agrees that then they may return to settle in the lands which they have chosen.

The book ends with the last period in the life of Moses. Virtually his last command is that the children of Israel should destroy all the idolatry in the land when they conquer it. Moses now stands in the plains of Moab by the river Jordan in sight of the city of Jericho, in the land in which he is never to dwell. The book therefore marks the end of the desert wandering and concludes with the words: "These are the commandments and the ordinances which the Lord commanded by the hand of Moses unto the children of Israel in the plains of Moab by the Jordan at Jericho."

DEUTERONOMY
GENERAL OUTLINE

The fifth book of the Torah, known in English (through the Greek) as Deuteronomy, is generally called in Hebrew *D'vorim*, "words," which is taken from the opening sentence of the book, "These are the words." The name Deuteronomy, which means repetition of the law, is related to an old Hebrew description of the book, *Mishne Torah*, "the repetition of the law." The justification for the title lies in the fact that in this book Moses repeats many of the laws which are found in the earlier books; there are, however, many laws in this book which are not found in the four previous ones.

In the opinion of critical scholars, the Book of Deuteronomy is pre-exilic, but dates from the time of King Josiah. The statement in the Second Book of Kings, chapter 22:10, that the priests found a book in the Temple and that book aroused the king to cleanse the country of idolatry and to institute other reforms, is taken by modern scholars to refer to the Book of Deuteronomy. It is not the entire book which they say dates from those days but only its nucleus; the Deuteronomic code, referred to as *D*, was written about the year 620 before the present era, that is to say, seven hundred years after the time of Moses. The bulk of the book is said, however, to have been written after the Exile. They consider that this Deuteronomic code itself (the core of the present book) was written under prophetic influence, thus accounting for the broad spirit of justice and philanthropy in it and its eloquent writing. It is, according to critical opinion, essentially a prophetic rewriting of the older codes described as *J* and *E*. Of course, even if this be so, the editor of the book fitted it into the other books of the Torah so that it forms a logical sequence with them.

The Book of Numbers extends to the end of the forty years' wandering through the desert and to the close of the career of Moses as he and the people stand at the Jordan, just across from the Promised Land. The Book of Deuteronomy contains the three final speeches of Moses, his farewell words to the people in the plains of Moab. The first part of the book, from chapter 1 near the end of chapter 4, reviews for the people the journeying through the wilderness these many years. Moses, reminding them of their murmurings and rebellions, calls upon them to strengthen their attachment to God, the only true God who has revealed Himself by signs and wonders and by His voice unto Israel.

The second address of Moses constitutes the bulk of the book. It extends from chapter 5 to chapter 29. Here Moses renews the divine covenant with Israel by repeating many of the laws which were mentioned in Exodus, beginning again with the Ten Commandments. Among these laws are some which are not mentioned in Exodus or Leviticus or in Numbers at all. For example, the detailed laws as to how to deal with idolatory, and also the laws concerning the appointment and the conduct of a king, specific laws about prophets (chapter 18), the complete judicial system with judges in every city and a supreme court, and a considerable number of other new laws are introduced here. Even those laws which are found in the earlier books of the Torah are not merely repetitions as given here in Deuteronomy. The mood in which the law is proclaimed, the language in which it is expressed, the motivation given for obedience to it, all are unique in this book. There is a broad spirit of noble benevolence in the Book of Deuteronomy, a generosity to slaves, to captives in war, and to strangers. The appeal for kind treatment is based upon fellow feeling: remember that you too suffered in Egypt.

This beautiful generosity of spirit, this humaneness and kindliness, so characteristic of the Book of Deuteronomy, is expressed with moving eloquence. The book is really an oration and can best be appreciated when read aloud. The sentences flow into each other till all the duties of man to fellow man are exalted to the grandeur of man's love to an ever-loving God.

SYNOPSIS OF TEXT

A.   And it came to pass in the fortieth year, in the eleventh month, on the first day of the month, that Moses spoke unto the children of Israel, according unto all that the Lord had given him in commandment unto them; . . .

The Lord our God spoke unto us in Horeb, saying: 'Ye have

dwelt long enough in this mountain; turn you, and take your journey, and go to the hill-country of the Amorites . . .'

And we journeyed from Horeb and went through all that great and dreadful wilderness which ye saw, by the way to the hill-country of the Amorites, as the Lord our God commanded us; and we came to Kadesh-barnea. . . .

Then I said unto you: 'Dread not, neither be afraid of them. The Lord your God who goeth before you, He shall fight for you, according to all that He did for you in Egypt before your eyes; and in the wilderness, where thou hast seen how that the Lord thy God bore thee, as a man doth bear his son, in all the way that ye went, until ye came unto this place. Yet in this thing ye do not believe the Lord your God. . . .'

Also the Lord was angry with me for your sakes, saying: 'Thou also shalt not go in thither; Joshua the son of Nun, who standeth before thee, he shall go in thither; encourage thou him, for he shall cause Israel to inherit. . . .'

And I besought the Lord at that time, saying: . . . 'Let me go over, I pray Thee, and see the good land that is beyond the Jordan, that goodly hill-country, and Lebanon.' But the Lord was wroth with me for your sakes, and hearkened not unto me; and the Lord said unto me: 'Let it suffice thee; speak no more unto Me of this matter. Get thee up into the top of Pisgah, and lift up thine eyes westward, and northward, and southward, and eastward, and behold with thine eyes; for thou shalt not go over this Jordan. But charge Joshua, and encourage him, and strengthen him . . .' – 1:3, 6-7a, 19, 29-32, 37, 38; 3:23, 25-28.

B.   And Moses called unto all Israel, and said unto them:

Hear, O Israel, the statutes and the ordinances which I speak in your ears this day, that ye may learn them, and observe to do them. The Lord our God made a covenant with us in Horeb. The Lord made not this covenant with our fathers, but with us, even us, who are all of us here alive this day. . . .

I am the Lord thy God, who brought thee out of the land of Egypt, out of the house of bondage.

Thou shalt have no other gods before Me. . . .

HEAR, O ISRAEL: THE LORD OUR GOD, THE LORD IS ONE. And thou shalt love the Lord thy God, with all thy heart, and with all thy soul, and with all thy might. And these words, which I command thee this day, shall be upon thy heart; . . .

When thy son asketh thee in time to come, saying: 'What mean the testimonies, and the statutes, and the ordinances, which the Lord our God hath commanded you?' then thou shalt say unto thy son: 'We were Pharaoh's bondmen in Egypt; and the Lord brought us out of Egypt with a mighty hand. . . . And the Lord commanded us to do all these statutes, to fear the Lord our God, for our good always, that He might preserve us alive, as it is at this day. . . .'

All the commandment which I command thee this day shall ye observe to do, that ye may live, and multiply, and go in and possess the land which the Lord swore unto your fathers. And thou shalt remember all the way which the Lord thy God hath led thee these forty years in the wilderness, that He might afflict thee, to prove thee, to know what was in thy heart, whether thou wouldest keep His commandments, or no. . . . And thou shalt consider in thy heart, that, as a man chasteneth his son, so the Lord thy God chasteneth thee.—5: 1-3, 6, 7; 6: 4-6, 20, 21, 24; 8: 1, 2, 5.

C.   At that time the Lord said unto me: 'Hew thee two tables of stone like unto the first, and come up unto Me into the mount; and make thee an ark of wood. And I will write on the tables the words that were on the first tables which thou didst break, and thou shalt put them in the ark.'

And now, Israel, what doth the Lord thy God require of thee, but to fear the Lord thy God, to walk in all His ways, and to love Him, and to serve the Lord thy God with all thy heart and with all thy soul; For the Lord your God, He is God of gods, and the Lord of lords, the great God, the mighty, and the awful, who regardeth not persons, nor taketh reward . . . Love ye therefore the stranger; for ye were strangers in the land of Egypt. . . .

These are the statutes and the ordinances, which ye shall observe to do in the land which the Lord, the God of thy fathers, hath given thee to possess it, all the days that ye live upon the earth. Ye shall surely destroy all the places, wherein the nations that ye are to dispossess served their gods, upon the high mountains, and upon the hills, and under every leafy tree. And ye shall break down their altars, and dash in pieces their pillars, and burn their Asherim with fire; and ye shall hew down the graven images of their gods; and ye shall destroy their name out of that place. Ye shall not do so unto the Lord your God. But unto the place which the Lord your God shall choose out of all your tribes to put His name there, even unto His habitation shall ye seek, and thither thou shalt come; and thither ye shall bring your burnt-offerings, and your sacrifices, and your tithes, and the offering of your hand, and your vows and your freewill-offerings, and the firstlings of your herd and of your flock; . . .

All this word which I command you, that shall ye observe to do; thou shalt not add thereto, nor diminish from it.

If there arise in the midst of thee a prophet, or a dreamer of dreams—and he give thee a sign or a wonder, and the sign or the wonder come to pass, whereof he spoke unto thee, saying: 'Let us go after other gods, which thou hast not known, and let us serve them'; thou shalt not hearken unto the words of that prophet, or unto that dreamer of dreams; for the Lord your God putteth you to proof, to know whether ye do love the Lord your God with all your heart and with all your soul. . . .

At the end of every seven years thou shalt make a release. And this is the manner of the release: every creditor shall release that which he hath lent unto his neighbour; he shall not exact it of his neighbour and his brother; because the Lord's release hath been proclaimed.

Judges and officers shalt thou make thee in all thy gates, which the Lord thy God giveth thee, tribe by tribe; and they shall judge the people with righteous judgment. . . . Justice, justice shalt thou follow, that thou mayest live, and inherit the land which the Lord thy God giveth thee. . . .

If there arise a matter too hard for thee in judgment, between blood and blood, between plea and plea, and between stroke and stroke, even matters of controversy within thy gates; then shalt thou arise, and get thee up unto the place which the Lord thy God shall choose. . . .

When thou goest forth to battle against thine enemies, and seest horses, and chariots, and a people more than thou, thou shalt not be afraid of them; for the Lord thy God is with thee, who brought thee up out of the land of Egypt. And it shall be, when ye draw nigh unto the battle, that the priest shall approach and speak unto the people, and shall say unto them: 'Hear, O Israel, ye draw nigh this day unto battle against your enemies; let not your heart faint; fear not, nor be alarmed, neither be ye affrighted at them; . . .'

When thou drawest nigh unto a city to fight against it, then proclaim peace unto it. And it shall be, if it make thee answer of peace, and open unto thee, then it shall be, that all the people that are found therein shall become tributary unto thee.

And it shall come to pass, if thou shalt hearken diligently unto the voice of the Lord thy God, to observe to do all His commandments which I command thee this day, that the Lord thy God will set thee on high above all the nations of the earth. And all these blessings shall come upon thee, and overtake thee, if thou shalt hearken unto the voice of the Lord thy God. Blessed shalt thou be in the city, and blessed shalt thou be in the field. . . . Blessed shalt thou be when thou comest in, and blessed shalt thou be when thou goest out. . . .

But it shall come to pass, if thou wilt not hearken unto the voice of the Lord thy God, to observe to do all His commandments and His statutes which I command thee this day; that all these curses shall come upon thee, and overtake thee. Cursed shalt thou be in the city, and cursed shalt thou be in the field. —10:1-2, 12, 17, 19; 12:1-6; 13:1-4; 15:1-2; 16:18, 20; 17:8; 20:1-3, 10, 11; 28:1-3, 6, 15, 16.

D.   And Moses called unto all Israel, and said unto them:

Ye have seen all that the Lord did before your eyes in the land of Egypt unto Pharaoh, and unto all his servants, and unto all his land; the great trials which thine eyes saw, the signs and those great wonders; but the Lord hath not given you a heart to know, and eyes to see, and ears to hear, unto this day. . . .

Ye are standing this day all of you before the Lord your God, your heads, your tribes, your elders, and your officers, even all the men of Israel, . . . that He may establish thee this day unto Himself for a people, and that He may be unto thee a God, as He spoke unto thee, and as He swore unto thy fathers, to Abraham, to Isaac, and to Jacob. Neither with you only do I make this covenant and this oath; but with him that standeth here with us this day before the Lord our God, and also with him that is not here with us this day— . . .

For this commandment which I command thee this day, it is not too hard for thee, neither is it far off. It is not in heaven, that thou shouldest say: 'Who shall go up for us to heaven, and bring it unto us, and make us to hear it, that we may do it?' . . . But the word is very nigh unto thee, in thy mouth, and in thy heart, that thou mayest do it.

I call heaven and earth to witness against you this day, that I have set before thee life and death, the blessing and the curse; therefore choose life, that thou mayest live, thou and thy seed; to love the Lord thy God, to hearken to His voice, and to cleave unto Him; for that is thy life, and the length of thy days; that thou mayest dwell in the land which the Lord swore unto thy fathers, to Abraham, to Isaac, and to Jacob, to give them. – 29: 1-3, 9, 12-14; 30: 11, 12, 14, 19-20.

E.   For when I shall have brought them into the land which I swore unto their fathers, flowing with milk and honey; and they shall have eaten their fill, and waxen fat; and turned unto other gods, and served them, and despised Me, and broken My covenant; . . .

> Give ear, ye heavens, and I will speak;
> And let the earth hear the words of my mouth.
> My doctrine shall drop as the rain,
> My speech shall distil as the dew;
> As the small rain upon the tender grass,
> And as the showers upon the herb.
> For I will proclaim the name of the Lord;
> Ascribe ye greatness unto our God. . . .
> And this is the blessing, wherewith Moses the man of
> God blessed the children of Israel before his death. . . .
> Moses commanded us a law,
> An inheritance of the congregation of Jacob. . . .
> Let Reuben live, and not die
> In that his men become few.
> And this for Judah, and he said:
> Hear, Lord, the voice of Judah, . . .
>   – 31:20; 32:1-3; 33:1, 4, 6, 7.

F.   And Moses went up from the plains of Moab unto mount Nebo, to the top of Pisgah, that is over against Jericho. And the

Lord showed him all the land, even Gilead as far as Dan; . . . So Moses the servant of the Lord died there in the land of Moab, according to the word of the Lord. And he was buried in the valley in the land of Moab over against Bethpeor; and no man knoweth of his sepulchre unto this day. . . . And Joshua the son of Nun was full of the spirit of wisdom; for Moses had laid his hands upon him; and the children of Israel hearkened unto him. . . . And there hath not arisen a prophet since in Israel like unto Moses, whom the Lord knew face to face. – 34: 1, 5, 6, 9, 10.

COMMENTARY

A.   Moses begins his first address by reviewing the history of the wanderings in the wilderness, and tells why he is not permitted to cross the Jordan and that Joshua will lead the people into the Promised Land. *Horeb* is another name for Sinai. Some scholars say that Sinai was really the name of the district (the Wilderness of Sinai) and Horeb was the actual name of the mountain itself.

B.   In his second address, which occupies the bulk of the Book of Deuteronomy (chapters 5-29), Moses speaks again of the covenant which God made with Israel at Sinai. And since he is speaking to the new generation which did not come out of Egypt, but was born and raised in the desert, he explains to them that this is an eternal covenant: "The Lord made not this covenant with our fathers [alone] but with us who are all of us here alive this day." This covenant involves Israel's obedience to God and the fulfillment of the laws which he had given hitherto. But the motive for obeying God for fulfilling the covenant is typical of Deuteronomy. "Thou shalt love the Lord thy God with all thy heart, and these words which I command thee this day shall be upon thy heart." The afflictions which Israel endured in the desert, described chiefly in the history of the thirty-eight year period in the Book of Numbers, were for the purpose of testing Israel, "to prove thee, to know what was in thy heart." All this constitutes an introduction to the actual commandments which now follow.

C.   The commandments in this renewal of the covenant at the end of Moses' career, at the end of the period of wilderness-wandering, parallel closely the covenant at the beginning of Israel's wilderness-wandering at Mount Sinai soon after it came out of Egypt. Here, as there, the long list of laws begins with the Ten Commandments, which are to be looked upon as the basic principles inherent in all the other detailed laws. Many of the laws here, as has been mentioned, are given for the first time in Deuteronomy.

D.   Just as in the Book of Leviticus, after the commandments have been stated, there is a statement of blessing and curse, depending upon Israel's fulfillment or rejection of the word of God.

E.   The end of the book contains two great poems, the second one a blessing by Moses to the people. This parallels the blessing that ends the biographies of the patriarchs. The blessing of Jacob given at the end of the Book of Genesis is now paralleled by the blessing of Moses before Israel enters the Promised Land.

F.   The book closes with a narrative, the story of the death of Moses, a story which tradition says was written by the hand of Joshua. Here Moses, the great lawgiver, is described as the greatest of all the prophets. "And there hath not arisen a prophet since in Israel like unto Moses, whom the Lord knew face to face."–Deut. 34:10.

ESSENCE OF THE TORAH

GENERAL OUTLINE

There is a consistency of thought from the beginning of the Torah to the end. This is taken for granted by those who adhere to the traditional view that the Torah had mainly one author; that Moses wrote it all, except for a few verses which may have crept in later, and the closing part of the last chapter describing Moses' death. Since the Torah had one author, it stands to reason that the author, who meant it to be one book, since the books refer to each other and are connected with each other, had in mind one general idea which he expressed in them all.

Even according to the modern critical theory, it must be taken for granted that the Torah as it now stands has one consistent idea, or at least a general thesis which unites it. While the critical hypothesis is more concerned with analyzing the Torah down to what is considered its original documents or fragments of documents, nevertheless it also is interested in the synthesis or the putting together of the Torah by an editor or a series of editors. When in any modern critical commentary on the five books of the Torah we look at the list of the verses as they are divided among the various original manuscripts, we observe that there is a general agreement on the part of most critical scholars as to the distribution of the verses among these manuscripts. A close inspection of such a list (see chapter 5, *The Modern Study of Scripture*) would reveal that the various original documents are minutely intermingled—a half verse from one document follows a half verse from another, then a verse or two verses from a third document and then a half verse from the first, etc. In other words, the editing was not done by taking one document and inserting it whole into another or placing it after another, and then writing a few connecting verses. There was, according to the critical theory, a most painstaking, minute, verse-by-verse, and in some cases word-by-word reconstruction of the original material. Whether a book ever could have been put together out of such tiny fragments, in other words, whether the theory of such a synthesis is believable, is another question. According to that theory, however, the editing was done in a most painstakingly careful manner and therefore it may be well taken for granted that the editor, selecting his material with such care and putting it together with such precision, had a specific aim in mind, a general idea which he wished to express.

Thus, as we try to arrive at the basic idea of the Torah, it is almost immaterial whether one follows the traditional or the modern critical point of view, except that according to one the Torah as a whole was written thirty-three hundred years ago and according to the other it dates back only twenty-three hundred years. Both ways of looking at the Bible finally come down to one author or editor, or to a closely knit group of editors.

The essential idea of the Torah is implied in its opening chapters. God, the Creator of man, sets man upon this earth with His blessing, but man, through his sin, brings curse upon the earth, and so must always rediscover the lost blessings which are his heritage as a child of God. To achieve the moral training which alone can restore blessing to man, God proceeds to select one branch of the human race. This process of selection begins early in Scripture. Cain is rejected; Abel is selected. The corrupt generations of the Flood are rejected; Noah and his descendants are selected. And at the selection of Noah, God again blesses mankind through him. From the time of Noah, as human evil again manifests itself through the Tower of Babel, etc., the selection proceeds at a faster rate, and the very genealogies in Scripture reveal the process. In each succeeding family only one child is mentioned; the rest remain anonymous. Thus (in chapter 11 of Genesis), Shem begot Arpachshad, and the rest of Shem's descendants are merely described as "sons and daughters." Then Arpachshad begot Shelah, and the rest are just referred to as "sons and daughters." So Shelah begot Eber, and the rest are referred to as "sons and daughters." Thus down to Terah, all of whose three sons are mentioned because all these three sons are part of the story of Abraham, but the story really concerns Abraham, the object and goal of the whole genealogical chart. As soon as the career of Abraham begins, God makes a covenant with him, promising him that his seed will be blessed and that through him all the children of man will find their blessing. Thus we are told that the process of selection is completed and the true story of the Bible is about to begin. "And in thee shall all the families of the earth be blessed." (Genesis 12:13.)

Thus it is clear that while the aim of God as revealed in Scripture is the blessing of all men, Scripture does not intend to give the history of mankind. The history which Scripture gives is the history of the selection of the seed of Abraham, who will be set aside for the moral training needed to restore God's blessing to the children of men. The rest of the story of the Book of Genesis is the story of the patriarchs, ending with Jacob's journey to Egypt, where the story of the individuals will end and the story of their descendants, the people of Israel, will begin.

*　　*　　*

The Book of Exodus is no longer the biography of individuals but is the history of the people of Israel. God speaks to Moses and to them through Moses of the covenant that He made with the patriarchs. Israel is redeemed from Egypt and brought at once to Mount Sinai, where the covenant now is renewed with the entire people, as if all the world were God's sanctuary and all the children of men were bringing offerings and worshipping God in it. Israel will be its kingdom of priests. The Ten Commandments introduce all the other laws which constitute the details of Israel's part of the covenant of their moral training. Accepting the covenant (which needed to be renewed after the sin of the golden calf), they build the tabernacle that they may be aware of the presence of God in their midst. And with the glory of God filling the tabernacle in the midst of the covenanted people, the Book of Exodus ends.

*　*　*

The Book of Exodus ending with the tabernacle dedicated and sanctified by the divine glory, the third book, Leviticus, logically continues with the sacrifices to be offered in the tabernacle. These sacrifices, the sacred ritual, are not the only evidence of sacredness in the life of the people. They must be personally holy in their family relationships, in the food that they eat, in their freedom from disease. Should they violate God's word they will be cursed: "I will break the pride of your power." Should they obey God's law, they will be blessed. But the spirit of their obedience must always be part of the aim of emulating the holiness of God. "Ye shall be holy, for I the Lord your God, am holy." (Lev. 19:2.)

*　*　*

All these laws and warnings were understood to be given in the period of a little more than a year that they remained around Mount Sinai. The fourth book of the Torah, Numbers, begins with their actual wandering through the desert, which was to last for thirty-eight years, to bring the total period of desert wandering to forty years. Now they suffer trials and tribulations in the arduous journey and wandering which continue until the whole generation which came out of Egypt dies. In this period their weaknesses become manifest. They murmur. They rebel. They are punished. They are forgiven. But through their sorrows and blundering they are trained to the service of God. The book ends with the end of their journeying, the end of the career of their leader, Moses, who was not to enter the Promised Land.

Exactly at the point where the fourth book ends, the fifth book, Deuteronomy, begins. Moses, the leader of the Israelites, makes his last three addresses to the people. He speaks in the plains of Moab on the east side of the Jordan, repeating the obligation to confirm the covenant with this new generation which is now entering into the Holy Land. "The Lord made not this covenant with our fathers [alone] but with us who are all of us here alive this day." (Deut. 5:3.) While many of the laws given in the previous books are repeated, now many new laws are given. There is also an additional motivation (or at least a new emphasis) besides the one given in the Book of Leviticus. In Leviticus the leading motivation is the ideal of holiness, in imitation of God. Here it is the warm bond of love of God for Israel and Israel for God. The training of Israel, selected by God, through it "the families of the earth be blessed," always hindered by the weaknesses of the human material, is ever reinspired by the ideal of personal holiness and sealed with the bond of an abiding love for God.

SYNOPSIS OF TORAH TEXT

A.   In the beginning God created the heaven and the earth. . . . This is the book of the generations of Adam. In the day that God created man, in the likeness of God made He him; male and female created He them, and blessed them, . . .

And the Lord saw that the wickedness of man was great in the earth, and that every imagination of the thoughts of his heart was only evil continually. . . . And the Lord said: 'I will blot out man whom I have created from the face of the earth; both man, and beast, and creeping thing, and fowl of the air; for it repenteth Me that I have made them.' But Noah found grace in the eyes of the Lord. . . .

And the Lord said unto Noah: 'Come thou and all thy house into the ark; for thee have I seen righteous before Me in this generation. . . .' And He blotted out every living substance which was upon the face of the ground, both man, and cattle, and creeping thing, and fowl of the heaven; and they were blotted out from the earth; and Noah only was left, and they that were with him in the ark. . . .

And God blessed Noah and his sons, and said unto them: 'Be fruitful, and multiply, and replenish the earth. . . .'

Now the Lord said unto Abram: 'Get thee out of thy country, and from thy kindred, and from thy father's house, unto the land that I will show thee. And I will make of thee a great nation, and I will bless thee, and make thy name great; and be thou a blessing. And I will bless them that bless thee, and him that curseth thee will I curse; and in thee shall all the families of the earth be blessed.' . . .

In that day the Lord made a covenant with Abram, saying: 'Unto thy seed have I given this land, from the river of Egypt unto the great river, the river Euphrates; . . .'

And Jacob went out from Beer-sheba, and went toward Haran. . . . And, behold, the Lord stood beside him, and said: 'I am the Lord, the God of Abraham thy father, and the God of Isaac. The land whereon thou liest, to thee will I give it, and to thy seed. . . . And in thee and in thy seed shall all the families of the earth be blessed. . . .'

And God spoke unto Israel in the visions of the night, and said: 'Jacob, Jacob.' And He said: 'Here am I.' And He said: 'I am God, the God of thy father; fear not to go down into Egypt; for I will there make of thee a great nation. I will go down with thee into Egypt; and I will also surely bring thee up again; . . .' – Genesis 1:1; 5:1-2a; 6:5, 7, 8; 7:1, 23; 9:1; 12:1-3; 15:18; 28:10, 13, 14b; 46:2-4a.

B. And it came to pass in the course of those many days that the king of Egypt died; and the children of Israel sighed by reason of the bondage, and they cried, and their cry came up unto God by reason of the bondage. And God heard their groaning, and God remembered His covenant with Abraham, with Isaac, and with Jacob. . . .

Then the Lord said unto Moses: 'Go in unto Pharaoh, and tell him: Thus saith the Lord, the God of the Hebrews: Let My people go, that they may serve Me. . . .'

In the third month after the children of Israel were gone forth out of the land of Egypt, the same day came they into the wilderness of Sinai. . . . And Moses went up unto God, and the Lord called unto him out of the mountain, saying: 'Thus shalt thou say to the house of Jacob, and tell the children of Israel: Ye have seen what I did unto the Egyptians, and how I bore you on eagles' wings, and brought you unto Myself. Now therefore, if ye will hearken unto My voice indeed, and keep My covenant, then ye shall be Mine own treasure from among all peoples; for all the earth is Mine; and ye shall be unto Me a kingdom of priests, and a holy nation. . . .'

And God spoke all these words, saying:

I am the Lord thy God, who brought thee out of the land of Egypt, out of the house of bondage.

Thou shalt have no other gods before Me. . . .

And let them make Me a sanctuary, that I may dwell among them. . . .

And he reared up the court around about the tabernacle and the altar, and set up the screen of the gate of the court. So Moses finished the work.

Then the cloud covered the tent of meeting, and the glory of the Lord filled the tabernacle. – Exodus 2:23, 24; 9:1; 19:1, 3-6a; 20:1-3; 25:8; 40:33, 34.

C.   Speak unto the children of Israel, and say unto them: When any man of you bringeth an offering unto the Lord, ye shall bring your offering of the cattle, even of the herd or of the flock. . . .

And the Lord spoke unto Moses, saying: Command Aaron and his sons, saying:

This is the law of the burnt-offering: it is that which goeth up on its firewood upon the altar all night unto the morning; and the fire of the altar shall be kept burning thereby. . . .

And the Lord spoke unto Moses, saying: Speak unto the children of Israel, and say unto them:

I am the Lord your God. After the doings of the land of Egypt, wherein ye dwelt, shall ye not do; and after the doings of the land of Canaan, whither I bring you, shall ye not do; neither shall ye walk in their statutes. Mine ordinances shall ye do, and My statutes shall ye keep, to walk therein: I am the Lord your God. . . .

And the Lord spoke unto Moses, saying: Speak unto all the congregation of the children of Israel, and say unto them:

Ye shall be holy; for I the Lord your God am holy. Ye shall fear every man his mother, and his father, and ye shall keep My sabbaths: I am the Lord your God. Turn ye not unto the idols, nor make to yourselves molten gods: I am the Lord your God. . . .

If ye walk in My statutes, and keep My commandments, and do them; . . . And I will give peace in the land, and ye shall lie down, and none shall make you afraid. . . .

But if ye will not hearken unto Me, and will not do all these commandments; and if ye shall reject My statutes, and if your soul abhor Mine ordinances, so that ye will not do all My commandments, but break My covenant; . . . And I will break the pride of your power; and I will make your heaven as iron, and your earth as brass. And your strength shall be spent in vain; . . . – Leviticus 1:1-2; 6:1-2; 18:1-4; 19:1-4; 26:3, 6a, 14, 15, 19, 20a.

D.   For all the first-born among the children of Israel are Mine, both man and beast; on the day that I smote all the first-born in the land of Egypt I sanctified them for Myself. And I have taken the Levites instead of all the first-born among the children of Israel. . . .

And the people were as murmurers, speaking evil in the ears of the Lord; . . .

And the mixed multitude that was among them fell a lusting; and the children of Israel also wept on their part, and said: 'Would that we were given flesh to eat! We remember the fish, which we were wont to eat in Egypt for nought; . . .'

And they spread an evil report of the land which they had spied out unto the children of Israel, saying: 'The land, through which we have passed to spy it out, is a land that eateth up the inhabitants thereof; and all the people that we saw in it are men of great stature. . . .'

And all the children of Israel murmured against Moses and against Aaron; and the whole congregation said unto them: 'Would that we had died in the land of Egypt! . . .'

And the Lord spoke unto Moses and unto Aaron, saying: 'How long shall I bear with this evil congregation, that keep murmuring against Me? . . . Say unto them: As I live, saith the Lord, surely as ye have spoken in Mine ears, so will I do to you: your carcasses shall fall in this wilderness, . . . But your little ones, that ye said would be a prey, them will I bring in, and they shall know the land which ye have rejected. . . .' – Numbers 8:17, 18; 11:1a, 4, 5a; 13:32; 14:2, 26, 27a, 28, 29a, 31.

E.   And it came to pass in the fortieth year, in the eleventh month, on the first day of the month, that Moses spoke unto the children of Israel, according unto all that the Lord had given him in commandment unto them; . . .

And Moses called unto all Israel, and said unto them:

Hear, O Israel, the statutes and the ordinances which I speak in your ears this day, that ye may learn them, and observe to do them. The Lord our God made a covenant with us in Horeb. The Lord made not this covenant with our fathers, but with us, even us who are all of us here alive this day. . . .

HEAR, O ISRAEL: THE LORD OUR GOD, THE LORD IS ONE. And thou shalt love the Lord thy God with all thy heart, and with all thy soul, and with all thy might. . . .

And now, Israel, what doth the Lord thy God require of thee, but to fear the Lord thy God, to walk in all His ways, and to love Him, and to serve the Lord thy God with all thy heart and with all thy soul; . . .

For thou art a holy people unto the Lord thy God, and the Lord hath chosen thee to be His own treasure out of all peoples that are upon the face of the earth. . . .

Thou shalt not pervert the justice due to the stranger, or to the fatherless; nor take the widow's raiment to pledge. . . .

Ye are standing this day all of you before the Lord your God: your heads, your tribes, your elders, and your officers, even all the men of Israel; . . . that thou shouldest enter into the covenant of the Lord thy God—and into His oath—which the Lord thy God maketh with thee this day; that He may establish thee this day unto Himself for a people, and that He may be unto thee a God, as He spoke unto thee, and as He swore unto thy fathers, to Abraham, to Isaac, and to Jacob. . . .

For this commandment which I command thee this day, it is not too hard for thee, neither is it far off. . . . But the word is very nigh unto thee, in thy mouth, and in thy heart, that thou mayest do it. . . . I call heaven and earth to witness against you this day, that I have set before thee life and death, the blessing and the curse; therefore choose life, that thou mayest live, thou and thy seed, to love the Lord thy God, to hearken to His voice, and to cleave unto Him; for that is thy life, and the length of thy days; that thou mayest dwell in the land which the Lord swore unto thy fathers, to Abraham, to Isaac, and to Jacob, to give them. – Deuteronomy 1:3; 5:1-3; 6:4-5; 10:12; 14:2; 24:17; 29:9, 11, 12; 30:11, 14, 19, 20.

CHAPTER III

The Historical Books

JOSHUA, JUDGES, SAMUEL, KINGS

PALESTINE is one of the most continuously settled lands on earth. Every day the spade of the archaeologist discovers evidences which push back the date of its earliest civilization. These archaeological discoveries are mostly pieces of pottery and foundations of buildings; there is almost no writing. For a land civilized for so many thousands of years, it is astonishing how few inscriptions are turned up by the archaeologist. In recent years there was a great find of Canaanitish writing on the coast of Phoenicia (Ras-shamra) north of Palestine. But the ancient Israelites themselves have left almost no inscriptions. Some fragments of letters were found at the city of Lachish a few years ago, written by an officer who lived about the time of Jeremiah. Before that time an inscription was found commemorating the completion of an underground water tunnel in the time of King Hezekiah (the Siloam inscription) and that is about all. The Egyptians, the Babylonians, and the Assyrians have left innumerable inscriptions of the victories, of the conquests, of the buildings erected by their kings. But there is not an official boastful inscription of this kind anywhere in Palestine coming from the Israelite or Judean kings except the single one on the walls of the water tunnel, and that was underground! This can hardly be an accident. It is too striking a fact, too sharp a contrast with the wealth of royal inscriptional boastings which are still being found in all the neighboring lands.

This remarkable absence of royal inscriptions, in spite of the fact that the kings of Israel had built palaces and had waged wars and had conquered lands, cannot be explained on the basis that the people of Israel had no interest in preserving records or in the

· 58 ·

writing of history. The very contrary is true. The histories preserved in the Bible in the Books of Joshua, Judges, Samuel, and Kings are among the earliest histories ever written by man. They are more truly histories than are the boastful royal records which kings of other peoples carved in rock to perpetuate their glories. These Biblical books are histories of kings, nobles, priests, shepherds, and farmers. They are certainly among the first, if not the very first real histories of a people, histories which go beyond the mere archives of kings. If then the people of Israel had so strong a sense of history that they created the first history of an entire people, why is there so little inscriptional material found?

The answer must be that inscriptions were made by kings, engraved in rock, so as to be an indestructible evidence of the eternal grandeur of the monarch. Such sentiment was never prevalent in Israel. If it would ever have arisen it would have been sternly suppressed. The very status of the king, his right to govern, was seriously questioned, as is clear in the Book of Samuel from the denunciation by that Prophet of the people, when, in order to be like the surrounding nations, they demanded a king. He told them that their desire for a mortal king was a rebellion against God, the Eternal King. The Prophet Samuel indeed did yield to their insistence, but neither he nor his successors among the prophets ever gave up their right to denounce the king in the name of God for tyranny and iniquity. Some of the kings in Israel and Judah were very powerful and some were very tyrannical, but there was always a prophet to show them their place. Kings in Israel would hardly have permitted themselves the boastfulness of making permanent stone inscriptions to their own eternal glory, and, even if they did so, the stubbornly democratic people of Israel would hardly have been impressed.

It was not only that the essential democracy of Israel would have discouraged such self-glorification and such royal pretenses to eternal fame, but also that the usual subject matter of such royal boasting did not appeal to the people, or at least not to those who wrote its history. There were indeed royal archives which are mentioned frequently in the Book of Kings and which were used by the historians who wrote those books. They had these archives at their disposal but they seemed to be utterly unimpressed by the descriptions of royal grandeur, of military adventures which were found, undoubtedly, in them. We know, for example, from a Moabite inscription that Omri, the king of Israel, was from the military point of view quite a successful king. The historians had these records of his victories before them but they scornfully omitted them all and wrote down only what interested them, namely, that Omri was a wicked king, inclined to idolatry. In other words, these ancient writers of Jewish history, whose works were preserved by the people of Israel, were interested chiefly in spiritual facts and in ethical attitudes. Other matters did not particularly concern them. They simply said frequently that "the rest of the doings of this and that king are to be found in the 'records of the kings of Israel.'"

The impressive fact is that it was not the royal political and military archives which survived but that it was the religious history which became eternal. We would not even know that the royal archives ever existed if they had not been half-scornfully mentioned in the spiritual histories which ignored most of their contents. It is interesting to note that this absorption in religious and spiritual matters and this ignoring of military glory remained as a lasting attitude in Israel. From the books of the Maccabees we learn of all the military victories of the Maccabees, and so too from the books of Josephus. But neither of these books ever became part of the Sacred Scripture of Israel. In the Talmudic literature which continued the tradition of Israel's ideals, all that is told of the Maccabees is the miracle of the lamp which burned with pure oil for eight days, just as if the Maccabeans had never drawn a sword or shot an arrow.

What these ancient historians wrote were not political annals but religious history. Only those political or military facts concerned them which indicated God's fulfillment of His promise to Israel to give it the land, or the defeats which they considered evidences of Israel's moral weakness due to idolatry and injustice. Of course we may well regret from the standpoint of the preservation of ancient records that the "Chronicles of the Kings of Israel" and the "Chronicles of the Kings of Judah" which are referred to in the Bible were not completely preserved. But it is a vain regret. Why should a people going through all the vicissitudes which Israel had endured maintain the mere records of past wars? What they preserved was a religious history which revealed, as they saw it, the hand of God in the life of the nation and which therefore could be a guide and an encouragement for its future.

The modern reader may be pardoned some impatience as he reads these religious histories, in which every victory is the reward of virtue and every defeat the punishment for evil. He may be inclined to some skepticism as to the justice of this point of view. As a matter of fact, there is a great deal of Biblical writing which likewise questions whether the righteous are always triumphant and the wicked always defeated. This questioning comes up in the Book of Jeremiah and is the theme of the entire Book of Job. Indeed, we may well agree with these earnest questioners that the righteous often suffer unjustly and the wicked often triumph unfairly and that this "problem of evil" is a crucial one.

But this must be said in behalf of these ancient historians: the unfair suffering of the righteous and the unjust triumph of the wicked is most frequently a problem in the life of the individual because the life of an individual is so brief. Before justice can be done to a victim of injustice his life comes to an end. That is why the great philosopher, Immanuel Kant, said that he believed in immortality, because the logic of life requires that there be both ethics and justice. A life may be ethical and yet, alas, may end before it receives justice. Therefore, said the philosopher, we must assume that life has actually a grander scope and continues after death so there be enough time for justice to crown ethical living.

But the problem of the unjust suffering of the righteous does not become so aggravated a problem in the long course of human history. When we take the life of fifty generations together, we are more likely to see the working out of a divine plan. If not in individual biography, then at least in world history, we see that evil does become national weakness and a corrupted nation does not endure; that inner moral decency does become social strength and that a community can outlast its misfortunes.

This was the faith of the Prophets and this is the basis for the philosophy which underlies these histories of Israel. The historical books are essentially prophetic books. They voice the Prophets' conviction that in the life of a nation evil is a prelude to destruction and righteousness a guarantee of group immortality. That is why in Jewish tradition these books are not called histories but are given the title *Neviim Rishonim*, the "earlier prophets."

But are they to be considered histories? They are histories because they do preserve the records of many ancient events. Yet how can books be histories when they have obviously omitted many events that we are accustomed to call historical, such as wars, defeats, and victories? But the fact is that no history is a mere collection of events. A million events occur every day. They are real facts but they are not history. History is always a selection of important facts, of significant facts. Which facts are to be considered significant and which insignificant depends upon the philosophy of the historian. That is why the great Greek historian, Thucydides, said that "history is philosophy taught by example." That is to say that the facts which the philosopher records are merely those which can serve as examples to prove the philosophy which he believes is expressed through the experiences of the past. That is exactly what these Biblical histories are. They represent the philosophy of the Prophets, namely, that ethical living, that obedience to the Divine Law, is the crucial factor in determining the destiny of a people. The facts that they selected were only such facts as could clearly exemplify this prophetic philosophy. If, then, history is "philosophy taught by example," these histories in the Bible may be described as "prophecy taught by example."

JOSHUA

Although the Talmud says (b. Baba Bathra 14a) that this book was written by Joshua himself, the book itself does not have a heading in the opening verse, as many of the books of the literary prophets have, which would imply that Joshua wrote it. In other words, the Book of Joshua itself does not make the claim that it was written by Joshua. Moreover, it is clear from its contents that much of it was written after his time. The book is a compilation of many ancient historical memories, all grouped around the character of Joshua, the servant and successor of Moses.

Joshua had had quite a career before the events described in his book take place. He led in the battle against Amalek, who attacked Israel as it came out of Egypt (Exodus 17:8 ff.). He and Caleb were the only two of the twelve spies sent out by Moses who brought back encouraging reports (Numbers 14:6-10). He was the servant of Moses and was designated as Moses' successor. He was not merely appointed as successor, but Moses had placed his hands upon him in the ceremony of ordination and the spirit of God was therefore in him. "And Joshua the son of Nun was full of the spirit of wisdom for Moses had laid his hands upon him; and the children of Israel hearkened unto him and did as the Lord commanded Moses." (Deuteronomy 34:9.)

Joshua was therefore not only the successor to Moses but the continuation of the divine leadership of which Moses was the instrument. Therefore it is to be observed that many of the dramatic events which occurred to Moses are also described as having occurred to Joshua. Moses was selected for his task by the vision of the burning bush at which God said, "Put off thy shoes from off thy feet for the place whereon thou standest is holy ground." (Exodus 3:5.) An almost identical event occurs with Joshua. This time it is not a burning bush but the vision "of the captain of the hosts of the Lord," who likewise says to Joshua, "Put off thy shoes from off thy foot for the place whereon thou standest is holy." (Joshua 5:15.) One of the outstanding miracles performed through Moses was the splitting of the Red Sea so that the Israelites coming out of Egypt could cross dry shod into the desert. The identical miracle is described of Joshua through whom the Jordan river is divided and the children of Israel cross dry shod from the desert into the Promised Land. Moses at the end of his career gathered the people and made a final address to them and renewed the covenant. So does Joshua at the end of his career summon the people. He renews the covenant and gives them counsel to love the Lord and to be loyal to Him. In fact, the language which he uses is very much like the language of the final speeches of Moses in Deuteronomy. He tells them to love the Lord with all their heart and calls them to be witness themselves to the fact that they have chosen to serve the Lord.

This similarity of the career of Joshua to that of his master, which in effect extends the career of Moses for one more generation through Joshua, tends to unite this book with the Five Books of Moses which precede it. In fact, modern critical scholars unite this book with the Five Books of the Torah and call the whole group the "Hexateuch," meaning the six scrolls, instead of the Pentateuch, the five scrolls (see Part Two, chapter 1). The ground for this grouping is that the book is the fulfillment of the promise made in the Five Books that the land of Canaan would be given to Israel. Furthermore, these scholars find in this book a continuation of the original documents called *E* and *J* and *D* which they found in the Five Books of Moses.

Yet there is no reason for us to turn away from the tradition which leaves the Five Books of Moses in a separate classification of their own, namely, the Torah, and which considers this book the first of the earlier prophets. While it is true, as many modern scholars say, that the Book of Joshua is the fulfillment of the promise of the Five Books, it is also the beginning of Israel's dwelling in the land of Canaan. The Five Books of the Torah bring them up to the river Jordan. With the Book of Joshua begins the new era, Israel's life in the Promised Land.

The Book of Joshua may be divided into three parts, the first section, from chapters 1-12, describes the conquest of Canaan beginning with the fall of the city of Jericho. The second section, chapters 13-21, deals with the dividing of the land among the tribes by lot. And the rest of the book, chapters 22-23, is in the nature of an appendix, dealing with the granting of the land on the eastern side of the Jordan to the tribes of Reuben and Gad and half of Manasseh. This land was promised to them by Moses, to be given them after they had helped their brethren in the conquest of Canaan. Then there is the final address of Joshua to the people and their renewal of the covenant. Just as the Book of Deuteronomy ends with the death of Moses, "the servant of the Lord," so the Book of Joshua ends with the death of his successor, Joshua: "and it came to pass after these things that Joshua the son of Nun, the servant of the Lord, died, being a hundred and ten years old and Israel served the Lord all the days of Joshua and all the days of the elders that outlived Joshua who had known all the work of the Lord that he had wrought for Israel."

SYNOPSIS OF TEXT

A.   Now it came to pass after the death of Moses the servant of the Lord, that the Lord spoke unto Joshua the son of Nun, Moses' minister, saying: 'Moses My servant is dead; now therefore arise, go over this Jordan, thou, and all this people, unto the land which I do give to them, even to the children of Israel. . . . Be strong and of good courage; for thou shalt cause this people to inherit the land which I swore unto their fathers to give them. Only be strong and very courageous, to observe to do according to all the law, which Moses My servant commanded thee; turn not from it to the right hand or to the left, that thou mayest have good success whithersoever thou goest. This book of the law shall not depart out of thy mouth, but thou shalt meditate therein day and night, that thou mayest observe to do according to all that is written therein; . . .'

And Joshua rose up early in the morning, and they removed from Shittim, and came to the Jordan, he and all the children of Israel; and they lodged there before they passed over. . . .

*　　*　　*

And the Lord said unto Joshua: 'This day will I begin to magnify thee in the sight of all Israel, that they may know that, as I was with Moses, so I will be with thee. And thou shalt command the priests that bear the ark of the covenant, saying: When ye are come to the brink of the waters of the Jordan, ye shall stand still in the Jordan.' . . .

And the priests that bore the ark of the covenant of the Lord stood firm on dry ground in the midst of the Jordan, while all Israel passed over on dry ground, . . .

And the children of Israel encamped in Gilgal; and they kept the passover on the fourteenth day of the month at even in the plains of Jericho. And they did eat of the produce of the land on the morrow after the passover, unleavened cakes and parched corn, in the selfsame day. And the manna ceased on the morrow, after they had eaten of the produce of the land; . . .

And it came to pass, when Joshua was by Jericho, that he lifted up his eyes and looked, and behold, there stood a man over against him with his sword drawn in his hand; and Joshua went unto him, and said unto him: 'Art thou for us, or for our adversaries?' And he said: 'Nay, but I am captain of the host of the Lord; I am now come!' And Joshua fell on his face to the earth, and bowed down, and said unto him: 'What saith my Lord unto his servant?' And the captain of the Lord's host said unto Joshua: 'Put off thy shoe from off thy foot; for the place whereon thou standest is holy.' And Joshua did so. – 1:1-2, 6-8a; 3:1, 7, 8, 18; 5:10, 12a, 13-15.

B.   Now Jericho was straitly shut up because of the children of Israel; none went out, and none came in.—And the Lord said unto Joshua: 'See, I have given into thy hand Jericho, and the king thereof, even the mighty men of valour. . . .'

And it came to pass at the seventh time, when the priests blew with the horns, that Joshua said unto the people: 'Shout; for the Lord hath given you the city. . . .'

And the Lord said unto Joshua: 'Fear not, neither be thou dismayed; take all the people of war with thee, and arise, go up to Ai; see, I have given into thy hand the king of Ai, and his people, and his city, and his land. And thou shalt do to Ai and her king as thou didst unto Jericho, and her king; . . .'

Then spoke Joshua to the Lord in the day when the Lord delivered up the Amorites before the children of Israel; and he said in the sight of Israel:

'Sun, stand thou still upon Gibeon;
And thou, Moon, in the valley of Aijalon.'
And the sun stood still, and the moon stayed,
Until the nation had avenged themselves of their enemies.

Is not this written in the book of Jashar? And the sun stayed in the midst of heaven, and hasted not to go down about a whole day. And there was no day like that before it or after it, that the Lord hearkened unto the voice of a man; for the Lord fought for Israel. . . .

So Joshua smote all the land, the hill-country, and the South, and the Lowland, and the slopes, and all their kings; . . .—6:1-2, 16; 8:1-2a; 10:12-14, 40.

C.   Now Joshua was old and well stricken in years; and the Lord said unto him: 'Thou art old and well stricken in years, and there remaineth yet very much land to be possessed. This is the land that yet remaineth: all the regions of the Philistines, and all the Geshurites; . . .'

And these are the inheritances which the children of Israel took in the land of Canaan, which Eleazar the priest, and Joshua the son of Nun, and the heads of the fathers' houses of the tribes of the children of Israel, distributed unto them, by the lot of their inheritance, as the Lord commanded by the hand of Moses, for the nine tribes, and for the half-tribe. . . .

And the lot for the tribe of the children of Judah according to their families was unto the border of Edom, even to the wilderness of Zin southward, at the uttermost part of the south. . . .

And as for the Jebusites, the inhabitants of Jerusalem, the children of Judah could not drive them out; but the Jebusites dwelt with the children of Judah at Jerusalem, unto this day. . . .

And the Lord spoke unto Joshua, saying: 'Speak to the children of Israel, saying: Assign you the cities of refuge, whereof I spoke unto you by the hand of Moses; that the manslayer that killeth any person through error and unawares may flee thither; and they shall be unto you a refuge from the avenger of blood. . . .'

And they set apart Kedesh in Galilee in the hill-country of Naphtali, and Schechem in the hill-country of Ephraim, and Kiriath-arba—the same is Hebron—in the hill-country of Judah. . . .

So the Lord gave unto Israel all the land which He swore to give unto their fathers; and they possessed it, and dwelt therein. . . . There failed not aught of any good thing which the Lord had spoken unto the house of Israel; all came to pass. —13:1-2; 14:1-2; 15:1, 63; 20:1-3, 7; 21:43, 45.

D.   And it came to pass after many days, when the Lord had given rest unto Israel from all their enemies round about, and Joshua was old and well stricken in years; that Joshua called for all Israel, for their elders and for their heads, and for their judges and for their officers, and said unto them: 'I am old and well stricken in years. And ye have seen all that the Lord your God hath done unto all these nations because of you; for the Lord your God, He it is that hath fought for you. . . . Therefore be ye very courageous to keep and to do all that is written in the book of the law of Moses, that ye turn not aside therefrom to the right hand or to the left; . . . but cleave unto the Lord your God, as ye have done unto this day; . . . And it shall come to pass, that as all the good things are come upon you of which the Lord your God spoke unto you, so shall the Lord bring upon you all the evil things, until He have destroyed you from this good land which the Lord your God hath given you. When ye transgress the covenant of the Lord your God, which He commanded you, and go and serve other gods, and worship them; . . .'

And the people said unto Joshua: 'Nay; but we will serve the

Lord.' And Joshua said unto the people: 'Ye are witnesses against yourselves that ye have chosen you the Lord, to serve Him.'—And they said: 'We are witnesses.'— . . .

And it came to pass after these things, that Joshua the son of Nun, the servant of the Lord, died, being a hundred and ten years old.—And Israel served the Lord all the days of Joshua, and all the days of the elders that outlived Joshua, and had known all the work of the Lord, that He had wrought for Israel.—23:1-3, 6, 8, 11, 15-16a; 24:21, 22, 29, 31.

COMMENTARY

A.   God reassures Joshua that He will be with him as He was with Moses. He urges Joshua to be courageous and to observe the law of Moses. As Moses crossed the Red Sea with the people of Israel by means of a miracle, so did Joshua cross the Jordan. As the Exodus from Egypt began with the observance of the first commandant given to the people, namely, the observance of Passover, so did the first observance in the Promised Land follow the same pattern. They observe the Passover at Gilgal. As Moses was inspired at the holy ground of the burning bush, so Joshua receives inspiration by standing at the holy ground around the "Captain of the Hosts" of the Lord.

B.   The first conquest is that of Jericho. Then follows a series of conquests. In all of them we are told that God fought for Israel and at one of them, miraculously, the sun and the moon stood still. This poem, describing the miracle of the standing still of the sun and the moon, is followed by the statement, "Is this not written in the book of Jasher?" This is one of the ancient books cited in Scripture. Others are the books of the "Chronicles of the Kings of Israel," the book of the "Chronicles of the Kings of Judah," etc. The writers of these historical books had older books which they used as sources for their rewriting of the story of the people.

C.   After Joshua conquers the land (i.e., most of it), he divides it among the tribes by lot, and as was required in the last book of the Bible, he sets aside refuge cities in which those who have accidentally killed someone may be saved from vengeance.

D.   As Moses did at the end of his days, Joshua calls the people together, addresses them, calls attention to God's work in their behalf, and renews the covenant between God and Israel.

JUDGES

In the Book of Deuteronomy (Deuteronomy 20:16, 17), the Israelites were commanded to destroy the inhabitants of the land of Canaan. Such destruction of a conquered people was frequent in all ancient warfare and has, alas, become a practice in modern times. But there was this difference, at least, between the destruction ordered of the Canaanites and similar ruthlessness in war among other peoples. The destruction of nations in war was generally out of bloodthirstiness and for booty. The Israelites were ordered to destroy the inhabitants of Canaan because of the corruption of their idol worship and for fear that Israel would be corrupted by them. They were not to take any booty at all, and, in fact, in the Book of Joshua, when Achan kept for himself some booty from a defeated enemy, all of Israel was punished for it and was by God's command defeated in the very next battle.

Yet, of course, even though the purpose of the destruction of the inhabitants of Canaan was not for booty, since that was prohibited, nor for bloodthirstiness, but to remove their corrupting idolatry, this total type of war, though it is not against the practice of many nations in these modern times, is still against our conscience. Yet, as a matter of fact, such annihilation did not occur at all. The Canaanites were not destroyed. They lived side by side with the Israelites for centuries, and indeed the inevitable did happen—the children of Israel were constantly corrupted by these idolatrous neighbors. The pure spiritual worship of the Infinite God of whom "thou shalt make no graven image" might have been possible for philosophers but was too much for simple folk. There was an inevitable attraction in the little gods of the Canaanites, their household images and their folk practices at sowing and harvest time. Israel was thus corrupted time and time again. One can understand how, in later times, pious historians, thinking back on the continual relapsing into idolatry of the people of Israel, must have thought that all this spiritual tragedy could have been avoided if the idol-worshipping Canaanites with their corrupt superstitions had been completely removed in the days of the conquest of Canaan.

The Book of Judges begins therefore with the thought that because the Israelites did spare the Canaanites, they were corrupted by the Canaanite idolatry, and thus were punished in every generation. The book therefore is not cold, objective history. It is, like the other books in this series of "earlier prophets," a religious interpretation of certain historical facts. It is written to prove, as the Prophets constantly tried to prove, that apostasy from God, the corruption of life through idol worship, and its accompanying immorality, led to the misfortunes of the people. And this of course was quite correct. The idol worship of the Canaanites did not differ from the worship of God merely in the fact that the god was named Baal or the goddess Astarte or that there were many gods instead of one God, but also in that these gods were all worshipped by hideously immoral rites. It was impossible to worship the idols without participating in corrupting immorality. Idolatry was not only a confusion of the mind; it was in actual practice a corruption of the morals.

The introduction states the general thesis of the book, namely that the children of Israel spared the Canaanites, learned from them their idol worship, were corrupted by it, were punished, then repented and were delivered, and then were corrupted again; and then the process started all over again. The main part of the book (chapter 3:7 to chapter 16:30) tells the story of the successive judges who rescued the people when, because of their sins, they were conquered by their enemies. These judges then guided the people for the rest of their careers. Thus we are told about the judges Ehud, Deborah, Gideon, Jephtha, and Samson, and other minor judges. These named in this book were not the only men who judged Israel. The careers of two of the great judges, Eli and Samuel, are described in the next Biblical book, the Book of Samuel.

The judges then were the leaders and deliverers and rulers of the people from the days of Joshua, who conquered the land, to the beginning of the kingdom under King Saul. The story of each judge begins virtually in the same formula which explains the significance, as the historians saw it, of the tribulation and the deliverances of Israel. Thus (Judges 3:7): "The children of Israel did that which was evil—and served the Baalim . . . therefore the anger of the Lord was kindled and He gave them into the hand of the king of Aram . . . and when the children of Israel cried unto the Lord, He raised up a saviour . . . Othniel the son of Kenaz and he judged Israel, and the Lord delivered the king of Aram into his hand . . . and the land had rest for forty years, and Othniel the son of Kenaz, died." This formula is repeated through the book with almost every judge.

The end of the book gives a series of miscellaneous stories which are told at this point because they occurred in the time of the Judges.

SYNOPSIS OF TEXT

A.   Now when Joshua had sent the people away, the children of Israel went every man unto his inheritance to possess the land. And the people served the Lord all the days of Joshua, and all the days of the elders that outlived Joshua, who had seen all the great work of the Lord, that He had wrought for Israel. . . . And also all that generation were gathered unto their fathers; and there arose another generation after them, that knew not the Lord, nor yet the work which He had wrought for Israel.

And the children of Israel did that which was evil in the sight of the Lord, and served the Baalim. And they forsook the Lord, the God of their fathers, who brought them out of the land of Egypt, and followed other gods, of the gods of the peoples that were round about them, and worshipped them; and they provoked the Lord. . . . And the anger of the Lord was kindled against Israel, and He delivered them into the hands of spoilers that spoiled them, and He gave them over into the hands of their enemies round about, so that they could not any longer stand before their enemies. . . . And the Lord raised up judges, who saved them out of the hand of those that spoiled them. . . . But it came to pass, when the judge was dead, that they turned back, and dealt more corruptly than their fathers, in following other gods to serve them, and to worship them; they left nothing undone of their practices, nor of their stubborn way. And the anger of the Lord was kindled against Israel; and He said: 'Because this nation have transgressed My covenant which I commanded their fathers, and have not hearkened unto My voice; I also will not henceforth drive out any from before them of the nations that Joshua left when he died . . .' – 2:6, 7, 10-12, 14, 16, 19-21.

B.   And the children of Israel again did that which was evil in the sight of the Lord, when Ehud was dead. And the Lord gave them over into the hand of Jabin king of Canaan, that reigned in Hazor; the captain of whose host was Sisera, who dwelt in Harosheth-goiim. And the children of Israel cried unto the Lord; for he had nine hundred chariots of iron; and twenty years he mightily oppressed the children of Israel.

Now Deborah, a prophetess, the wife of Lappidoth, she judged Israel at that time. And she sat under the palm-tree of Deborah between Ramah and Beth-el in the hill-country of Ephraim; and the children of Israel came up to her for judgment. And she sent and called Barak the son of Abinoam out of Kedesh-naphtali, and said unto him: 'Hath the Lord, the God of Israel, commanded, saying: Go and draw toward mount Tabor, and take with thee ten thousand men of the children of Naphtali and of the children of Zebulun? . . .'

And Deborah said unto Barak: 'Up, for this is the day in which the Lord hath delivered Sisera into thy hand; is not the Lord gone out before thee?' So Barak went down from mount Tabor, and ten thousand men after him. And the Lord discomfited Sisera, and all his chariots, and all his hosts, with the edge of the sword before Barak; and Sisera alighted from his chariot, and fled away on his feet. . . .

Then sang Deborah and Barak the son of Abinoam on that day, saying:
When men let grow their hair in Israel,
When the people offer themselves willingly,
Bless ye the Lord.
Hear, O ye kings; give ear, O ye princes;
I, unto the Lord will I sing;
I will sing praise to the Lord, the God of Israel. . . .
Awake, awake, Deborah;
Awake, awake, utter a song;
Arise, Barak, and lead thy captivity captive, thou son of Abinoam. . . .

They fought from heaven,
The stars in their courses fought against Sisera.
The brook Kishon swept them away,
That ancient brook, the brook Kishon. – 4:1-6, 14-15; 5:1-3, 12,
20, 21a.

C.   And the children of Israel again did that which was evil
in the sight of the Lord: and the Lord delivered them into the
hand of the Philistines forty years.

And there was a certain man of Zorah, of the family of the
Danites, whose name was Manoah; and his wife was barren; and
bore not. And the angel of the Lord appeared unto the woman,
and said unto her: 'Behold now, thou art barren, and hast not
borne; but thou shalt conceive, and bear a son. . . .'

And the woman bore a son, and called his name Samson; and
the child grew, and the Lord blessed him. . . . And it came to pass
afterward, that he loved a woman in the valley of Sorek, whose
name was Delilah. And the lords of the Philistines came up unto
her, and said unto her: 'Entice him, and see wherein his great
strength lieth, and by what means we may prevail against him,
that we may bind him to afflict him; and we will give thee every
one of us eleven hundred pieces of silver.' And Delilah said to
Samson: 'Tell me, I pray thee, wherein thy great strength lieth,
and wherewith thou mightest be bound to afflict thee.' . . . And
he told her all his heart, and said unto her: 'There hath not come
a razor upon my head; for I have been a Nazirite unto God from
my mother's womb; if I be shaven, then my strength will go from
me, and I shall become weak, and be like any other man.' . . . And
she made him sleep upon her knees; and she called for a man, and
had the seven locks of his head shaven off; and she began to afflict
him, and his strength went from him. And she said: 'The Philistines
are upon thee, Samson.' And he awoke out of his sleep, and said: 'I
will go out as at other times, and shake myself.' But he knew not
that the Lord was departed from him. And the Philistines laid hold
on him, and put out his eyes; and they brought him down to Gaza,
and bound him with fetters of brass; and he did grind in the prison-
house. . . .

And the lords of the Philistines gathered them together to offer
a great sacrifice unto Dagon their god, and to rejoice; for they

· 73 ·

said: 'Our god hath delivered Samson our enemy into our hand.' . . .
And it came to pass, when their hearts were merry, that they said:
'Call for Samson, that he may make us sport.' And they called for
Samson out of the prison-house; and he made sport before them;
and they set him between the pillars. . . . And Samson called unto
the Lord, and said: 'O Lord God, remember me, I pray Thee, and
strengthen me, I pray Thee, only this once, O God, that I may
be this once avenged of the Philistines for my two eyes.' And Samson took fast hold of the two middle pillars upon which the house
rested, and leaned upon them, the one with his right hand, and
the other with his left. And Samson said: 'Let me die with the
Philistines.' And he bent with all his might; and the house fell
upon the lords, and upon all the people that were therein. So the
dead that he slew at his death were more than they that he slew
in his life. Then his brethren and all the house of his father came
down, and took him, and brought him up, and buried him between
Zorah and Eshtaol in the burying-place of Manoah his father. And
he judged Israel twenty years. —13:1-3, 24; 16:4-6, 17, 19-21, 23,
25, 28-31.

COMMENTARY

A.   The opening of the book is connected with the end of the
preceding book. We are told at the end of Joshua that the people
served the Lord as long as Joshua and the leaders of his generation
lived. After he died, they were led astray to the corrupt idolatrous
practice of the Canaanites, and were punished "because this nation
has transgressed My covenant."

B.   This is a typical story of one of the judges, Deborah, the
Prophetess. Included in this story is an ancient song, the type of
many ancient epic songs found in the earlier Biblical books.

C.   One of the most dramatic of the stories in the Book of
Judges, the story of Samson, his heroic life and his tragic death,
is told here.

SAMUEL

The Prophet Jeremiah, in the depths of his spiritual depression,
seeing before him the cumulating sins of the people, tells his

listeners that nothing can avert the inevitable end, national tragedy. Because they must have known from ancient tradition that
Moses, the first of the Prophets, had frequently pleaded for the
people and averted destruction; Jeremiah tells them that even
Moses himself could not successfully plead now in their behalf.
It is interesting that he does not mention Moses alone as advocate
in behalf of the people. He says (Jeremiah 15:1): "Though Moses
and Samuel stood before Me, My mind could not be toward this
people." Thus the Prophet Jeremiah, looking back over all of
Israel's past, thinking of the two men closest to God, mentions the
Prophet Samuel with Moses himself.

This indicates in what high reverence Samuel was held in ancient Israelitish tradition. He is to be looked upon as the greatest
as well as the last of the judges. His authority was more than local.
He travelled through the land as Judge of all Israel. "And Samuel
judged Israel all the days of his life and he went from year to
year in circuits to Beth-el and Gilgal and Mizpah and he judged
Israel in all those places." (1 Samuel 7:15, 16.) He was also a
prophet. The Book of Samuel tells us that whereas in the past the
men who performed prophetical functions had been called "seers,"
now, beginning with Samuel, they were called prophets. (1 Samuel
9:9.) There are great prophetic passages in the Book of Samuel,
words which he speaks in the mood of the literary prophets of
later times. Thus when Samuel rebukes Saul, he says:

"Hath the Lord as great delight in burnt-offerings and sacrifices,

As in hearkening to the voice of the Lord?
Behold, to obey is better than sacrifice." (Samuel 15:22.)

It seems also that Samuel organized bands of prophets to serve,
perhaps, as prophetic schools. Thus 1 Samuel 19:20 speaks of "The
company of the Prophets prophesying and Samuel standing as
head over them." Samuel was not only a judge and prophet but
he guided Israel through the transition from the loosely knit tribal
life to the organized national life ruled and regulated by kings.

The Talmud says (b. Baba Bathra 14b) that Samuel wrote the
Book of Samuel as well as the Book of Judges. Yet it is to be
noted that nowhere in the book itself is it said that Samuel wrote
the book. Moreover, many of the events of the Second Book of
Samuel happened after his death. It is also clear, as many scholars

have pointed out, that the style of writing changes a number of times. Furthermore, some of the events are given in two or sometimes three different forms. For example, the end of the family of Eli is really given twice, and the coronation of King Saul, the first king, is given twice, and indeed, three times. There are two different accounts of how David was introduced to the household of Saul, and so for a number of historical events in the book. It is evident that, as with all history books, different sources were used by the author.

The two books of Samuel (I and II Samuel) were originally one book. The Talmud speaks simply of the Book of Samuel. Similarly, First and Second Kings were also one book. An interesting evidence of this is offered by the Masora. This ancient tradition which counted the words in every Biblical book as a protection against any words falling out or others being put in provides at the end of each Biblical book a statistical summary which gives the number of the words and the sentences in the book and also records which is the middle sentence (see Part One, chapter III). Now there is no such statistical Masoretic note at the end of First Samuel but only at the end of Second Samuel, and this Masora at the end of Second Samuel declares that the middle verse of the book is the verse which is in our present division I Samuel 28:24. In other words, the Masoretic tradition, like the Talmud, considers both present books of Samuel to be one book. The same is true of the two books of Kings.

The present division of the book goes back to the ancient Greek translation of the Bible. In the Greek translation the Books of Samuel and Kings are united into one large book called "Kingdoms" (since the Book of Samuel includes the kingdoms of Saul and David). Now it was the custom in the Greek and Roman classical period to have, for commercial convenience, rolls of a certain size equivalent roughly to about twenty-six average chapters in the present Bible. Hence the Greek translation of the Bible divided this combined book into four standard rolls of the current commercial size. This made two books of Samuel and two books of Kings, except, of course, that the Greek translation called the four books First, Second, Third, and Fourth Book of Kings. It was not until the sixteenth century that this Greek and Latin division came into our Hebrew Bibles.

The Book of Samuel begins with the story of the house of Eli and the birth of Samuel. It continues with Samuel's judgeship, the people's demand for a king, the anointing of Saul as king, the rift between Samuel and Saul. Then the book continues with the joint history of the young David and the aging Saul, and with this the First Book of Samuel ends. The Second Book of Samuel begins with the kingdom of David, and tells how he united the entire family of Israel under his control. The book ends with the rebellions of certain sons of David against him, and concludes with David at the end of his career.

Students of the book have endeavored to analyze the book into various sources. They generally agree that one of the sources was an ancient history of Saul and David, and that another source may have been a history of the Prophets Samuel, Nathan, and Gad. But as the book now stands it reads well as a unit, though there is some repetition of certain narratives. This book contains some of the finest narrative writing in all of Scripture. The story of the rebellion of Absalom and of old king David's mourning for his death is one of the grandest narratives which have come down to us from antiquity.

FIRST SAMUEL

SYNOPSIS OF TEXT

A.   And Hannah prayed, and said:
My heart exulteth in the Lord, ..
There is none holy as the Lord;
For there is none beside Thee;
Neither is there any rock like our God. ....
The Lord killeth, and maketh alive;
He bringeth down to the grave, and bringeth up.
The Lord maketh poor, and maketh rich;
He bringeth low, He also lifteth up.
He raiseth up the poor out of the dust,
He lifteth up the needy from the dung-hill,
To make them sit with princes,
And inherit the throne of glory;
For the pillars of the earth are the Lord's,
And He hath set the world upon them. ....

And the child Samuel ministered unto the Lord before Eli. And the word of the Lord was precious in those days; there was no frequent vision. And it came to pass at that time, when Eli was laid down in his place—now his eyes had begun to wax dim, that he could not see—and the lamp of God was not yet gone out, and Samuel was laid down to sleep in the temple of the Lord, where the ark of God was, . . . And the Lord came, and stood, and called as at other times: 'Samuel, Samuel.' Then Samuel said: 'Speak; for Thy servant heareth.' . . .

And Samuel grew, and the Lord was with him, and did let none of his words fall to the ground. And all Israel from Dan even to Beer-sheba knew that Samuel was established to be a prophet of the Lord. And the Lord appeared again in Shiloh; for the Lord revealed Himself to Samuel in Shiloh by the word of the Lord.

And Samuel spoke unto all the house of Israel, saying: 'If ye do return unto the Lord with all your heart, then put away the foreign gods and the Ashtaroth from among you, and direct your hearts unto the Lord, and serve Him only; and He will deliver you out of the hand of the Philistines.' Then the children of Israel did put away the Baalim and the Ashtaroth, and served the Lord only. . . .

And Samuel judged Israel all the days of his life. And he went from year to year in circuit to Beth-el, and Gilgal, and Mizpah; and he judged Israel in all those places. And his return was to Ramah, for there was his house; and there he judged Israel; and he built there an altar unto the Lord. . . .

And Samuel said unto all Israel: 'Behold, I have hearkened unto your voice in all ye said unto me, and have made a king over you. And now, behold, the king walketh before you; and I am old and gray-headed; . . .'

'Now therefore behold the king whom ye have chosen, and whom ye have asked for; and, behold, the Lord hath set a king over you. If ye will fear the Lord, and serve Him, and hearken unto His voice, and not rebel against the commandment of the Lord, and both ye and also the king that reigneth over you be followers of the Lord your God—; but if ye will not hearken unto the voice of the Lord, but rebel against the commandment of the Lord, then shall the hand of the Lord be against you, and against your fathers. . . . For the Lord will not forsake His people for

His great name's sake; because it hath pleased the Lord to make you a people unto Himself. . . . But if ye shall still do wickedly, ye shall be swept away, both ye and your king.' – 2:1a-2, 6-8; 3:1-3, 10, 19-21; 7:3-4, 15-17; 12:1, 2a, 13-15, 22, 25.

B.   And it came to pass, when he had made an end of speaking unto Saul, that the soul of Jonathan was knit with the soul of David, and Jonathan loved him as his own soul. And Saul took him that day, and would let him go no more home to his father's house. Then Jonathan made a covenant with David, because he loved him as his own soul. And Jonathan stripped himself of the robe that was upon him, and gave it to David, and his apparel, even to his sword, and to his bow, and to his girdle. And David went out whithersoever Saul sent him, he had good success; and Saul set him over the men of war; and it was good in the sight of all people, and also in the sight of Saul's servants.

And it came to pass as they came, when David returned from the slaughter of the Philistines, that the women came out of all the cities of Israel, singing and dancing, to meet king Saul, with timbrels, with joy, and with three-stringed instruments. And the women sang one to another in their play, and said:

Saul hath slain his thousands,
And David his ten thousands.

And Saul was very wroth, and this saying displeased him; and he said: 'They have ascribed unto David ten thousands, and to me they have ascribed but thousands; and all he lacketh is the kingdom!' And Saul eyed David from that day and forward.

And it came to pass on the morrow, that an evil spirit from God came mightily upon Saul, and he raved in the midst of the house; and David played with his hand, as he did day by day; and Saul had his spear in his hand. And Saul cast the spear; for he said: 'I will smite David even to the wall.' And David stepped aside out of his presence twice. And Saul was afraid of David, because the Lord was with him, and was departed from Saul. Therefore Saul removed him from him, and made him his captain over a thousand; and he went out and came in before the people. And David had great success in all his ways; . . . And when Saul saw that he had great success, he stood in awe of him. But all Israel and Judah loved David; for he went out and came in before them. . . .–18:1-16.

SECOND SAMUEL

And David lamented with this lamentation over Saul and over
Jonathan his son, and said —

Thy beauty, O Israel, upon thy high places is slain!
How are the mighty fallen!
Tell it not in Gath,
Publish it not in the streets of Ashkelon; . . .
How are the mighty fallen in the midst of the battle!
I am distressed for thee, my brother Jonathan;
Very pleasant hast thou been unto me;
Wonderful was thy love to me,
Passing the love of women.
How are the mighty fallen,
And the weapons of war perished! –1:17-20a, 25a, 26, 27.

C.   Now David sat between the two gates; and the watchman
went up to the roof of the gate unto the wall, and lifted up his
eyes, and looked, and behold a man running alone: And the watchman cried, and told the king. And the king said: 'If he be alone,
there is tidings in his mouth.' And he came apace, and drew near.
And the watchman saw another man running; and the watchman
called unto the porter, and said: 'Behold another man running
alone.' And the king said: 'He also bringeth tidings.' And the
watchman said: 'I think the running of the foremost is like the
running of Ahimaaz the son of Zadok.' And the king said: 'He is a
good man, and cometh with good tidings.'

     And Ahimaaz called, and said unto the king: 'All is well.' And
he bowed down before the king with his face to the earth, and
said: 'Blessed be the Lord thy God, who hath delivered up the
men that lifted up their hand against my lord the king.' . . .

     And, behold, the Cushite came; and the Cushite said: 'Tidings
for my lord the king; for the Lord hath avenged thee this day of
all them that rose up against thee.' And the king said unto the
Cushite: 'Is it well with the young man Absalom?' And the Cushite
answered: 'The enemies of my lord the king, and all that rise up
against thee to do thee hurt, be as that young man is.'

     And the king was much moved, and went up to the chamber

over the gate, and wept; and as he went, thus he said: 'O my son Absalom, my son, my son Absalom! would I had died for thee, O Absalom, my son, my son!'–18:24-28, 31-32; 19:1.

D.   And David spoke unto the Lord the words of this song in the day that the Lord delivered him out of the hand of all his enemies, and out of the hand of Saul; and he said:

The Lord is my rock, and my fortress, and my deliverer;
The God who is my rock, in Him I take refuge;
My shield, and my horn of salvation, my high tower, and my refuge;
My saviour, Thou savest me from violence.
Praised, I cry, is the Lord,
And I am saved from mine enemies. . . .
A tower of salvation is He to His king;
And showeth mercy to His anointed,
To David and to his seed, for evermore. – 22:1-4, 51.

COMMENTARY

A.   The thanksgiving prayer of Hannah after her child Samuel is born begins the book. The name Samuel means "God has heard [my prayer]." The central idea of this song of praise is repeated in Psalm 113, verse 7 ff.: "He raiseth up the poor out of the dust," etc. The child Samuel is dedicated from birth to the service of God just as the Prophet Jeremiah felt that he himself was dedicated. Thus Jeremiah says: "The word of the Lord came unto me, saying, 'Before thou camest forth from the womb, I sanctified thee; I have appointed thee a prophet unto the nations.'" (Jeremiah 1:5.) Perhaps because of this tradition that Samuel was dedicated to God from birth, Jeremiah felt a special kinship with his ancient predecessor; and perhaps that is why he names him with Moses. "Though Moses and Samuel stood before Me." (Jeremiah 15:1.)

Samuel becomes judge over all of Israel after the death of his teacher Eli. It is he who finally yields to the people's demand and appoints a king over them, anointing Saul to be the first King of Israel. At the end of his life ("and I am old and gray-headed," 12:2) he assembles the people as Moses and Joshua did before him, reviews his career before them, and urges them to revere God and

· 81 ·

not forsake Him; then God will keep His part of the covenant to them: "For the Lord will not forsake His people because it hath pleased the Lord to make you a people unto Himself." (12:22.)

B.   The career of King Saul is an unhappy one almost from the beginning, and its end is overshadowed with the rising career of David. The people soon prefer David to Saul, and the end of Saul's life is a series of pursuits of David and occasional recon-ciliations. The Book of Samuel ends with Saul and Jonathan losing their lives in a battle against the Philistines on Mount Gilboa. The Second Book of Samuel begins with the lament of David for Saul and Jonathan.

C.   The Second Book of Samuel deals entirely with the life of King David and ends with the rebellions against David which arose in his own household. The section quoted is the magnificent narrative of the last battle in Absalom's rebellion and his death.

D.   David ends his career with a song of praise to God, just as Jacob (at the end of Genesis) and Moses (at the end of Deuter-onomy) did. This hymn of David's is found twice in the Bible, here at the end of the Second Book of Samuel and in the Psalms (Psalm 18).

KINGS

As is the case with most of the historical books, the author of the Book of Kings used many older sources. The book makes frequent mention of the sources which were used. Thus in 1 Kings (14:29) we read: "Now the rest of the acts of Rehoboam, are they not written in the book of the chronicles of the kings of Judah?" In 1 Kings (15:31): "Now the rest of the acts of Nadab, are they not written in the book of the chronicles of the kings of Israel?" These books of royal chronicles are mentioned many times in the Biblical Book of Kings. Some scholars are of the opinion that there must also have been a separate history of the Prophets because it would seem unlikely that the royal chronicles, which were con-cerned chiefly with the acts of the kings, would contain such large and extensive narratives concerning the Prophets Elijah and Elisha as are contained in the present book, especially since these prophets, particularly Elijah, were in frequent opposition to many of the actions of the kings. There may well have been a history of the prophets which included the stories of the Prophets Samuel, Nathan, and Gad (spoken of in the Book of Samuel), and Elisha and Elijah (spoken of in the Book of Kings).

As has already been indicated, the Book of Kings can hardly be called simply a history. Many of the events which other historians would have included were simply omitted with a reference made to the chronicles of the kings of Judah or of Israel, where those facts might be found. The historian was a religious historian whose aim was to demonstrate that evil led to national destruction, and righteousness to God's help. Therefore, the method of writing and the organization of the material is similar to that in the Book of Judges. There the career of every judge is enclosed in a literary formula which reveals the aim of the author, namely, that the people sinned, that they were therefore defeated in war, that the judge redeemed them after they had repented. Here in Kings the formula accompanies the career of every ruler. Thus: "Rehoboam was forty-one years old when he began to reign . . . and Judah did evil in the sight of the Lord . . . they built high places and pillars and Asherim on every hill [i.e., for the worship of idols] and it came to pass that Shishak king of Egypt came up against Jerusalem and took away the treasures of the house of the Lord. . . . Now the rest of the acts of Rehoboam, are they not written in the book of the chronicles of the kings of Judah?" (1 Kings 14:21 ff.)

First and Second Kings, although divided in our present Bible, are really one book (see introduction to the Book of Samuel). The book begins with the last days of David, his selection of Solomon to succeed him, and Solomon's building of the Temple. Then follows the division of the kingdom, with Solomon's son Rehoboam ruling in the southern kingdom, Judah, and Jeroboam ruling as the first king of the northern kingdom. From then on, the histories of the two kingdoms are intermingled, the kings of one kingdom being dated according to the year of the reign of the king of the other kingdom when they came to the throne. Most of the great stories of Elijah the Prophet are found in the First Book of Kings. The Second Book of Kings begins with the last days of Elijah the Prophet and tells the various narratives of his successor, Elisha. It continues with the history of both kingdoms until the northern kingdom is destroyed by the Assyrians, and then goes on with the history of the southern kingdom till it is destroyed by the Babylonians. The last chapter of the Book of Kings covers the same material as the thirty-ninth chapter of Jeremiah, the description of the capture of the last king of Judah, Zedekiah, and the destruction of Jerusalem.

The Talmud (b. Baba Bathra 15a) says that Jeremiah wrote his own book of prophecies and the Book of Lamentations and also the Book of Kings. However, he could hardly have written the last paragraph of the book which tells that in the thirtieth year of the captivity of Jehoyachin, King of Judah, the King of Babylon released him from prison. Jehoyachin was captured eleven years before the final destruction described by Jeremiah, and the liberation of Jehoyachin took place nineteen years after the destruction. Of course, Jeremiah may have lived that long. We do not know just when he died. At all events, the Talmud reveals its awareness of the fact that the book was written late, towards the end of the kingdom or the beginning of the Exile. This is approximately the same opinion as that to which modern scholars have come.

FIRST KINGS

SYNOPSIS OF TEXT

A.   And Solomon ruled over all the kingdoms from the River unto the land of the Philistines, and unto the border of Egypt; they brought presents, and served Solomon all the days of his life. . . . And Judah and Israel dwelt safely, every man under his vine and under his fig-tree from Dan even to Beer-sheba, all the days of Solomon. . . .

And God gave Solomon wisdom and understanding exceeding much, and largeness of heart, even as the sand that is on the sea-shore. And Solomon's wisdom excelled the wisdom of all the children of the east, and all the wisdom of Egypt. . . . And he spoke three thousand proverbs; and his songs were a thousand and five. And he spoke of trees, from the cedar that is in Lebanon even unto the hyssop that springeth out of the wall; he spoke also of beasts, and of fowl, and of creeping things, and of fishes. And there came of all peoples to hear the wisdom of Solomon, from all kings of the earth, who had heard of his wisdom. . . .

And Solomon stood before the altar of the Lord in the presence of all the congregation of Israel, and spread forth his hand toward heaven; and he said: 'O Lord, the God of Israel, there is no God like Thee, in heaven above, or on earth beneath; who keepest covenant and mercy with Thy servants, that walk before Thee with all their heart; . . .

'But will God in very truth dwell on the earth? behold, heaven and the heaven of heavens cannot contain Thee; how much less this house that I have builded! Yet have Thou respect unto the prayer of Thy servant, and to his supplication, O Lord my God, to hearken unto the cry and to the prayer which Thy servant prayeth before Thee this day; . . . And hearken Thou to the supplication of Thy servant, and of Thy people Israel, when they shall pray toward this place; yea, hear Thou in heaven Thy dwelling-place; and when Thou hearest, forgive. . . .

'Moreover concerning the stranger that is not of Thy people Israel, when he shall come out of a far country for Thy name's sake—for they shall hear of Thy great name, and of Thy mighty hand, and of Thine outstretched arm—when he shall come and pray toward this house; hear Thou in heaven Thy dwelling-place, and do according to all that the stranger calleth to Thee for; that all the peoples of the earth may know Thy name, to fear Thee, as doth Thy people Israel, and that they may know that Thy name is called upon this house which I have built. . . .'

And when the queen of Sheba heard of the fame of Solomon because of the name of the Lord, she came to prove him with hard questions. And she came to Jerusalem with a very great train, with camels that bore spices and gold very much, and precious stones; and when she was come to Solomon, she spoke with him of all that was in her heart. And Solomon told her all her questions; there was not any thing hid from the king which he told her not. And when the queen of Sheba had seen all the wisdom of Solomon, and the house that he had built, . . . she said to the king: 'It was a true report that I heard in mine own land of thine acts, and of thy wisdom. Howbeit I believed not the words, until I came, and mine eyes had seen it; and, behold, the half was not told me; thou hast wisdom and prosperity exceeding the fame which I heard. Happy are thy men, happy are these thy servants, that stand continually before thee, and that hear thy wisdom. Blessed be the

Lord thy God, who delighted in thee, to set thee on the throne of Israel; because the Lord loved Israel for ever, therefore made He thee king, to do justice and righteousness.'– 5:1, 5, 9, 10, 12-14; 8:22, 23, 27, 28, 30, 41, 42, 43; 10:1-4, 6-9.

B.   So Jeroboam and all the people came to Rehoboam the third day, as the king bade, saying: 'Come to me again the third day.' And the king answered the people roughly, and forsook the counsel of the old men which they had given him; and spoke to them after the counsel of the young men, saying: 'My father made your yoke heavy, but I will add to your yoke; my father chastised you with whips, but I will chastise you with scorpions.' So the king hearkened not unto the people; for it was a thing brought about of the Lord, that He might establish His word, which the Lord spoke by the hand of Ahijah the Shilonite to Jeroboam the son of Nebat.

And when all Israel saw that the king hearkened not unto them, the people answered the king, saying: 'What portion have we in David? neither have we inheritance in the son of Jesse; to your tents, O Israel; now see to thine own house, David.' So Israel departed unto their tents. But as for the children of Israel that dwelt in the cities of Judah, Rehoboam reigned over them. . . . So Israel rebelled against the house of David, unto this day. And it came to pass, when all Israel heard that Jeroboam was returned, that they sent and called him unto the congregation and made him king over all Israel; there was none that followed the house of David, but the tribe of Judah only. And Rehoboam the son of Solomon reigned in Judah. Rehoboam was forty and one years old when he began to reign, and he reigned seventeen years in Jerusalem, the city which the Lord had chosen out of all the tribes of Israel, to put His name there; and his mother's name was Naamah the Ammonitess. And Judah did that which was evil in the sight of the Lord; and they moved Him to jealousy with their sins which they committed, above all that their fathers had done. For they also built them high places, and pillars, and Asherim, on every high hill, and under every leafy tree; and there were also sodomites in the land; they did according to all the abominations of the nations which the Lord drove out before the children of Israel. . . .

Now in the eighteenth year of king Jeroboam the son of Nebat

began Abijam to reign over Judah. Three years reigned he in Jerusalem; and his mother's name was Maacah the daughter of Abi-
shalom. And he walked in all the sins of his father, which he had
done before him; and his heart was not whole with the Lord his
God, as the heart of David his father. Nevertheless for David's
sake did the Lord his God give him a lamp in Jerusalem, to set
up his son after him, and to establish Jerusalem; because David
did that which was right in the eyes of the Lord, and turned not
aside from anything that He commanded him all the days of his
life, save only in the matter of Uriah the Hittite. Now there was
war between Rehoboam and Jeroboam all the days of his life.

And the rest of the acts of Abijam, and all that he did, are they
not written in the book of the chronicles of the kings of Judah?
And there was war between Abijam and Jeroboam. And Abijam
slept with his fathers; and they buried him in the city of David;
and Asa his son reigned in his stead. . . . –12:12-17, 19-20; 14:21-24;
15:1-8.

C.   And it came to pass, when Ahab saw Elijah, that Ahab
said unto him: 'Is it thou, thou troubler of Israel?' And he answered: 'I have not troubled Israel; but thou, and thy father's
house, in that ye have forsaken the commandments of the Lord,
and thou hast followed the Baalim. Now therefore send, and gather
to me all Israel unto mount Carmel, and the prophets of Baal four
hundred and fifty, and the prophets of the Asherah four hundred,
that eat at Jezebel's table.'

And Ahab sent unto all the children of Israel, and gathered
the prophets together unto mount Carmel. And Elijah came near
unto all the people, and said: 'How long halt ye between two
opinions? if the Lord be God, follow Him; but if Baal, follow
him.' And the people answered him not a word. . . .

Then the fire of the Lord fell, and consumed the burnt-offering,
and the wood, and the stones, and the dust, and licked up the
water that was in the trench. And when all the people saw it, they
fell on their faces; and they said: 'The Lord, He is God; the Lord,
He is God.'

And he came thither unto a cave, and lodged there; and, behold,
the word of the Lord came to him, and He said unto him: 'What
doest thou here, Elijah?' And he said: 'I have been very jealous

for the Lord, the God of hosts; for the children of Israel have forsaken Thy covenant, thrown down Thine altars, and slain Thy prophets with the sword; and I, even I only, am left; and they seek my life, to take it away.' And He said: 'Go forth, and stand upon the mount before the Lord.' And, behold, the Lord passed by, and a great and strong wind rent the mountains, and broke in pieces the rocks before the Lord; but the Lord was not in the wind; and after the wind an earthquake; but the Lord was not in the earthquake; and after the earthquake a fire; but the Lord was not in the fire; and after the fire a still small voice. And it was so, when Elijah heard it, that he wrapped his face in his mantle, and went out, and stood in the entrance of the cave. And there came a voice unto him, and said: 'What doest thou here, Elijah?'

And it came to pass after these things, that Naboth the Jezreelite had a vineyard, which was in Jezreel, hard by the palace of Ahab, king of Samaria. And Ahab spoke unto Naboth, saying: 'Give me thy vineyard, that I may have it for a garden of herbs, because it is near unto my house; and I will give thee for it a better vineyard than it; or, if it seem good to thee, I will give thee the worth of it in money.' And Naboth said to Ahab: 'The Lord forbid it me, that I should give the inheritance of my fathers unto thee.' And Ahab came into his house sullen and displeased because of the word which Naboth the Jezreelite had spoken to him; for he had said: 'I will not give thee the inheritance of my fathers.' And he laid him down upon his bed, and turned away his face, and would eat no bread.

And Jezebel his wife said unto him: 'Dost thou now govern the kingdom of Israel? arise, and eat bread, and let thy heart be merry; I will give thee the vineyard of Naboth the Jezreelite.' So she wrote letters in Ahab's name, and sealed them with his seal, and sent the letters unto the elders and to the nobles that were in his city, and that dwelt with Naboth. And she wrote in the letters, saying: 'Proclaim a fast, and set Naboth at the head of the people; and set two men, base fellows, before him, and let them bear witness against him, saying: Thou didst curse God and the king. And then carry him out, and stone him, that he die.'

And it came to pass, when Ahab heard that Naboth was dead, that Ahab rose up to go down to the vineyard of Naboth the Jezreelite, to take possession of it.

And the word of the Lord came to Elijah the Tishbite, saying: 'Arise, go down to meet Ahab king of Israel, who dwelleth in Samaria; behold, he is in the vineyard of Naboth, whither he is gone down to take possession of it. And thou shalt speak unto him, saying: Thus saith the Lord; Hast thou killed, and also taken possession? and thou shalt speak unto him, saying: Thus saith the Lord: In the place where dogs licked the blood of Naboth shall dogs lick thy blood, even thine.' And Ahab said to Elijah: 'Hast thou found me, O mine enemy?' And he answered: 'I have found thee; because thou hast given thyself over to do that which is evil in the sight of the Lord. . . .'—18: 17-21, 38, 39; 19:9-13; 21: 1-4, 7-10, 16-20.

SECOND KINGS

Now there cried a certain woman of the wives of the sons of the prophets unto Elisha, saying: 'Thy servant my husband is dead; and thou knowest that thy servant did fear the Lord; and the creditor is come to take unto him my two children to be bondmen.' And Elisha said unto her: 'What shall I do for thee? tell me; what hast thou in the house?' And she said: 'Thy handmaid hath not any thing in the house, save a pot of oil.' Then he said: 'Go, borrow thee vessels abroad of all thy neighbours, even empty vessels; borrow not a few. And thou shalt go in, and shut the door upon thee and upon thy sons, and pour out into all those vessels; and thou shalt set aside that which is full.' So she went from him, and shut the door upon her and upon her sons; they brought the vessels to her, and she poured out. And it came to pass, when the vessels were full, that she said unto her son: 'Bring me yet a vessel.' And he said unto her: 'There is not a vessel more.' And the oil stayed. Then she came and told the man of God. And he said: 'Go, sell the oil, and pay thy debt, and live thou and thy sons of the rest.' . . .

And Pekah the son of Remaliah, his captain, conspired against him (i.e., against Pekahiah) and smote him in Samaria, in the castle of the king's house, by Argob and by Arieh; and with him were fifty men of the Gileadites; and he slew him, and reigned in his stead. Now the rest of the acts of Pekahiah, and all that he did, behold, they are written in the book of chronicles of the kings of Israel.

In the two and fiftieth year of Azariah king of Judah Pekah the son of Remaliah began to reign over Israel in Samaria, and reigned twenty years. And he did that which was evil in the sight of the Lord; he departed not from the sins of Jeroboam the son of Nebat, wherewith he made Israel to sin. In the days of Pekah king of Israel came Tiglath-pileser king of Assyria, and took Ijon, and Abel-beth-maacah, and Janoah, and Kedesh, and Hazor, and Gilead, and Galilee, all the land of Naphtali; and he carried them captive to Assyria. And Hoshea the son of Elah made a conspiracy against Pekah the son of Remaliah, and smote him, and slew him, and reigned in his stead, in the twentieth year of Jotham the son of Uzziah. Now the rest of the acts of Pekah, and all that he did, behold, they are written in the book of the chronicles of the kings of Israel. – 4: 1-7; 15:25-31.

D.   In the ninth year of Hoshea, the king of Assyria took Samaria, and carried Israel away unto Assyria, and placed them in Halah, and in Habor, on the river of Gozan, and in the cities of the Medes.

And it was so, because the children of Israel had sinned against the Lord their God, who brought them up out of the land of Egypt from under the hand of Pharaoh king of Egypt, and had feared other gods, and walked in the statutes of the nations, whom the Lord cast out from before the children of Israel, and of the kings of Israel, which they practiced; . . . and they served idols, whereof the Lord had said unto them: 'Ye shall not do this thing'; . . . and they rejected His statutes, and His covenant that He made with their fathers, and His testimonies wherewith He testified against them; and they went after things of nought, and became nought, and after the nations that were round about them, concerning whom the Lord had charged them that they should not do like them; . . . and they caused their sons and their daughters to pass through the fire, and used divination and enchantments, and gave themselves over to do that which was evil in the sight of the Lord, to provoke Him; that the Lord was very angry with Israel, and removed them out of His sight; there was none left but the tribe of Judah only . . . until the Lord removed Israel out of His sight, as He spoke by the hand of all His servants the prophets. So Israel was carried away out of their own land to Assyria, unto this day.

Now in the fifth month, on the seventh day of the month, which was the nineteenth year of king Nebuchadnezzar, king of Babylon, came Nebuzaradan the captain of the guard, a servant of the king of Babylon, unto Jerusalem. And he burnt the house of the Lord, and the king's house; and all the houses of Jerusalem, even every great man's house, burnt he with fire. And all the army of the Chaldeans, that were with the captain of the guard, broke down the walls of Jerusalem round about. And the residue of the people that were left in the city, and those that fell away, that fell to the king of Babylon, and the residue of the multitude, did Nebuzaradan the captain of the guard carry away captive. But the captain of the guard left of the poorest of the land to be vine-dressers and husbandmen. –17:6-8, 12, 15, 17, 18, 23; 25:8-12.

COMMENTARY

A.   The grandeur of Solomon's kingdom, his great wisdom, his building of the Temple, and the magnificent prayer which he utters, pleading also that when strangers "not of thy people Israel" shall come to this house and pray, that God may hear their prayer, begin the book. This is the same idealism found in many of the Prophets, that nations shall "flow unto" the house of the Lord to worship the one true God.

B.   The description of Rehoboam's idolatry, learned from the nations of the land, and the division of the kingdom are told here.

C.   The great test on Mount Carmel in which Elijah brings the people back to the worship of God is described here.
The prophetic career of Elisha, the pupil of Elijah, is full of miracles and wonders. The story of the widow and the vessel of oil here quoted is one of Elisha's many miracles found in the Book of Kings.
The northern kingdom was not ruled by one family as the southern kingdom was ruled by the family of David. Its kings came to the throne usually by means of revolt and assassination. Hoshea, who slew Pekah, was the last king of the northern kingdom. It was in his reign, in the year 722 B.C.E., that the northern kingdom was destroyed by the Assyrians.

D.   The ten northern tribes were carried away and the As-syrians settled them in various places of their vast empire. They disappeared, never forming part of Jewish history again. These are the so-called "ten lost tribes." At the end of the story of the north-ern kingdom, the historian explains why this tragedy happened and his explanation is in line with the prophetic doctrine. Idolatry and sinfulness among the people were the source of national weakness: "And the children of Israel walked in all the sins of Jeroboam . . . until the Lord removed Israel out of His sight as He spoke by the hand of all His servants the prophets."

Although the Book of Kings ends with the tragic story of the fall of the northern and then of the southern kingdom, the Bible continues with the works of the later prophets who, though they had predicted this destruction, soon saw through the curtain of tragedy to the time when Israel would be spiritually regenerated and restored.

Chapter IV

The Prophetic Movement

THE Prophets of Israel are unique in the history of religion. Before their times there were none quite like them, and succeeding generations, although they had the prophets themselves as models, have never produced their equal. They are clothed in such moral majesty that the most stubborn skeptic, scorning the science, the legislation, or the history found in Scripture, is moved to admiration for them. The most radical, critical students of Scripture, who are careful to explain all leading Scriptural ideas and institutions as the outcome of a slow evolution from paganism, speak of the Prophets in amazement, as of a sudden, dramatic, and unprecedented appearance upon the stage of history.

Indeed, there is no precedent for the Prophets, and so far there have been no successors. It is almost impossible to compare them with other religious teachers, for none resemble them sufficiently to be classified with them.

The Prophets were lonely men, every one of them. It has indeed frequently occurred in history that a handful of men have stood against the opinions and the power of an entire nation, provided this little group was banded together and met as a revolutionary unit for mutual encouragement and strength. But when has it ever happened that men belonging to no group at all, having no intellectual or spiritual companionship, solitaries, with only God at their side, should have the courage to face the prejudices and the delusions of their day and speak their mind before an entire nation? And furthermore, these solitary prophets, organizing no party, training no young disciples to follow them (some exceptions are discussed later in this chapter), except sometimes one solitary disciple, nevertheless achieved a genealogy of inspiration, one prophet following another, generation after generation. There is a succession of great literary prophets for four unbroken centuries. This combination of solitude and continuity is unprecedented in the history of the growth of ideas.

The Prophets were not only solitary; they were deeply meditative. Their inspiration came from within. They did not use, as others did, group chanting, dervish-dancing, or mass hypnotism. They spent long periods in silent thought and in their hearts they heard the Voice and the Mandate of God. Such men would be expected to live like the hermits of many great religions, away from the moral filth of the haunts of men in order to seek the nearness of God in the loneliness of cave or desert. Or if they spoke at all, they would be expected to speak to some worshipful individuals who would come in time of trouble to ask their guidance. But it was not so with the Prophets. Lonely seekers of God though they were, their inspiration drove them back into the market-place, to the great gathering of the people at their temples, and their message almost invariably concerned the nation, and, indeed, all the nations of the earth. They were hermits, but unlike the hermits in other religions. They were solitary men driven to become spiritual statesmen.

Another strange phenomenon about the Prophets is the mood of their utterances. Except for an occasional utterance of pity or consolation, their messages are mainly denunciatory. In blazing words, prophet after prophet points to the sins of Israel. These denunciations were not written in some hidden place in safe secrecy, but were given as public addresses to the people denounced. The people were, of course, deeply disturbed, and not a little indignant at these men who, instead of rebuilding their morale in time of danger and trouble, denounced them for their iniquities, and what is worse, not only failed to console them with promises of victories, but predicted dire destruction, conquest, spoliation, fire, and exile. One would expect such men, preaching so heart-breaking a message in a time of trouble, to be sternly suppressed and promptly forgotten. But, strangely enough, the very nation which was denounced and discouraged recognized that there was something unique in these prophecies and preserved them. As a result, Scripture is today unlike any other of the chronicles of antiquity. Whereas these others invariably praised the people and their rulers, enumerating their victories, boasting of their superiority, Scripture alone preserves the somber catalogue of Israel's iniquities. There is an unequalled national confessional mood in the Bible, an unprecedented and awesome sincerity, all because the Prophets, who denounced and prophesied doom, were nevertheless preserved as a permanent part of Sacred Scripture by the very people whose heart these indignant prophets seem to have broken when they lived and preached on earth.

Remarkable as it was that the words of the Prophets should have been reverently preserved by a people whom they so violently denounced, it was still more remarkable to what an extent the teachings of the Prophets achieved their purposes. After all, the Prophets had no actual authority. They had no official positions. On the contrary, almost all the kings and priests in Israel and in Judah opposed them and occasionally imprisoned them. Yet these lone men, without authority and under official disapproval, eventually won the hearts of Israel. An essential element in the Prophets' preachment was the denunciation of the sin of idolatry. They predicted national destruction to Israel for its sin of abandoning God. When the Exile came and then later when the people returned from the Exile, they returned purified. There was no more idolatry left among them. Whereas hitherto they had the unique character of the one people in which monotheism was widely taught and was the official religion, now they became truly the first people among which monotheism was not only taught but deeply believed. The idols of Canaan were not only removed from high places and from groves, they were removed from the hearts of Israel. Faith in the One and Only God, which was occasionally found among rare and exalted souls in other nations, was now for the first time the abiding faith of an entire people. Israel had truly become a kingdom of priests and a holy people. When prophecy ceased, it had died triumphant.

This was the unique character of the Prophets. Solitary men, without party and without groups of disciples, they achieved a continuity of language and thought which persisted for four centuries. Although their thoughts were turned inward, seeking the voice of God, their inspired energies were turned outward, declaring the fate of Israel and the world. Often detested as enemies of the people, their messages were preserved by the populace as its highest spiritual treasure. Seemingly voices lost in the wilderness of their times, they became, unaided except by God, the triumphant, transforming power in the life of Israel, making of it a world-changing force which, by direct influence and through its daughter religions, destroyed idolatry in half of the world.

Such a spiritual and literary phenomenon is beyond explanation. Professor Arnold Toynbee, in his *Study of History*, finds that in every great civilization there come centuries of tragedy which he calls "time of trouble," and that it is these "times of trouble" which are the creative periods in any civilization. The phrase "time of trouble" is a Biblical one (Psalm 10:1; Psalm 27:5), and clearly the Biblical "time of trouble" was when the great empires of Mesopotamia fought against the great empire of the Nile, and Palestine was a battle-field for century after century. That time of trouble produced the grandeur of prophecy. But this explains only the soil, not the wondrous plant which grew from it. How many countless "times of trouble" were there in the history of mankind which ended only in destruction, despair and in death? Just why this "time of trouble" in Israel produced the Prophets remains a mystery.

This might be said by way of partial explanation. The Prophets did not rise entirely without precedent. Before the time of the great literary prophets, beginning with Amos and ending with Malachi, there were other prophets whose preachments were not preserved for us. These men were akin to the literary prophets and in some cases hardly to be distinguished from them. There is, for example, Elijah, like them a solitary, like them emerging from his solitude to denounce the people for their sins, and like them hated by the dominant classes. There was the Prophet Nathan, whose message was like theirs, denouncing the king for his sins. The Prophet Samuel denounced the king for his sins, and the few words that are preserved are of blazing, ethical nature: "Behold, obedience to God is nobler than sacrifice." There was the lesser known Prophet Micaiah, the son of Imlah (1 Kings 22), who, like the classic prophets, dared to give the king a dire prediction about a national enterprise. In the time of the Prophet Jeremiah, when officers of the court and the king were indignant at his prophecies of national doom, one group wanted to put Jeremiah to death, but another group recalled similar prophets in the past who had made similar dire prophecies and yet had lived. Two are mentioned (Jeremiah 26:16-24), Micah and Uriah. Both are described in the same way as giving the same sort of message. Micah is among our literary prophets. Uriah, the Prophet, is not mentioned elsewhere. Had it happened that Micah's addresses were forgotten and Uriah's addresses, which evidently were of the same nature, were preserved, it would have been Uriah who would have been listed among our literary prophets. Evidently the literary prophets were part of a larger movement of men similarly minded and similarly devoted who voiced a similar message, but unfortunately all of the prophecies were not preserved.

Some of the men, then, who might be described as belonging to the same group as the literary prophets, had, unlike them, official status. Samuel was himself the leading authority in Israel in his time; Nathan the Prophet was in a sense an official. Elisha had at least a semi-official status. But the great literary prophets never sought such status and the nature of their prophecy made such status unattainable even if they desired it. Had they attained it, their prophecy would have lost its grandeur. Prophets who kept close touch with the government, who gradually developed official status, inevitably came to reflect the official point of view. When a government prepared for war it was essential to build up national morale, and the predictions of victory and a general optimism as to the future became the easy and the inevitable prophecy of official prophets. Thus were truth and sincerity destroyed in them, and they grew corrupt. The literary prophets frequently refer scornfully to these official prophets, coupling them with the official priests. They indicate how these prophets inevitably began to preach flattering, popular messages. Thus the Prophet Isaiah (30:9, 10) indicates how the people detest the stern truths of the true prophets and prefer and demand smooth, optimistic words:

> For it is a rebellious people,
> Lying children,
> Children that refuse to hear the teaching of the Lord;
> That say to the seers: 'See not,'
> And to the prophets: 'Prophesy not unto us right things,
> Speak unto us smooth things, prophesy delusions.'

The Prophet Jeremiah speaks of this cheap optimism which prophesies peace when the true prospect is destruction and war. Thus (Jeremiah 6:13, 14):

> And from the prophet even unto the priest
> Every one dealeth falsely.
> They have healed also the hurt of My people lightly,
> Saying: 'Peace, peace,' when there is no peace.

Therefore, the great literary prophets couple these official prophets with the official priesthood and denounced priest and prophet together. While, therefore, some of the nobler early prophets, who were akin in spirit to the great literary prophets, had official status, the official status proved to be a blind alley on the road of the development of prophecy. The official prophets soon became insincere time-servers, while the great prophets went on their solitary roads with no authority but that of God speaking through their conscience.

Some of the earlier prophets were surrounded by a prophetic social organization. They developed groups of prophets whom they trained. Thus even in the time of Moses, revered by tradition as the first and the greatest of the prophets, all the seventy elders prophesied *en masse* (Numbers 11:25):

"And the Lord came down in the cloud, and spoke unto him [i.e., Moses], and took of the spirit which was upon him, and put it upon the seventy elders; and it came to pass, that, when the spirit rested upon them, they prophesied."

In the time of Samuel there is frequent mention of companies or schools of prophets (1 Samuel 10:10). Thus when Saul is anointed king by Samuel, Samuel himself tells him that he will come upon a company of prophets of whom Samuel speaks approvingly (1 Samuel 10:5, 6):

"Thou shalt meet a band of prophets coming down from the high place with a psaltery, and a timbrel, and a pipe, and a harp, before them; and they will be prophesying. And the spirit of the Lord will come mightily upon thee, and thou shalt prophesy with them, and shalt be turned into another man."

Samuel himself joined such a company of prophets and prophesied with them (1 Samuel 19:20):

"They saw the company of the prophets prophesying and Samuel standing as head over them."

So too Elisha, the pupil and successor of Elijah, was the head of a company of prophets (1 Kings 2:15), where the company is called "sons of the prophets."

This mass prophesying was as bound to degenerate as was the official prophesying of the court prophets. There was the spiritual danger in using music and dance to create a sort of mass hypnotism, and under this excitement a contagion of the spirit developed like that of dervishes and like the "speaking with tongues" at revivals. Thus, while some of the noble prophets in earlier times were associated with such companies of prophets, this too became a blind alley and the Prophets grew more and more solitary. Only one of them had as much as one disciple (Jeremiah and Baruch). The true creative prophecy could only come when God the Only One spoke to man alone. The true Prophet was alone with God.

Among all people there were men who prophesied the future by magical methods, divination, enchantments, and mediumistic procedures with the dead, and such practices were found in Israel. When Saul, towards the end of his reign, in the midst of a dangerous invasion by the Philistines, wished to know the future, he consulted the mediumistic witch because there were no prophets who would give him answer. So Saul says to the ghost of Samuel (1 Samuel 28:15): "I am sore distressed; for the Philistines make war against me, and God is departed from me, and answereth me no more, neither by prophets, nor by dreams; therefore have I called thee (from the dead), that thou mayest make known unto me what I shall do." Of course, magic and spells might have been originally merely auxiliaries to some genuine prophecy, but they were corrupting procedures and sank into superstition. True prophecy quickly veered away from that seductive and dangerous path. And the great prophets attacked false prophets in the same breath as they did the magicians. The Prophet Micah speaks to these false prophets: "Therefore it shall be night unto you and you shall have no vision, and it shall be dark unto you that ye shall not make divination, and the sun shall go down upon the prophets." So Ezekiel (12:24): "For there shall be no more any vain vision nor smooth divination within the house of Israel." So too Ezekiel (chapter 13) attacks the old prophets who used such magic methods:

"Son of man, prophesy against the prophets of Israel that prophesy . . . woe unto the vile prophets . . . they have seen vanity and lying divination and say, 'the Lord sayeth.' " Such magical practices found among all people never formed a part of the great tradition of prophecy. Among the great prophets there might be material objects used as part of a prophecy—a basket of grapes, a pitcher, a flowering almond rod—but these were not magic; they were visual symbols of an ethical idea. The Prophets needed no magic tricks. The word of God was marvelous enough.

In the early days of prophecy, the Prophet frequently served as a guide and counsellor to the individuals who came and consulted them. Thus Samuel is consulted by Saul for as simple a purpose as to find the animals lost by his father. The Israelitish maiden, captive in Syria, suggests that her master Naaman go to the Prophet in Israel to be cured of his leprosy (II Kings 5:3): Jeroboam sends his wife to Ahija, the prophet, to Shiloh, to achieve a cure for their sick son. Elijah heals the widow's son (I Kings 17). And even Isaiah, the great literary prophet, is requested by King Hezekiah to cure him of his mortal sickness (II Kings 20).

While this seemed a natural function for the Prophet, this personal pastoral work proved to be also a blind alley in the development of prophecy. The king's request of Isaiah was perhaps the last of such personal requests which were frequent in earlier days. The Prophets turned their attention to national and international matters. While each individual was precious in God's sight, Israel, its failures and its function, its fate and the destiny of all mankind, became the sole message and activity of the Prophets. God said to Amos: "Go, prophesy to my people Israel" (Amos 7:15). Also Jeremiah was told: "I have appointed thee over nations and kingdoms" (Jeremiah 19:10).

Thus prophecy found itself. It grew in an ancient soil which it shared with kindred plants. But it developed in an original direction. Very early the great prophets turned away from official connection with the government, from group prophecy, from auxiliary devices of magical type, and from individual problems of personal nature. They became lonely men, preaching righteousness on the authority of God speaking through their own consciences, speaking to the entire people, relying solely upon the power and the majesty of the living word of God.

The order of the prophetic books as given in the Bible is not the order in which the books were written. For example, Amos, who was the first of the literary prophets, comes sixth in the present Biblical arrangement. It is difficult to know exactly how the present arrangement came about. The first three books (the "Major Prophets": Isaiah, Jeremiah, and Ezekiel) come first because they are the largest books and are at present in the order in which the authors (of the main part of each book) lived. Yet the Talmud (b. Baba Bathra 14b) gives these three books in a different order (Jeremiah, Ezekiel, and Isaiah) and also offers some explanation of the order of the twelve "Minor Prophets."

Modern scholarship has not come to a unanimous decision as to the relative dates of all of the Prophets, but there is a fair consensus of opinion. Since, in the next two chapters, we shall follow the Biblical order of the books, the following list of the approximate dates of the prophets in chronological order will be of help to the reader.

Amos	about 750 B.C.E.
Hosea	about 740 B.C.E.
Isaiah	about 730 B.C.E.
Micah	a younger contemporary of Isaiah
Zephaniah	about 630 B.C.E.
Nahum	about 611 B.C.E.
Jeremiah	just before the Exile. (The Exile is generally dated as from 586 B.C.E. to 539 B.C.E.)
Ezekiel	early in the Exile
Habakkuk	during the Exile
Obadiah	immediately before or during the Exile
"Deutero-Isaiah"	near the end of the Exile
Haggai	520 B.C.E.
Zechariah	a younger contemporary of Haggai
Malachi	about 450 B.C.E.
Joel	
Jonah	well after the Exile

Although the message of the Prophet is clear in its outlines, the texts of the prophecies which have been preserved are not easy to read. Students spending a great deal of time and energy on the texts as we have them now have been able to work out the meanings of the prophecies of the successive prophets. There is a temptation, therefore, for one who would try to understand the message of the Prophets, to get the material second hand from books about them. Yet their own words are before us, even though the text is sometimes difficult to read. It should be possible for the general reader with some guidance to have the joy of understanding the Prophets after reading the Prophets' own words. The general introduction as given above may be of some assistance. It might be of still greater assistance to select the telling sentences from each prophet and put them together in a mosaic, thus enabling the reader to follow the prophecy at first hand as a preparation for more complete reading later.

CHAPTER V

The Major Prophets

THE term "major prophets" is not known in the older Hebrew literature. The only classification which it uses is the "earlier prophets" and the "later prophets," the "earlier prophets" referring to the Books of Joshua, Judges, Samuel, and Kings, with all the Books of the Prophets, Isaiah through to Zechariah being called "the later prophets." The relatively modern terms, "major prophets" for Isaiah, Jeremiah, and Ezekiel, and "minor prophets" for the prophets from Hosea to Malachi must not be taken to mean that Isaiah, Jeremiah and Ezekiel are more important than the Prophets Hosea, Joel, etc., to Malachi, but merely that their works are larger.

The three "major" prophets, Isaiah, Jeremiah, and Ezekiel, follow each other in this order in the Hebrew Scriptures. This is the correct chronological order and it forms a logical sequence.

ISAIAH

GENERAL OUTLINE

Isaiah is perhaps the greatest of the Prophets for vividness of imagery and brilliant style, for rich variety of ideas, for his extraordinary blending of practical wisdom and exalted vision, for the long sweep of his career, and for his enduring influence on later Hebrew literature. None of the literary prophets has quite equalled him. He is the prince of prophets.

The period of his prophetic activity extends from about the year 760 of the pre-Christian era to the end of that century. He was a young man when Amos, the first of the literary prophets, gave his great address at Beth-el, the capital city and shrine of the northern kingdom (Israel). It might help to an understanding of Isaiah if he be contrasted with Amos, the pioneer of literary prophecy. Amos preached in a city that was strange to him, in which he, a Judean (a native of the southern kingdom), felt alien and deeply disturbed. Isaiah preached at home, in his beloved city of Jerusalem. Amos was a herdsman and a pruner of sycamore trees, while Isaiah was a citizen of Jerusalem, the great capital of the southern kingdom. There is very little of the mood of the field and farm in Isaiah's preaching. Amos came like Elijah from the countryside. He detested the luxurious life of the great city of Beth-el. He disliked the material refinements of the great capital. But Isaiah loved the great city of Jerusalem. It was precious to him. In his dreams of the blessed future, the city of Jerusalem and Mount Zion within it would be the center of restoration and of inspiration to all the peoples of the world. People would flow unto it to worship and to learn righteousness. Yet precisely because he loved Jerusalem, he was all the more enraged at the wickedness of the city. "How is the faithful city become a harlot, she that was full of justice . . . but now [is full of] murderers."

Amos belonged to the poor, while Isaiah, judging by his easy relationships with the kings and his at-homeness in the royal court, was clearly one of the aristocrats of Jerusalem. Yet no less than his simple-hearted countryman, Amos, does he denounce the luxury and the tyranny of the powerful. It is clear, then, that prophecy was not a class phenomenon. It was not primarily a revolt of "masses against the classes"; it was a revolt of conscience against evil. The sin of all classes was denounced and the prophets who denounced the people sometimes came from one social class and sometimes from another. Whoever received the word of God as mandate spoke out courageously, fearlessly denouncing the people for their sins.

There is, therefore, no basic difference in the prophecies of Amos and Isaiah. Everything that Amos was impelled to say came from the same exalted source as did the preachments of Isaiah. We find in both of them the same proclamation of the God of Justice, the same denunciation of the people for their sins, the same scornful denial that mere ritual will save them from punishment, the same prediction of inevitable national calamity because of moral weakness. These thoughts are found among all the prophets, but each prophet added something which was his own to the common store of prophetic preachment.

Since God is Infinite, no one man can grasp the fullness of the divine grandeur. Yet each of the great prophets, meditating long and deeply on the thought of God, tended to realize some additional element of God's Infinite Personality. Amos primarily saw and felt that God was a God of Justice, and so he spoke of God's exacting of punishment from those who are unjust. Hosea saw Him as the God of Love, pleading with His people which has gone astray to come back to His forgiving tenderness and be reconciled. "Return O Israel to the Lord your God." These differing ideas of God's infinitude are both found in Isaiah, but, in addition, more than any other prophet he sees God as holy, pure without a stain, perfect in goodness and truth. "Holy, holy, holy is the Lord of hosts" (Isaiah 6:3). More frequently than any other prophet, he speaks of God as "The Holy One of Israel" before whose perfect sanctity men must be humble and never walk in haughty pride.

Like Amos, he sees clearly that moral weakness will bring about national destruction, but for him a ray of hope begins to shine in the darkness and he speaks with confidence of the remnant of Israel which will never be destroyed, the saving remnant that will return to be the beginning of new growth, the seed of the future.

Like all the prophets, he was concerned with the fate of the nation and saw that the cause of national destruction lay in the character of the individual. But unlike them, he was concerned with practical problems of statesmanship and applied the doctrine of the saving power of righteousness to actual political problems. He gave stern advice to kings, denouncing their plans, mocking their intentions. He was opposed to all alliances either with or against the growing political power of the age, Assyria. He advised that the people build up their own inner, moral strength in order to outlast the inevitable political misfortunes of a dangerous and bloody age. "Unless ye have faith, ye will not endure" (Isaiah 7:9).

The vision of the saved and the saving remnant expands in the vision of Isaiah into a picture of a great world future. The beloved house of David will be purified of its sins; a descendant of David will once more ascend the throne in Jerusalem. He will be a righteous king who will do justice and promote peace. His rulership will send its blessing beyond the confines of Israel and all nations will come like flowing rivers to the beloved city of Jerusalem, to Zion, God's holy mountain, to learn of the ways of God.

Thus early in the great prophetic movement, as early as Isaiah, an indomitable vision begins to pierce the dark curtain of inevitable destruction and to see a future in which righteousness will stem from a people purified of its sins by its suffering and will spread over all the earth till "nation will no longer take up sword against nation."

This vision of the righteous king spreading the message of peace and the knowledge of God remained clear in the minds of later prophets and was extended in the works of the "second" Isaiah, the unknown exilic prophet, whose writings were quite properly appended to the prophecies of Isaiah of Jerusalem. According to the second Isaiah the prince of peace, the source of the world's blessing, is no longer to be an individual, a royal descendant on the throne of David, but the entire people of Israel, purified in exile, becoming a light unto the nations.

SYNOPSIS OF TEXT

The arrangement of the verses in the following synopsis, and in the synopsis of the words of the other prophets, does not imply that the order given is the original order and that the present order in the Bible is the result of erroneous misplacement. Of course, in some cases this may be true. The only reason that a verse is taken from a later chapter and quoted after an earlier chapter is that it makes the sequence of thought clearer. In the full detailed expression of his utterance, the prophet may frequently revert to thoughts which he had originally stated and thus may repeat (as is natural in all public addresses and in writing), but in a short epitome such as we are giving, such restatements would be confusing. Therefore, the best statements of a certain idea of the prophet are placed together even though in the book itself they are widely scattered.

A.   Hear, O heavens, and give ear, O earth,
      For the Lord hath spoken:
      Children I have reared, and brought up,
      And they have rebelled against Me.

The ox knoweth his owner,
And the ass his master's crib;
But Israel doth not know,
My people doth not consider.
Ah sinful nation,
A people laden with iniquity,
A seed of evil-doers,
Children that deal corruptly;
They have forsaken the Lord,
They have contemned the Holy One of Israel,
They are turned away backward. –1:2-4.

B.   To what purpose is the multitude of your sacrifices unto
         Me,
Saith the Lord;
I am full of the burnt-offerings of ram,
And the fat of fed beasts;
And I delight not in the blood
Of bullocks, or of lambs, or of he-goats.
When ye come to appear before Me,
Who hath required this at your hand,
To trample My courts?
Bring no more vain oblations;
It is an offering of abomination unto Me;
New moon and sabbath, the holding of convocations—
I cannot endure iniquity along with the solemn assembly. . . .
And when ye spread forth your hands,
I will hide Mine eyes from you;
Yea, when ye make many prayers,
I will not hear;
Your hands are full of blood.
Wash you, make you clean,
Put away the evil of your doings
From before Mine eyes,
Cease to do evil;
Learn to do well;
Seek justice, relieve the oppressed,
Judge the fatherless, plead for the widow. –1:11, 12, 13, 15-
    17.

C.   Let me sing of my well-beloved,
A song of my beloved touching his vineyard.
My well-beloved had a vineyard
In a very fruitful hill; . . .
And he looked that it should bring forth grapes,
And it brought forth wild grapes. . . .
For the vineyard of the Lord of hosts is the house of Israel,
And the men of Judah the plant of His delight;
And he looked for justice, but behold violence;
For righteousness, but behold a cry. . . .
Therefore My people are gone into captivity.
For want of knowledge;
And their honourable men are famished,
And their multitude are parched with thirst. . . .
And man is bowed down,
And man is humbled,
And the eyes of the lofty are humbled;
But the Lord of hosts is exalted through justice,
And God the Holy One is sanctified through righteousness.
        −5:1, 2, 7, 13, 15, 16.

D.   In the year that king Uzziah died I saw the Lord sitting upon a throne high and lifted up, and His train filled the temple.
Above Him stood the seraphim; . . .
And one called unto another, and said:
    Holy, holy, holy, is the Lord of hosts;
    The whole earth is full of His glory. . . .
Then said I:
    Woe is me! for I am undone;
    Because I am a man of unclean lips,
    And I dwell in the midst of a people of unclean lips;
    For mine eyes have seen the King.
    The Lord of hosts. . . .
And I heard the voice of the Lord, saying:
    Whom shall I send,
    And who will go for us?
Then I said: 'Here am I; send me.'
And He said: 'Go, and tell this people:
    Hear ye indeed, but understand not;

And see ye indeed, but perceive not. . . .
Then said I: 'Lord, how long?'
And He answered:
    'Until cities be waste without inhabitant,
    And houses without man,
    And the land become utterly waste. . . .'– 6: 1-3, 5, 8, 9, 11.

E.   And it came to pass in the days of Ahaz the son of Jotham,
the son of Uzziah, king of Judah, that Rezin the king of Aram,
and Pekah the son of Remaliah, king of Israel, went up to Jerusalem
to war against it; but could not prevail against it. And it was told
the house of David, saying: 'Aram is confederate with Ephraim.'
And his heart was moved, and the heart of his people, as the trees
of the forest are moved with the wind.

    Then said the Lord unto Isaiah: 'Go forth now to meet Ahaz . . .
and say unto him: Keep calm, and be quiet; fear not, neither let
thy heart be faint, . . .
    If ye will not have faith, surely ye shall not be established.' . . .
    Forasmuch as this people hath refused
    The waters of Shiloah that go softly,
    And rejoiceth with Rezin and Remaliah's son;
    Now therefore, behold, the Lord bringeth up upon them
    The waters of the River, mighty and many,
    Even the king of Assyria and all his glory;
    And he shall come up over all his channels,
    And go over all his banks; . . .
    O Asshur, the rod of Mine anger,
    In whose hand as a staff is Mine indignation!
    I do send him against an ungodly nation,
    And against the people of My wrath do I give him a charge,
    To take the spoil, and to take the prey,
    And to tread them down like the mire of the streets. . . .
Wherefore it shall come to pass, that when the Lord hath
performed His whole work upon mount Zion and on Jerusalem, I will punish the fruit of the arrogant heart of the
king of Assyria, and the glory of his haughty looks. For he
hath said:
    By the strength of my hand I have done it,
    And by my wisdom, for I am prudent;

In that I have removed the bounds of the peoples,
And have robbed their treasures,
And I have brought down as one mighty the inhabitants.
 — 7:1-4, 9; 8:6, 7; 10:5, 6, 12, 13.

F.   And it shall come to pass in that day,
That the remnant of Israel,
And they that are escaped of the house of Jacob,
Shall no more again stay upon him that smote them;
But shall stay upon the Lord, the Holy One of Israel, in
    truth,
A remnant shall return, even the remnant of Jacob,
Unto God the Mighty.
For though thy people, O Israel, be as the sand of the sea,
Only a remnant of them shall return; . . .
And it shall come to pass in that day,
That the Lord will set His hand again the second time
To recover the remnant of His people,
That shall remain from Assyria, and from Egypt. . . .
And He will set up an ensign for the nations,
And will assemble the dispersed of Israel,
And gather together the scattered of Judah
From the four corners of the earth. — 10:20-22; 11:11, 12.

G.   The people that walked in darkness
Have seen a great light;
They that dwelt in the land of the shadow of death,
Upon them hath the light shined. . . .
For a child is born unto us,
A son is given unto us;
And the government is upon his shoulder;
And his name is called
'Wonderful in counsel is God the Mighty,
The everlasting Father, the Ruler of peace';
That the government may be increased,
And of peace there be no end,
Upon the throne of David, and upon his kingdom,
To establish it, and to uphold it
Through justice and through righteousness

From henceforth even for ever. . . .
And there shall come forth a shoot out of the stock of Jesse,
And a twig shall grow forth out of his roots.
And the spirit of the Lord shall rest upon him,
The spirit of wisdom and understanding,
The spirit of counsel and might,
The spirit of knowledge and of the fear of the Lord.
And his delight shall be in the fear of the Lord;
And he shall not judge after the sight of his eyes,
Neither decide after the hearing of his ears;
But with righteousness shall he judge the poor,
And decide with equity for the meek of the land; . . .
And the wolf shall dwell with the lamb,
And the leopard shall lie down with the kid;
And the calf and the young lion and the fatling together;
And a little child shall lead them. . . .
They shall not hurt nor destroy
In all My holy mountain;
For the earth shall be full of the knowledge of the Lord,
As the waters cover the sea. . . .
And it shall come to pass in the end of days,
That the mountain of the Lord's house shall be established as
    the top of the mountains,
And shall be exalted above the hills;
And all nations shall flow unto it.
And many peoples shall go and say:
'Come ye, and let us go up to the mountain of the Lord,
To the house of the God of Jacob;
And He will teach us of His ways,
And we will walk in His paths.'
For out of Zion shall go forth the law,
And the word of the Lord from Jerusalem.
And He shall judge between the nations,
And shall decide for many peoples;
And they shall beat their swords into plowshares,
And their spears into pruning-hooks;
Nation shall not lift up sword against nation,
Neither shall they learn war any more. – 9:1, 5, 6; 11:1-4, 6,
    9; 2:2-4.

COMMENTARY

A.   As Amos, the first of the literary prophets, had said, Israel had received special training from God and should, therefore, be especially righteous, hence, "I will visit your iniquities upon you"; so Isaiah says, I have reared Israel as a child of mine but they have rebelled against me; they have become children that deal corruptly.

B.   As Amos denounced over-reliance upon ritual as a means of discharging one's obligation to God, "I hate, I despise your feasts . . . though ye offer me burnt offerings I will not accept them . . . but let justice well up as water and righteousness as a mighty stream" (Amos 5:21-24), so Isaiah here denounces the reliance of the people upon ritual: "To what purpose the multitude of your sacrifices unto Me; I delight not in the blood of bullocks." This scorn for the ritual runs through the entire succession of literary prophecy, but there is some doubt or disagreement as to exactly what the Prophets meant by it. Some critical scholars are inclined to believe that the Prophets were entirely opposed to the sacrificial cult as a mode of worship, saying that God did not ask of the people this sort of sacrifice. Yet this hardly seems to be a justified conclusion. After all, the offering of sacrifices was not the only mode of worship which the Prophets denounced. Amos also says, "Take away from me the noise of thy songs. Let me not hear the melody of thy psalteries." Are we to conclude from that denunciation that the Prophet opposed vocal and instrumental music in worship? Isaiah, when he denounces the sacrifices, also says, "Who hath required this at your hand to trample My courts?" He also speaks slightingly of "new moon and Sabbath." Are we then to conclude that Isaiah was opposed to people coming to God's court to worship or that he did not believe in the celebration of special sacred days, like new moons and Sabbaths? He also says, "When ye make many prayers I will not hear." Are we to conclude that the Prophet was opposed to prayer as a mode of worship? Surely not.

What the Prophets clearly opposed was the superstitious idea that these ritual observances, if scrupulously followed, would in themselves make up for injustice and evil. Isaiah says it clearly: "I cannot endure iniquity along with the solemn assembly." Also: "When ye make many prayers, I will not hear; your hands are full

of blood." The Prophets were concerned chiefly with righteousness. They did not oppose ritual as such; they did oppose mere ritual unaccompanied by sanctity. Thus too did later generations
understand their message, for many of these very denunciatory passages from the Prophets were embodied as part of the regular ritual. As, for example, the denunciation of the Prophet (Isaiah 58)
against fasting was introduced into the Yom Kippur service, where
fasting was an important part of the ritual. The early post-prophetic
generations understood the Prophets better than many modern critics do. They realized that the Prophets meant that righteousness is
essential. No ritual can make up for unrighteousness, but obviously
the Prophets did not oppose sacrifices, songs, solemn assemblies and
prayers when righteous people participated in such worship.

C.   When Amos said, "You only have I known from among all
people, therefore I will visit your iniquities upon you" (3:2), he
did not mean to deny his basic principle that the God of Justice
seeks justice equally among all peoples, but he meant to say that
Israel, taught by the Lord, should be all the more just and that
therefore, when unjust, merits greater punishment. So Isaiah taught
that God's love extends to all mankind, but Israel, whom God
taught and lovingly raised like a plant, should, like the good vine,
have produced noble grapes, but has produced only wild grapes
and hence will be especially punished.

D.   The conception of God which appeals most to Isaiah, to
which he reverts time and again throughout his prophecies, is that
of the pure holiness of God. For that reason the uncleanliness of the
people glares in sharp contrast. Sin is a visible, ugly defilement.
Hence the Prophet says, "Wash yourselves; make yourselves clean."

E.   Here is described the Prophet's conviction as to the proper
policy for this small nation in a world of turmoil. It must learn
where its strength really is. It is a mistake to imagine that by political adroitness it can find security. There is no use making alliance
with Assyria against Aram or with Egypt against Assyria. The only
strength is inner strength. A nation that has inner faith in God and
follows righteousness in its action can outlast calamity and will endure. God works through history. Assyria, the great conquering

power, is God's instrument: "O Asshur, rod of Mine anger." Assyria, God's rod, will serve to prove the helplessness and the worthlessness of all the idols of all the nations whom Assyria will destroy. And then Assyria, in its arrogance and pride, will itself be destroyed.

F.   Perhaps Judah will be unable by military strength to resist the great conqueror Assyria, but if the people maintain their moral strength they cannot be wholly destroyed. A remnant will always remain to become the nucleus for the future.

G.   This remnant returning will build the hope of mankind. A righteous king, a descendant born to the house of David, will establish his throne in wisdom, understanding, and righteousness. From Jerusalem, always the beloved city, now the world-revered center of God's spirit of justice and mercy, will become the source of blessing for all people. "All nations shall flow unto it." "Nation shall not lift up sword against nation." "Out of Zion shall go forth the laws of justice." "And the earth shall be filled with the knowledge of God as the waters cover the sea."

DEUTERO-ISAIAH

GENERAL OUTLINE

There is no prophet whose name was Deutero-Isaiah, but students of Scripture were compelled to invent the name (i.e., the Second Isaiah) for the author of the prophecies which begin with chapter 40 of our present Book of Isaiah and go on for at least fifteen chapters. It has long been recognized by scholars as far back as Abraham ibn Ezra in the eleventh century that the later parts of the present Book of Isaiah were written after the time of the First Isaiah. The Talmud itself does not say that Isaiah wrote this entire book. These chapters refer to Israel's exile as an accomplished fact, as having lasted for a long time and now drawing to a close. They speak of Cyrus, the Persian king who lived at the time of the end of the Exile and overthrew the Babylonian kingdom.

These prophecies, written in the Exile long after the time of the First Isaiah, were, for some reason, appended by some editor or scribe to a book of the prophecies of the Isaiah who lived centuries earlier. No name of the author is given. Therefore we can only say the "unknown prophet," or call him the "Second Isaiah," or "Deutero-Isaiah," although there is not the slightest reason to believe that Isaiah was his name.

The entire background of the preachment of Deutero-Isaiah is different from that of Amos and the earlier prophets. Most of them, especially Amos, spoke in a period of national independence and social luxury. Deutero-Isaiah spoke in a period of exile and misery. Since it was characteristic of the Prophets never to be misled by outer circumstances but to look to the roots of the present in order to understand the development of the future, Amos, who saw the luxury of the northern kingdom, predicted its collapse and exile, while Deutero-Isaiah, who lived in the time of exile, predicted the end of exile and Israel's redemption. There is, therefore, a jubilant note in Deutero-Isaiah in sharp contrast to the somberness in Amos and the earlier prophets. Amos and the earlier prophets point out the many iniquities of the people and their rulers. Deutero-Isaiah speaks of their moral purification in the suffering they have endured. In Amos and the earlier prophets, the prophet was a lonely man, speaking at God's command to the people, enduring suffering because of his message, but obeying the mandate nevertheless to speak God's truth. In Deutero-Isaiah the Prophet as a personality seems to have disappeared. There is no mention of personal experience as in Amos ("I am a herdsman, and God commanded me to speak to my people Israel"). Instead, the role of the prophet ceases to be confined to an individual and becomes the role of the entire people. It is Israel now, purified by suffering, who has God's mandate to go forth and be a light unto the nations. In the triumph of prophecy, the whole nation becomes a prophetic people.

SYNOPSIS OF TEXT

A.   Comfort ye, comfort ye My people,
Saith your God.
Bid Jerusalem take heart,
And proclaim unto her,
That her time of service is accomplished,
That her guilt is paid off;
That she hath received of the Lord's hand
Double for all her sins. . . .

Hark! one calleth:
Clear ye in the wilderness the way of the Lord, . . .
O thou that tellest good tidings to Jerusalem,
Lift up thy voice with strength;
Lift it up, be not afraid;
Say unto the cities of Judah:
'Behold your God!'—40: 1-3, 8, 9.

B.   Why sayest thou, O Jacob,
And speakest, O Israel:
'My way is hid from the Lord,
And my right is passed over from my God'?
Hast thou not known? hast thou not heard
That the everlasting God, the Lord,
The Creator of the ends of the earth,
Fainteth not, neither is weary?
His discernment is past searching out. . . .
They that wait for the Lord shall renew their strength;
They shall mount up with wings as eagles;
They shall run, and not be weary;
They shall walk, and not faint.—40: 27, 28, 31.

C.   Lift up your eyes on high,
And see: who hath created these?
He that bringeth out their host by number,
He calleth them all by name; . . .
To whom then will ye liken God?
Or what likeness will ye compare unto Him?
The image perchance, which the craftsman hath melted,
And the goldsmith spread over with gold,
The silversmith casting silver chains? . . .
Ye that hire a goldsmith, that he make it a god,
To fall down thereto, yea, to worship.
He is borne upon the shoulder, he is carried,
And set in his place, . . .
Yea, though one cry unto him, he cannot answer,
Nor save him out of his trouble. —40: 26, 18, 19; 46: 6b-7.

D.   I have roused up one from the north, and he is come,

From the rising of the sun one that calleth upon My name;
And he shall come upon rulers as upon mortar,
And as the potter treadeth clay. . . .
Thus saith the Lord to His anointed,
To Cyrus, whose right hand I have holden,
To subdue nations before him, . . .
For the sake of Jacob My servant,
And Israel Mine elect,
I have called thee by thy name,
I have surnamed thee, though thou hast not known Me.
—41:25; 45:1, 4.

E. Come down, and sit in the dust,
O virgin daughter of Babylon,
Sit on the ground without a throne, . . .
For thou shalt no more be called
The mistress of kingdoms.
I was wroth with My people, . . .
And gave them into thy hand;
Thou didst show them no mercy;
Upon the aged hast thou very heavily
Laid thy yoke. — 47:1, 5, 6.

F. Behold My servant, whom I uphold;
Mine elect, in whom My soul delighteth;
I have put My spirit upon him,
He shall make the right to go forth to the nations. . . .
He shall make the right to go forth according to the truth. . . .
I the Lord have called thee in righteousness,
And have taken hold of thy hand,
And kept thee, and set thee for a covenant of the people,
For a light of the nations; . . .
Yea, He saith: 'It is too light a thing that thou shouldest be
    My servant
To raise up the tribes of Jacob,
And to restore the offspring of Israel;
I will also give thee for a light of the nations,
That My salvation may be unto the end of the earth.'
—42:1-3, 6; 49:6.

G.   But Zion said: 'The Lord hath forsaken me,
And the Lord hath forgotten me.'
Can a woman forget her sucking child,
That she should not have compassion on the son of her
    womb?
Yea, these may forget,
Yet will not I forget thee. . . .
Thus saith the Lord God:
Behold, I will lift up My hand to the nations,
And set up Mine ensign to the peoples,
And they shall bring thy sons in their bosom,
And thy daughters shall be carried upon their shoulders.
    —49:14, 15, 22.

H.   Hearken to Me, ye that follow after righteousness,
Ye that seek the Lord;
Look unto the rock whence ye were hewn,
And to the hole of the pit whence ye were digged.
Look unto Abraham your father,
And unto Sarah that bore you;
For when he was but one I called him,
And I blessed him, and made him many. . . .
But thou, Israel, My servant,
Jacob whom I have chosen,
The seed of Abraham My friend; . . .
And said unto thee: 'Thou art My servant,
I have chosen thee and not cast thee away';
Fear thou not, for I am with thee,
Be not dismayed, for I am thy God;
I strengthen thee, yea, I help thee;—51:1-2; 41:8-10.

I.   Remember these things, O Jacob,
And Israel, for thou art My servant;
I have formed thee, thou art Mine own servant;
O Israel, thou shouldest not forget Me.
I have blotted out, as a thick cloud, thy transgressions,
And, as a cloud, thy sins;
Return unto Me, for I have redeemed thee. . . .
Behold, I have refined thee, but not as silver;

I have tried thee in the furnace of affliction. – 44:21-22;
   48:10.

J.   He was despised, and forsaken of men,
A man of pains, and acquainted with disease,
And as one from whom men hide their face:
He was despised, and we esteemed him not.
Surely our diseases he did bear, and our pains he carried; . . .
All we like sheep did go astray,
We turned every one to his own way;
And the Lord hath made to light on him
The iniquity of us all. . . .
Yet it pleased the Lord to crush him by disease;
To see if his soul would offer itself in restitution,
That he might see his seed, prolong his days,
And that the purpose of the Lord might prosper by his
   hand. – 53:3, 4, 6, 10.

COMMENTARY

A.   In contrast to the earlier prophets, who predicted the coming of the Exile, Deutero-Isaiah predicts the ending of the Exile and preaches consolation.

B.   The exiles are, of course, discouraged. They think God has forgotten them, to which the Prophet says, trust in the Lord; your strength and courage will return.

C.   God is great and can be trusted to deliver them. He is the only God. All the idols are as nothing. An important contrast is to be noted between the treatment of idolatry in the earlier prophets and its treatment in Deutero-Isaiah. All the Prophets oppose idolatry. It is an essential part of their messages. But the earlier prophets mention specific idols—Baal, and the queen of heaven—and specific modes of worship—groves, high places, human sacrifice, etc. All this specific mention has vanished from Deutero-Isaiah. No names, no modes of worship are specifically referred to. It is no longer necessary. The idolatry has now become something vague and distant. The Prophets are winning their battle. Israel is being emancipated from the Baalim and the other gods and their worship. The Prophet now discusses the matter on theoretical, philosophic grounds. God is All, idols are nothing. The Prophet, speaking of the redemption of Israel from Babylon, reveals their redemption from the sin of idolatry. The specific gods and the specific practices are gone. The Prophet now is able to brush away idolatry as a general belief.

D.   God, the Master of history, calls upon Cyrus, the Persian king, as His messenger, to fulfill His word. So among the earlier prophets Babylon and Assyria were the instruments of God's purpose. "O Asshur, the rod of My anger" (Isaiah 10:5). Cyrus, God's messenger, will redeem Israel.

E.   First Cyrus will destroy Babylon. As Amos wept for the virgin daughter of Israel, doomed to destruction, so Deutero-Isaiah sings a dirge for the Babylonians. It is true that Babylon was an instrument of God's purpose, but she carried out that task in brutality and cruelty. "Thou didst show them no mercy, hence you will now be punished."

F.   As the Prophet was the voice of God to Israel, so Israel now becomes the voice of God to all the nations.

G.   This grand destiny may seem unbelievable to a scattered, exiled people, but the Prophet assures Israel that God has not forgotten them and they shall return.

H.   Even though Israel overcomes the despair of exile, the proffered destiny of being a light to the nations seems too great because Israel is so few in number. Therefore God reminds them that Abraham was only one and yet God called him to his tasks. So: "Fear thou not for I am with you."

I.   And should the consciousness of Israel's own unworthiness assail it and the memory of the sins pointed out by the earlier prophets weaken Israel's faith in itself as God's voice of the world, God answers that He forgives the sins, since they are now purified "in the furnace of affliction."

J.   The task of being God's messenger is a heavy one. As the

Prophets suffered when they spoke to Israel, so Israel will suffer, but the nations will come to realize that Israel has endured suffering in order to redeem mankind. The sins of mankind, corrupting the world, weigh heavily on Israel, but these sufferings too, due to world evil, have helped purify and ennoble the messenger of God.

JEREMIAH

GENERAL OUTLINE

More biographical facts are available about the Prophet Jeremiah than about any other of the literary prophets. Perhaps this is because Jeremiah was the only one of them known to have had a disciple who was also his secretary. It may well have been Baruch, Jeremiah's disciple-scribe, who recorded the many biographical details of Jeremiah's career which we now have in the Book of Jeremiah. Whether this available information was due to Baruch, who devotedly recorded many of the events in the life of his beloved teacher, or whether it just simply so happened, the fact is that not one of the books of the other literary prophets has anywhere near the amount of biographical detail about its author as has the Book of Jeremiah.

We learn, for example, that he belonged to an honored priestly family, perhaps that branch of the priesthood which was descendant of Eli, the family which was the guardian of the Ark. He lived in the city of Anathoth, a few miles from Jerusalem. Evidently even there his tragic and pessimistic preachments must have aroused hostility because we are told that in his native city there were men who sought his death. We hear of the assemblage which was convoked to condemn him to death, and how he escaped. We hear of the many times that he was arrested and placed into a pit or into the stocks, and who rescued him. We are present at the various interviews that he had with priests and officers and the king himself, of his dictating his prophecies twice, and how the first book of prophecies was burnt in anger by the king.

Besides all these biographical data for which Baruch may have been responsible, we learn of his inner history, the emotional life of Jeremiah which no secretary could well record. These inward, emotional moods are revealed by Jeremiah himself. The Prophet was so introspective and so sensitive that many of his prophecies do not concern the people but himself and his sorrows and his disappointments. There are many dialogues between Jeremiah and God. In these plaints directed to God (often called "confessions" by modern scholars) he bemoans the sorrows which are his because he has so tragic a message to preach and because so many people hate him because of it. These outcries of the heart-broken Prophet, who in his deepest sorrows has not lost his faith in God, this lyrical, somber self-expression, were brought into Hebrew literature and perhaps into world literature by this sensitive man who lived in a time of national tragedy. Scores of psalms copy this spirit of the sad plaint of the suffering poet pouring out his sorrows before God. One great modern scholar (Wellhausen) says that the Psalms could never have been written if Jeremiah had not lived. It is not only the Psalms that show the influence of the profound and solemn introspection and self-expression of Jeremiah, but also the Book of Job, the great philosophic tragedy of Scripture, which repeats and develops themes found in this book. The Prophet's wish that he had never been born, the deep and bitter question as to why the righteous suffer and the evil prosper: all these ideas of Jeremiah are repeated in the Book of Job.

It was indeed a heart-breaking time for a brooding, sensitive man, compelled by the command of God to proclaim the tragic truths in the midst of a people bitter and broken-hearted by their imminent fate. The other prophets before Jeremiah also lived in times of trouble, but the troubles did not seem quite insurmountable. They did indeed preach that if the people did not repent, the destruction and the exile of the nation would inevitably ensue. But they were predicting a future event. Jeremiah saw the destruction, not as a future event, but as a rapidly approaching tragedy. He lived during the last days of the Hebrew commonwealth. In his time he saw the good King Josiah killed. He saw Josiah's son, Shalum (also called Yehoyahaz) captured by the Egyptians. He saw the Babylonian armies capture Jerusalem (in the year 597 B.C.E.) and take the young King Yehoyachin captive to Babylon together with a large number of priests and nobles. He saw the last king of Judah, Zedekiah, who was placed on the throne by the Babylonian king, rebel against his Babylonian master with the result that the city was besieged again, captured a second time, and this time the Temple destroyed and the Jewish state overthrown (586 B.C.E.).

He knew the bitter taste of exile and died either in Egypt or Babylon, we know not which.

This sensitive man, seeing destruction rapidly approaching, was compelled by his prophetic mandate to take away the last pathetic illusions of his people, to compel them to face the inescapable national destruction and to understand the part which their own evil had played. He is the most tragic, the most somber, the most expressive of all the Prophets. Yet his doctrine, though deeply personal, is harmonious with that of all the Prophets who preceded him. He is called to prophecy; he cannot escape the bitter task. He is commanded to announce the destruction of the people. He speaks as they all do of Israel's turning away from God toward the idols and toward moral evil. In his description of Israel's relationship to God, he takes up the theme first expressed by the Prophet Hosea, of the family relationship between Israel and God. Israel is symbolized as a beloved wife who abandons her husband and goes astray. This theme will be continued by the Prophet Ezekiel and later by Deutero-Isaiah. For the sin of betrayal, destruction is inevitable. There is no value in self-delusion, in crying, "Peace, peace," when there is no peace, or in seeking political alliances. Nothing will avert the destruction.

But God loves Israel "with an everlasting love" and Israel will be restored. God will make a new covenant with them to take the place of the covenant of old which they had broken. The new covenant will endure: "It will be written in their hearts." And Israel will never again, after its restoration, be parted from God.

SYNOPSIS OF TEXT

A.   And the word of the Lord came unto me, saying: . . . before thou camest forth out of the womb I sanctified thee; I have appointed thee a prophet unto the nations.
Then I said: 'Ah, Lord God! Behold, I cannot speak; for I am a child.' But the Lord said unto me:
Say not: I am a child;
For to whomsoever I shall send thee thou shalt go,
And whatsoever I shall command thee thou shalt speak. . . .
See, I have this day set thee over the nations and over the kingdoms,

To root out and to pull down,
And to destroy and to overthrow;
To build, and to plant. —1:4-7, 10.

B.   Woe is me, my mother, that thou hast borne me
A man of strife and a man of contention to the
        whole earth!
I have not lent, neither have men lent to me;
Yet every one of them doth curse me. . . .
O Lord, Thou hast enticed me, and I was enticed,
Thou hast overcome me, and hast prevailed;
I am become a laughing-stock all the day,
Every one mocketh me.
For as often as I speak, I cry out,
I cry: 'Violence and spoil';
Because the word of the Lord is made
A reproach unto me, and a derision, all the day.
Cursed be the day
Wherein I was born;
The day wherein my mother bore me,
Let it not be blessed. . . .
Wherefore came I forth out of the womb
To see labour and sorrow,
That my days should be consumed in shame? . . .
My heart moaneth within me!
I cannot hold my peace!
Because thou hast heard, O my soul, the sound of
        the horn,
The alarm of war.
Destruction followeth upon destruction,
For the whole land is spoiled; . . .
How long shall I see the standard,
Shall I hear the sound of the horn? . . .
Is there no balm in Gilead?
Is there no physician there?
Why then is not the health
Of the daughter of my people recovered?
Oh that my head were waters,
And mine eyes a fountain of tears,

That I might weep day and night
For the slain of the daughter of my people –15:10; 20:7, 8,
    14, 18; 4:19b-21; 8:22, 23.

C.   1 Heal me, O Lord, and I shall be healed;
    2 Save me, and I shall be saved;
    3 For Thou art my praise.
    4 Behold, they say unto me:
    5 'Where is the word of the Lord? let it come now.'
    6 As for me, I have not hastened from being a shepherd after
       Thee;
    7 Neither have I desired the woeful day; Thou knowest it;
    8 That which came out of my lips was manifest before Thee.
    9 Be not a ruin unto me;
   10 Thou art my refuge in the day of evil.
   11 Let them be ashamed that persecute me, but let not me
       be ashamed;
   12 Let them be dismayed, but let not me be dismayed; . . .
       –17:14-18.

D.   I have forsaken My house,
     I have cast off My heritage;
     I have given the dearly beloved of My soul
     Into the hand of her enemies.
     My heritage is become unto Me
     As a lion in the forest;
     She hath uttered her voice against Me;
     Therefore have I hated her. . . .–12:7, 8.

E.   1 Hear ye the word of the Lord, O house of Jacob,
    2 And all the families of the house of Israel: Thus saith the
       Lord:
    3 What unrighteousness have your fathers found in Me,
    4 That they are gone far from Me,
    5 And have walked after things of nought, and are become
       nought? . . .
    6 The priests said not: 'Where is the Lord?'
    7 And they that handle the law knew Me not,
    8 And the rulers transgressed against Me;

9 The prophets also prophesied by Baal,
10 And walked after things that do not profit. . . .
11 And they have healed the hurt of the daughter of My people
   lightly,
12 Saying: 'Peace, peace,' when there is no peace. . . .
13 Wherefore I will yet plead with you, saith the Lord,
14 And with your children's children will I plead. . . .
15 They have forsaken Me, the fountain of living waters,
16 And hewed them out cisterns, broken cisterns,
17 That can hold no water.
18 . . . Have I been a wilderness unto Israel?
19 Or a land of thick darkness?
20 Wherefore say My people: 'We roam at large;
21 We will come no more unto Thee'? . . .
22 Also in thy skirts is found the blood
23 Of the souls of the innocent poor; . . .
24 For My people is foolish,
25 They know Me not;
26 They are sottish children,
27 And they have no understanding;
28 They are wise to do evil,
29 But to do good they have no knowledge. . . .
30 Woe unto him that buildeth his house by unrighteousness,
31 And his chambers by injustice;
32 That useth his neighbour's service without wages,
33 And giveth him not his hire;
34 That saith: 'I will build me a wide house
35 And spacious chambers,'
36 And cutteth him out windows,
37 And it is ceiled with cedar, and painted with vermilion.
38 Shalt thou reign, because thou strivest to excel in cedar?
39 Did not thy father eat and drink, and do justice and righteousness?
40 Then it was well with him. . . .
41 But thine eyes and thy heart
42 Are not but for thy covetousness,
43 And for shedding innocent blood,
44 And for oppression, and for violence, to do it. – 2:4, 5, 8, 9;
   8:11; 2:13, 31, 34; 4:22; 22:13, 14, 15, 17.

F.   The word that came to Jeremiah from the Lord, saying: Stand in the gate of the Lord's house, and proclaim there this word, and say: Hear the word of the Lord, all ye of Judah, that enter in at these gates to worship the Lord. Thus saith the Lord of hosts, the God of Israel:

Amend your ways and your doings, and I will cause you to dwell in this place. Trust ye not in lying words, saying: 'The temple of the Lord, the temple of the Lord, the temple of the Lord, are these.' Nay, but if ye thoroughly amend your ways and your doings; if ye thoroughly execute justice between a man and his neighbour; if ye oppress not the stranger, the fatherless, and the widow, and shed not innocent blood in this place, neither walk after other gods to your hurt; then will I cause you to dwell in this place, in the land that I gave to your fathers, for ever and ever. Behold, ye trust in lying words, that cannot profit. Will ye steal, murder, and commit adultery, and swear falsely, and offer unto Baal, and walk after other gods whom ye have not known, and come and stand before Me in this house, whereupon My name is called, and say: 'We are delivered,' that ye may do all these abominations? Is this house, whereupon my name is called, become a den of robbers in your eyes? ... And I will cast you out of My sight, as I have cast out all your brethren, even the whole seed of Ephraim. – 7:1-11, 15.

G.   How greatly dost thou cheapen thyself
      To change thy way?
      Thou shalt be ashamed of Egypt also,
      As thou wast ashamed of Asshur.
      From him also shalt thou go forth,
      With thy hands upon thy head;
      For the Lord hath rejected them in whom thou didst trust,
      And thou shalt not prosper in them. – 2:36-37.

H.   1 O Jerusalem, wash thy heart from wickedness,
     2 That thou mayest be saved.
     3 How long shall thy baleful thoughts
     4 Lodge within thee? ...
     5 Be thou corrected, O Jerusalem,
     6 Lest My soul be alienated from thee,

7 Lest I make thee desolate,
9 A land not inhabited. . . .
9 Can the Ethiopian change his skin,
10 Or the leopard his spots?
11 Then may ye also do good,
12 That are accustomed to do evil . . .
13 O Lord, I know that man's way is not his own;
14 It is not in man to direct his steps as he walketh. – 4:14; 6:8;
13:23; 10:23.

I.   Go, and cry in the ears of Jerusalem, saying: Thus saith
the Lord:
I remember for thee the affection of thy youth,
The love of thine espousals;
How thou wentest after Me in the wilderness,
In a land that was not sown.
Israel is the Lord's hallowed portion,
His first-fruits of the increase;
All that devour him shall be held guilty,
Evil shall come upon them,
Saith the Lord. . . .
Surely as a wife treacherously departeth from her husband,
So have ye dealt treacherously with Me, O house of Israel,
Saith the Lord. . . .
Didst thou not just now cry unto Me: 'My father,
Thou art the friend of my youth. . . .'
Is Ephraim a darling son unto Me?
Is he a child that is dandled?
For as often as I speak of him,
I do earnestly remember him still;
Therefore My heart yearneth for him,
I will surely have compassion upon him, saith the Lord.
– 2:2-3; 3:20; 3:4; 31:20.

J.   Thus saith the Lord:
The people that were left of the sword
Have found grace in the wilderness,
Even Israel, when I go to cause him to rest.
'From afar the Lord appeared unto me.'

'Yea, I have loved thee with an everlasting love;
Therefore with affection have I drawn thee.
Again will I build thee, and thou shalt be built, . . .'
Hear the word of the Lord, O ye nations,
And declare it in the isles afar off, and say:
'He that scattered Israel doth gather him,
And keep him, as a shepherd doth his flock.'
For the Lord hath ransomed Jacob,
And he redeemeth him from the hand of him that is stronger
    than he. . . .
Thus saith the Lord:
A voice is heard in Ramah,
Lamentation, and bitter weeping,
Rachel weeping for her children;
She refuseth to be comforted for her children,
Because they are not.
Thus saith the Lord:
Refrain thy voice from weeping,
And thine eyes from tears;
For thy work shall be rewarded, saith the Lord;
And they shall come back from the land of the enemy.
And there is hope for thy future, saith the Lord;
And thy children shall return to their own border. – 31:2-4a,
    10, 11, 15, 16, 17.

K.   Build ye houses, and dwell in them, and plant gardens, and eat the fruit of them; take ye wives, and beget sons and daughters; and take wives for your sons, and give your daughters to husbands, that they may bear sons and daughters; and multiply ye there, and be not diminished. And seek the peace of the city whither I have caused you to be carried away captive, and pray unto the Lord for it; for in the peace thereof shall ye have peace.

Behold, the days come, saith the Lord, that I will make a new covenant with the house of Israel, and with the house of Judah; not according to the covenant that I made with their fathers in the day that I took them by the hand to bring them out of the land of Egypt; forasmuch as they broke My covenant, although I was a lord over them, saith the Lord. But this is the covenant that I will make with the house of Israel after those days, saith the

Lord, I will put My law in their inward parts, and in their heart will I write it; and I will be their God, and they shall be My people; and they shall teach no more every man his neighbour, and every man his brother, saying: 'Know the Lord'; for they shall all know Me, from the least of them unto the greatest of them, saith the Lord; for I will forgive their iniquity, and their sin will I remember no more. – 29:5-7; 31:31-34.

COMMENTARY

A.   The Prophet is destined for his task. He cannot escape it. Isaiah complained (Isaiah, chapter 6) that he was unworthy to be the voice of the holy God. Jeremiah here complains that he is too immature to be the bearer of God's words. But the Prophet receives the mandate. He cannot evade it.

B.   How bitter it is to live at such a time! The Prophet wishes he had never been born to see the destruction of his people. Is there none to heal them? Is there no medicine in Gilead or no physician? Because of the nation's present sorrow and coming sorrow, he would weep "day and night" for the slain of his people.

C.   The prophetic task is difficult not only because he is saddened by having to prophesy a woeful day, but because people hate him for his tragic message. He asks that God heal him and save him from their hatred.

D.   God, as it were, is Himself grieved. He voices His infinite sorrow that His beloved Israel must be destroyed.

E.   The sins of the people, their abandoning God for idols, their persecution of the innocent, their living in luxury are here described.

F.   The Prophet calls upon the people not to deceive themselves by false optimism. The only possible hope, that God may yet save them, may come if they repent: "If ye oppress not the fatherless and the widow." But how can they imagine that if they "steal, murder and offer unto Baal" that they may yet be delivered?

G.   In vain it is that Israel tries to evade the coming destruction by means of alliances with Egypt and with Asshur. Here the Prophet takes up the leading theme of his predecessor, Isaiah: the folly of political maneuvers when the only real security is the inner moral strength to endure an evil time.

H.   He pleads again for Israel's repentance but fears that his pleading is in vain: "Can the leopard change his spots?"

I.   But God remembers his love for Israel in spite of its treachery to Him; God still thinks of Ephraim as a darling son and will have compassion.

J.   After the destruction, God's love will again assert itself and Israel will be gathered. Let mother Rachel cease to weep. Her children will return from the land of the enemy. Isaiah also speaks of the restoration, but it is as a saving remnant which will be the seed of growth. Jeremiah seems to emphasize a return of all the exiles.

K.   God will make a new covenant with Israel. The old covenant was broken by Israel. The new one will be unbreakable, being written in the heart. Isaiah, in his thought of the future, speaks of a world at peace, knowing the Lord; Jeremiah speaks of a people eternally possessing the presence of God in its heart. Isaiah is the spiritual statesman; Jeremiah is the visionary mystic.

EZEKIEL

GENERAL OUTLINE

The Prophet Ezekiel lived among the exiles in Babylon. He was brought there in the first exile, when the young King Yehoyachin was captured by the Babylonians during the first of the two Babylonian conquests of Jerusalem (597 B.C.E.). The king and many of the nobles, the priests and the other leaders of the community were carried away to Babylon. Meanwhile, the shriveled-up Jewish state, a small territory around the capital city of Jerusalem, continued under the rulership of Zedekiah, Yehoyachin's uncle, whom the Babylonian king had established as a vassal monarch. This ghostlike existence of Jerusalem, quasi-independent, continued for eleven years, until the year 586 B.C.E., when, after a rebellion by Zedekiah, the Babylonians again captured the city, finally destroyed the

Temple, left Jerusalem in ruins and took Zedekiah with the rest of the leaders of the community to Babylon, where they joined their predecessors in exile.

It was during this eleven-year period when Jeremiah was preaching in the doomed city of Jerusalem that Ezekiel was preaching to the first group of exiles in Babylon. Ezekiel continued his preachments after the final destruction of Jerusalem in the second and complete exile. Thus he was a later contemporary of Jeremiah, the early part of his career overlapping the later part of Jeremiah's career. In contrast with our relatively complete knowledge of the personal career of Jeremiah, we know very little about the biography of Ezekiel, the Prophet of the Exile. As was suggested, we know much more about Jeremiah because his disciple and secretary, Baruch, may well have been responsible for the many historical, biographical notes concerning the Prophet which we find in his book. But Ezekiel had no secretary, and, like the Prophets, was more concerned with God's message than with his own adventures and experiences.

However, some few biographical facts can be gleaned from the book. Ezekiel belonged to the priesthood of Jerusalem, the descendants of Zadok, as Jeremiah belonged to a priestly family, the descendants of Eli. He was married. His wife died during the Exile. He lived in a village called Tel Aviv on the river Chabar, one of the rivers or canals of Babylon where there was a settlement of the exiles. We know that the elders of the people came frequently to consult him. Already this fact indicates a change in the status of prophecy. Up to the time of Jeremiah the Prophets were perforce lone men. Their prophecy of the inevitable doom alienated them from the people and certainly was contrary to the desire of the ruling classes, who wanted to buoy up the people with visions of victory. Thus the Prophets were scorned by the leaders as dangerous men who broke public morale and by the people as gloomy men who depressed their hearts and denounced them for all sorts of sins. But in the Exile it was evident that the people underwent a change of heart. The very fact that the Exile did come was a vindication of the preachments of the Prophets whom they had scorned at home. The Exile was, in a sense, a triumph of the word of God as spoken through His Prophets. Therefore the people began to turn to the Prophets, a phenomenon which had never occurred before except occasionally in the case of the good King Hezekiah and Isaiah, and once in the case of Zedekiah and Jeremiah. Now the leaders of the people came to Ezekiel and consulted him; for the first time the prophet became an accepted guide, a sort of spiritual pastor.

This change foreshadows the future development of Judaism when prophecy, which at first seemed to be outside the channels of at least official religion, became an important and influential part in later Judaism. In Ezekiel we see the first evidence of the victory of prophecy and the conversion of the people of Israel to prophetic ideas. Thus Ezekiel may be called the first prophet who became an accepted guide, and this in spite of the fact that, in true prophetic tradition, he continued to denounce them for their sins and to call them a "house of rebellion."

As did Isaiah and Jeremiah before him, the prophet Ezekiel describes the great emotions of the moment when he felt the call to become a prophet, and his description of that mystic, ecstatic time seems like a vast and complex elaboration of the vision which Isaiah saw. Isaiah beheld (Isaiah, chapter 6) cherubim standing in the Temple over the throne of God, chanting, "Holy, holy, holy," then the voice of God calling, "Whom shall I send?" and the Prophet answering, "Here am I, send me." This vision in Isaiah is immensely elaborated and complicated in Ezekiel, who describes not only angels but strange creatures, half-human, half-animal, chariots and wheels, the sound of thunder and lightning; but all that vision comes to the same conclusion as does the simpler vision of Isaiah, namely, that God sends the Prophet to speak unto the children of Israel the words which God puts into his heart.

As was the case with Jeremiah, who had to live and preach in a time when Jerusalem was clearly doomed, so it was with Ezekiel. As the people in Jerusalem were hoping for some miraculous victory, so too were these first exiles in Babylon hoping that somehow Jerusalem and the Temple would be spared. But Ezekiel's task, like that of Jeremiah and other literary prophets, was to show that the destruction was inevitable and in harmony with the classic, prophetic doctrine. He indicates that the source of national weakness is in the heart and the behavior of individuals. In the same mood as all his predecessors, he denounces the idolatry and the social injustice of the people.

Like Isaiah and Jeremiah, he sees beyond the smoke and flames of destruction into the clearer air of the coming restoration. In this regard he is closer to Jeremiah than to Isaiah. Isaiah speaks of national restoration following national repentance. Jeremiah, because of his own contemplative, subjective nature, thinks more of the individual's repentance and speaks of God's covenant which will now be written in every heart. This idea of individual, personal spiritual reconstruction appearing in Jeremiah becomes a cornerstone of Ezekiel's thought. To a people crushed by national calamity, feeling helpless because of the great forces unleashed against them, he voices the great message that history depends upon the individual. The nation was guilty; it was punished. But let not any man think that he will be punished for the sins of the past. Let each man now repent and live righteously, and God, "who desireth not the death of the sinner but that he shall return from his sin and live," will abundantly pardon. Out of this regeneration of the individuals of Israel there will come a restoration of the entire people. The latter part of the Book of Ezekiel describes the restoration in full and rich detail. True, as Isaiah said, a descendant of David will be restored to the throne; but it will be God Himself who will be the real king, guiding, teaching and defending His people.

The book is more systematic than the books of his two predecessors, Isaiah and Jeremiah. It evidently was written down by Ezekiel himself and comes to us very much as he wrote it.

It is true that we do not have many biographical details in the book since the Prophet, in all likelihood, wrote the book himself, and the Prophets were not prone to write about themselves; but something of the inner nature of Ezekiel is revealed to us by his book. The richness and detail of his ecstatic visions, richer and more imaginative than that of any of his predecessors, the many symbolic actions which he portrays, the dramatizing of the siege of Jerusalem by building a little wall and laying siege to it, the uniting two sticks to prove the future reunion of the two Jewish kingdoms, Israel and Judah, all these reveal to us that Ezekiel was a man of intense emotion, deep visualizing power, ecstatic, who could see his dreams in vivid, visual image. This much of his individuality is discernible from his writing. He was also the first whose whole known career took place in exile, and the first who was listened to and consulted in friendly spirit by the leaders of the people. Yet the main prophetic message of evil leading to de-struction, righteousness to restoration, idolatry leading to estrange-ment, and that God alone should be accepted as King—all these thoughts which went on from prophet to prophet are clearly voiced in Ezekiel's prophecies. Ezekiel, for all the mystic imagery at the beginning of his book, and all the ritual detail at its end, is in the mainstream of literary prophecy.

SYNOPSIS OF TEXT

A.   In the fifth day of the month, which was the fifth year of king Jehoiachin's captivity, the word of the Lord came expressly unto Ezekiel the priest, the son of Buzi, in the land of the Chaldeans . . . ; and the hand of the Lord was there upon him.

And I looked, and, behold, a stormy wind came out of the north, a great cloud, with a fire flashing up, so that a brightness was round about it; and out of the midst thereof as the colour of electrum, out of the midst of the fire. And out of the midst thereof came the likeness of four living creatures. And this was their appearance: they had the likeness of a man. . . .

And He said unto me: 'Son of man, stand upon thy feet, and I will speak with thee.' And spirit entered into me when He spoke and set me upon my feet; and I heard Him that spoke unto me.

And He said unto me: 'Son of man, I send thee to the children of Israel, to rebellious nations, that have rebelled against Me; they and their fathers have transgressed against Me, even unto this very day; and the children are brazen-faced and stiff-hearted, I do send thee unto them; and thou shalt say unto them: Thus saith the Lord God. And they, whether they will hear, or whether they will forbear—for they are a rebellious house—yet shall know that there hath been a prophet among them.

And thou, son of man, be not afraid of them, neither be afraid of their words, though defiers and despisers be with thee, and thou dost dwell among scorpions; be not afraid of their words, nor be dismayed at their looks, for they are a rebellious house. . . .'—1:2-5; 2:1-6.

B.   Thou also, son of man, take thee a tile, and lay it before thee, and trace upon it a city, even Jerusalem; and lay siege against it, and build forts against it, and cast up a mound against it; set camps also against it, and set battering rams against it round about. This shall be a sign to the house of Israel.

Moreover lie thou upon thy left side, and lay the iniquity of the house of Israel upon it; according to the number of the days that thou shalt lie upon it, thou shalt bear their iniquity. . . .

Moreover He said unto me: 'Son of man, behold, I will break the staff of bread in Jerusalem, and they shall eat bread by weight, and with anxiety; and they shall drink water by measure, and in appalment; . . .'– 4: 1-4, 16.

C.   Thus saith the Lord God: This is Jerusalem! I have set her in the midst of the nations, and countries are round about her. And she hath rebelled against Mine ordinances in doing wickedness more than the nations, and against My statutes more than the countries that are round about her; for they have rejected Mine ordinances, and as for My statutes, they have not walked in them. . . . Wherefore, as I live, saith the Lord God, surely, because thou hast defiled My sanctuary with all thy detestable things, and with all thine abominations, therefore will I also diminish thee; neither shall Mine eye spare, and I also will have no pity. . . .

And the word of the Lord came unto me, saying: 'Son of man, set thy face toward the mountains of Israel, and prophesy against them, and say: Ye mountains of Israel, hear the word of the Lord God: Thus saith the Lord God concerning the mountains and concerning the hills, concerning the ravines and concerning the valleys: Behold, I, even I, will bring a sword upon you, and I will destroy your high places. And your altars shall become desolate, and your sun-images shall be broken; and I will cast down your slain men before your idols. And I will lay the carcasses of the children of Israel before their idols; and I will scatter your bones round about your altars. In all your dwelling-places the cities shall be laid waste, and the high places shall be desolate; that your altars may be laid waste and made desolate, and your idols may be broken and cease, and your sun-images may be hewn down, and your works may be blotted out. . . .'

'Make the chain; for the land is full of bloody crimes, and the city is full of violence. . . . Horror cometh; and they shall seek peace, and there shall be none.

The king shall mourn, and the prince shall be clothed with appalment, and the hands of the people of the land shall be enfeebled; I will do unto them after their way, and according to their deserts will I judge them; and they shall know that I am the Lord.'–5:5, 6, 11; 6:1-6; 7:23, 25, 27.

D.   Therefore, thou son of man, prepare thee stuff for exile, and remove as though for exile by day in their sight; and thou shalt remove from thy place to another place in their sight; it may be they will perceive, for they are a rebellious house. . . .
'Son of man, hath not the house of Israel, the rebellious house, said unto thee: What doest thou? Say thou unto them: Thus saith the Lord God: Concerning the prince, even this burden, in Jerusalem, and all the house of Israel, among whom they are, say: I am your sign: like as I have done, so shall it be done unto them—they shall go into exile, into captivity. . . .'–12:3, 9, 10, 11.

E.   And the word of the Lord came unto me, saying: 'Son of man, prophesy against the prophets of Israel that prophesy, and say thou unto them that prophesy out of their own heart: Hear ye the word of the Lord: Thus saith the Lord God: Woe unto the vile prophets, that follow their own spirit, and things which they have not seen! O Israel, thy prophets have been like foxes in ruins. . . . They have seen vanity and lying divination, that say: The Lord saith; and the Lord hath not sent them, yet they hope that the word would be confirmed! . . . And My hand shall be against the prophets that see vanity, and that divine lies; they shall not be in the council of My people, neither shall they be written in the register of the house of Israel, neither shall they enter into the land of Israel; and ye shall know that I am the Lord God. Because, even because they have led My people astray, saying: Peace, and there is no peace; . . .'–13:1-4, 6, 9, 10a.

F.   And the word of the Lord came unto me, saying: 'What mean ye, that ye use this proverb in the land of Israel, saying:

> The fathers have eaten sour grapes,
> And the children's teeth are set on edge?

As I live, saith the Lord God, ye shall not have occasion any more to use this proverb in Israel. Behold, all souls are Mine; as the soul of the father, so also the soul of the son is Mine; the soul that sinneth, it shall die. . . .

But if the wicked turn from all his sins that he hath committed, and keep all My statutes, and do that which is lawful and right, he shall surely live, he shall not die. . . . Have I any pleasure at all that the wicked should die: saith the Lord God; and not rather that he should return from his ways, and live? . . .

Therefore I will judge you, O house of Israel, every one according to his ways, saith the Lord God. Return ye, and turn yourselves from all your transgressions; so shall they not be a stumblingblock of iniquity unto you.

Cast away from you all your transgressions, wherein ye have transgressed; and make you a new heart and a new spirit; for why will ye die, O house of Israel? For I have no pleasure in the death of him that dieth, saith the Lord God; wherefore turn yourselves, and live. . . .'–18:1-4, 21, 23, 30-32.

G.   So thou, son of man, I have set thee a watchman unto the house of Israel; therefore, when thou shalt hear the word at My mouth, warn them from Me. When I say unto the wicked: O wicked man, thou shalt surely die, and thou dost not speak to warn the wicked from his way: that wicked man shall die in his iniquity, but his blood will I require at thy hand. Nevertheless, if thou warn the wicked of his way to turn from it, and he turn not from his way; he shall die in his iniquity, but thou hast delivered thy soul.

Therefore, O thou son of man, say unto the house of Israel: Thus ye speak, saying: Our transgressions and our sins are upon us, and we pine away in them; how then can we live? Say unto them: As I live, saith the Lord God, I have no pleasure in the death of the wicked, but that the wicked turn from his way and live; turn ye, turn ye from your evil ways; for why will ye die, O house of Israel? – 33:7-11.

H.   And the word of the Lord came unto me, saying: 'Son of man, set thy face toward the children of Ammon, and prophesy against them; and say unto the children of Ammon: Hear the word of the Lord God: Thus saith the Lord God: Because thou saidst: Aha! against My sanctuary, when it was profaned, and against the land of Israel, when it was made desolate, and against the house of Judah, when they went into captivity; . . .'

And it came to pass in the eleventh year, in the first day of the month, that the word of the Lord came unto me, saying: 'Son of man, because that Tyre hath said against Jerusalem:

Aha, she is broken that was the gate of the peoples;

She is turned unto me;

I shall be filled with her that is laid waste;

Therefore thus saith the Lord God:

Behold, I am against thee, O Tyre, . . .'

In the tenth year, in the tenth month, in the twelfth day of the month, the word of the Lord came unto me, saying: 'Son of man, set thy face against Pharaoh king of Egypt, and prophesy against him, and against all Egypt; speak, and say: Thus saith the Lord God:

Behold, I am against thee, Pharaoh, King of Egypt. . . .'– 25:1-3; 26:1-3a; 29:1-3a.

I.   And it came to pass in the twelfth year of our captivity, in the tenth month, in the fifth day of the month, that one that had escaped out of Jerusalem came unto me, saying: 'The city is smitten.' . . .

For thus saith the Lord God: Behold, here am I, and I will search for My sheep, and seek them out. As a shepherd seeketh out his flock in the day that he is among his sheep that are separated, so will I seek out My sheep; and I will deliver them out of all places whither they have been scattered in the day of clouds and thick darkness. And I will bring them out from the peoples, and gather them from the countries, and will bring them into their own land; and I will feed them upon the mountains of Israel, by the streams, and in all the habitable places of the country. I will feed them in a good pasture. . . .

And I will set up one shepherd over them, and he shall feed them, even My servant David; he shall feed them, and he shall be their shepherd. And I the Lord will be their God, and My servant David prince among them; I the Lord have spoken. . . . And they shall no more be a prey to the nations, neither shall the beast of the earth devour them; but they shall dwell safely, and none shall make them afraid. . . .

The hand of the Lord was upon me, and the Lord carried me out in a spirit, and set me down in the midst of the valley, and it was full of bones; and He caused me to pass by them round about, and, behold, there were very many in the open valley; and, lo, they were very dry. And He said unto me: 'Son of man, can these bones live?' And I answered: 'O Lord God, Thou knowest.' Then He said unto me: 'Prophesy over these bones, and say unto them: O ye dry bones, hear the word of the Lord: Thus saith the Lord God unto these bones: Behold, I will cause breath to enter into you, and ye shall live. . . .' Then He said unto me: 'Son of man, these bones are the whole house of Israel; behold, they say: Our bones are dried up, and our hope is lost; we are clean cut off. Therefore prophesy, and say unto them: Thus saith the Lord God: Behold, I will open your graves, and cause you to come up out of your graves, O My people; and I will bring you into the land of Israel. And ye shall know that I am the Lord, when I have opened your graves, and caused you to come up out of your graves, O My people. And I will put My spirit in you, and ye shall live, and I will place you in your own land; and ye shall know that I the Lord have spoken, and performed it, saith the Lord.' . . . 'My dwelling-place also shall be over them; and I will be their God, and they shall be My people. And the nations shall know that I am the Lord that sanctify Israel, when My sanctuary shall be in the midst of them for ever.'—33:21; 34:11-14a, 23-24, 28; 37:1-5, 11, 14, 27-28.

J.   In the five and twentieth year of our captivity, in the beginning of the year, in the tenth day of the month, in the fourteenth year after that the city was smitten, in the self-same day, the hand of the Lord was upon me, and He brought me thither. In the visions of God brought He me into the land of Israel, and set me down upon a very high mountain, whereon was as it were the frame of a city on the south. . . .

But the priests the Levites, the sons of Zadok, that kept the charge of My sanctuary when the children of Israel went astray from Me, they shall come near to Me to minister unto Me; . . . they shall enter into My sanctuary, and they shall come near to My table, to minister unto Me, and they shall keep My charge. —40:1-2; 44:15a, 16.

COMMENTARY

A.   The vision which he saw when he was consecrated a prophet is described. This vision is more detailed and more ecstatic than the vision of Isaiah in the Temple in which he merely saw angels around the throne of God. As in the case of Isaiah and Jeremiah, the Prophet is told to be unafraid when he would meet with the stubbornness and the rebelliousness of the people in exile.

B.   The Prophet and his fellow exiles are carried off to Babylon while the Temple still stands and is to stand for eleven years. The prophet now speaks of the siege and of the inevitable fall of Jerusalem. It is typical of all the Prophets to educate the people by visible symbols. Isaiah wore a yoke on his shoulders and walked around with it that the people might see that they were destined to bear the yoke of the Assyrians. Jeremiah took a clay bottle which he broke in the valley of Hinnom to indicate how Israel would be broken by God, the Potter, who formed it. This symbolism, found in all the Prophets, is richly elaborated in Ezekiel. Here he builds up a little city and sets little battering rams against it. He subsists on strictly rationed food to indicate the hunger of the people during the siege. He enacts the departure of the people into exile, and so forth. There is more symbolic dramatization of the prophetic message in Ezekiel than in any other prophet.

C.   Here Ezekiel continues the classic prophetic teaching that the misfortunes come to the people because of their sins, their idolatry and their violence to the weak.

D.   Therefore exile is inevitable, and the Prophet dramatizes a picture of exile by his own garb and demeanor.

E.   Like all his predecessors, he denounces the official prophets of whom Jeremiah said "they preach 'peace, peace, peace,' when there is no peace." Ezekiel repeats Jeremiah's phrase and calls down upon these prophets the punishment of God because they delude the people.

F. This is Ezekiel's central religious doctrine: individual responsibility for sin and the individual obligation to repentance. It was an enlightening and enheartening doctrine. The exiles felt a great weight of the national calamity. They remembered now the teaching of the Prophets, how the repeated sins of many generations of the children of Israel have brought this calamity as the prophets foretold; now they must feel that all this accumulation of sin is too big a burden for them to escape. Therefore, the Prophet says that each man will suffer only for his own sins; each man can repent and God will gladly receive him.

G. In order that each man should be stirred to repentance, God sets the prophet up to be "a watchman unto the house of Israel." As a sentinel warns of the approach of danger, so the Prophet must warn of the disintegrating power of moral evil and must lead people to repentance and inner righteousness which alone can give courage and fortitude.

H. Oracles against the nations, Tyre, Egypt, etc., are included here. Such oracles are already found among the earlier prophets. In fact, the very opening words of the first literary Prophet, Amos, are in essence an oracle against the nations which surround Israel. God is the Lord of all the earth; His law of justice is incumbent upon all. Since the nations have violated it, they will be punished. Besides this general idea, that a just God punishes injustice among all nations, the Prophets add the thought that many of the nations whom God used as the instrument of His anger, such as Assyria, Babylonia, etc., had carried out their mission with cruelty and unjustified pride. For that they will now be punished. Also, other nations, which were not used as the instrument of God's punishment, but who rejoiced at the tragedies of Israel, will be punished for that. It is this idea which dominates the oracles of the nations found in Ezekiel.

I. This prophecy was given when the final part of the tragedy was enacted and Jerusalem was destroyed and the tidings of that destruction reached Ezekiel and the exiles already in Babylon. Immediately the Prophet begins his preachment of hope and restoration. The destruction of the Temple was the punishment for sin. Now God holds out hope to His children. He will restore the dynasty of David. But God will be the real Ruler of Israel. The people in their tragedy believe that such restoration is impossible. Their spirit is broken; their hopes are gone. Therefore Ezekiel preaches his sermon of the dry bones in the desert valley which miraculously come alive.

J.   Ezekiel is much more specific in his picture of the restored people than are any of his predecessors. They saw the destruction and the calamity clearly and described it in vivid detail. But as for the restoration, they saw it only as a bright vision whose very radiance blotted out the details. Only Isaiah among the predecessors of Ezekiel described something of the detail of the future restoration, but that too only in general terms, a vision of righteousness radiating from Zion all over the world. But Ezekiel is already in the Exile and therefore feels that the restoration is close and can be clearly and specifically envisaged. The whole latter part of the book therefore is a detailed picture of the building of the Temple, of the division of the land.

Thus the cycle of prophecy becomes complete. The Prophet becomes not only a spiritual statesman, as Isaiah was, but an inspired legislator as Moses was who was revered as the first and the greatest of prophets. With Ezekiel prophecy goes beyond preachment and becomes legislation, not only inspiring the mind but disciplining the life of Israel.

ChAPTER VI

The Minor Prophets

THE Hebrew name for what, in our modern usage, we now call the "minor prophets" is simply "The Twelve," because twelve of these prophets are combined in one large subdivision of Scripture. The first of these is Hosea, and the last Malachi. We will discuss them in the order in which they appear in Scripture.

HOSEA

GENERAL OUTLINE

When Amos, the pioneer of literary prophecy, preached in Beth-el, it was a period of prosperity in the northern kingdom (Israel). Yet it was clear to the Prophet, although it may not have been apparent at the time to the people and their rulers, that the violation of God's moral laws would soon bring an end to the kingdom. So it was. The northern kingdom was destroyed by the Assyrians in the year 722 B.C.E., and Amos preached about the year 750, only twenty-eight years before the destruction which is foretold. Thus the northern kingdom could have been blessed with only a small fragment of the entire prophetical movement which lasted for a number of centuries. Yet in this brief period of twenty-eight years, at the very beginning of literary prophecy, there were in the northern kingdom two great prophets, Amos and Hosea, one closely following the other, who together formed the vanguard of the entire procession of literary prophets.

Why the first two literary prophets should have appeared in the northern kingdom is not too difficult to explain. The northern kingdom was more highly developed economically than the southern kingdom. It had greater wealth, greater luxury, greater oppression and injustice. Morever, its eventual destruction at the hands of the Assyrians was becoming increasingly clear. Thus the northern kingdom presented clearly two of the chief elements of prophetic preachment, moral evil and national destruction, both the sin and its punishment. So Amos, the herdsman from Judea, came up to the luxuriant north to preach, and Hosea, a native of the northern kingdom, followed closely in the footsteps of his Judean predecessor.

It is quite clear that Hosea was a citizen of the northern kingdom. All the cities that he mentions are cities in the northern kingdom—Jezreel, Gilgal, Beth-el, etc. When he refers to the northern kingdom in general, he calls it "the land," and when he refers to the king of the northern kingdom, he says "our king." In addition to these facts gleaned from his prophecy, we have a description of his family life, a broken, unhappy family which was taken to be a symbol of Israel's relationship with God. Hosea married a woman of bad character and she bore his children. She abandoned him to follow her lovers. Eventually he forgave her and brought her back. All these events were to him a parallel to the relationship of Israel to God. God, as it were, had espoused Israel to him. The covenant between God and Israel was like a covenant of marriage. Israel broke faith and sought other worship, the idols and their corruptions.

This picture of the family relationship between Israel and God, Israel's broken covenant, and later her restoration and return to her beloved Lord, first described in Hosea, became a permanent metaphor in all the prophetic literature. The Prophet Isaiah speaks of Israel: "I will sing of my beloved." Jeremiah speaks tenderly to Israel: "I remember for thee the affection of thy youth, the love of thine espousals, how they wentest after Me in the wilderness"; and then, speaking of Israel's sin, Jeremiah says: "Surely as a wife treacherously departeth from her husband, so have ye dealt treacherously with Me, O house of Israel." In Ezekiel, Israel and Samaria are described as adulterous, sinful women, an elaboration of the thought of Hosea. And in Deutero-Isaiah, who was among the last of the great prophets, the theme of restoration is again, as in Hosea, the bringing back home, the forgiveness of the once sinful but now repentant wife: "For thy Maker is thy Husband; the Lord of hosts is His name; for the Lord hath called thee as a wife forsaken and grieved in spirit and as a wife of youth; can she be rejected, saith the Lord." Thus, out of the personal experience of this early northern kingdom prophet, the sinfulness of his wife and his forgiveness, there developed an idea which became not only the central thought of his own prophecy but a leading thought in the entire prophetic literature.

It is interesting to note the individual differences as well as the similarities among the Prophets, and nowhere among the Prophets is a difference in mood clearer than between Amos and Hosea, both of whom preached in the northern kingdom in the same span of twenty-eight years. Amos is stern; Hosea is tender. Amos thunders of God's justice; Hosea speaks pleadingly of God's love. With Amos the cardinal sin is cruelty and oppression; with Hosea the cardinal sin is the violation of the love-bond between Israel and God, the betrayal and desertion of God for the worship of idols.

These two differing preachments, that of Amos against oppression, and that of Hosea against idolatry, are not mutually exclusive. They are in fact closely related to each other. God was a God of justice and righteousness and those who abandoned him abandoned the commands: "righteousness shall ye pursue" and "thou shalt not bear a grudge," and "thou shalt love the stranger for strangers were ye in the land of Egypt." Idolatry meant abandoning the One and Only God, and therefore also the doctrine that all men are brothers. Amos and Hosea preached basically the same message, Amos showing the cruel result of idolatry, and Hosea giving the cause for the moral decay.

That each one took his own side of this unitary doctrine, that abandoning God meant moral decay, was due, of course, to a difference in temperament and to a difference in personal experience. Although Amos and Hosea lived within the same score of years, those years were years of rapid change. When Amos preached, the northern kingdom was at the height of its prosperity, and only the keen prophetic conscience could see that moral corruption would some day bring about national destruction. But as far as the people could see, it was a time of victory and security. They were confident and smug, and needed to be shocked and denounced. Therefore he denounced them for their sins. But in the few years between the preachment of Amos and that of Hosea, the giant destructive armies of Assyria were already coming close. Security had vanished. Destruction was imminent. Therefore Hosea, while he, like all the Prophets, denounced the people for their sins, already began to see beyond the destruction to a time of restoration. Thus his message was analogous in mood to that of the great Jeremiah who lived a century later. Jeremiah, in the southern kingdom (Judah), lived at a time when the doom foretold by his predecessors was already at hand and therefore he too began to plead, and enhearten and encourage and see beyond the destruction to a time of consolation. "Yea I have loved thee with an everlasting love and again will I build thee and thou shalt be built, O virgin of Israel" (Jeremiah 31:4). Similarly, Hosea, in the northern kingdom which was destroyed almost a century and a half before the southern kingdom, also assures the people that although God has rejected them, He will yet forgive them. "I will betroth thee unto Me in righteousness. I will betroth thee unto Me forever" (Hosea 2:21). It was in times of prosperity that the Prophets preached their harshest words, and in times of tragedy that they gave their promises of consolation. Thus Hosea and Jeremiah are akin. Each of them lived in the time of national danger and destruction and preached the promise of God's forgiving love.

SYNOPSIS OF TEXT

A.   When the Lord spoke at first with Hosea, the Lord said unto Hosea: 'Go, take unto thee a wife of harlotry and children of harlotry; for the land doth commit great harlotry, departing from the Lord.' So he went and took Gomer the daughter of Diblaim; and she conceived, and bore him a son. And the Lord said unto him: 'Call his name Jezreel; for yet a little while, and I will visit the blood of Jezreel upon the house of Jehu, and will cause to cease the kingdom of the house of Israel. And it shall come to pass at that day, that I will break the bow of Israel in the valley of Jezreel.' And she conceived again, and bore a daughter. And He said unto him: 'Call her name Lo-ruhamah; for I will no more have compassion upon the house of Israel, that I should in any wise pardon them.'—1:2-6.

B. Hear the word of the Lord, ye children of Israel!
For the Lord hath a controversy with the inhabitants of the
    land,
Because there is no truth, nor mercy,
Nor knowledge of God in the land.
Swearing and lying, and killing, and stealing, and commit-
    ting adultery!
They break all bounds, and blood toucheth blood.
Therefore doth the land mourn,
And every one that dwelleth therein doth languish,
With the beasts of the field and the fowls of heaven;
Yea, the fishes of the sea also are taken away.
Harlotry, wine, and new wine take away the heart.
My people ask counsel at their stock,
And their staff declareth unto them;
For the spirit of harlotry hath caused them to err,
And they have gone astray from under their God.
They sacrifice upon the tops of the mountains,
And offer upon the hills,
Under oaks and poplars and terebinths,
Because the shadow thereof is good;
Therefore your daughters commit harlotry,
And your daughters-in-law commit adultery. – 4:1-3, 11,
    12, 13.

C. And when Ephraim saw his sickness,
And Judah his wound,
Ephraim went to Assyria,
And sent to King Contentious;
But he is not able to heal you,
Neither shall he cure you of your wound. . . .
And Ephraim is become like a silly dove, without under-
    standing;
They call unto Egypt, they go to Assyria. . . .
Ephraim striveth after wind, and followeth after the east
    wind;
All the day he multiplieth lies and desolation;
And they make a covenant with Assyria,
And oil is carried into Egypt. – 5:13; 7:11; 12:2.

D.   And I said unto her: 'Thou shalt sit solitary for me many days; thou shalt not play the harlot, and thou shalt not be any man's wife; nor will I be thine.' For the children of Israel shall sit solitary many days without king, and without prince, and without sacrifice, and without pillar, and without ephod or teraphim; – 3:3-4.

E.   And the Lord said unto me: 'Go yet, love a woman beloved of her friend and an adultress, even as the Lord loveth the children of Israel, though they turn unto other gods, . . .'

> When Israel was a child, then I loved him,
> And out of Egypt I called My son.
> The more they called them, the more they went from them;
> They sacrificed unto the Baalim,
> And offered to graven images.
> And I, I taught Ephraim to walk,
> Taking them by their arms;
> But they knew not that I healed them.
> I drew them with cords of a man,
> With bands of love; – 3:1; 11:1-4a.

F.   For I will take away the names of the Baalim out of her mouth,
> And they shall no more be mentioned by their name.
> And in that day will I make a covenant for them
> With the beasts of the field, and with the fowls of heaven,
> And with the creeping things of the ground;
> And I will break the bow and the sword and the battle out of the land,
> And will make them to lie down safely.
> And I will betroth thee unto Me forever;
> Yea, I will betroth thee unto Me in righteousness, and in justice,
> And in lovingkindness, and in compassion.
> And I will betroth thee unto Me in faithfulness;
> And thou shalt know the Lord. . . .
> And I will say to them that were not My people: 'Thou art My people';
> And they shall say: 'Thou art my God.'–2:19-22, 25b.

G.   For I desire mercy, and not sacrifice.
And the knowledge of God rather than burnt-offerings. . . .
Sow to yourselves according to righteousness,
Reap according to mercy,
Break up your fallow ground;
For it is time to seek the Lord,
Till he come and cause righteousness to rain upon you. . . .
Return, O Israel, unto the Lord thy God;
For thou hast stumbled in thine iniquity.
Take with you words,
And return unto the Lord;
Say unto Him: 'Forgive all iniquity,
And accept that which is good;
So will we render for bullocks the offering of our lips.
Asshur shall not save us;
We will not ride upon horses;
Neither will we call any more the work of our hands our
    gods;
For in thee the fatherless findeth mercy.'
I will heal their backsliding,
I will love them freely;
For Mine anger is turned away from him.
I will be as the dew unto Israel;
He shall blossom as the lily,
And cast forth his roots as Lebanon. . . .
'Come, and let us return unto the Lord;
For He hath torn, and He will heal us,
He hath smitten, and He will bind us up. . . .'– 6:6; 10:12;
    14:2-6; 6:1.

COMMENTARY

A.   Many of the prophets considered their lives symbolical of the destiny of Israel. This idea of a prophet as a symbol of Israel begins here in Hosea. His adulterous wife is a symbol of Israel's faithlessness to God. His sons and daughter are given names symbolical of Israel's destiny. So later Isaiah names his children as a symbol of what will happen to the people of Israel. Ezekiel goes through the ritual of mourning as a symbol of Israel's mourning.

He fasts as a symbol of the famine of Jerusalem when under siege of the enemy.

B.   The Prophet describes the moral sins of the people, but whenever he mentions these evils he connects them with the abandonment of God for the worship of idols: "they have gone astray from their God; they sacrifice on the top of the mountain."

C.   It is in vain for Israel to seek its deliverance through political alliances. The only source of national strength is moral strength. There is no other way of surviving, especially in a time of world turmoil; hence, alliances are delusions. This thought of Hosea became a central thought in Isaiah and the essence of his advice to the kings of Judah.

D.   As the Prophet, taking back his faithless wife, will keep her isolated that she may have time for repentance, so will God give Israel a time "when Israel shall sit solitary, many days without king and without prince and without sacrifice," that it may meditate on its repentance and then return to God.

E.   Here the metaphor changes. Israel, described as a wife to God, is now described in another metaphor in family life, namely, as God's beloved child. "When Israel was a child I loved him . . . I taught Ephraim to walk," as a father lovingly plays and teaches his child. This description of God, the loving Father of Ephraim (the chief tribe of the northern kingdom of Israel, as Judah is the chief tribe of the southern kingdom), is developed also in Jeremiah. "Is Ephraim a darling child unto Me? As often as I speak of him, I do earnestly remember him still. Therefore My heart yearneth for him" (Jeremiah 31:20).

F.   When Hosea describes the restoration, he speaks of Israel being cured of idolatry and of the coming of a period of peace, an end of war. This vision of enduring peace becomes a leading thought in all the Prophets. Though they preached, almost all of them, in the midst of endless wars, the struggles between empires, they saw beyond the present and visualized that picture which Hosea describes as "I will break the bow and the sword and the battle out of the land," and which Isaiah and Micah describe as "they will beat their swords into plowshares."

G.   As all the Prophets taught, so Hosea teaches that the essential worship of God is not ritual—this is but the symbol at best—but righteousness and mercy. The way to worship God, the God of justice and mercy, is to be like God, just and merciful. This exalted idea, that character is the noblest offering to God, was brought into world religion at the very beginning of the prophetic movement. Samuel and Elijah, Nathan, and all the literary prophets from Amos down, reiterate, each in his own words, that what the Lord requires of us is "to do justly and to love mercy." It is characteristic of the difference in temperament between Amos and Hosea that Amos says: "Let justice flow forth like water" and Hosea speaks of mercy rather than sacrifice.

In the closing preachment of Hosea which the synagogue has adopted for reading on the Sabbath of Repentance, the Prophet sums up his entire doctrine. Israel, which has gone astray, is now asked to return, confident that God in His love will "forgive all iniquity," and that in Him they will find mercy and He will "love them freely." They will not turn any more to Assyria or to Egypt, but will rely upon God's love alone.

Hosea must have loved the countryside. His whole book breathes with nature, the mist and the rain and the dew, the blossoming flowers and the tenacious cedar trees on the rocky mountain tops. All the country scenes so familiar and so beloved to him become the text in the story of the love between God and Israel, a story becoming tragic but destined to be triumphant.

JOEL

GENERAL OUTLINE

The opening sentence of the Book of Joel is: "The word of the Lord that came to Joel the son of Pethuel." That is all we know of him, his own name and his father's name. We may infer some additional facts about him: since he refers to Zion and to the priests in the Temple, it is likely that he was a Judean. This possibility is strengthened by the fact that he speaks of restoring the captivity of Judah and Jerusalem and makes no mention of the northern kingdom. Scholars have carefully studied this booklet of prophecy and are still far from any agreement as to when the author lived or when this book was written.

It may, perhaps, be of interest to the reader to become acquainted with the type of arguments which scientific students of the Bible use in trying to determine the date of a book whenever there is almost no definite evidence available. All scholars have observed that Joel makes no mention of kings but calls upon the priests to lead the people to repentance (Joel 2:17); also, that he makes no mention of Assyria or Babylon. From these two facts one group of scholars draws conclusions entirely opposite from those drawn by another group of scholars. One group says that the book must be very late, written in fact after the Exile, when the memory of the old warring armies of Assyria and Babylonia had disappeared from the minds of men, both these military powers having been swallowed up by the Persian empire. Joel's appeals to the priests indicate that the kings had long since disappeared. In the Persian period (i.e., the post-exilic period) it was the priests who dominated Jewish life. Moreover, the fact that he does not mention the northern kingdom (Israel) at all is taken to be a further corroboration of the lateness of the book because by that time (the post-exilic period) the separate existence of the northern kingdom was only a memory and not a real fact, which could be used as a moral lesson by a prophet who could refer to its sins and its fate.

But other scholars come to an entirely different opinion based upon the same facts. They say that this book, far from being as late as the post-exilic period, is very early—in fact, is the earliest of all the literary prophecies, earlier even than Amos. They argue as follows: the fact that Assyria and Babylonia are not mentioned is a proof that the book was written before these two nations became a menace to Israel. The fact that only the priests are referred to as leading the people to repentance points to the infancy of King Joash (836-798) who, according to the Book of Kings (II Kings 12:2-3), became king as a child with the priests as the virtual regents of the kingdom. As for the fact that he does not mention the northern kingdom, that is simply because he came from the southern kingdom. He was a Judean. All this does not mean to imply that Biblical scholarship is always so inconclusive,

but it is an example, though rather an extreme one, of how difficult it sometimes is to assign a definite date to a Biblical book when
there is nothing but negative evidence upon which to base a conclusion.

Some scholars, dividing the book into various parts, date each
part differently. For our purpose it is simply sufficient to take the
book as it stands and to describe its contents. It is a description
of a time of a great locust plague and a famine. The locusts are
described as a vast army moving in regular platoons, marching
irresistibly forward. Joel calls upon the people to repent of their
sins and promises that God will restore prosperity and abundance.
"I will restore to you the years that the locusts have eaten."

The second part of the book, beginning with chapter 3, describes the great future in which the spirit of prophetic inspiration will descend upon young and old and God will summon
the wicked nations to the valley of Jehoshaphat and there will judge
them for their evil deeds "because they have shed innocent blood."
Then God will restore Judah "and Jerusalem from generation to
generation."

SYNOPSIS OF TEXT

A.   The word of the Lord that came to Joel the son of Pethuel.
Hear this, ye old men,
And give ear, all ye inhabitants of the land.
Hath this been in your days,
Or in the days of your fathers? . . .
That which the palmer-worm hath left hath the locust
  eaten;
And that which the locust hath left hath the canker-worm
  eaten;
And that which the canker-worm hath left hath the cater-
  pillar eaten. . . .
The appearance of them is as the appearance of horses;
And as horsemen, so do they run. . . .
They leap upon the city,
They run upon the wall,
They climb up into the houses;
They enter in at the windows like a thief. . . .

For a people is come up upon my land,
Mighty, and without number;
His teeth are the teeth of a lion,
And he hath the jaw-teeth of a lioness. . . .
The vine is withered,
And the fig-tree languisheth;
The pomegranate-tree, the palm-tree also, and the apple-
tree,
Even all the trees of the field are withered;
For joy is withered away from the sons of men. — 1: 1-2, 4;
2:4, 9; 1:6, 12.

B.   Gird yourselves, and lament, ye priests,
Wail, ye ministers of the altar;
Come, lie all night in sackcloth,
Ye ministers of my God; . . .
Sanctify ye a fast,
Call a solemn assembly,
Gather the elders
And all the inhabitants of the land
Unto the house of the Lord your God,
And cry unto the Lord. . . .
Unto Thee, O Lord, do I cry;
For the fire hath devoured
The pastures of the wilderness,
And the flame hath set ablaze
All the trees of the field. — 1:13a, 14, 19.

C.   Then was the Lord jealous for His land,
And had pity on His people.
And the Lord answered and said unto His people:
'Behold, I will send you corn, and wine, and oil,
And ye shall be satisfied therewith;
And I will no more make you a reproach among the na-
tions; . . .'
And I will restore to you the years that the locust hath
eaten,
The canker-worm, and the caterpillar, and the palmer-worm,
My great army which I sent among you.

And ye shall eat in plenty and be satisfied,
And shall praise the name of the Lord your God, . . . – 2:18,
19, 25, 26a.

D.   And it shall come to pass afterward,
That I will pour out My spirit upon all flesh;
And your sons and daughters shall prophesy,
Your old men shall dream dreams,
Your young men shall see visions;
And also upon the servants and upon the handmaids
In those days will I pour out My spirit.
And I will show wonders in the heavens and in the earth,
Blood, and fire, and pillars of smoke. – 3:1-3.

E.   And also what are ye to Me, O Tyre, and Zidon, and all
the regions of Philistia? will ye render retribution on My behalf?
and if ye render retribution on My behalf, swiftly, speedily will I
return your retribution upon your own head. . . . the children also
of Judah and the children of Jerusalem have ye sold unto the sons
of the Jevanim, that ye might remove them far from their border; . . .

Proclaim ye this among the nations,
Prepare war;
Stir up the mighty men;
Let all the men of war draw near,
Let them come up.
Beat your plowshares into swords,
And your pruning-hooks into spears;
Let the weak say: 'I am strong.'
Haste ye, and come, all ye nations round about,
And gather yourselves together;
Thither cause Thy mighty ones to come down, O Lord!
Let the nations be stirred up, and come up
To the valley of Jehoshaphat;
For there will I sit to judge
All the nations round about. . . .
Multitudes, multitudes in the valley of decision!
For the day of the Lord is near in the valley of decision. . . .
The sun and the moon are become black,

And the stars withdraw their shining. . . .
And the heavens and the earth shall shake;
But the Lord will be a refuge unto His people.
Egypt shall be a desolation,
And Edom shall be a desolate wilderness,
For the violence against the children of Judah,
Because they have shed innocent blood in their land.
But Judah shall be inhabited forever,
And Jerusalem from generation to generation. – 4:4, 6, 9-12,
    14, 15, 16b, 19, 20.

COMMENTARY

A.   Joel describes the plague of locusts who march in regular
military formation and eat up the produce of the land.

B.   He calls upon the priests to summon the inhabitants of the
land to fasting and prayer.

C.   God's promise to restore the land to abundance is given
in answer to their repentance.

D.   The great future will be ushered in by the prophetic spirit
inspiring old and young, servants and handmaids. This idea of
wide-spread prophecy is a familiar idea in Scripture. The seventy
elders prophesied in the presence of Moses (Numbers 11:25). And
Moses says: "would that all the Lord's people were prophets and
that the Lord would put His spirit upon them" (Numbers 11:29).
It is this prayerful hope of Moses which Joel says will come in the
great future to a grand fulfillment.

E.   Many of the prophets have oracles against the nations. This
is, in fact, one of the leading thoughts in prophecy. It begins with
Amos, who opens his book with a denunciation of the nations.
Great sections of the oracles against the nations are found in Jere-
miah, Isaiah, and Ezekiel. Often the nations are denounced for
their cruelty to Israel, particularly in times of Israel's misfortunes.
Here then the nations will be gathered together to the valley of
Jehoshaphat and God will render judgment against them.

AMOS

GENERAL OUTLINE

The book of Amos begins with this sentence: "The words of Amos, who was among the herdmen of Tekoa, which he saw concerning Israel in the days of Uzziah king of Judah, and in the days of Jeroboam the son of Joash king of Israel, two years before the earthquake."

Since the dates of some of the kings of Israel have been closely determined in relationship with certain monuments, historians are able to come rather close to the dates of many of the literary prophets. Amos' address (or addresses), which is preserved in the Book of Amos, was delivered at Beth-el in the northern kingdom (Israel) about 750 B.C.E. He is the first of the literary prophets.

Amos begins with a declaration of God's world-wide justice. God punishes the sins of all the nations round about Israel—Damascus, the Philistines, Tyre, Edom, Ammon, Moab, and also Judah and Israel (that is, both the southern and the northern kingdoms of the children of Israel). Since the Prophet is addressing a gathering in the kingdom of Israel, the northern kingdom, he mentions their punishment last, as a climax. In every case the sin which the various nations have committed is an ethical sin, chiefly brutality in war. The sin of Israel for which they will be punished is its oppression of the poor. For that sin God will bring defeat and exile upon them. The Prophet knows that this is a tragic prophecy to give to his brethren but he has no choice. God compels him to speak. He pleads with the people to practice righteousness that they may yet be saved. Amaziah, the priest of Beth-el, the great sanctuary in Israel, tells Amos to go back home and not preach such treachery, to which Amos says, "I am not a professional prophet; I do not trim my words to please people; I am simply a herdman whom God has commanded to bring this message to you: For their sins, Israel will be exiled."

SYNOPSIS OF TEXT

A.   Thus saith the Lord:
     For three transgressions of Damascus,

Yea, for four, I will not reverse it:
Because they have threshed Gilead with sledges of iron. . . .
And I will break the bar of Damascus, . . .
And the people of Aram shall go into captivity unto Kir,
Saith the Lord. . . .
For three transgressions of Gaza, . . .
For three transgressions of Tyre, . . . of Edom, . . . of Am-
    mon, . . . of Moab, . . .
For three transgressions of Judah, . . .
For three transgressions of Israel, . . . I will not reverse it;
Because they sell the righteous for silver,
And the needy for a pair of shoes (from chapters 1 and 2);
Are ye not as the children of the Ethiopians unto Me,
O children of Israel? saith the Lord.
Have I not brought up Israel out of the land of Egypt,
And the Philistines from Caphtor,
And Aram from Kir? – 9:7.

B.   Hear this word, ye kine of Bashan,
      That are in the mountain of Samaria,
      That oppress the poor, that crush the needy,
      That say unto their lords: 'Bring, that we may feast.'– 4:1.

C.   I brought you out of the land of Egypt,
      And led you forty years in the wilderness,
      To possess the land of the Amorite.
      And I raised up of your sons for prophets,
      And of your young men for Nazirites.
      Is it not even thus, O ye children of Israel?
      Saith the Lord (chapter 2).
      And I also have withholden the rain from you,
      When there were yet three months to the harvest; . . .
      Yet have ye not returned unto Me,
      Saith the Lord.
      I have smitten you with blasting and mildew; . . .
      I have sent among you the pestilence . . .
      Yet have ye not returned unto Me,
      Saith the Lord. . . .
      Therefore thus will I do unto thee, O Israel; . . .

Prepare to meet thy God, O Israel. . . .
Hear ye this word which I take up for a lamentation over
you,
O house of Israel:
The virgin of Israel is fallen,
She shall no more rise;
She is cast down upon her land,
There is none to raise her up.—From chapters 4 and 5.
You only have I known of all the families of the earth;
Therefore I will visit upon you all your iniquities.—3:2.

D.   For the Lord God will do nothing,
But He revealeth His counsel unto His servants the
prophets.
The lion hath roared,
Who will not fear?
The Lord God hath spoken,
Who can but prophesy?—3:7, 8.

E.   Seek good, and not evil, that ye may live;
And so the Lord, the God of hosts, will be with you as
ye say.
Hate the evil, and love the good,
And establish justice in the gate;
It may be that the Lord, the God of hosts,
Will be gracious unto the remnant of Joseph. . . .
But let justice well up as waters,
And righteousness as a mighty stream.—5:14, 15, 24.

F.   Then Amaziah the priest of Beth-el sent to Jeroboam king
of Israel, saying: 'Amos hath conspired against thee in the midst of
the house of Israel; the land is not able to bear all his words. For thus
Amos saith: Jeroboam shall die by the sword, And Israel shall surely
be led away captive out of his land.' Also Amaziah said unto Amos:
'O thou seer . . . prophesy not again any more at Beth-el . . .' Then
answered Amos . . . 'I was no prophet, neither was I a prophet's
son; but I was a herdman . . . and the Lord took me from following
the flock, and the Lord said unto me: Go, prophesy unto My
people Israel. Now therefore hear thou the word of the Lord: . . .

thou thyself shalt die in an unclean land, and Israel shall surely be led away captive out of his land.'– 7:10-17.

COMMENTARY

A.   God is king of all the world. His moral law is valid for all the nations. All nations who sin will be punished with destruction and exile. Israel's sin is social injustice and oppression; hence it shall suffer as will all others. Israel should not consider itself an exception, a special favorite of God. It is true that God brought Israel out of Egypt, but He also led other nations out of their slaveries. All are His children, all should obey His laws of righteousness, and all must suffer for their sinfulness.

B.   Amos specifies the ways in which the rich oppress the poor in order that they may live in luxury.

C.   There is one regard in which Israel is different from the other peoples. God has given Israel special guidance through prophets, but they have disregarded it. God has attempted in many ways to bring Israel to repentance from the sins of oppression. He has sent them drought and mildew on their crops, but they have not repented and now destruction must come to them.

D.   The Prophet is aware of the bitter taste of his prophecy. It is as difficult for him to preach as it is for them to hear. But he has no choice. He is merely the voice of God. God compels him to prophesy.

E.   He pleads with the people to give up their evil ways, to establish justice. He suggests that perhaps God will yet have mercy upon them.

F.   But the authorities consider his preachment subversive and ask him to go back to the land from which he came (Judah). He says that he is speaking at the command of God. God's dire intention will certainly be fulfilled and Israel will surely be exiled for its sins.

OBADIAH

GENERAL OUTLINE

This is the shortest book in the Bible. It consists of only one chapter, containing twenty-one verses. Most scholars assign this book to the time just before the destruction of the Temple—in other words, about the time of Jeremiah. They base it upon the fact that the denunciation of Edom in Jeremiah 49:7-11 is almost identical with the first seven verses of Obadiah. The book is an oracle against one nation only, Edom. Edom is denounced for having been unsympathetic and unbrotherly to Judah in "the day of their destruction," which is taken to refer to the two conquests of Jerusalem by the Babylonians.

SYNOPSIS OF TEXT

A. The vision of Obadiah.
Thus saith the Lord God concerning Edom:
We have heard a message from the Lord,
And an ambassador is sent among the nations:
'Arise ye, and let us rise up against her in battle.'
Behold, I make thee small among the nations;
Thou art greatly despised. . . .
Though thou make thy nest as high as the eagle,
And though thou set it among the stars,
I will bring thee down from thence, saith the Lord.—1:1,
2, 4.

B. For the violence done to thy brother Jacob
Shame shall cover thee,
And thou shalt be cut off for ever.
In the day that thou didst stand aloof,
In the day that strangers carried away his substance,
And foreigners entered into his gates,
And cast lots upon Jerusalem,
Even thou wast as one of them. . . .
Thou shouldest not have entered into the gate of My
people

In the day of their calamity;
Yea, thou shouldest not have gazed on their affliction
In the day of their calamity,
Nor have laid hands on their substance
In the day of their calamity. —1:10, 11, 13.

C.   But in mount Zion there shall be those that escape,
And it shall be holy;
And the house of Jacob shall possess their possessions. . . .
And saviours shall come up on mount Zion
To judge the mount of Esau;
And the kingdom shall be the Lord's. —1:17, 21.

COMMENTARY

A.   Edom should not rely upon her inaccessible mountain fastnesses; God will summon the nations against her.

B.   Her sin was that she helped the invaders (understood to mean the Babylonians) in their conquest of Jerusalem. Edom, which is descendant from Esau, is looked upon as a kindred tribe. It should have felt kinship with Israel—hence the words: "for violence done to thy brother Jacob [Esau to Jacob] shame shall cover thee." As Amos, in his catalogue of denunciation of nations for their sins, when he comes to the transgressions of Edom, says: "Because he did pursue his brother with the sword" (Amos 1:11), so too a later prophet than Obadiah, Ezekiel, accuses Edom of the same unbrotherly cruelty. "Thus saith the Lord, because Edom hath dealt against the house of Judah by taking vengeance, . . . I will stretch out My hand upon Edom" (Ezekiel 25:13).

C.   Obadiah tells how God will restore Zion and judgment will go forth from Zion against Edom.

JONAH

GENERAL OUTLINE

The opening sentence of the Book of Jonah reads: "Now the word of the Lord came to Jonah, the son of Amittai." This Jonah, the son of Amittai, is also mentioned in the Book of Kings (II Kings 14:25): "According to the word of the Lord, the God of Israel, which He spoke by the hand of His servant Jonah the son of Amittai, the prophet." This book does not contain any prophecies by this prophet nor is there any claim made in the book itself that Jonah, the son of Amittai, is its author.

The book is not a series of prophecies, but is a story concerning the Prophet. It would seem that this book, being a narrative about a prophet rather than a series of addresses or writings by a prophet, should not belong in this collection of literary prophecies but should belong in the Book of Kings, where there are narratives about other prophets, especially Elijah and Elisha. It may well be that Jonah, the son of Amittai, was the last of that group of pre-literary prophets to which Elijah and Elisha belong. This book, written about him, is put here among the literary prophets even though it does not contain any prophecies as all the other such books do. It is placed among the prophetic books because its essential theme is one typical of the literary prophets, namely, that God is the God of all nations, that the people of Nineveh, a Gentile city, has sinned, and therefore God will punish them with national destruction. But God offers them the opportunity of repentance, and when they repent, God forgives them and spares them.

The Prophet Jonah is sent by God to preach to the Gentile city of Nineveh, to tell it that its destruction is imminent because of its sins. The Prophet refuses to go. He flees from the presence of the Lord. On board ship he is cast overboard in the midst of a storm. A huge fish swallows him, and after three days casts him back again on shore. This time Jonah obeys the command of God and goes to Nineveh and preaches to it. Nineveh is moved to repentance by the preaching and God forgives it. Jonah, angered that he should be sent to preach destruction and then have his preachment belied, is rebuked by God, who reminds him of His pity for all His children.

It is obvious that this book is one of the latest books of the Bible. It was written at a time long after the destruction of the Assyrian empire, the capital of which was Nineveh. This is evident from the vague and fanciful way in which Nineveh is referred to as impossibly vast, it taking three full days' journey to traverse the city. It speaks of the king of Nineveh. There was no king of Nineveh, only an Assyrian king whose capital was Nineveh. The idea of the beasts as well as man being covered with the sackcloth and fasting and praying to God is simply an imaginative overstatement. Besides, the style and the language seem to indicate its late origin. The purpose of the book, however, is clear. Related as the story of a real pre-exilic prophet, it indicates that the task of Israel and of the Prophets is to bring all mankind to repentance, and thus to peace and security.

SYNOPSIS OF TEXT

A.   Now the word of the Lord came unto Jonah the son of Amittai, saying: 'Arise, go to Nineveh, that great city, and proclaim against it; for their wickedness is come up before Me.' But Jonah rose up to flee unto Tarshish from the presence of the Lord; and he went down to Joppa, and found a ship going to Tarshish; so he paid the fare thereof, and went down into it, to go with them unto Tarshish, from the presence of the Lord. –1:1-3.

B.   But the Lord hurled a great wind into the sea, and there was a mighty tempest in the sea, so that the ship was like to be broken. . . . So they took up Jonah, and cast him forth into the sea; and the sea ceased from its raging.

And the Lord prepared a great fish to swallow up Jonah; and Jonah was in the belly of the fish three days and three nights. . . .

And the Lord spoke unto the fish, and it vomited out Jonah upon the dry land. –1:4, 15; 2:1, 11.

C.   And the word of the Lord came unto Jonah the second time, saying: 'Arise, go unto Nineveh, that great city, and make unto it the proclamation that I bid thee.' So Jonah arose, and went unto Nineveh, according to the word of the Lord. Now Nineveh was an exceeding great city, of three days' journey. And Jonah began to enter into the city a day's journey, and he proclaimed, and said: 'Yet forty days, and Nineveh shall be overthrown.'

And the people of Nineveh believed God; and they proclaimed a fast and put on sackcloth, from the greatest of them even to the least of them. . . .

And God saw their works, that they turned from their evil way; and God repented of the evil, which He said He would do unto them; and He did it not. – 3: 1-5, 10.

D.   Then Jonah went out of the city, and sat on the east side of the city, and there made him a booth, and sat under it in the shadow, till he might see what would become of the city. And the Lord God prepared a gourd, and made it come up over Jonah, that it might be a shadow over his head, to deliver him from his evil. So Jonah was exceeding glad because of the gourd. But God prepared a worm when the morning rose the next day, and it smote the gourd, that it withered. . . . And God said to Jonah: 'Art thou greatly angry for the gourd?' And he said: 'I am greatly angry, even unto death.' And the Lord said: 'Thou hast had pity on the gourd, for which thou hast not laboured, neither madest it grow, which came up in a night, and perished in a night; and should not I have pity on Nineveh, that great city, wherein are more than six-score thousand persons . . . ?'– 4: 5-7, 9-11a.

COMMENTARY

A.   The classic prophetic theme, that God, being the moral Ruler of the whole world, will punish all nations for their evil, is repeated here. This theme begins with the first literary prophet Amos and is the basic theme of this story.

B.   The heathen sailors are described sympathetically, each praying to his own god during the storm while Jonah sleeps. They cast him into the sea at his own request and pray that they may be forgiven.

C.   At the repetition of God's command, Jonah now goes to tell the city that its sins necessitate its destruction. The literary prophets reiterated this message to Israel so that Israel might repent in time and be saved, or at least be restored when suffering had purified it. Jonah brings the same message to a Gentile nation. Yet this is not as exceptional as some commentators believe. In many of the oracles against the nations in the other prophets, the nations are denounced for their sins and then promised that if they repent they will be restored. A magnificent example of this promise to the Gentile nations with the promise of restoration is found at the end of the nineteenth chapter of Isaiah, where it is said that the time will come when the Egyptians in the midst of deserved suffering "shall cry unto the Lord because of the oppressors" (Isaiah 19:20), "and they shall return unto the Lord and He will heal them" (verse 22). In that day Israel will be united with its former enemies, Egypt and Assyria. All of them will be redeemed from sin. "Blessed be Egypt, My people, and Assyria, the work of My hands and Israel, Mine inheritance" (verse 24). The idea of Jonah, therefore, is not new. All that is new is that it is a whole narrative devoted entirely to a theme which is found scattered among other themes throughout the writings of the prophets.

D.   Jonah does not want to preach that message at all. But when he finally goes and does preach the destruction of Nineveh and then sees that God does not destroy the city after all, he feels peevishly annoyed. God rebukes Jonah and reminds him of His love and pity for all His children.

MICAH

GENERAL OUTLINE

It is remarkable how little mention there is of the literary prophets in the other books of the Bible. Except for the mention of Isaiah in the Book of Kings, which was almost inevitable, since he played a great part in the statesmanship of his day, and some mention of Jeremiah in the Book of Chronicles, and Haggai and Zechariah in the Book of Ezra, the Prophets are not mentioned except each in his own book. In fact, one would imagine that at least they would refer to each other in their books since there is a clear continuity of thought from prophet to prophet. They certainly must have been aware of each other's teachings. Nevertheless, the fact remains: one literary prophet never mentions another unless we count the mention of Moses in Malachi 3:22: "Remember the law of Moses My servant," where Moses is mentioned not as the greatest of prophets, as tradition takes him to be, but as the great lawgiver.

To this fact that the literary prophets do not mention each

other there is one outstanding exception, namely that the Prophet Micah is clearly referred to in Jeremiah. Not only is he quoted by name but a verse of his prophecy (found actually in the Book of Micah) is quoted almost precisely in the statement in Jeremiah. Thus in Jeremiah 26:18 we read as follows: "Micah the Morash-tite prophesied in the days of Hezekiah king of Judah; and he spoke to all the people of Judah, saying:

Thus saith the Lord of hosts:
Zion shall be plowed as a field,
And Jerusalem shall become heaps,
And the mountain of the house as the high places of a forest."

This verse is found in our present book of Micah 3:12.

The heading of the Book of Micah describes him as the Morash-tite, which means that he came from the Judean city of Moresheth-Gath, a town near the Egyptian border. He himself refers to his village in chapter one, verse fourteen. The statement in Jeremiah refers to the fact that Micah preached in the days of Hezekiah, which is confirmed in this verse which heads the Book of Micah. He was, therefore, a contemporary (and most scholars say that he was a younger contemporary) of Isaiah. In fact, there are many parallel phrases and passages in Isaiah and Micah which indicate that Micah either heard or read prophecies of his older and great contemporary, Isaiah.

There is one discernible difference between the two contemporary Prophets Isaiah and Micah, and this difference is due to their different backgrounds. Isaiah was a native of the great city of Jerusalem; Micah came from a tiny village. Isaiah was from a well-known family; Micah was evidently from a humble family, the fact that his father's name is not given indicating his family was not well known. He is referred to merely as Micah from the village of Moresheth. So the Prophet Nahum is referred to by his village, with his father's name not mentioned. Evidently he too came from a little-known family.

This contrast in background between the two contemporary Prophets, Isaiah being a Jerusalem aristocrat and Micah being a humble villager, explains the difference in emphasis found in their prophecies. Both preach the same general prophetic message, but Isaiah is chiefly concerned with statecraft, alliances, and whether Judah should declare war or remain at peace. When Isaiah rebukes the king and his officers, it is chiefly because they do not trust in God but trust in alliances. When Micah rebukes the ruling classes, he rebukes them not for matters dealing with statecraft but for their violence and oppression of the poor. Isaiah also mentions violence and oppression, but the humble villager Micah, among the classes who suffered from the oppressor, makes this the center of his message. It is noteworthy that that other great villager, Amos, was likewise deeply sensitive to the suffering and oppression of the humble.

SYNOPSIS OF TEXT

A.   The word of the Lord that came to Micah the Morashtite in the days of Jotham, Ahaz, and Hezekiah, kings of Judah, which he saw concerning Samaria and Jerusalem.
>   Hear, ye peoples, all of you;
>   Hearken, O earth, and all that therein is;
>   And let the Lord God be witness against you,
>   The Lord from His holy temple. . . .
>   For the transgression of Jacob is all this,
>   And for the sins of the house of Israel. . . .
>   Therefore shall Zion for your sake be plowed as a field,
>   And Jerusalem shall become heaps,
>   And the mountain of the house as the high places of a
>   forest. —1:1-2, 5a; 3:12.

B.   Woe to them that devise iniquity
>   And work evil upon their beds!
>   When the morning is light, they execute it,
>   Because it is in the power of their hand.
>   And they covet fields, and seize them;
>   And houses, and take them away;
>   Thus they oppress a man and his house,
>   Even a man and his heritage.
>   Therefore thus saith the Lord:
>   Behold, against this family do I devise an evil,
>   From which ye shall not remove your necks,
>   Neither shall ye walk upright; for it shall be an evil time. . . .
>   For the rich men thereof are full of violence,

And the inhabitants thereof have spoken lies,
And their tongue is deceitful in their mouth,
Therefore I also do smite thee with a grievous wound;
I do make thee desolate because of thy sins. . . .
Trust ye not in a friend,
Put ye not confidence in a familiar friend;
Keep the doors of thy mouth from her that lieth in thy
      bosom.
For the son dishonoureth the father,
The daughter riseth up against her mother,
The daughter-in-law against her mother-in-law;
A man's enemies are the men of his own house. – 2:1-3;
    6:12, 13; 7:5, 6.

C.   If a man walking in wind and falsehood do lie:
'I will preach unto thee of wine and of strong drink';
He shall even be the preacher of this people. . . .
Thus saith the Lord concerning the prophets that make my
      people to err;
That cry: 'Peace,' when their teeth have any thing to bite;
And whoso putteth not into their mouths,
They even prepare war against him:
Therefore it shall be night unto you, that ye shall have no
      vision;
And it shall be dark unto you, that ye shall not divine;
And the sun shall go down upon the prophets,
And the day shall be black over them. . . .
Do I change, O house of Jacob?
Is the spirit of the Lord straitened?
Are these His doings?
Do not My words do good to him that walketh up-
      rightly? . . .
But I truly am full of power by the spirit of the Lord,
And of justice, and of might,
To declare unto Jacob his transgression,
And to Israel his sin. – 2:11; 3:5, 6; 2:7; 3:8.

D.   Hear ye now what the Lord saith:
Arise, contend thou before the mountains,

And let the hills hear thy voice.
Hear, O ye mountains, the Lord's controversy,
And ye enduring rocks, the foundations of the earth;
For the Lord hath a controversy with His people,
And He will plead with Israel.
O My people, what have I done unto thee?
And wherein have I wearied thee?
Testify against Me.
For I brought thee up out of the land of Egypt,
And redeemed thee out of the house of bondage,
And I sent before thee Moses, Aaron and Miriam. – 6: 1-4.

E.   'Wherewith shall I come before the Lord,
And bow myself before God on high?
Shall I come before Him with burnt-offerings,
With calves of a year old? . . .'
It hath been told thee, O man, what is good,
And what the Lord doth require of thee:
Only to do justly, and to love mercy, and to walk humbly
    with thy God. – 6:6, 8.

F.   He retaineth not His anger for ever,
Because He delighteth in mercy.
He will again have compassion upon us;
He will subdue our iniquities;
And Thou wilt cast all their sins into the depths of the sea.
Thou wilt show faithfulness to Jacob, mercy to Abraham,
As Thou hast sworn unto our fathers from the days of
    old. . . .
Rejoice not against me, O mine enemy;
Though I am fallen, I shall arise;
Though I sit in darkness, the Lord is a light unto me.
I will bear the indignation of the Lord,
Because I have sinned against Him;
Until He plead my cause, and execute judgment for me;
He will bring me forth to the light,
And I shall behold His righteousness. . . .
There shall be a day when they shall come unto thee,
From Assyria even to the cities of Egypt, . . .

And from sea to sea, and from mountain to mountain. . . .
But in the end of days it shall come to pass,
That the mountain of the Lord's house shall be established
    as the top of the mountains,
And it shall be exalted above the hills;
And people shall flow unto it.
And many nations shall go and say:
'Come ye, and let us go up to the mountain of the Lord,
And to the house of the God of Jacob;
And He will teach us of His ways,
And we will walk in His paths';
For out of Zion shall go forth the law,
And the word of the Lord from Jerusalem.
And He shall judge between many peoples,
And shall decide concerning mighty nations afar off;
And they shall beat their swords into plowshares,
And their spears into pruning-hooks;
Nation shall not lift up sword against nation,
Neither shall they learn war any more.
But they shall sit every man under his vine and under his
    fig-tree;
And none shall make them afraid;
For the mouth of the Lord of Hosts hath spoken. – 7: 18b-20;
    7:8, 9, 12; 4:1-4.

COMMENTARY

A.   Micah begins with the theme of God's coming to punish both the northern and the southern kingdoms for their sins. He refers to them sometimes by their capital cities, Samaria and Jerusalem, and sometimes as Israel for the northern kingdom, and Zion and Jerusalem for the southern.

B.   He lists the sins for which they have earned the inevitable punishment, the extortion and the oppression of the powerful. "The rich men thereof are full of violence." As a result of all this sinful oppression, morality gives way to cynicism and even the comradeship within the home is broken up. "The son dishonoureth the father; the daughter riseth up against the mother."

C.   He attacks the false prophets. Their chief sin is that they lure the sinful people with visions of safety. They cry "Peace." This theme of the prophets falsely predicting peace is taken up and elaborated by Jeremiah: "They have healed the hurt of the daughter of My people lightly, saying 'Peace, peace' when there is no peace" (8:12). Likewise, Ezekiel says of the prophets: "Because they have led My people astray, saying: 'Peace' and there is no peace" (13:10).The true function of the Prophet is not to flatter the people to their own ultimate hurt but to heal them with the bitter medicine of truth, "To declare unto Jacob his transgression and to Israel his sin" (Micah 3:8).

D.   The Lord has a controversy with His people and He pleads with them. The same idea is used by Micah's contemporary, Isaiah: "Come now let us reason together, saith the Lord" (Isaiah 1:18). And the last prophet, Malachi, writes his whole booklet in the form of a debate between God and sinful Israel.

E.   This great passage deals with the classic prophetic idea that the true worship of God is not necessarily in ritual but essentially in righteousness. It is interesting to observe that Amos, the stern preacher at Beth-el, denounces reliance upon the sacrificial rites and urges in contrast "but let justice well up as water" (Amos 5:24). Hosea, the gentle Prophet of God's love and mercy, expressing the same theme, says: "I desire mercy rather than sacrifice" (Hosea 6:6). Isaiah, whose central concept of God was not predominantly Amos' God of Justice nor Hosea's God of Love, although he believed, of course, in both, had as his central idea of God, God's absolute holiness. "Holy is the Lord of Hosts" (Isaiah 6:3). Because God is holy and exalted, man must be humble. Isaiah constantly preaches against haughtiness and the sin of pride. All three ethical virtues, each based upon a different emphasis of God's infinity—justice with Amos, mercy with Hosea, humility with Isaiah—are combined here in Micah, the younger contemporary of Isaiah. "What doth the Lord require of thee: to do justly, to love mercy and to walk humbly with thy God" (Micah 6:8).

F.   The Prophet says that God will lead Israel to forgiveness. As Israel repents, it will be restored. The vision of the restoration is identical almost word for word with that vision in Isaiah (chapter 2, verse 2 and following), namely, that it shall come to pass that all nations shall come to the mountain of the Lord to learn the ways of justice and peace, and they shall beat their swords into plowshares and never again learn the art of war. Scholars, discussing the fact that these two parallel sections occur both in Isaiah and his younger contemporary Micah, come to various explanations of this repetition. Some say that Isaiah quotes Micah. Others say that Micah quotes Isaiah. Still others say it was an older prophecy which both cite. However this may have been, one interesting fact is to be observed. The passage in Micah has one significant verse added to the passage as it is found in Isaiah. Micah is a country man. He has seen the marauding armies march through the countryside, ravaging at will, while the inhabitants of Jerusalem are still safe behind their massive city walls. So to the vision of peace found in Isaiah he adds this beautiful countryside picture of peace: "And they shall sit each man under his vine and his fig-tree and none shall make them afraid" (4:4).

NAHUM

GENERAL OUTLINE

The opening verse of this prophecy reads: "The burden of Nineveh. The book of the vision of Nahum, the Elkoshite." The word "burden" is generally used for a solemn and denunciatory vision, often concerning the punishment of the nations for their sins. The oracle or preachment against the various nations was from the very beginning a theme among the literary prophets. Amos, the first of the literary prophets, begins with a series of brief oracles against the nations. Such oracles are found in the succeeding prophets. Whereas most of the prophets utter oracles against many of the nations, this address is directed against one nation only, Assyria, and its capital city, Nineveh, just as the prophecy of Obadiah was against Edom alone.

The fact that we have here an oracle against the city of Nineveh and the Assyrians enables us to date at least approximately this work of Nahum. It is assumed that the Prophet already saw the first evidence of the break-down of this warlike and ferocious nation which with its implacable cruelties and irresistible military skill conquered all of west Asia and also Egypt. It is further assumed that since the Prophet speaks of the coming destruction of Nineveh, the capital of Assyria, that the destruction has not yet occurred, although it seems near. Since the date of the destruction of Nineveh by the alliances of Media and Babylonia took place around the year 611, it is generally agreed that these prophecies of Nahum were written a little before that time. Therefore Nahum may be placed between the periods of Isaiah and Jeremiah.

Nothing further is known of Nahum, the Elkoshite. The village of Elkosh from which he came is unknown. Various suggestions have been made as to its location, but none of them are convincing. The text itself reveals that the Prophet had great poetic power. This booklet contains some of the most vividly descriptive passages in all the prophetic literature.

SYNOPSIS OF TEXT

A.   The burden of Nineveh. The book of the vision of Nahum
          the Elkoshite. . . .
      Thus saith the Lord;
      Though they be in full strength, and likewise many,
      Even so shall they be cut down, and he shall pass away;
      And though I have afflicted thee, I will afflict thee no more.
      And now will I break his yoke from off thee,
      And will burst thy bonds in sunder.
      And the Lord hath given commandment concerning thee,
      That no more of thy name be sown;
      Out of the house of thy god will I cut off
      The graven image and the molten image;
      I will make thy grave; for thou art become worthless. —1: 1,
          12, 13, 14.

B.   The shield of his mighty men is made red,
      The valiant men are in scarlet;
      The chariots are fire of steel in the day of his preparation,
      And the cypress spears are made to quiver.
      The chariots rush madly in the streets,
      They jostle one against another in the broad places;
      The appearance of them is like torches,

They run to and fro like the lightnings. . . .
Yet they flee away;
'Stand, stand';
But none looketh back.
Take ye the spoil of silver, take the spoil of gold; . . .
Where is the den of the lions;
Which was the feeding-place of the young lions,
Where the lion and the lioness walked,
And the lion's whelp, and none made them afraid? . . .
And it shall come to pass, that all they that look upon thee
Shall flee from thee,
And say: 'Nineveh is laid waste;
Who will bemoan her?
Whence shall I seek comforters for thee?' – 2:4, 5, 9, 10,
    12; 3:7.

C.   Art thou better than No-amon,
        That was situate among the rivers,
        That had the waters round about her;
        Whose rampart was the sea, and of the sea her wall? . . .
        Yet was she carried away,
        She went into captivity; . . .
        Thou also shalt be drunken,
        Thou shalt swoon;
        Thou also shalt seek a refuge
        Because of the enemy. . . .
        Thy shepherds slumber, O king of Assyria,
        Thy worthies are at rest;
        Thy people are scattered upon the mountains,
        And there is none to gather them. . . .
        A maul is come up before thy face;
        Guard the defences,
        Watch the way, make thy loins strong,
        Fortify thy power mightily! – 3:8, 10a, 11, 18; 2:2.

COMMENTARY

A.   Nahum announces the coming destruction of Nineveh together with all its idols.

B.   A vivid picture of the preparations for defense of the city and the destruction of the city is given. The description of Nineveh as the den of lions is particularly apt. During their dominance of western Asia, the Assyrians were ferocious and irresistible. From the den of Nineveh, these beasts marched forth and the very rumor of their coming, like the roaring of a lion, struck terror in the hearts of their victims.

C.   The city of No-amon (Thebes) had recently been destroyed by the Assyrians on one of their forays into Egypt. This took place about the year 664 B.C.E. The poet-prophet says to Nineveh: "You are no better and no stronger than No-amon which in spite of its fortification and its allies fell to your assault. So will your kingdom and your city be assaulted and destroyed."

HABAKKUK

GENERAL OUTLINE

The opening sentence of this prophecy reads: "The burden which Habakkuk the Prophet did see." The name "Habakkuk" is a curious one. Some derive it from the Hebrew word meaning "to embrace." Others say that it is an Assyrian word meaning "garden plant." And since it is mentioned without any reference either to the city from which the Prophet came, as with some of the prophets, or the name of his father, it is assumed that Habakkuk is a pseudonym and therefore is used alone.

The fact that the name may be an Assyrian pseudonym and also that scholars have found in the prophecy references to Assyrian mythology has led some scholars to assume that the Prophet was a Judean prince who was living as a hostage in Nineveh, the capital of Assyria. This, however, is only a surmise. Scholars are uncertain as to the date of his preachment. Some place him early, as a young disciple of Isaiah, and some place him later, as a contemporary of Jeremiah in Jerusalem. This variation in date is based upon variations in interpretation of passages in the prophecy, some saying that the nation that he denounces is Assyria, therefore placing him early, and others saying that the nation that he denounces is Chaldea (or Babylonia), which overthrew the Assyrians, hence placing him later, in the time of Jeremiah. Some combine both ideas and say that he refers both to the Assyrians and the Babylonians and announces the coming destruction of the Assyrians by the Chaldeans.

Let us take the prophecy just as it stands. Since it is difficult to determine its exact date, we may describe it as an oracle, "a burden" against the nations, in which the Chaldeans are the instruments of God's punishment, who will in turn be punished for their crimes. The Prophet takes up one of the most troublesome problems in religious philosophy, namely, why do the evil triumph, why does a just God allow wrongdoing to go unpunished? This problem was already discussed by Jeremiah (12:1), "Wherefore doth the way of the wicked prosper?" and becomes the entire theme of the Book of Job. The answer of God is that the Prophet must be patient, that God will send his Chaldeans to punish the wicked but that in the meantime the righteous must be patient and live by his faith. The closing chapter is an exultant psalm.

SYNOPSIS OF TEXT

A.   The burden which Habakkuk the prophet did see.
How long, O Lord, shall I cry,
And Thou wilt not hear?
I cry out unto Thee of violence,
And Thou wilt not save.
Why dost Thou show me iniquity,
And beholdest mischief?
And why are spoiling and violence before me?
So that there is strife, and contention ariseth.
Therefore the law is slacked,
And right doth never go forth;
For the wicked doth beset the righteous;
Therefore right goeth forth perverted. . . .
Art not Thou from everlasting,
O Lord my God, my Holy One?
We shall not die.
O Lord, Thou hast ordained them for judgment,
And Thou, O Rock, hast established them for correction.
Thou that art of eyes too pure to behold evil,
And that canst not look on mischief,

Wherefore lookest Thou, when they deal treacherously,
And holdest Thy peace, when the wicked swalloweth up
The man that is more righteous than he? —1: 1-4, 12, 13.

B.   For lo, I raise up the Chaldeans,
That bitter and impetuous nation,
That march through the breadth of the earth,
To possess dwelling-places that are not theirs.
They are terrible and dreadful;
Their law and their majesty proceed from themselves.
Their horses also are swifter than leopards,
And are more fierce than the wolves of the desert;
And their horsemen spread themselves;
Yea, their horsemen come from far,
They fly as a vulture that hasteth to devour. . . .
Shall they therefore empty their net,
And not spare to slay the nations continually? —1: 6-8, 17.

C.   I will stand upon my watch,
And set me upon the tower,
And will look out to see what He will speak by me,
And what I shall answer when I am reproved.
And the Lord answered me, and said:
'Write the vision,
And make it plain upon tables,
That a man may read it swiftly.
For the vision is yet for the appointed time,
And it declareth of the end, and doth not lie;
Though it tarry, wait for it;
Because it will surely come, it will not delay.'
Behold, his soul is puffed up, it is not upright in him;
But the righteous shall live by his faith. — 2: 1-4.

D.   Because thou hast spoiled many nations,
All the remnant of the peoples shall spoil thee;
Because of men's blood, and for the violence done to the
    land,
To the city and to all that dwell therein.
Woe to him that gaineth evil gains for his house,

That he may set his nest on high, . . .
Thou hast devised shame to thy house,
By cutting off many peoples,
And hast forfeited thy life.
For the stone shall cry out of the wall,
And the beam out of the timber shall answer it. . . .
For the earth shall be filled
With the knowledge of the glory of the Lord,
As the waters cover the sea. — 2:8-11, 14.

COMMENTARY

A.   As the Prophet Jeremiah complained that he was born to look upon tragedy and cruelty, so Habakkuk complains that God shows him all this heart-breaking iniquity in the world. And he asks God why He looks on when people deal treacherously and the "wicked swalloweth up the righteous."

B.   God says He will send the Chaldeans, whose horsemen will ride to destroy those who have earned punishment.

C.   The Prophet is to be a watchman for coming events. This theme is found frequently in the Prophets. Thus, for example, Ezekiel (3:17): "Son of man, I have appointed thee as a watchman over the house of Israel." The Prophet on watch writes down his vision which will yet be fulfilled.

D.   That vision is that the Chaldeans who have destroyed many peoples will, although they were instruments of God, be punished for their cruelty and presumption. And in the end, as many of the prophets have predicted, "the earth will be filled with the knowledge of God as the waters cover the sea." This phrase is virtually identical with a phrase in Isaiah (11:9).

ZEPHANIAH
GENERAL OUTLINE

Those prophets who came from humble families which were not well known are described by their own names and the villages from which they came. Thus Micah, the Morashtite, and Nahum, the Elkoshite. Prophets who came from well-known families are referred to by their fathers' names, as Isaiah, the son of Amoz; Jeremiah, son of Hilkiah; Joel, the son of Pethuel. Zephaniah is given a long genealogy, with the name of his father, his grandfather, his great-grandfather and his great-great-grandfather. It is clear that he must have come from a very noble and possibly royal family, particularly since his great-grandfather is Hezekiah, the same name as that of the king of Judah. It is also clear that this son of the royal house or of an exalted noble family lived in Jerusalem. He mentions the many districts within the city. (See 1:10.)

The prophecy of Zephaniah is, as a whole, not difficult to date. The opening verse clearly says that he preached in the days of Josiah, the King of Judah. And since he describes many corruptions and idolatries, it is assumed that the period of his activities was before the time when Josiah instituted the reforms described in the Second Book of Kings (chapter 23), where it is mentioned that Josiah destroyed the idol worship. Hence it is usually taken that Zephaniah preached in the early days of the reign of Josiah. In other words, he was somewhat earlier than the Prophet Jeremiah (i.e., around the year 630 B.C.E.).

Zephaniah's book shows clearly the influence of both Amos and Isaiah. From Amos comes the sweeping oracle against all the surrounding nations for their wickedness, and from Isaiah the doctrine that the remnant of Israel will survive to grow into a blessed and a righteous people. It seems from his prophecy that the great destructive kingdom of Assyria, whose menace overshadowed the prophecies of Isaiah, is about to fall, and the Prophet speaks of the "great coming day of God" when this mighty military empire will collapse into ruins, and in that fall other wicked nations, on the day of God's judgment, will receive their punishments.

SYNOPSIS OF TEXT

A.   The word of the Lord which came unto Zephaniah the son of Cushi, the son of Gedaliah, the son of Amariah, the son of Hezekiah, in the days of Josiah the son of Amon, king of Judah.

I will utterly consume all things
From off the face of the earth, . . .

And I will stretch out My hand upon Judah,
And upon the inhabitants of Jerusalem;
And I will cut off the remnant of Baal from this place,
And the name of the idolatrous priests with the priests; . . .
And it shall come to pass in the day of the Lord's sacrifice,
That I will punish the princes, and the king's sons,
And all such as are clothed with foreign apparel. . . .
And it shall come to pass at that time,
That I will search Jerusalem with lamps;
And I will punish the men that are settled on their lees,
That say in their heart;
'The Lord will not do good, neither will He do evil.'
Therefore their wealth shall become a booty,
And their houses a desolation;
Yea, they shall build houses, but shall not inhabit them, . . .

    —1:1, 2, 4, 8, 12, 13a.

B.   Gather yourselves together, yea, gather together,
O shameless nation;
Before the decree bring forth . . .
Seek ye the Lord, all ye humble of the earth,
That have executed His ordinance;
Seek righteousness, seek humility.
It may be ye shall be hid in the day of the Lord's anger.
For Gaza shall be forsaken,
And Ashkelon a desolation;
They shall drive out Ashdod at the noonday,
And Ekron shall be rooted up. . . .
I have heard the taunt of Moab,
And the revilings of the children of Ammon,
Wherewith they have taunted My people,
And spoken boastfully concerning their border.
Therefore as I live,
Saith the Lord of hosts, the God of Israel:
Surely Moab shall be as Sodom,
And the children of Ammon as Gomorrah,
Even the breeding-place of nettles, and saltpits,
And a desolation, for ever;
The residue of My people shall spoil them,

And the remnant of My nation shall inherit them. . . .
Because they have taunted and spoken boastfully
Against the people of the Lord of hosts.
And He will stretch out His hand against the north,
And destroy Assyria;
And will make Nineveh a desolation,
And dry like the wilderness. . . .
This is the joyous city
That dwelt without care,
That said in her heart:
'I am, and there is none else beside me';
How is she become a desolation,
A place for beasts to lie down in!
Every one that passeth by her
Shall hiss, and wag his hand. — 2:1, 2a, 3, 4, 8, 9, 10, 13, 15.

C.   For then will I turn to the peoples
A pure language,
That they may all call upon the name of the Lord,
To serve Him with one consent.
From beyond the rivers of Ethiopia
Shall they bring My suppliants,
Even the daughter of My dispersed,
As Mine offering.
And I will leave in the midst of thee
An afflicted and poor people,
And they shall take refuge in the name of the Lord.
The remnant of Israel shall not do iniquity,
Nor speak lies,
Neither shall a deceitful tongue be found in their mouth;
For they shall feed and lie down,
And none shall make them afraid. . . .
At that time will I bring you in,
And at that time will I gather you;
For I will make you to be a name and a praise
Among all the peoples of the earth,
When I turn your captivity before your eyes,
Saith the Lord. — 3:9, 10, 12, 13, 20.

COMMENTARY

A.   There will be wide-spread destruction during which God will sweep away the idol worship in Israel. The day of the Lord's judgment is at hand. Those people who have become skeptical, who say that God neither punishes nor rewards, will see the evidence of His mighty judgment.

B.   He calls upon the children of Israel to gather and see the destruction of all the surrounding nations, and as a climax even the fall of the mighty Assyria.

C.   When the Prophet speaks of the return of the remnant of Israel, he extends the vision of the blessed future to include all the peoples of the earth. All peoples will "speak a pure language" and God's suppliants will come from everywhere and the remnant of Israel shall find peace and joy.

HAGGAI

GENERAL OUTLINE

The three Prophets Haggai, Zechariah, and Malachi are the last of the literary prophets. They lived after the return from the Exile. Jewish tradition (b. Yoma 9b) says that when these three died, the holy spirit of prophetic inspiration died with them in Israel. They are properly put at the end of the list of literary prophets in the Bible.

Haggai and Zechariah both are mentioned in the first verse of the fifth chapter of Ezra, who, with Nehemiah, was one of the reorganizers of the reestablished Palestinian community. These two Prophets (Haggai and Zechariah) lived in the early days of the return, in the time of Zerubbabel, the returning prince of the house of David, and Joshua the high priest, before the time of Ezra and Nehemiah. Ezra and Nehemiah came a little less than a century after the first group of returning exiles who came under the leadership of Zerubbabel and Joshua. The last of the three post-exilic prophets, Malachi, lived in the time of Ezra and Nehemiah, therefore almost a century after Haggai and Zechariah.

We are able to date exactly the time of Haggai's preaching. He gives the exact date during the reign of the Persian king Darius when he preached. The year of his preachment, his whole prophecies lasting only a few months, was 520 B.C.E. Since he refers, as if he were an eye-witness, to the beauty of the original temple which had been destroyed seventy years previously by the Babylonians, it is assumed that he was now a very old man, having lived through the entire period of the Exile. Perhaps this accounts for the brief period of his prophecy. It was toward the end of his life that he spoke.

The aim of his prophecy is a practical one. The people had returned from the Exile. They managed to build houses for themselves, but neglected to begin rebuilding the Temple of God. The Prophet says that they will never have real security and prosperity until they reestablish their religious life by reestablishing the Temple. His preachment seemed to have moved Zerubbabel, the governor, and Joshua, the high priest, and the people, as they started to rebuild the Temple. The last part of the prophecy is a typical theme found among many of the Prophets, that God will disturb and shake up many nations, and he adds that Israel will be restored to an independent government and Zerubbabel will be chosen by God to be an independent king.

It may seem strange to the reader of the works of the great literary prophets that a series of addresses urging the people to rebuild the Temple should be considered harmonious with the rest of literary prophecy. After all, most of the preceding prophets preached of the breakdown of national independence and the destruction of the Temple. Yet here a prophet urges its reconstruction. But it is perfectly in harmony. The earlier prophets spoke of the idolatry of the people even in the very Temple. Also Ezekiel, who lived in the Exile, referred to it. The original Temple was beyond purification. It had to be destroyed. With its destruction Israel in exile was purified, "in the furnace of suffering." Idolatry disappeared among them. The Prophets had won that battle and now it was necessary to rebuild the Temple for the purer worship of God.

Even the Prophet Isaiah, who was one of the earlier prophets, visualized the distant time when to Zion purified would flow the nations of the earth, seeking inspiration from an ennobled Israel. Now Israel, returning from exile purified from idolatry, must rebuild God's house. To urge them to that task was the function of the Prophet Haggai.

A.   In the second year of Darius the king, in the sixth month, in the first day of the month, came the word of the Lord by Haggai the prophet unto Zerubbabel the son of Shealtiel, governor of Judah, and to Joshua the son of Jehozadak, the high priest, saying: 'Thus speaketh the Lord of hosts, saying: This people say: The Lord's house should be built.' Then came the word of the Lord by Haggai the prophet, saying: 'Is it a time for you yourselves to dwell in your ceiled houses, while this house lieth waste? Now therefore thus saith the Lord of hosts:

> Consider your ways.
> Ye have sown much, and brought in little,
> Ye eat, but ye have not enough,
> Ye drink, but ye are not filled with drink,
> Ye clothe you, but there is none warm;
> And he that earneth wages earneth wages
> For a bag with holes. . . .

And I called for a drought upon the land, and upon the mountains, and upon the corn, and upon the wine, and upon the oil, and upon that which the ground bringeth forth, and upon men, and upon cattle, and upon all the labour of the hands.' . . .

And the Lord stirred up the spirit of Zerubbabel the son of Shealtiel, governor of Judah, and the spirit of Joshua the son of Jehozadak, the high priest, and the spirit of all the remnant of the people; and they came and did work in the house of the Lord of hosts, their God. —1:6, 11, 14.

B.   In the seventh month, in the one and twentieth day of the month, came the word of the Lord by Haggai the prophet, saying: 'Speak now to Zerubbabel the son of Shealtiel, governor of Judah, and to Joshua the son of Jehozadak, the high priest, and to the remnant of the people, saying: Who is left among you that saw this house in its former glory? and how do ye see it now? is not such a one as nothing in your eyes? Yet now be strong, O Zerubbabel, saith the Lord; and be strong, O Joshua, son of Jehozadak, the high priest; and be strong, all ye people of the land, saith the Lord, and work; for I am with you, saith the Lord of hosts. The word that I covenanted with you when ye came out of Egypt have I established, and My spirit abideth among you; fear ye not.

The glory of this latter house shall be greater than that of the former, . . . and in this place will I give peace. – 2 : 1-5, 9.

C.   And the word of the Lord came the second time unto Haggai in the four and twentieth day of the month, saying: 'Speak to Zerubbabel, the governor of Judah, saying: I will shake the heavens and the earth, and I will overthrow the throne of kingdoms, and I will destroy the strength of the kingdoms of the nations; . . . In that day, saith the Lord of hosts, will I take thee, O Zerubbabel, My servant, the son of Shealtiel, saith the Lord, and will make thee as a signet; for I have chosen thee. . . .' – 2 : 20-22a, 23.

COMMENTARY

A.   Although the people have built houses to live in, they are not secure and prosperous. They will continue to deserve punishment and poverty until they rebuild God's house.

B.   Those old people, probably Haggai among them, who remembered the glories of the pre-exilic Temple, are depressed at the sight of the tiny impoverished community. The Prophet enheartens them and says "be strong all ye people of the land."

C.   When the Prophet gives this address, there is a series of rebellions in Persia, and the entire kingdom of which the newly returned community is a part is profoundly shaken. It is this time of disturbance which the Prophet sees as the occasion for Israel's restoration of independence and Zerubbabel's return as king on his ancestor's throne.

ZECHARIAH

GENERAL OUTLINE

Zechariah was a younger contemporary of Haggai. It is very likely that he was born during the Exile in Babylon. The main purpose of his preachment was the same as that of Haggai's, the rebuilding of the Temple and the restoration of the community. His style is entirely different from that of his older contemporary. Haggai spoke in simple prose wherein, too, he was different from the earlier prophets, whose sermons were mostly in poetry. Zechariah speaks in visions, which come as dreams of the night. Every sermon of his in the first eight chapters is based upon a strange vision. He sees horses of different colors, four oxhorns, a flying scroll, a candlestick of gold. The Prophet whom he most resembles in this regard is Ezekiel, who likewise lived in Babylon. Some scholars therefore feel that it was the Persian-Babylonian influence, with its love of rich imagery, which influenced both these men.

Another difference between this very late Prophet and his great predecessors is that God spoke with them directly and they spoke to God. Here Zechariah no longer speaks with God but through an intermediary. It is the angel who speaks to him and explains the visions. Also Satan appears as a sort of a mischief maker. In spite of these mystic visions, Zechariah has great flashes of the old prophetic fervor, denouncing evil and opposing mere ritual in favor of justice and mercy. "Thus hath the Lord of hosts spoken: show mercy and compassion; oppress not the widow, the orphan, the stranger nor the poor."

The last six chapters of the book are in poetry and are chiefly oracles against the nations. Most scholars are in agreement that these last chapters (from 9-14) were not written by Zechariah and, just as the section in Isaiah from chapter 40 on is called "Deutero-Isaiah," so this part of Zechariah is often called "Deutero-Zechariah." There is, however, this difference. Deutero-Isaiah lived after the Isaiah who preached the sermons in the first part of the book, whereas many scholars are of the opinion that the last six chapters now found at the end of Zechariah were written much earlier than the rest of the book. Some scholars, on the other hand, say these six chapters were written much later. But most of them say that since they refer to Israel and to Judah, they were written before the Exile.

SYNOPSIS OF TEXT

A.   In the eighth month, in the second year of Darius, came the word of the Lord unto Zechariah the son of Berechiah, the son of

Iddo, the prophet, saying: 'The Lord hath been sore displeased with your fathers. Therefore say thou unto them: Thus saith the Lord of hosts: Return unto Me, saith the Lord of hosts, and I will return unto you, saith the Lord of hosts. Be ye not as your fathers, unto whom the former prophets proclaimed, saying: Thus saith the Lord of hosts: Return ye now from your evil ways, and from your evil doings; but they did not hear, nor attend unto Me, saith the Lord. Your fathers, where are they? and the prophets, do they live for ever? But My words and My statutes, which I commanded My servants the prophets, did they not overtake your fathers? so that they turned and said: Like as the Lord of hosts purposed to do unto us, according to our ways, and according to our doings, so hath He dealt with us.'–1:1-6.

B.   Upon the four and twentieth day of the eleventh month, which is the month Shebat, in the second year of Darius, came the word of the Lord unto Zechariah the son of Berechiah, the son of Iddo, the prophet, saying—I saw in the night, and behold a man riding upon a red horse, and he stood among the myrtle-trees that were in the bottom; and behind him there were horses, red, sorrel, and white. Then said I: 'O my Lord, what are these?' And the angel that spoke with me said unto me: 'I will show thee what these are.' . . .

Then the angel of the Lord spoke and said: 'O Lord of hosts, how long wilt Thou not have compassion on Jerusalem and on the cities of Judah, against which Thou hast had indignation these threescore and ten years?' . . .

Therefore thus saith the Lord: I return to Jerusalem with compassions: My house shall be built in it, saith the Lord of hosts, and a line shall be stretched forth over Jerusalem. –1:7-9, 12, 16.

C.   And the angel that spoke with me returned, and waked me, as a man that is wakened out of his sleep. And he said unto me: 'What seest thou?' And I said: 'I have seen, and behold a candlestick all of gold, with a bowl upon the top of it, and its seven lamps thereon; there are seven pipes, yea, seven, to the lamps, which are upon the top thereof; and two olive-trees by it, one upon the right side of the bowl, and the other upon the left side thereof.' And I answered and spoke to the angel that spoke with me, saying: 'What are these, my Lord?' Then the angel that spoke with me answered and said unto me: 'Knowest thou not what these are?' And I said: 'No, my lord.' Then he answered and spoke unto me, saying: 'This is the word of the Lord unto Zerubbabel, saying: Not by might, nor by power, but by My spirit, saith the Lord of hosts.'– 4: 1-6.

D.   Then came the word of the Lord of hosts unto me, saying: 'Speak unto all the people of the land, and to the priests, saying: When ye fasted and mourned in the fifth and in the seventh month, even these seventy years, did ye at all fast unto Me, even to Me? . . .'

And the word of the Lord came unto Zechariah, saying: 'Thus hath the Lord of hosts spoken, saying: Execute true judgment, and show mercy and compassion every man to his brother; and oppress not the widow, nor the fatherless, the stranger, nor the poor; and let none of you devise evil against his brother in your heart. . . .'– 7:4, 8, 9, 10.

E.   And the word of the Lord of hosts came unto me, saying: 'Thus saith the Lord of hosts: It shall yet come to pass, that there shall come peoples, and the inhabitants of many cities; and the inhabitants of one city shall go to another, saying: Let us go speedily to entreat the favour of the Lord, and to seek the Lord of hosts; I will go also. Yea, many peoples and mighty nations shall come to seek the Lord of hosts in Jerusalem, and to entreat the favour of the Lord. . . .'– 8: 18-22.

COMMENTARY

A.   The Prophet begins in the mood of many of the earlier prophets, pointing out that Israel had failed to repent. He reviews the work of the prophets and says that what the prophets had predicted would occur has occurred. The destruction of the state and the Exile, which they foretold would come as a result of Israel's continuous backsliding and moral weakness, have indeed been tragically fulfilled.

B.   This is a typical vision of Zechariah. It evidently was a dream "I saw in the night." The angel explains the dream and says that it means that God will rebuild Jerusalem. The builder's measuring line will be stretched over Jerusalem and the city will be reconstructed.

C.   This famous vision is read on Chanuko. The candlestick, the light of pure worship, and the two olive trees which feed it with their olive oil are the secular and the priestly rulership, Zerubbabel and Joshua.

D.   This is a classic preachment of the prophets: Not sacrifice, not songs, not fasting in themselves are the true worship of God, but mercy and justice are the essentials of the worship of the merciful and just God.

E.   The vision of restoration is described, and as is frequent among the prophets, the statement is made that when Israel will be restored—purified—other peoples will be inspired to seek true worship of God. "Let us go speedily to entreat the favour of the Lord, and to seek the Lord of hosts; I will go also."

MALACHI

GENERAL OUTLINE

There was, very likely, no prophet by the name of Malachi. The true name of the Prophet who preached the prophecies now headed "Malachi" in our Bible is not known. There must not have been a name or heading on these prophecies when the book of the twelve minor prophets was compiled. The word *malachi* means "my messenger." The third chapter of the book begins, "Behold, I send My messenger." Either by mistake or for lack of any other specific name, this word "My messenger," *Malachi*, was put at the head of the book.

Rabbis in the Talmud (b. Megilla 15a) offer some theories as to what Malachi's real name was. One says it was Mordecai, who of course lived in the Persian period. Others say it was Ezra. It was indeed in the time of Ezra the scribe that Malachi lived. It is almost certain that Malachi preached in the time of Ezra and Nehemiah, the reorganizers of the community which had returned to Palestine almost a century before. The prophecies of Malachi can best be understood in relation to the book of Nehemiah. Nehemiah (13:9) had to fight against the defilement of the house of God and so did Malachi speak of the corrupted priests. Nehemiah denounced the people for putting aside their Jewish wives and marrying heathens; so did Malachi. Nehemiah had to urge the people to bring their tithes to the Temple; so did Malachi. It was his task to help in the reformation of the Temple whose worship had become slack.

Thus the last of the Prophets advocates a reforming of the ritual, whereas the earlier prophets seemed to have scorned it. What the earlier prophets objected to was mere ritual as a substitute for righteous living. But the ritual had its place in a normal, established community. It was the function of the last three prophets, Malachi among them, to reestablish the ritual interrupted by the Exile and to put it upon a high level.

The style of Malachi is unique among the Prophets. Just as in the case of Haggai and Zechariah, his fellow exilic Prophets, the old intense poetic preachment has disappeared. Haggai speaks in prose as a matter-of-fact lecturer. Zechariah speaks in visions, as a man awakened from sleep; Malachi speaks like a schoolmaster with questions and answers, test problems, objections and correct solutions. Thus prophecy completes its cycle from the impassioned orator to the patient teacher.

SYNOPSIS OF TEXT

A.   The burden of the word of the Lord to Israel by Malachi . . .
A son honoureth his father,
And a servant his master;
If then I be a father,
Where is My honour?
And if I be a master,
Where is My fear?
Saith the Lord of hosts
Unto you, O priests, that despise My name.
And ye say: 'Wherein have we despised Thy name?'
Ye offer polluted bread upon Mine altar.
And ye say: 'Wherein have we polluted Thee?'
In that ye say: 'The table of the Lord is contemptible.'
And when ye offer the blind for sacrifice, it is no evil!
And when ye offer the lame and sick, it is no evil!

Present it now unto thy governor;
Will he be pleased with thee?
Or will he accept thy person?
Saith the Lord of hosts. . . .
For from the rising of the sun even unto the going down of
the same
My name is great among the nations;
And in every place offerings are presented unto My name,
Even pure oblations;
For My name is great among the nations,
Saith the Lord of hosts.
But ye profane it,
In that ye say:
'The table of the Lord is polluted,
And the fruit thereof, even the food thereof, is contempt-
ible.'—1:1, 6-8, 11-12.

B.   And now, this commandment
Is for you, O ye priests.
If ye will not hearken, and if ye will not lay it to heart,
To give glory unto My name,
Saith the Lord of hosts,
Then will I send the curse upon you,
And I will curse your blessings;
Yea, I curse them,
Because ye do not lay it to heart. . . .
Know then that I have sent
This commandment unto you,
That My covenant might be with Levi,
Saith the Lord of hosts.
My covenant was with him
Of life and peace, and I gave them to him,
And of fear, and he feared Me,
And was afraid of My name.
The law of truth was in his mouth,
And unrighteousness was not found in his lips;
He walked with Me in peace and uprightness,
And did turn many away from iniquity.
For the priest's lips should keep knowledge,

And they should seek the law at his mouth;
For he is the messenger of the Lord of hosts.
  — 2:1, 2, 4-7.

C.   Have we not all one father?
      Hath not one God created us?
      Why do we deal treacherously every man against his brother,
      Profaning the covenant of our fathers?
      Judah hath dealt treacherously,
      And an abomination is committed in Israel and in Jerusalem;
      For Judah hath profaned the holiness of the Lord which He
          loveth,
      And hath married the daughter of a strange god. . . .
      And this further ye do:
      Ye cover the altar of the Lord with tears,
      With weeping, and with sighing,
      Insomuch that He regardeth not the offering any more,
      Neither receiveth it with good will at your hand.
      Yet ye say: 'Wherefore?'
      Because the Lord hath been witness
      Between thee and the wife of thy youth,
      Against whom thou hast dealt treacherously,
      Though she is thy companion,
      And the wife of thy covenant. . . .
      Ye have wearied the Lord with your words.
      Yet ye say: 'Wherein have we wearied Him?'
      In that ye say: 'Every one that doeth evil
      Is good in the sight of the Lord,
      And He delighteth in them;
      Or where is the God of justice?'
          — 2:10, 11, 13, 14, 17.

D.   Your words have been all too strong against Me,
      Saith the Lord.
      Yet ye say: 'Wherein have we spoken against Thee?'
      Ye have said: 'It is vain to serve God;
      And what profit is it that we have kept His charge,
      And that we have walked mournfully
      Because of the Lord of hosts?

And now we call the proud happy;
Yea, they that work wickedness are built up;
Yea, they try God, and are delivered.'– 3:13-15.

E.   Then they that feared the Lord
Spoke one with another;
And the Lord hearkened, and heard,
And a book of remembrance was written before Him,
For them that feared the Lord, and that thought upon His
    name . . .
Remember ye the law of Moses My servant,
Which I commanded unto him in Horeb for all Israel,
Even statutes and ordinances.
Behold, I will send you
Elijah the prophet
Before the coming
Of the great and terrible day of the Lord.
And he shall turn the heart of the fathers to the children,
And the heart of the children to their fathers;
Lest I come and smite the land with utter destruction. – 3:16,
    22-24.

COMMENTARY

A.   The Temple is restored. It lacks the grandeur of the old,
pre-exilic Temple. The priests and Levites and the people seem to be
uninspired by it. The ritual is observed in a careless manner.
Worthless animals and polluted bread are grudgingly given. For
this the Prophet denounces them. He reminds them that this little
Temple will some day be the center of inspiration for all the peoples
of the earth, and Israel should surely honor it. The beginning of
this section follows the typical schoolmaster method of question
and answer.

B.   He is particularly indignant at the priests whose duty it is to
fulfill the covenant which God made with them, to teach the law
of truth and to be, instead of bored ministrants at an indifferently
honored little shrine, the inspired and inspiring "messengers of the
Lord of hosts."

C.   Many men have cruelly set aside their wives and married heathen women from the surrounding peoples. He denounces them for this treachery to the bonds of marriage. "Ye cover the altar of the Lord with tears" by brutally setting aside the covenant of wedlock. Deal not treacherously with each other. How dare ye deal treacherously? "Have we not all one Father?"

D.   The people, in their gloom and disheartenment at this tiny community, surrounded by enemies, ask the question which has been asked since the days of Jeremiah: why are the wicked successful and the righteous suffering?

E.   Those who revere God speak to each other and encourage each other, confident that there will come a day, "the great and terrible day of God," when wickedness will be destroyed. That day will be ushered in by Elijah the Prophet, who will unite the hearts of fathers to the hearts of children. Thus Malachi, the messenger, the last of the Prophets, invokes as a messenger Elijah the great predecessor of the literary prophets.

THE ESSENCE OF THE PROPHETS

The literary prophets constitute a spiritual, ethical and literary movement which endured for three centuries. Amos preached in the middle of the eighth pre-Christian century, and Malachi in the middle of the fifth. This is a very long period for a continuous literary movement.

But is it really a continuity? There is little evidence that the Prophets taught each other. Sometimes we find a repetition of a sentence or a passage from one prophet in another, indicating that they may have seen some of each other's writings. But there is no evidence at all that Amos actually taught Hosea, or that Isaiah taught Micah, or that Jeremiah taught Ezekiel. One would think that with so many diverse personalities, living over such a vast stretch of time, particularly a time so disturbed that there was no opportunity for calm contemplation and instruction, that there would be comparatively little similarity between the Prophets. Nevertheless it is remarkable how much identity of doctrine and literary methods there was among them. They varied indeed in personality and in the circumstances under which they lived, but there is a classic, prophetic doctrine which somehow carried over from prophet to prophet over these long centuries.

In our discussion of the various prophets we have indicated many similarities of teaching. We will now attempt to sum up the main ideas which were found in almost all of them and we will attempt to do it in the same way in which we treated each individual prophet, namely to provide first a general outline of the main range of prophetic ideas and then to follow it with a mosaic of verses, taken from all the Prophets, which, in the words of the Prophets themselves, will give the essence of prophecy.

GENERAL OUTLINE

A.   God, the Holy God, the God of justice and love, is the Lord of all the earth. His law is incumbent upon all people, and whichever nation violates His law will inevitably be punished by Him.

B.   Israel will be punished among all other nations for its sins. But Israel has a special place in God's plan for the world. God trained Israel, loved him like a parent loves a child, nurtured him gently. Because of this special training Israel should have been more just and more merciful. Therefore when, in spite of this training, Israel is unjust and cruel, he deserves greater punishment than all the other nations.

C.   The Prophet's task is to tell this truth unto Israel. It is not a task which the Prophet chooses of his own accord. He is conscripted for this mission, and though his heart may break at the bitter message he must give, he cannot evade the mandate which God has put upon him.

D.   The chief sins of Israel which the Prophet is compelled to bring to the people's attention is social injustice and treachery to God, abandoning Him for other gods, the worthless idols.

E.   For that sin Israel must be punished. The nation will be overthrown, the countryside ruined, the Temple destroyed.

F.   Israel will not believe this message. It is too unpleasant to be easily accepted. Besides, Israel is lulled into a false security by false prophets who will cry "Peace, peace when there is no peace."

G.   Nevertheless, in spite of the deceitful assurances of the false prophets, punishment will surely come. God has selected mighty nations, Assyria and Chaldea, as the instruments of His just anger, and when the time will come for Israel to be restored, He will again select a great nation, Persia, to be the instrument of His merciful purpose.

H.   God's intended punishment of the people cannot be diverted by political devices. In vain it is to seek alliances with Rezin, King of Syria, or with Egypt or with Assyria.

I.   It is equally vain to imagine that the mere ritual at the Temple will save Israel. Sacrifices and fasting are not enough.

J.   The only possible deliverance from misfortune would be a complete change of conscience. Only justice and mercy can save Israel or any nation.

K.   When Israel will have been punished, God, who chastises them in love, will awaken their hearts to repentance and they will be purified "in the furnace of suffering."

L.   Then God will restore them. They will be a united people, and God's eternal covenant will be recorded on their hearts.

M.   Israel is not restored for its own sake. God, who punishes all nations for their sins, will lead them too in happiness and righteousness. Israel reclaimed, and Zion restored will be the vehicle of the redemption of all of God's children in the nations of the earth.

SYNOPSIS OF TEXT

A.   Thus saith the Lord: for three transgressions of Damascus, I will not reverse it because they have threshed Gilead with sledges of iron. For three transgressions of Gaza, yea for four, I will not reverse it because they carried away captive a whole captivity. For three transgressions of Israel, I will not reverse it, because they sell the righteous for silver and the needy for a pair of shoes. – Amos 1:3, 6; 2:6.

Are ye not as the children of Ethiopians unto me, O children of Israel? Have I not brought up Israel out of the land of Egypt and the Philistines from Caphtor and Aram from Kir? – Amos 9:7.

B.   Let Me sing a song of My well beloved concerning his vineyard, the vineyard of the Lord of hosts, the house of Israel. – Isaiah 5:1, 7.

When Israel was a child I loved him and out of Egypt I called My son. – Hosea 11:1.

Is Ephraim a darling son unto me? As often as I speak of him, My heart yearneth for him. – Jeremiah 31:20.

Children I have reared and brought up and they have rebelled against Me. – Isaiah 1:1.

You only have I known of all the families of the earth; therefore I will visit upon you all your iniquities. – Amos 3:2.

C.   The Lord God will do nothing but He revealeth His counsel unto His servants the prophets. The lion hath roared. Who will not fear? The Lord God hath spoken. Who can but prophesy? – Amos 3:7, 8.

And I said, 'Here am I, send me.' And He said: 'Go and tell this people.' – Isaiah 6:8, 9.

Before thou camest from the womb, I sanctified thee. I have appointed thee a prophet unto the nations. To whomsoever I send you, thou shalt go, and whatsoever I shall command you, thou shalt speak. – Jeremiah 1:5, 6.

D.   They sell the righteous for silver and the needy for a pair of shoes. – Amos 2:6.

What mean ye that ye crush My people and grind the face of the poor? – Isaiah 3:15.

Hath a nation changed its gods which yet are no gods but My people hath changed its glory for that which doth not profit. They have forsaken Me, the fountain of living waters. – Jeremiah 2:11, 13.

E. And Israel shall surely be led away captive out of his land.
– Amos 7:17.

Until cities be waste without inhabitants and houses without man and the land become utterly waste. – Isaiah 6:11.

F. They have healed the hurt of the daughter of my people lightly, saying 'Peace, peace when there is no peace.'– Jeremiah 8:11.

Son of man, prophesy against the prophets of Israel that prophesy. Thus saith the Lord God: Woe unto the vile prophets because they have led My people astray, saying 'Peace' and there is no peace. – Ezekiel 13:2, 3, 10.

Thus saith the Lord: concerning the prophets that make My people to err, that cry 'Peace' when their teeth have anything to bite. – Micah 3:5.

G. O Asshur, the rod of Mine anger. – Isaiah 10:5.

O daughter of the Chaldeans, . . . I was wroth with My people and gave them into thy hand. – Isaiah 47:5, 6.

Thus saith the Lord to His anointed.

To Cyrus whose right hand I have holden, . . .

For the sake of Jacob My servant . . .

I have called thee by thy name. – Isaiah 45:1, 4.

H. And Ephraim has become like a silly dove without under- standing. They call unto Egypt, they go to Assyria. – Hosea 7:11.

Forasmuch as this people hath refused the waters of Shiloah that go softly and rejoiceth with Rezin and Remaliah's son, now there- fore the Lord bringeth upon them, the waters of the River, the king of Assyria. – Isaiah 8:6, 7.

How greatly dost thou cheapen thyself. Thou shalt be ashamed of Egypt also, as thou wast ashamed of Asshur. – Jeremiah 2:36.

I. Yea though ye offer Me burnt-offerings and your meal- offerings, I will not accept them. Take away from Me the noise of thy songs. – Amos 5:22, 23.

For I desire mercy and not sacrifice, the knowledge of God rather than burnt-offering. – Hosea 6:6.

To what purpose is the multitude of your sacrifices unto Me, saith the Lord? I delight not in the blood of bullocks, or of lambs. . . .

Who hath required this at your hand to trample My courts? – Isaiah 1:11, 12.

For I spoke not unto your fathers, nor commanded them in the day that I brought them out of Egypt concerning burnt-offerings or sacrifices. – Jeremiah 7:22.

Wherewith shall I come before the Lord? Shall I come before Him with burnt-offerings? Will the Lord be pleased with thousands of rams, with ten thousand rivers of oil? – Micah 6:6, 7.

J.   It hath been told thee, O man, what is good, and what the Lord doth require of thee: Only to do justly, and to love mercy, and to walk humbly with thy God. – Micah 6:8.

Seek good and not evil that ye may live. Let justice well up as water and righteousness as a mighty stream. – Amos 5:14, 24.

Sow to yourselves, according to righteousness, reap according to mercy. – Hosea 10:12.

Wash you, make you clean, put away the evil of your doings, seek justice, relieve the oppressed, judge the fatherless and plead for the widow.

Zion shall be redeemed with justice and they that return to her with righteousness. – Isaiah 1:16, 17, 27.

If ye oppress not the stranger and shed not innocent blood in this place, neither walk after other gods to your hurt, then I will cause you to dwell in this place, in the land that I gave to your fathers for ever and ever. But this thing I commanded them saying: Hearken unto My voice and I will be your God and ye shall be My people. – Jeremiah 7:22, 23.

K.   Come, let us return unto the Lord, for He hath torn and He will heal us. – Hosea 6:1.

Behold I have refined thee but not as silver. I have tried thee in the furnace of affliction. – Isaiah 48:10.

L.   And it shall come to pass in that day that the remnant of Israel shall stay upon the Lord, the holy One of Israel in truth. A remnant shall return unto God the Mighty. – Isaiah 10:21.

And I will make them one nation in the land, . . . and they shall no more be two nations, neither shall they be divided into two kingdoms any more at all; neither shall they defile themselves any more with their idols . . . so shall they be My people and I will be their God. – Ezekiel 37:22, 23.

Behold the days come, saith the Lord that I make a new covenant with the house of Israel and with the house of Judah. I will put My law in their inward parts, in their heart will I write it; and I will be their God and they shall be My people. – Jeremiah 31:33.

The remnant of Israel shall not do iniquity nor speak lies and none shall make them afraid. – Zephaniah 3:13.

M.   And many nations shall go and say, 'Come ye, let us go up to the mountain of the Lord, and He will teach us of His ways and we will walk in His paths. For out of Zion shall go forth the law and the word of the Lord from Jerusalem. – Isaiah 2:3.

And the Lord shall make Himself known to Egypt and the Egyptians shall know the Lord in that day; in that day Israel will be the third with Egypt and with Assyria, a blessing in the midst of the earth: 'Blessed be Egypt, My people, and Assyria, the work of My hands, and Israel, Mine inheritance.' – Isaiah 19:21, 24, 25.

For from the rising of the sun even unto the going down of the same, My name is great among the nations, and in every place offerings are presented unto My name. – Malachi 1:11.

Also the aliens that join themselves to the Lord, and to love the name of the Lord, to be His servants . . . their burnt-offerings and their sacrifices shall be acceptable upon Mine altar for My house shall be called a house of prayer for all peoples. – Isaiah 56:6, 7.

I will also give thee for a light unto the nations that my salvation may be unto the ends of the earth. – Isaiah 49:6.

CHAPTER VII

Psalms, Proverbs, Job

T HE Book of Psalms is the first book in the third part of the
Bible—the *K'suvim,* "The Writings." The name in the Greek
Bible is *Hagiographa,* which means "Holy Writings." It is
the last part of the Bible to be embodied into the entire collection.
Not all the books which in the Hebrew Bible are in the "Holy
Writings" are included in them in the Christian Bible. For example,
Ruth, which is one of the *K'suvim* in our Hebrew Bible, is counted
as one of the "Earlier Prophets," and is placed after Judges in the
Christian Bible. Also, the Book of Lamentations is included, in the
Christian Bible among the "Later Prophets," immediately following
the prophecies of Jeremiah, who is said by tradition to have been its
author.

Not all the books in the Hagiographa are different in content
or type from the books in the two earlier parts of the Bible, the
Torah and the Prophets. For example, Ezra, Nehemiah, and Chronicles, being historical books, could well have been classified with
the earlier historical books in the Bible, Samuel, Kings, etc. Daniel,
which is a species of prophecy, could be included among the
Prophets. In fact, this whole third part of the Bible is a rather
miscellaneous collection. The Psalms are poetry; the Proverbs, as
the name implies, are terse sayings of popular wisdom; Ecclesiastes
and Job are religious philosophy; Ruth is narrative; Ezra and
Chronicles are history. Thus the third section of Scripture is a mis-
cellany of various books. The bond which unites this group of
books is the fact that they are later in composition than the books
in the first two sections of Scripture and hence are gathered into
this final part of the Bible.

· 203 ·

PSALMS

One can recognize at a glance that the Psalms belong to a type of literature which is different from the rest of the Bible. It is not merely because the Psalms are poetry; the Bible has a great deal of poetry scattered through the various books—many of the great orations of the Prophets are in poetic form. The main difference between the Psalms and the earlier books is in the person addressed. In the earlier books, the Torah and the Prophets, it is generally Israel who is addressed by the prophet or by God Himself. But in the Psalms it is Israel who speaks, chiefly to God. Thus in the Torah Israel is asked to hearken to the laws and to the God-given ordinances. In the earlier Prophets (the historical books), Israel is called upon to listen to the lessons derived from Israel's past history. In the Prophets, Israel is rebuked, pleaded with, and urged to loyalty, to mercy, and to justice. In the Psalms, too, there are certain poems which voice the mood of the historical books, many which glorify the Torah and its laws, and also a number which express the prophetic fervor for righteousness. But in most of the Psalms it is the human heart which expresses its own sorrows, its disappointments, its sufferings. The individual, either in his own behalf or for the people Israel, pleads to God for help, or chants his song of thanks for blessings and deliverance. The people of Israel, exhorted and admonished in the rest of the Bible, find at last in the Psalms its response and its self-expression.

This makes the book rather unique in ancient literature. Poetry which expresses the inner mood of the individual (lyric poetry) was virtually unknown in antiquity. There was plenty of epic poetry—the story of the triumph of a nation symbolized by a great hero—but there is almost no poetry, other than the Psalms themselves, which voice the sorrows and the hope of the individual man. The chief reason for this lack of self-expressive or lyric poetry is that the sense of individuality, of personal uniqueness, was not very well developed in antiquity. People thought of themselves as part of their tribe or their nation. They were not schooled to look within. Their inward moods, even to the extent that they were observed, were not deemed important enough for permanent literary expression. It was first of all in Israel that the individual soul, the unique child of God, felt that his own moods, his own hopes, and his own fears deserved expression in enduring literary form. The Psalms, therefore, are the world's first great collection of personal poetry. An English writer, Rowland E. Prothero, said of the Psalms:

The Book of Psalms contains the whole music of the heart of man, swept by the hands of his Maker. In it are gathered the lyrical burst of his tenderness, the moan of his penitence, the pathos of his sorrow, the triumph of his victory, the despair of his defeat, the firmness of his confidence, the rapture of his assured hope.

The present Book of Psalms is considered by tradition to have been collected by King David. It is easy to see why this tradition arose. David is described in the Book of Samuel as the "sweet singer in Israel." In the Book of Chronicles he is credited with having organized the choirs of Levites which sang the Psalms in the Temple. There are many individual psalms in the collection which are ascribed to him as author. The book is divided into five subdivisions which tradition considers parallel to the five books of the Torah. Thus, it is said, that as Moses gave us the Torah, so David gave us the five books of the Psalms.

Of course, the tradition did not mean that David wrote all the Psalms himself. Many of the Psalms in the book have headings which indicate other authors. There is one which is ascribed to Moses, one ascribed to Solomon, quite a number to the Levite family of Assaf, others to the Levite family of Korah, etc. In fact, the Talmud recognizes this multiple authorship by saying that David and ten others collected the Psalms (b. Baba Bathra 15a).

The Book as it stands is clearly a collection of previous smaller collections. Psalm 72 ends with the words: "The prayers of David son of Jesse are ended." The sentence indicates that this first part of the Book of Psalms belongs to an independent collection which was called "The Prayers of David." In the next section of Psalms, from 73 on, there is a large group in succession with the heading "Assaf," indicating that the Levite family of Assaf must have had a collection of its own. Students are divided as to the date of the individual Psalms and the final date of completion of the entire collection. Many of the Psalms may well be old, dating back to the time of David. Others clearly reveal the ritual of the Second

Temple, where they were chanted by the Levites in connection with the sacrifice. The end of the third pre-Christian century is generally accepted as the period in which the Book of Psalms attained its present form, although some scholars say that certain individual psalms are as late as the Maccabean era, therefore a half a century later.

The Greek word *psalm* implies instrumental music, since many of the Psalms were played to the accompaniment of instrumental music by the Levites. Thus *psalm* is related to the Hebrew word *mizmor*, a term found in the heading of numerous psalms and which also means instrumental music. The generally current word for the book is *T'hilim* (popularly *tilim*) which means "songs of praise." The following Psalms selected may serve as a fair sampling of the more prevalent types of poetry in this great collection.

SYNOPSIS OF TEXT

A.　For the Leader. A Psalm of David.
　　The heavens declare the glory of God,
　　And the firmament showeth His handiwork;
　　Day unto day uttereth speech,
　　Night unto night revealeth knowledge; ...
　　And their words to the end of the world.
　　O Lord, our Lord,
　　How glorious, is Thy name in all the earth!
　　Whose majesty is rehearsed above the heavens. ...
　　The Lord reigneth; He is clothed in majesty;
　　The Lord is clothed, He hath girded Himself with strength;
　　Yea, the world is established, that it cannot be moved.
　　Thy throne is established of old;
　　Thou art from everlasting. ...
　　For all the gods of the peoples are things of nought;
　　But the Lord made the heavens. ...
　　O worship the Lord in the beauty of holiness;
　　Tremble before Him, all the earth.
　　Say among the nations: 'The Lord reigneth.'
　　The world also is established that it cannot be moved;
　　He will judge the peoples with equity. – 19:1-3, 5; 8:2;
　　　93:1-2; 96:5, 9, 10.

B.   Happy is the man that hath not walked in the counsel of
the wicked,
Nor stood in the way of sinners,
Nor sat in the seat of the scornful. . . .
And he shall be like a tree planted by streams of water,
That bringeth forth its fruit in its season, . . .
Not so the wicked;
But they are like the chaff which the wind driveth away. . . .
Why standeth Thou afar off, O Lord?
Why hidest Thou Thyself in times of troubles?
Through the pride of the wicked the poor is hotly pursued,
They are taken in the devices that they have imagined. . . .
The wicked, in the pride of his countenance (saith): 'He
will not require';
All his thoughts are: 'There is no God.'
His ways prosper at all times;
Thy judgments are far above out of his sight; . . .
Why art thou cast down, O my soul?
And why moanest thou within me?
Hope thou in God; for I shall yet praise Him
For the salvation of His countenance. . . .
[A Psalm] of David.
The Lord is my light and my salvation; whom shall I fear?
The Lord is the stronghold of my life; of whom shall I be
afraid?
When evil-doers came upon me to eat up my flesh,
Even mine adversaries and my foes, they stumbled and fell.
Though a host should encamp against me,
My heart shall not fear;
Though war should rise up against me,
Even then will I be confident. — 1:1, 3a, 4; 10:1, 2, 4, 5a;
42:6; 27:1-3.

C.   For the Leader; Maschil of the sons of Korah.
As the hart panteth after the water brooks,
So panteth my soul after Thee, O God.
My soul thirsteth for God, for the living God:
'When shall I come and appear before God?' . . .
Great is the Lord, and highly to be praised,

In the city of our God, His holy mountain,
Fair in situation, the joy of the whole earth;
Even mount Zion, the uttermost parts of the north,
The city of the great King. . . .
We have thought on Thy lovingkindness, O God,
In the midst of Thy temple. – 42: 1-3; 48: 2, 3, 10.

D.   Maschil of Asaph.
Give ear, O my people, to my teaching;
Incline your ears to the words of my mouth. . . .
We will not hide from their children,
Telling to the generation to come the praises of the Lord,
And His strength, and His wondrous works that He hath
     done. . . .
That they might put their confidence in God,
And not forget the works of God,
But keep His commandments; . . .
'Because he hath set his love upon Me, therefore will I de-
     liver him;
I will set him on high, because he hath known My name.
He shall call upon Me, and I will answer him;
I will be with him in trouble;
I will rescue him, and bring him to honour.
With long life will I satisfy him,
And make him to behold My salvation.' – 78: 1, 4, 7; 91: 14-16.

COMMENTARY

A.   These selections are from the nature poetry in the Psalms.
All of nature is seen as a revelation of God's presence, for it speaks
of His power and His dominion. Nature calls upon man to be
humble before His greatness and to worship the beauty of His
holiness.

B.   The righteous shall flourish like a tree firmly planted near
streams of water. The wicked will be blown away like chaff by
the wind. This general conviction, based upon the assurance of
God's justice, runs through most of the Bible. The Psalmist never
doubts it. That is why he pleads so earnestly with God in his time

of trouble. If he has sinned, he asks for forgiveness. When he is certain that he has been righteous, he asks: Why does God "stand afar off," and pleads: "Come to my help, O God." Even in the deepest sorrow, he never loses faith that "The Lord is the stronghold of my life; of whom shall I be afraid?"

C. Almost all of the Psalms by the Levite family Korah (that is to say, the psalms in the Korah collection) have the same theme, namely, longing for the presence of God, a homesickness for the Temple, and for the city of Jerusalem. "When shall I come and appear before God . . . in the city of our God . . . the joy of the whole earth."

D. The Psalms of Assaf (the collection of this family of Levites) are generally historical, in the mood of Deuteronomy and the earlier prophets (the historical books). The poems review the history of Israel in Egypt and in the desert, interpreting the story, as do the historical books, so as to indicate that God's providence has preserved and tested Israel "that they might put their confidence in God and keep His commandments."

PROVERBS

The Book of Proverbs (in Hebrew, *Mishle*) is the second of the Holy Writings (Hagiographa). It is also the first of another group of books called "The Wisdom Literature," in which are included also Job and Ecclesiastes. The Wisdom Literature, especially as exemplified in the Book of Proverbs, is noticeably different in content and mood from the other literature in the Bible. The other books of the Bible center about the people of Israel, the laws and special commandments of their religion, their spiritual struggles, their political history and destiny. But in the Wisdom Literature there is no reference at all to anything specifically Jewish. The books deal with general human affairs as if the books were written by non-Jews for non-Jews.

The Book of Proverbs represents the Wisdom Literature in its most confident mood before it began to restudy its own philosophy in the Book of Job and before it arrived at skepticism in the Book of Ecclesiastes. Characteristic of this self-assured Wisdom

Book is its calm, material mood. There is in it none of the intense self-expression of the Psalms or of the high dedication of the Prophets. There is no great sense of mission, of spiritual oneness with God. The Book of Proverbs is hardly to be considered a spiritual book at all. It is not inward; it is not emotional. It deals out practical counsel for earthly happiness: if one is righteous, one will be happy. Even the definition of happiness is practical and earthy: happiness is long life, good health, wealth and contented family living. The books therefore are merely practical counsel as to how to attain success in life. This matter-of-fact practicality applies especially to the Book of Proverbs where the Wisdom Literature is at its most confident mood. It applies somewhat to the Book of Ecclesiastes, less to the Book of Job in which the depth of human suffering is plumbed. The book most akin to Proverbs in the Wisdom Literature is the Book of Sirach, one of the books excluded from the Bible (the Apocrypha, see Part One, chapter ii). But in all of the Wisdom Literature, Israel and Jerusalem and the Temple play no part at all. The Wisdom Books deal with the problems of human happiness for the average man.

Yet, although Israel is not present as a specific theme, the Wisdom Books are nevertheless Jewish wisdom, at least by implication. There is no complete agnosticism in them. God is real and He is just. Even Job who suffers never abandons his conviction of God's justice. The books are Jewish also in their concreteness. When the Greek writers deal with themes such as these, they are inclined to be theoretical. They will ask: What is happiness? What is ethics? and will try to work out exact definitions for these ideas. The Jewish Wisdom Books are not interested in theoretical definitions but in practical experience taken from daily life, and in simple and direct counsel on how to live.

The Book of Proverbs, then, is the most confident of the Wisdom Books. Later wisdom books will begin to doubt the thesis that a wise understanding of the practical technique of life will necessarily lead to happiness. But Proverbs is still sure that caution in human relationships, energy, and the willingness to accept counsel will lead on to happiness, and that happiness consists of material success and contentment.

The book is ascribed by tradition to King Solomon, inasmuch as the Book of Kings says of King Solomon that: "He spoke three thousand proverbs" (1 Kings 5:12). The opening sentence of the book is: "The proverbs of Solomon the son of David king of Israel." However, the book itself gives evidence that it is composed of parts from other books. Chapter 10 in our present Book of Proverbs begins with the words, "The proverbs of Solomon," indicating that the preceding nine chapters belonged to some previous collection. Chapter 24, verse 23, reads: "These also are the sayings of the wise." This evidently is a heading from another group of proverbs. Chapter 25 begins with the sentence: "These also are the proverbs of Solomon which the men of Hezekiah king of Judah copied out," which marks still another collection of proverbs. Thus it is clear that just as the Book of Psalms is a collection of previous collections of poems, so is our present Book of Proverbs a collection of various previous collections of proverbs. Some of these proverbs are quite clear in their reference to God and His commandments; others merely give practical advice without reference to religious motivation, although in all of them there is the implied conviction that the world is managed in justice and that wisdom and virtue will bring earthly happiness.

SYNOPSIS OF TEXT

A. The proverbs of Solomon the son of David, king of Israel;
To know wisdom and instruction;
To comprehend the words of understanding;
To receive the discipline of wisdom,
Justice, and right, and equity; . . .
To understand a proverb, and a figure;
The words of the wise, and their dark sayings.
The fear of the Lord is the beginning of knowledge;
But the foolish despise wisdom and discipline. . . .
Wisdom crieth aloud in the street,
She uttereth her voice in the broad places;
She calleth at the head of the noisy streets,
At the entrances of the gates, in the city, she uttereth her
  words:
'How long, ye thoughtless, will ye love thoughtlessness?
And how long will scorners delight them in scorning,
And fools hate knowledge? . . .'

My son, forget not my teaching;
But let thy heart keep my commandments;
For length of days, and years of life,
And peace, will they add to thee.
Let not kindness and truth forsake thee;
Bind them about thy neck,
Write them upon the table of thy heart;
So shalt thou find grace and good favour
In the sight of God and man. . . .
The Lord by wisdom founded the earth;
By understanding He established the heavens. —1:1-3, 6, 7,
    20-22; 3:1-4, 19.

B.   The proverbs of Solomon.
A wise son maketh a glad father;
But a foolish son is the grief of his mother.
Treasures of wickedness profit nothing;
But righteousness delivereth from death.
The Lord will not suffer the soul of the righteous to famish;
But He thrusteth away the desire of the wicked. . . .
When pride cometh, then cometh shame;
But with the lowly is wisdom. . . .
Behold, the righteous shall be requited in the earth;
How much more the wicked and the sinner! . . .
A righteous man regardeth the life of his beast;
But the tender mercies of the wicked are cruel.
He that tilleth his ground shall have plenty of bread;
But he that followeth after vain things is void of under-
    standing. . . .
Lying lips are an abomination to the Lord;
But they that deal truly are His delight. . . .
The hand of the diligent shall bear rule;
But the slothful shall be under tribute. . . .
Better is a dry morsel and quietness therewith,
Than a house full of feasting with strife. . . .
Death and life are in the power of the tongue;
And they that indulge it shall eat the fruit thereof. . . .
Seest thou a man wise in his own eyes?
There is more hope of a fool than of him. . . .

Whoso diggeth a pit shall fall therein;
And he that rolleth a stone, it shall return upon him. –10:1-3;
  11:2, 31; 12:10, 11, 22, 24; 17:1; 18:21; 26:12, 27.

C.   A woman of valour who can find?
For her price is far above rubies.
The heart of her husband doth safely trust in her,
And he hath no lack of gain.
She doeth him good and not evil
All the days of her life. . . .
Her children rise up, and call her blessed;
Her husband also, and he praiseth her:
'Many daughters have done valiantly,
But thou excellest them all.'
Grace is deceitful, and beauty is vain;
But a woman that feareth the Lord, she shall be praised.
Give her of the fruit of her hands;
And let her works praise her in the gates. – 31:10-12, 28-31.

COMMENTARY

A.   The introductory part of the book expresses the purpose of the whole collection. Wisdom is personified as if she were a wise mother pleading with her erring sons to turn back from the path of folly. "Wisdom crieth aloud in the streets . . . how long ye thoughtless will ye love thoughtlessness." She calls upon youth to accept the guidance of wisdom and, as a reward, "length of days and years of life will they add to thee." Wisdom is also looked upon as a co-worker with God in Creation. God founded the world by the aid of Wisdom and therefore Wisdom must be obeyed as the law of life for all the children of men.

B.   The main group of the Proverbs of Solomon from chapter 10 to chapter 22 are all in the form of two-line poetry-like statements, similar to the style of writing in the poetic parts of the Prophets. Generally the second line gives "the opposite side of the coin," the contrast to the first line. Thus, "a wise son maketh a glad father, but a foolish son is the grief of his mother." Or, "The hand of the diligent shall bear rule, but the slothful shall be under tribute."

C.   This famous chapter, closing the Book of Proverbs, has long been part of the Friday evening Home Ritual. It describes the noble woman who looks after the affairs of her household in wisdom and in diligence. Her husband's heart delights in her. Her children rise up and call her blessed. Thus the beginning and the end of the book balance each other. The book opens with wisdom personified as a gracious motherly guide, and closes with the true mother, the queen and the guide of her household.

JOB

The Book of Job belongs to the Wisdom Literature. Like all Wisdom Books it does not mention the specific history or problems of the household of Israel. It deals with those problems which apply equally to all men. But unlike the Book of Proverbs, it lacks the rather easy-going confidence that any life can be happy if it is managed with wisdom and motivated by righteousness. The very contrary is the mood of the Book of Job. It declares that a man may be completely righteous and yet suffer endless misery. The book therefore may be considered to be an answer to the confidence of the Book of Proverbs, and in a sense, also a refutation of the popular misunderstanding of the teaching of the Prophets. The Prophets taught that God is just and that man is in duty bound to obey Him. The popular opinion concluded that if a man suffers misfortunes, then it must be because he has violated the will of God, in other words, that all sufferers must be sinners. This seems like a reasonable inference but it surely is not what the Prophets intended to say. It is true that the Prophets insisted that certain specific suffering is a punishment for evil, as, for example, the sufferings of Israel, already endured and yet to come, were due to their injustices and idolatry. But the Prophet Jeremiah speaks of his own suffering and demands to know why he is afflicted when he has done no harm. Certainly the Prophet Jeremiah at least realized that not all who suffer should be denounced as sinful.

The notion that suffering is always a punishment for sin ignores one of the most tragic questions in human life: why do the righteous suffer and the wicked prosper if God is just? The Book of Job faces this question squarely but it cannot be said that it answers this question successfully. Perhaps this question can never be fully answered by our limited human intellect, but the book at least deals with the problem honestly and reveals it in a more realistic light than ever before in Scriptural or in any other classic literature.

The book is a drama, the tragic story of a man whom God consents (at the suggestion of Satan) to put to the test of character by means of the fires of suffering. Job resembles many of the great Greek dramas in which man endures tragedy due to the actions of the gods or of fate. The book is also dramatic not only in content but in form. It is composed almost entirely of dramatic dialogue. Even the narrative introduction and conclusion are largely dialogue, as in a drama. Yet it is rather different from what we today would consider a play. There is almost no action in it. The bulk of the book is merely debate. The sole progress is the progress of the argument. Moreover, unlike modern dramatic dialogue, which consists of an interchange of rather brief speeches, this is a succession of long monologues. Each of the friends speaks and Job answers each of them in an address that is generally two chapters long. Perhaps the book is more correctly comparable to the dialogues of Plato than to the Greek dramas.

Job, the hero of the book, is described as a righteous man who lived long ago. The scene in the prologue, with its flocks and herds, recalls the period of the patriarchs who wandered with their herds over the land of Canaan. Thus the traditional literature considers Job to have been an ancient. Some say that he lived at the time of Abraham. There are as many as ten different periods suggested in the traditional literature as the time in which Job lived. Perhaps the most popular one is that Job lived in the time of Moses and indeed was one of the counsellors of Pharaoh. The Talmud says that Moses wrote the Book of Job. Yet one rabbi says that Job never really existed as an historical character but that he was a parable, i.e., that the book is dramatic fiction (b. Baba Bathra 15a).

The book describes the career of Job, one of the "righteous of the Gentiles" who lived in ancient times. The prologue and the epilogue of the book, which give the story of Job's life, are considered by some modern scholars to be much older than the main part of the book, the philosophic dialogue. Even if this be so, that the author of the dialogue used the older legend in the prologue and the epilogue as the framework of his drama, it is evident that he reworked them so as to fit them to the dialogues since the thought now expressed in the prologue is in full harmony with the dialogues. The whole purpose of the debate in the dialogues is to prove that a man (Job), although completely righteous, may nevertheless be visited with horrible suffering. Thus too the narrative prologue describes how Job was righteous and how, at the suggestion of Satan, God consented that Job be afflicted in order to test him. The prologue ends with the statement that when Job was sorely afflicted, his three friends, Eliphaz, Bildad, and Zophar came to comfort him. Then follow the dialogues between the three friends and Job.

Job begins by cursing that day on which he was born, wishing that he never would have lived, since life involves such suffering. Eliphaz says to him that all men are prone to sin and that God is now correcting whatever sin Job may have committed. Job rebukes Eliphaz and says that his friends should console him in his suffering, but that instead they are accusing him of being sinful. The two other friends are blunter in their accusation that Job must have sinned or he would not have suffered. This Job denies, but he adds that it is impossible for him to prove his innocence because who can argue successfully with an Almighty God? He wishes, however, that God would let him speak.

In spite of his suffering, he trusts in God's justice, even though he does not understand why he is being afflicted. "Yea, though He slay me, yet will I trust in Him" (13:15). He will trust in God's justice but he will never do as the friends do who try to flatter God thinking thus to please Him. "Will ye speak unrighteously for God? Will ye show Him favour?" (13:7, 8). Yes, he does believe that God is righteous but he will never give up the right to speak the truth that he is innocent and that he does not merit this suffering. "I trust in Him, but I will argue my ways before Him" (13:15).

In the end, after some speeches by an additional speaker, Elihu, God rebukes the friends because they did not speak truthfully as Job did. In other words, God says, Do not think that you are defending Me when you accuse every sufferer of being a sinner against Me. "The Lord said to Eliphaz: 'My wrath is kindled against thee, and against thy two friends; for ye have not spoken of Me the thing that is right as My servant Job hath'" (42:7). But God also rebukes Job in the words: "Who is this that darkeneth counsel?" (38:1). In other words, that Job's complaints darken the true understanding of the universe; but the true understanding of God's way is, actually, not made quite clear in the book.

God's speech beginning with chapter 38 is a description of His magnificent but mysterious work in the world. Man does not understand the depth of the divine purposes in nature. "Where wast thou when I laid the foundations of the earth?" (38:4). God's answer satisfies Job and he repents for his rebellious words.

But wherein is the answer satisfactory? What does it amount to? What does the author of the book give as a solution of the problem of why righteous people like Job suffer unjustly? Perhaps he means to say that the tragic experience of the righteous will remain a mystery just as many other great mysteries in the universe are beyond our understanding. We cannot solve all the problems involved in human life. Or perhaps he means to say further that in all these mysteries we see the grandeur of God's work and the manifest purposefulness of His way in the world. Therefore, even when what happens to us remains incomprehensible to us, we must still hold on to the confidence that there is some purpose and a just one. Realizing, however, that although God's ways are just we do not always understand His actions, we must never fall into the sin of despising and accusing the unfortunate and looking upon their misfortunes as proof of their wickedness.

The book, therefore, does not solve the problem of suffering, but it deepens our sympathies with suffering and humbles us with the sense that many of the great problems in life are beyond our understanding but that beyond those mysteries stands the Eternal Wisdom and Justice.

SYNOPSIS OF TEXT

A.   There was a man in the land of Uz, whose name was Job; and that man was whole-hearted and upright, and one that feared God, and shunned evil. . . .

And the Lord said unto Satan: 'Hast thou considered My servant Job, that there is none like him in the earth, a whole-hearted and an upright man, one that feareth God, and shunneth evil?' Then Satan answered the Lord, and said: 'Doth Job fear God for nought? . . . Thou hast blessed the work of his hands, and his possessions are increased in the land. But put forth Thy hand now, and touch all that he hath, surely he will blaspheme Thee to Thy face.' . . .

So Satan went forth from the presence of the Lord, and smote Job with sore boils from the sole of his foot even unto his crown. . . . Then said his wife unto him: 'Dost thou still hold fast thine integrity? blaspheme God, and die.' But he said unto her: 'Thou speakest as one of the impious women speaketh. What? shall we receive good at the hand of God, and shall we not receive evil?' For all this did not Job sin with his lips. — 1: 1, 8, 9, 10b, 11; 2:7, 9, 10.

B.   And Job spoke and said:
Let the day perish wherein I was born,
And the night wherein it was said:
   'A man-child is brought forth.' . . .
Why died I not from the womb?
Why did I not perish at birth? . . .
I should have slept; then had I been at rest— . . .
Then answered Eliphaz, the Temanite, and said:
Shall a mortal man be just before God?
Shall a man be pure before his Maker? . . .
Behold, happy is the man whom God correcteth;
Therefore despise not thou the chastening of the Almighty.
For He maketh sore, and bindeth up;
He woundeth, and His hands make whole. . . .
Then Job answered and said:
Oh that my vexation were but weighed,
And my calamity laid in the balances altogether! . . .
For the arrows of the Almighty are within me,
The poison whereof my spirit drinketh up;
The terrors of God do set themselves in array against me. . . .
How forcible are words of uprightness!
But what doth your arguing argue? . . .
Yea, ye would cast lots upon the fatherless,
And dig a pit for your friend. . . .
If I have sinned, what do I unto Thee, O Thou watcher of
   men?
Why hast Thou set me as a mark for Thee,
So that I am a burden to myself? . . . — 3: 2, 3, 11, 13; 4: 17;
    5: 17, 18; 6: 1, 2, 4, 25, 27; 7: 20.

C.   Then answered Bildad the Shuhite, and said: . . .
Doth God pervert judgment?
Or doth the Almighty pervert justice? . . .
If thou wert pure and upright;
Surely now He would awake for thee,
And make the habitation of thy righteousness prosperous.
Then Job answered and said:
Of a truth I know that it is so;
And how can man be just with God? . . .
How much less shall I answer Him,
And choose out my arguments with Him?
Whom, though I were righteous, yet would I not answer;
I would make supplication to Him that contendeth with
    me. . . .
Though I be righteous, mine own mouth shall condemn me;
Though I be innocent, He shall prove me perverse. . . .
Let Him take His rod away from me,
And let not His terror make me afraid;
Then would I speak, and not fear Him;
For I am not so with myself. – 8: 1, 3, 6; 9: 1, 2, 14, 15, 20,
    34, 35.

D.   Then answered Zophar the Naamathite, and said:
Should not the multitude of words be answered?
And should a man full of talk be accounted right? . . .
Thy boastings have made men hold their peace. . . .
And thou hast said: 'My doctrine is pure,
And I am clean in Thine eyes.' . . .
Canst thou find out the deep things of God?
Canst thou attain unto the purpose of the Almighty? . . .
If iniquity be in thy hand, put it far away,
And let not unrighteousness dwell in thy tents—
Surely then shalt thou lift up thy face without spot;
Yea, thou shalt be stedfast, and shalt not fear; . . .
Then Job answered: Hear now my reasoning.
And hearken to the pleadings of my lips.
Will ye speak unrighteously for God,
And talk deceitfully for Him?
Will ye show Him favour?

Will ye contend for God?
Would it be good that He should search you out?
Or as one mocketh a man, will ye mock Him? . . .
Have pity upon me, have pity upon me, O ye my friends;
For the hand of God hath touched me. . . .
But as for me, I know that my Redeemer liveth,
And that He will witness at the last upon the dust; . . . – 11:1,
    2, 3a, 4, 7, 14, 15; 13:6-9; 19:21, 25.

E.   Then the Lord answered Job out of the whirlwind, and said:
Who is this that darkeneth counsel
By words without knowledge? . . .
Where wast thou when I laid the foundations of the earth?
Declare, if thou hast the understanding. . . .
When the morning stars sang together,
And all the sons of God shouted for joy? . . .
Canst thou bind the chains of the Pleiades,
Or loose the bands of Orion? . . .
Knowest thou the ordinances of the heavens?
Canst thou establish the dominion thereof in the earth? . . .
Then Job answered the Lord, and said:
Behold, I am of small account; what shall I answer Thee?
I lay my hand upon my mouth.
Once have I spoken, but I will not answer again;
Yea, twice, but I will proceed no further. . . .
Then Job answered the Lord, and said:
I know that Thou canst do every thing,
And that no purpose can be withholden from Thee. . . .
I had heard of Thee by the hearing of the ear;
But now mine eye seeth Thee;
Wherefore I abhor my words, and repent,
Seeing I am dust and ashes. – 38:1, 2, 4, 7, 31, 33; 40:3-6;
    42:1, 2, 5, 6.

F.   And it was so, that after the Lord had spoken these words unto Job, the Lord said to Eliphaz the Temanite: 'My wrath is kindled against thee, and against thy two friends; for ye have not spoken of Me the thing that is right, as My servant Job hath. Now therefore, take unto you seven bullocks and seven rams, and go to My servant Job, and offer up for yourselves a burnt-offering; and My servant Job shall pray for you; for him will I accept, that I do not unto you aught unseemly; for ye have not spoken of Me the thing that is right, as My servant Job hath.' . . . And the Lord changed the fortune of Job, when he prayed for his friends; and the Lord gave Job twice as much as he had before. . . . and after this Job lived a hundred and forty years, and saw his sons, and his sons' sons, even four generations. So Job died, being old and full of days. – 42:7, 8, 10, 16.

COMMENTARY

A.   This is part of the narrative prologue. Job is righteous, but Satan, who is described as a sort of a prosecuting attorney, says that while Job is righteous, it is because he is prosperous. Satan says that if Job would suffer he would abandon his righteousness. God consents to this test of Job. Suffering comes but Job holds fast to his integrity.

B.   This is the opening address of the dialogue. Job gives a vivid, poetic description of how peaceful it would be never to have existed. Then Eliphaz's speech expresses the thought that no mortal can be just by God's standards, so Job should be happy that God corrects him. "Happy is the man whom God correcteth," to which Job replies that his words are not intended to comfort Job but to trap him into admitting that he is guilty. "You dig a pit for your friend."

C.   Bildad feels called upon to defend the justness of God: "Doth the Almighty pervert justice?" That is to say, the very fact that Job is suffering proves that he is evil, or else it would be a proof that God is unjust. Job responds that even though he is just, he cannot successfully argue with God the Almighty to prove his case.

D.   The third friend, Zophar, denounces Job for claiming to be righteous and assures him that if he really were righteous he would be confident and happy. Job, responding, says that Zophar is trying to defend God, who does not need such deceitful defense. "I know that my Redeemer liveth and He will witness." Job knows that some day God Himself will come to his defense and declare his innocence.

E.   God's answer is that Job should realize that he cannot know the great mysteries of life, the mysteries of creation and of the life of the animals of the field. The world is a mystery to man. The plans of God are wise and just. These great speeches bring so clear a vision of God's mighty purpose, mysterious but overwhelming, that Job says, "I had heard of Thee by the hearing of the ear, but now mine eye seeth Thee. I abhor my words and repent, seeing I am dust and ashes." In other words, Job admits that the mysteries are too great for him, but trusts in God's mighty purposes.

F.   The epilogue is in prose as was the prologue. God rebukes the friends for seeking to defend Him falsely by untruthfully accusing Job. God restores Job to happiness.

CHAPTER VIII

The Five Scrolls

THE five booklets following the Psalms, Proverbs, and Job are called "The Five Scrolls." They succeed each other in the following order: Song of Songs, Ruth, Lamentations, Ecclesiastes, and Esther. In the older Talmudic literature, the term "Scroll" (*Megillah*) was used exclusively for only one of them, namely the Book of Esther, which was read on Purim, and the Talmudic section which deals with the laws of Purim and the reading of the Scroll of Esther is called Megillah.

All of the five booklets are part of the synagogue ritual. The Song of Songs is read on Passover. The Book of Ruth is read on Shovuos. Lamentations is read on the Ninth of Ov, the anniversary of the destruction of the Temple. Ecclesiastes is read on Sukos, and Esther is read on Purim. In the Greek translation of the Bible these scrolls are not all placed here in the Hagiographa, and therefore, of course, are not together. The Book of Ruth follows the Book of Judges; Lamentations follows the Book of Jeremiah. As a matter of fact, the Talmud itself (b. Baba Bathra 14b), although it has all five of these scrolls in the Hagiographa, does not have them in the present sequence. Ruth precedes the Psalms, Ecclesiastes follows the Proverbs, and Esther follows Daniel.

Judging by their contents, these Five Scrolls do not actually belong together. Two of them are historical (Esther and Ruth); two may be described as poetry (Lamentations and the Song of Songs); and one is philosophical (Ecclesiastes). They are together presumably because all of them were used in the synagogue and all of them, being short scrolls, may have been combined in one fair-sized scroll, just as the twelve small books of the so-called minor prophets were put together in one scroll and are now in one book called "The Twelve."

SONG OF SONGS

The Song of Songs is a series of love songs, but there is no systematic arrangement of its material. Many scholars have endeavored to work out a unitary interpretation which would prove that the book is organized in logical sequence. Most of them have tried to interpret it as a drama and explain its successive dialogues as part of one dramatic plot. One modern scholar finds the custom even in modern-day Syria of a week's celebration with song during the marriage festival, with the bride and groom described as king and queen; therefore this scholar takes this book to be the songs to bride and groom in the week's marriage festival celebrations. A still more recent scholar recalls the ceremonial dances which took place in ancient times in the vineyards twice a year, at which the young men came and selected their brides, and he suggests that these songs, dating from those semi-religious observances, were sacred to the people and hence were preserved. But none of the explanations seems adequate. It is now fairly well accepted that the book is a collection of love songs which are not preserved in a systematic order.

The book is of high literary quality. The countryside of Palestine is vividly recreated. The end of the winter and the coming of the springtime, the shepherds and their flocks and the spices and fragrant air are also drawn. There is a bold description of physical beauty in the frank and ardent language of love.

Talmudic literature records the fact that there was serious question whether this book should be admitted among the sacred writings (Aboth of Rabbi Nathan, chapter 1). Indeed, what place is there for secular love lyrics in a book of sacred Scripture, especially when the name of God is mentioned only once in the entire book? But the rabbis were desirous of including this sweetly human and beautiful book, so they reinterpreted the entire work as a metaphor. It is to be looked upon as a symbolic book, describing the love of God, the Bridegroom, for Israel, the bride. This theme of course is found a number of times in the prophetic literature. It is first developed by the Prophet Hosea and comes to its fullest expression in the Second Isaiah (see Part Two, chapters v and vi). This symbolizing of the book's theme as God's love for Israel was borrowed and reinterpreted by early Christianity and became classic in the Christian church.

The custom arose to read this book on Friday evening, since the Sabbath is deemed to be a bride and Israel a bridegroom. It was made the regular reading for Passover, possibly because of the beautiful description in the second chapter of the end of the winter and the coming of the springtime.

SYNOPSIS OF TEXT

The song of songs, which is Solomon's.
Let him kiss me with the kisses of his mouth —
For thy love is better than wine. . . .
My beloved spoke, and said unto me:
'Rise up, my love, my fair one, and come away.
For, lo, the winter is past,
The rain is over and gone;
The flowers appear on the earth;
The time of singing is come,
And the voice of the turtle is heard in our land;
The fig-tree putteth forth her green figs,
And the vines in blossom give forth their fragrance.
Arise, my love, my fair one, and come away. . . .'
I am a rose of Sharon,
A lily of the valleys.
As a lily among thorns,
So is my love among the daughters.
As an apple-tree among the trees of the wood,
So is my beloved among the sons.
Under its shadow I delighted to sit,
And its fruit was sweet to my taste.
He hath brought me to the banqueting-house,
And his banner over me is love.
'Stay ye me with dainties, refresh me with apples;
For I am love-sick.'
Let his left hand be under my head,
And his right hand embrace me. . . .

Set me as a seal upon thy heart,
As a seal upon thine arm;
For love is strong as death,
Jealousy is cruel as the grave;
The flashes thereof are flashes of fire,
A very flame of the Lord.
Many waters cannot quench love,
Neither can the floods drown it;
If a man would give all the substance of his house for love,
He would utterly be contemned. —1:1, 2; 2:10-13; 2:1-6; 8:6, 7.

COMMENTARY

A vivid description of the beginning of the springtime. The "voice of the turtle" means the voice of the turtle-dove.

RUTH

Ruth is a short narrative set in the days of the Judges. The first verse of the book reads: "And it came to pass in the days when the judges judged, that there was a famine in the land." It is the story of Elimelech from Bethlehem in Judah, who, with his wife Naomi and his two sons, went to the land of Moab to live. The two sons married Moabite women. When Elimelech and the two sons died, Naomi resolved to return to the land of Judah. Of her two widowed daughters-in-law, only Ruth returned with her to the land of Judah. There she married a kinsman of her mother-in-law Naomi and founded an honored family in Israel. Her great-grandson was King David.

Modern scholars say that this book was written in the time of Ezra and Nehemiah as a protest against their stern policy of forbidding the members of the returned community to marry heathen wives. The story, therefore, says that the great-grandmother of King David himself was Ruth, a Moabite woman. While of course this idea is found in the story, it is not necessarily the entire or the chief purpose of the book. The main theme seems to be praise of the virtuous Ruth, who was willing to go into exile to remain by the side of her widowed mother-in-law Naomi. For that she was rewarded as the story indicates.

The book is beautifully written. Even if it were written as late as the time of Ezra and Nehemiah, as some modern scholars say, the author has given so vivid a picture of the early days in a little Judean village that the Talmud is convinced that the book was written by Samuel the Judge, and the Greek translation places the book after the Book of Judges.

SYNOPSIS OF TEXT

A.   And it came to pass in the days when the judges judged, that there was a famine in the land. And a certain man of Bethlehem in Judah went to sojourn in the field of Moab, he, and his wife, and his two sons. . . . And Elimelech Naomi's husband died; and she was left, and her two sons. And they took them wives of the women of Moab: the name of the one was Orpah, and the name of the other Ruth; and they dwelt there about ten years. And Mahlon and Chilion died both of them; and the woman was left of her two children and of her husband. . . . And Naomi said unto her two daughters-in-law: 'Go, return each of you to her mother's house; the Lord deal kindly with you, and with me. . . .' And Ruth said: 'Entreat me not to leave thee, and to return from following after thee; for whither thou goest, I will go; and where thou lodgest, I will lodge; thy people shall be my people, and thy God my God; where thou diest, will I die, and there will I be buried; the Lord do so to me, and more also, if aught but death part thee and me.' . . . So Naomi returned, and Ruth the Moabitess, her daughter-in-law, with her, who returned out of the field of Moab—and they came to Beth-lehem in the beginning of barley harvest. —1:1, 3-5, 8, 16, 17, 22.

B.   And Naomi had a kinsman of her husband's, a mighty man of valour, of the family of Elimelech, and his name was Boaz. And Ruth the Moabitess said unto Naomi: 'Let me now go to the field, and glean among the ears of corn after him in whose sight I shall find favour.' And she said unto her: 'Go, my daughter.' And she went, and came and gleaned in the field after the reapers; and her hap was to light on the portion of the field belonging unto Boaz, who was of the family of Elimelech. . . . Then said Boaz unto his servant that was set over the reapers: 'Whose damsel is this?' And the servant that was set over the reapers answered and said: 'It is a Moabitish damsel that came back with Naomi out of the field of Moab; and she said: Let me glean, I pray you, and gather after the reapers among the sheaves; . . .' Then said Boaz unto Ruth: 'Hearest thou not, my daughter? Go not to glean in another field, neither pass from hence, but abide here fast by my maidens. . . .' Then she fell on her face, and bowed down to the ground, and said unto him: 'Why have I found favour in thy sight, that thou shouldest take cognizance of me, seeing I am a foreigner?' And Boaz answered and said unto her: 'It hath fully been told me, all that thou hast done unto thy mother-in-law since the death of thy husband; . . . The Lord recompense thy work, and be thy reward complete from the Lord, the God of Israel, under whose wings thou art come to take refuge.'– 2: 1-3, 5, 6, 7a, 8, 10, 11a, 12.

COMMENTARY

A.   The introduction to the story leading to the widowhood of Naomi and of her two daughters-in-law is given. The story proper begins with Naomi's resolve to return to the land of Judah and Ruth's famous plea: "Entreat me not to leave thee."

B.   This is a vivid picture of how the poor were allowed to glean in the fields after the reapers, as is required in the Law: "When ye reap the harvest of your land, ye shall not wholly reap the corner of thy field, nor shalt thou gather the gleanings of thy harvest . . . thou shalt leave them for the poor and the stranger. I am the Lord your God" (Lev. 19:9, 10).

LAMENTATIONS

In the Hebrew Bible this book is entitled *Eicho*, which simply means "How." "Eicho" is the opening word of the first sentence: "How does the city sit solitary." The naming of a book by its opening word or by the important word in the opening sentence rather than a general description of its contents is a frequent practice in the Hebrew Bible. Thus the Book of Genesis is called "B'reshis," from the opening word, "In the beginning"; and the Book of Leviticus is called "Vayikro," from the opening word which means "and He called" (see Part Two, chapter 1). However, in the Talmud the book is called *Kinos,* which means "Lamentations," a description of its contents.

The traditional view is that the book was written by the prophet Jeremiah in lamentation for the destruction of Jerusalem. In the Greek, and therefore in the Christian Bibles, the book follows the Book of Jeremiah in the order of Biblical books. This traditional view seems to be confirmed by the statement in 11 Chronicles, chapter 35, verse 25: "And Jeremiah lamented for Josiah . . . and behold they are written in the lamentations." From this it is assumed that Jeremiah wrote lamentations not only for King Josiah but also for Jerusalem at the time of its destruction.

However, modern scholars are inclined to doubt that Jeremiah wrote these lamentations. They note a distinct difference in style between two parts of the book. Most of the book refers to Jerusalem and is written in the third person, but chapter 3 is written in the first person, as a man speaking of his personal unhappiness. It seems unlikely to critical scholars that Jeremiah would have written so short a book in two different styles. They are inclined to believe that part of the book was written during the Exile, but that the whole book was put into its final form after the Exile.

We know from a question which was asked by one of the returning exiles of the Prophet Zechariah that in the Exile the Jews did have a fast of lamentations on the Ninth of Ov, commemorating the destruction of Jerusalem: "Should I weep in the fifth month as I have done these many years?" The question meant, should the fast of weeping and lamentations cease now that we have returned from Babylon? It may well be, therefore, that this book, or much of the present book, was used in the Exile in these public services of lamentations for the destruction of Jerusalem. The fast day of the Ninth of Ov still observed in Jewish worship commemorates the destruction of Jerusalem, first by the Babylonians and then six hundred years later by the Romans, and this Book of Lamentations is recited during the services.

SYNOPSIS OF TEXT

How doth the city sit solitary,
That was full of people;

How is she become as a widow!
She that was great among the nations,
And princess among the provinces,
How is she become tributary! . . .
And gone is from the daughter of Zion
All her splendour;
Her princes are become like harts
That find no pasture,
And they are gone without strength
Before the pursuer. . . .
All her people sigh,
They seek bread;
They have given their pleasant things for food
To refresh the soul.
'See, O Lord, and behold,
How abject I am become.' . . .
I am the man that hath seen affliction
By the rod of His wrath.
He hath led me and caused me to walk
In darkness and not in light.
Surely against me He turneth His hand
Again and again all the day. . . .
Remember mine affliction and mine anguish,
The wormwood and the gall.
My soul hath them still in remembrance,
And is bowed down within me.
This I recall to my mind,
Therefore have I hope.
Surely the Lord's mercies are not consumed,
Surely His compassions fail not,
They are new every morning;
Great is Thy faithfulness.
'The Lord is my portion,' saith my soul;
'Therefore will I hope in Him.' . . .
Remember, O Lord, what is come upon us;
Behold, and see our reproach.
Our inheritance is turned unto strangers,
Our mothers are as widows. . . .
Thou, O Lord, art enthroned for ever,

Thy throne is from generation to generation.
Wherefore dost Thou forget us for ever,
And forsake us so long time?
Turn Thou us unto Thee, O Lord, and we shall be turned;
Renew our days as of old. —1:1, 6, 11; 3:1-3, 19-24; 5:1-3, 19-21.

COMMENTARY

The selection indicates the two types of dirges—the type of dirge in most of the book, speaking in the third person, of the suffering of the people, and the third chapter, the personal dirge, beginning here with the words: "I am the man that hath seen affliction."

ECCLESIASTES

The English word *Ecclesiastes* comes from the Greek and is a translation of the Hebrew name of the book, *Koheleth*, which seems to mean "he who assembles," or "he who gathers people to listen to his preachment," that is to say, the preacher. The book itself claims to be written by King Solomon, although Solomon's name is not expressly mentioned. The opening sentence reads: "The words of Koheleth, the son of David king in Jerusalem." Solomon was the only son of David who became king except during the temporary rebellions of two of David's other sons. Besides, Koheleth describes himself as possessing superlative wisdom. "I have gotten great wisdom more than all that were before me over Jerusalem" (Ecc. 1:16). And Solomon, by tradition, is supposed to have had superlative wisdom: "And Solomon's wisdom excelled the wisdom of all the children of the east for he was wiser than all men" (1 Kings 5:10, 11).

This book is the third of the three Wisdom Books, the other two being Proverbs and Job. Like all the wisdom books it is not specifically Jewish. There is no mention of Israel in it and God is never referred to in the terms used by the other books of the Bible, by the names which are specifically Jewish. Like the Book of Proverbs, it speaks of wisdom and of material happiness. The book may be looked upon as the somber climax of the Wisdom Literature, its final disappointment. The Book of Proverbs reveals the mood of wisdom at its most confident stage. It says with complete assurance: be wise and diligent and you will have material success and happiness. The Book of Job begins to express doubt of this connection between wisdom, goodness, and happiness, and demonstrates that even a righteous man can be miserably unhappy. Nevertheless, the Book of Job holds firm to its conviction of God's ultimate justice. Ecclesiastes, the third Wisdom Book, comes, at times, close to complete skepticism. It not only doubts, as Job does, the "Wisdom" doctrine that righteousness receives reward in life, it frequently doubts the value of wisdom itself. It says that life is meaningless, so one might as well have what pleasure he can, and soon it doubts even the satisfaction of pleasure itself, calling it folly. Everything ultimately is meaningless, says this pessimist-preacher: "Vanity of vanities, all is vanity."

Yet the book is not consistent. Intermingled with its pessimism are sentences which are religious and directly contradict the negativism of the rest of the book. Koheleth will say, for example (in order to indicate that it is useless to try to accomplish anything): "That which is crooked cannot be made straight" (1:15). Furthermore, this hopeless crookedness of the world is due to God Himself: "Consider the work of God for who can make that straight which He hath made crooked?" (7:13). Yet in direct contradiction with this pessimism that life is all twisted and meaningless, he says of God: "He hath made everything beautiful in its time" (3:11). Likewise he denies that there is any life after death and that man is possessed of a soul which makes him superior to the beasts: "Who knoweth the spirit of man whether it goeth upward and the spirit of the beast whether it goeth downward to the earth?" (3:21). And yet, in direct contradiction to that, he speaks of the immortality of the soul: "And the dust returneth to the earth as it was and the spirit returneth unto God who made it" (12:7).

The rabbis in the Talmud (b. Shabbas 30b) say that originally they wanted to keep this book out of the Bible because "its words contradicted each other." But somehow they were able to find a means of harmonizing these contradictions and as a result the book was included in the Sacred Scriptures.

Many explanations are given by modern scholars of these contradictions. The one generally accepted is that these religious statements were not original with Koheleth but were inserted later by some pious writer as an antidote to the poison of the author's pessimism and thus to make the book acceptable for inclusion in Holy Writ. A recent scholar has given another explanation. He says that these pious statements must be understood as being in quotation marks. Koheleth quotes them as popular sayings which he himself disbelieves and which he now proceeds to dispute. Another modern writer suggests that these contradictions are the work of the original author and are quite natural. When a man writes down the whole stream of his thought, sometimes he is inclined to believe the more religious doctrine and then again he turns to a skeptical mood.

Most modern scholars consider the book to be one of the latest in Scripture. They find in it a strong influence of Greek pessimistic thinking and therefore some of them say it was written in Alexandria where the great Jewish community was in constant contact with Greek thought. Whether it was written in Alexandria or not, the general opinion of present scholarship is that the book was written about the year 200 before the present era.

SYNOPSIS OF TEXT

A. The words of Koheleth, the son of David, king in Jerusalem.
Vanity of vanities, saith Koheleth;
Vanity of vanities, all is vanity.
What profit hath man of all his labour
Wherein he laboureth under the sun?
One generation passeth away, and another generation
   cometh;
And the earth abideth for ever. . . .
That which hath been is that which shall be,
And that which hath been done is that which shall be done;
And there is nothing new under the sun. . . .
I Koheleth have been king over Israel in Jerusalem. And I
   applied my heart to seek and to search out by wisdom
   concerning all things that are done under heaven; . . .
That which is crooked cannot be made straight;
And that which is wanting cannot be numbered. . . .
And I applied my heart to know wisdom, and to know madness and folly—

I perceived that this also was a striving after wind.
For in much wisdom is much vexation;
And he that increaseth knowledge increaseth sorrow. . . .
Then I saw that wisdom excelleth folly, as far as light ex-
celleth darkness.
The wise man, his eyes are in his head;
But the fool walketh in darkness. And I also perceived that
one event happeneth to them all. –1:1-4, 9, 12, 13a, 15,
17, 18; 2:13, 14.

B.   I said in my heart: 'Come now, I will try thee with mirth,
and enjoy pleasure'; and, behold, this also was vanity. I said of
laughter: 'It is mad'; and of mirth: 'What doth it accomplish?' . . .
I made me great works; I builded me houses; I planted me vineyards; . . . So I was great, and increased more than all that were
before me in Jerusalem; also my wisdom stood me in stead. – 2:1,
2, 4, 9.

C.   And moreover I saw under the sun, in the place of justice,
that wickedness was there; and in the place of righteousness, that
wickedness was there. I said in my heart: 'The righteous and the
wicked God will judge; for there is a time there for every purpose
and for every work.' . . . All go unto one place; all are of the dust,
and all return to dust. Who knoweth the spirit of man whether
it goeth upward, and the spirit of the beast whether it goeth downward to the earth? Wherefore I perceived that there is nothing
better, than that a man should rejoice in his works; for that is his
portion; for who shall bring him to see what shall be after him?
– 3:16, 17, 20-22.

D.   Go thy way, eat thy bread with joy,
And drink thy wine with a merry heart;
For God hath already accepted thy words.
Let thy garments be always white;
And let thy head lack no oil. . . .
A feast is made for laughter,
And wine maketh glad the life;
And money answereth all things. . . .
And the light is sweet,

And a pleasant thing it is for the eyes to behold the sun.
For if a man live many years,
Let him rejoice in them all,
Remember then thy Creator in the days of thy youth,
Before the evil days come,
And the years draw nigh, when thou shalt say:
'I have no pleasure in them.'– 9:7, 8; 10:19; 11:7, 8; 12:1.

COMMENTARY

A.   The chief basis for Koheleth's pessimism is that human life shows no progress. Though one generation goes and another comes, the world stays as it is. Furthermore, even the pursuit of wisdom brings no satisfaction to him. The more wisdom he gets, the more vexation comes to him. In this section there is one of the obvious contradictions to which we have referred. He says pessimistically: "He that increaseth knowledge increaseth sorrow." Then follows the very opposite thought: "Wisdom excelleth folly as far as light excelleth darkness."

B.   If there is no progress and if even wisdom is a source of sorrow, then at least, he says, I will try just to enjoy life: "I will try thee with mirth and enjoy pleasure." But he finds that even the life of hilarity is a source of boredom, and becomes meaningless.

C.   There is no real justice in the world and there is no use counting upon some future existence to make up for the sorrows of this one. "Who knoweth the spirit of man whether it goeth upward?"

D.   But after saying that mirth and enjoyment are likewise a weariness to the spirit, he ends by calling upon youth to enjoy its youth before old age comes and life loses its capacity for pleasure. "Remember thy Creator in the days of thy youth before the years draw nigh when thou shalt say: 'I have no pleasure in them.'" This verse became the text of the medieval Latin college song, *Gaudeamus igitur juvenes dum sumus*, "Let us therefore rejoice while we are yet young."

ESTHER

This book is the last one of the Five Scrolls and is the only one referred to in the Talmud as the Megillah, "the Scroll." It explains, by means of an historical narrative, the origin of the festival of Purim. The story is set in Persia in the time of Ahasuerus (or Artaxerxes), king of Persia, who is also mentioned in the Book of Ezra (Ezra 4:6). The Talmud (in b. Megillah 7a) expresses doubt as to whether the Book of Esther should be included among the inspired books in Scripture, namely, as to whether it was given "by the holy spirit." Indeed the book, although it speaks of Israel's miraculous deliverance from Haman who meant to destroy the entire people, actually does not mention the name of God even once. There even is no mention of any worship or any prayer, except that the people are asked to fast. Nor is the punishment which threatens Israel ascribed to any sin on their part, as is usually the case in the other books in the Bible. The book is a secular book; a persecution is threatened against the Jews on purely racial grounds and is averted by purely political methods. Most scholars are convinced that the book was written in the early Greek period at the time of bitter hostility between the Jews and the surrounding people.

SYNOPSIS OF TEXT

A.   After these things did king Ahasuerus promote Haman the son of Hammedatha the Agagite, and advanced him, and set his seat above all the princes that were with him. And all the king's servants, that were in the king's gate, bowed down, and prostrated themselves before Haman; for the king had so commanded concerning him. But Mordecai bowed not down, nor prostrated himself before him. . . . And when Haman saw that Mordecai bowed not down, nor prostrated himself before him, then was Haman full of wrath. But it seemed contemptible in his eyes to lay hands on Mordecai alone; for they had made known to him the people of Mordecai; . . .

And Haman said unto king Ahasuerus: 'There is a certain people scattered abroad and dispersed among the peoples in all the prov-

inces of thy kingdom; and their laws are diverse from those of
every people; neither keep they the king's laws; therefore it prof-
iteth not the king to suffer them. . . . and I will pay ten thousand
talents of silver into the hands of those that have the charge of
the king's business, to bring it into the king's treasuries.' – 3:1-2, 5,
6a, 8, 9b.

B.   Now when Mordecai knew all that was done, Mordecai rent
his clothes and put on sackcloth with ashes, and went out into the
midst of the city, and cried with a loud and a bitter cry and he came
even before the king's gate; . . .
Then Mordecai bade them return answer unto Esther: 'Think
not with thyself that thou shalt escape in the king's house, more
than all the Jews. For if thou altogether holdest thy peace at this
time, then will relief and deliverance arise to the Jews from another place, but thou and thy father's house will perish; and who
knoweth whether thou art not come to royal estate for such a
time as this?' Then Esther bade them return answer unto Mordecai: 'Go, gather together all the Jews that are present in Shushan,
and fast ye for me, and neither eat nor drink three days, night
or day; . . .' – 4:1, 2, 13, 14, 15, 16a.

C.   So they hanged Haman on the gallows that he had prepared
for Mordecai. Then was the king's wrath assuaged.
On that day did the king Ahasuerus give the house of Haman
the Jews' enemy unto Esther the queen. And Mordecai came before the king; for Esther had told what he was unto her. And the
king took off his ring, which he had taken from Haman, and gave
it unto Mordecai. And Esther set Mordecai over the house of
Haman. . . .
And Mordecai wrote these things, and sent letters unto all the
Jews that were in all the provinces of the king Ahasuerus, both
nigh and far, to enjoin them that they should keep the fourteenth
day of the month Adar, and the fifteenth day of the same, yearly,
the days wherein the Jews had rest from their enemies, and the
month which was turned unto them from sorrow to gladness, and
from mourning into a good day; that they should make them days
of feasting and gladness, and of sending portions one to another,
and gifts to the poor. – 7:10; 8:1-2; 9:20-22.

COMMENTARY

A.   Haman, the arch enemy of the Jews who plans their destruction, is described as the Agagite which tradition connects
with Agag, the king of the Amalakites (1 Samuel 15:8). In other
words, Haman is a descendant of the ancient enemy of Israel, the
Amalakites who attacked them without warning and without prov-
ocation when they came out of Egypt. The reason which Haman
gives for the destruction of the Jews is that they are different from
other people and that they are not law-abiding.

B.   The only approach to a religious idea appears when Mordecai says to Esther: "Who knoweth whether thou are not come
to royal estate for such a time as this?" He implies that destiny
(God) has put her in a position of power that she may save her
people.

C.   Here is recounted the institution of the festival of Purim
as the day in which the sorrow of the Jews was turned to gladness.
It was ordained to be ever afterward a time "of feasting and gladness, of sending portions to one another and gifts to the poor."
The Hebrew words here in Esther for sending portions is *mish-
loach monos*, from which comes the popular term *Shalach monos*
for the gifts that people exchange on Purim.

CHAPTER IX

Daniel, Ezra, Nehemiah, Chronicles

DANIEL

DANIEL represents a type of literature which is unique in the Hebrew Bible. It is a species of mystic prophecy which scholars call "apocalyptic" (i.e., "revelations"). There are a few passages of apocalyptic writing scattered elsewhere in Scripture. There are also a large number of apocalyptic books, but they have been excluded from the Bible, books such as the Book of Enoch, the Testament of the Twelve Patriarchs, the Second Book of Esdras. Also in the New Testament, the Book of Revelation is a typical Apocalyptic book.

Daniel is the only apocalyptic book in the Hebrew Bible, and may well be the first of this rather extensive literature. This literature is unique and has such characteristic methods of expression as to make it immediately recognizable. The purpose of apocalyptic writing is to reassure the people that the suffering which they now endure soon will end and that the evil nations which oppress them will be destroyed. This destruction will come on a certain great day, a Day of Judgment. Thus the Apocalypse carries over the idea of "The Day of the Lord" found in the Prophets. But whereas in the classic prophecies, the "Day of the Lord" is the day when God will bring punishment upon the sinful of His people, in the Apocalypse it is the day when the tyrannical nations of the world will receive their just punishment and Israel will be saved.

These apocalyptic books were all written at a time when the dominant Greek or Roman empires were masters of the Mediterranean world, and therefore any predictions of their coming doom had to be made in disguised fashion. Hence, the description of the evil nations who had been destroyed in the past or of the present tyrannical nations who will soon be destroyed is always carefully disguised. Generally the nations are symbolized by some strange mythological beasts, half lion or ram or goat. This sort of mythological vision has its root in the older and genuine prophecy. The visions of Ezekiel were more or less of this nature. These strange mythological visions symbolizing the nations are imparted to the speaker usually in a dream, and are interpreted by an angel. This technique was also borrowed from a prophet, from Zechariah, one of the last of the Prophets. In the classical age of prophecy, God spoke directly to the Prophet. To Zechariah, at the fading end of prophecy, there was an intermediary, an angel who interpreted the vision. This interpreting intermediary is constantly present in the Apocalypse.

These ideas in the Apocalypse, the visions of the great day of judgment, the mythological symbols, the intermediaries who interpret the visions are all borrowed from the prophetic books. But in the prophetic writing they are only chance ideas. They become the essential ideas in the apocalyptical writing, of which Daniel is a great example. To these elements just mentioned, the Apocalypse adds another. Unlike the Prophets, the apocalyptic writer never gives his own name. He always selects some great hero from the past and "quotes" the prophecies in that hero's name. Thus Moses or the twelve sons of Jacob or Enoch will speak the words which the anonymous author puts into their mouth.

The apocalyptic visions are all constructed in virtually the same way. There is a series of mythological word pictures, all of which are uttered by some great man in the distant past. Therefore, the events to which they disguisedly refer are all presented as prophecies of events which have not yet taken place at the time when that ancient author spoke. Since these supposed predictions will be recognized by the reader as having actually come true, therefore the reader must likewise accept as true the rest of the prophecies which have not yet been fulfilled. In other words, the author, in order to give credibility to the prophecies which he makes of the coming destruction of the present tyrants, describes actual past events as if they were still to take place, and he predicts, successfully of course, that they will take place. Therefore, the author is compelled to select as the supposed speaker a character who lived in the distant past before these events actually occurred.

Once we understand the construction of the apocalyptic writings, it is comparatively easy to discover the real date of their composition. At the point where the "successful" prediction ends and the actual future events are described, the author writes his book. In the present book, the one who tells the story, who utters the prophecies, is Daniel. Daniel already was known in the time of the Exile as a very wise and righteous man. The Prophet Ezekiel, wishing to say that even if the wisest men of antiquity, or the most righteous would plead for the people, they would not be able to avert the punishment which the people deserve. ("Though these three men, Noah, Daniel, and Job, were in it [the land] they should deliver but their own souls by their righteousness." Ezekiel 14:14.) Thus the author of the Apocalypse took a man revered by tradition, the honored equivalent of Job and Noah, and had him speak the prophecies. The early part of the book describes Daniel as one of the exiles in Babylon, his wisdom and the miracles which were performed to save him from the lion's death and fiery furnace. The latter part of the book then puts the apocalyptic visions in the mouth of Daniel.

The vision which is cited here from the eighth chapter of the book is carefully explained in the book itself and therefore serves us as a guide to understanding other apocalyptic visions here and in similar books. Also, it can be seen how such a book can be dated almost precisely. By interpreting the successive mythological symbols representing the succession of tyrannical powers which are overthrown, it is clear that he is writing in the time of the capture of the Temple and its defilement by Antiochus Epiphanes. He says that this beast will defile the Temple for 2300 half-days, or 1150 days, which is about the time the Temple remained defiled until it was cleansed by Judas Maccabeus. Obviously therefore the book was written close to 165 B.C.E.

In the Greek Bible the Book of Daniel is placed between Ezekiel and Hosea, since it is considered a prophetic book.

SYNOPSIS OF TEXT

In the third year of the reign of king Belshazzar a vision appeared unto me, even unto me Daniel, after that which apeared unto me at the first. . . . And I lifted up mine eyes, and saw, and, behold, there stood before the stream a ram which had two horns; and the two horns were high, but one was higher than the other, and the higher came up last. . . .

And as I was considering, behold, a he-goat came from the west over the face of the whole earth, and touched not the ground; and the goat had a conspicuous horn between his eyes. . . . And I saw him come close unto the ram, and he was moved with choler against him, and smote the ram, and broke his two horns; and there was no power in the ram to stand before him; but he cast him down to the ground, and trampled upon him; and there was none that could deliver the ram out of his hand. And the he-goat magnified himself exceedingly; and when he was strong, the great horn was broken; and instead of it there came up the appearance of four horns towards the four winds of heaven.

And out of one of them came forth a little horn, which waxed exceeding great, toward the south, and toward the east, and toward the beauteous land. . . . Yea, it magnified itself, even to the prince of the host; and from him the continual burnt-offering was taken away, and the place of his sanctuary was cast down. . . . Then I heard a holy one speaking; and another holy one said unto that certain one who spoke: 'How long shall be the vision concerning the continual burnt-offering, and the transgression that causeth appalment, to give both the sanctuary and the host to be trampled under foot?' And he said unto me: 'unto two thousand and three hundred evenings and mornings; then shall the sanctuary be victorious.'

And it came to pass, when I, even I Daniel, had seen the vision, that I sought to understand it; and, behold, there stood before me as the appearance of a man. And I heard the voice of a man between the banks of Ulai, who called, and said: 'Gabriel, make this man to understand the vision.' So he came near where I stood; and when he came, I was terrified, and fell upon my face; but he said unto me: 'Understand, O son of man; for the vision belongeth to the time of the end.' '. . . The ram which thou sawest having the two horns, they are the kings of Media and Persia. And the rough he-goat is the king of Greece; and the great horn that is between his eyes is the first king. And as for that which was broken in the place whereof four stood up, four kingdoms shall stand up out of the nation, but not with his power. And in the latter time of their kingdom, when the transgressors have completed their transgression, there shall stand up a king of fierce countenance, and understanding stratagems. . . . And through his cunning he shall cause craft to prosper in his hand; and he shall magnify himself in his heart, and in time of security shall he destroy many; he shall also stand up against the prince of princes; but he shall be broken without hand. . . . but thou, shut thou up the vision; for it belongeth to many days to come.' – 8: 1, 3, 5, 7-9, 11, 13-17, 20-23, 25, 26b.

COMMENTARY

The first mythological animal seen in the vision is the ram with two horns, one horn larger than the other. This is interpreted later in this chapter as the dual kingdom of the Medes and the Persians, the Persians being the dominant partner, the larger horn. The he-goat which comes from the west with the conspicuous horn between his eyes, who overthrows the two-horned ram, is the Macedonian-Greek army with Alexander (the great horn) who crushed the empire of the Medes and the Persians. Then the great horn was broken and in the place of it appeared four horns towards the four winds of heaven. When Alexander died (when the great horn was broken), his great kingdom was divided into four parts and each was governed by one of his generals. "Out of one of them came forth a little horn." This means that out of the kingdom of Seleucus, one of the four parts into which Alexander's kingdom was divided, there came the descendant of Seleucus, Antiochus Epiphanes, who attacked God's Temple in Jerusalem and ended its sacrificial ritual. "It magnified itself and from him the continual burnt-offering was taken away."

At this point, the prophecy changes and Daniel asks, how long will this continue, this defilement of the sanctuary, and the cessation of the worship of God? So it is clear that at this point the author has ended his "prophecies," which are really descriptions of past events, and begins actually to look into the future. Thus, as in all apocalyptic visions, there is the turning point from past to future which is the present moment in which the real author actually lives. The angel reassures Daniel that this little horn who has defiled the sanctuary, i.e., Antiochus, will not endure long.

"But he shall be broken without hand." This is the real purpose of the vision and of the book, to reassure the people that just as the other "beasts" were destroyed, so will destruction soon come to the present beast, Antiochus Epiphanes.

EZRA AND NEHEMIAH

Ezra and Nehemiah were originally one book. The Talmud calls this combined book "Ezra." The Masora, the tradition which safeguards Biblical texts by counting the words, has no statistical note as to the number of verses, etc., at the end of what is now called the Book of Ezra; but at the end of what is now the Book of Nehemiah, it gives the total number of verses and other statistics for both books as one.

Ezra the Scribe, and Nehemiah the Governor, were the rebuilders of the community which had returned to Palestine in the mid-fifth century before the present era. The first group of exiles from Babylon had returned a century earlier under Joshua the High Priest, and Zerubbabel the prince. This was the time of the Prophets Haggai and Zechariah. This first group of returning exiles reestablished the Temple, but apparently their community did not flourish. It needed reinforcement and reconstruction. Therefore a century later, Ezra the Priest, and after him, Nehemiah the Governor, came from Persia. Ezra brought about the solemn public acceptance of the Torah by the people. Nehemiah rebuilt the walls of Jerusalem. Both of them worked to convince the small community of the necessity of refraining from mixed marriages with the heathens.

Of all the Scriptural books, Ezra-Nehemiah comes closest to the modern idea of a history book, or rather, to an historical autobiography or memoir. Events are precisely dated, and the experiences of Ezra and Nehemiah are told in autobiographical manner. Authentic decrees of the Persian government are given in Aramaic, the diplomatic language of the day.

Ezra was of a noble, priestly family. He is sometimes referred to as Ezra the Priest, but more generally he is referred to as Ezra the Scribe. He was "a ready scribe" in the law of Moses. In the Persian king's decree which defines his mission to Palestine, he is told to appoint magistrates and judges and to teach those people who do not know the law of God. Tradition, recorded in the Talmud, pays profound reverence to Ezra. He is described as the founder of the Great Synagogue, the succession of scholars who are credited with establishing many of the institutions of Judaism. He is said to have instituted the public reading of Scripture during week-days and Sabbath afternoons. He was the first to record the Torah in the square Hebrew letters (the Assyrian script) in which it now is written, supplanting the older Hebrew writing (the writing found on ancient coins and inscriptions). The rabbis even say (b. Sanhedrin 21b) that had the Law not been given already to Moses, Ezra the Scribe would have been deemed worthy to have received it.

Nehemiah, who was an officer of King Artaxerxes in Persia, received permission to return to Palestine and served there as royal governor. In spite of opposition by the heathen neighbors of the little community, he succeeded in completing the walls of Jerusalem. His memoirs in the latter part of his book reveal him as a man of strong will and unselfish devotion.

The end of the book describes the solemn public reading of the Law and its formal acceptance by the people. Ezra read the Law before the entire people on the first day of the seventh month and then the people accepted the Law as a covenant and signed their names: "We make a sure covenant and subscribe it and our princes and our Levites and our priests set their seal unto it" (Nehemiah 10:1). Then follow the signatories, Nehemiah himself being the first to sign.

Scholars disagree as to how much of the Torah was read and accepted by the people on that great occasion. Some modern critics say that it was only the part that they call "The Priestly Code." The traditional view, however, is that it was the whole Torah. The Torah hitherto had been known only to a few of the learned. Ezra the Scribe, in the decade or more that he was in Jerusalem before this great event, had the Torah copied and recopied and had taught it to many as a decree of the king had suggested. Therefore, at the great assembly, the people formally accepted the Law of Moses and from now on it was read to the people regularly as part of their worship and taught to them all. Thus, forever after, the law, "which Moses had commanded, became the heritage of the congregation of Jacob."

SYNOPSIS OF TEXT

A.   Now in the first year of Cyrus king of Persia, that the word of the Lord by the mouth of Jeremiah might be accomplished, the Lord stirred up the spirit of Cyrus king of Persia, that he made a proclamation throughout all his kingdom, and put it also in writing, saying: 'Thus saith Cyrus king of Persia: All the kingdoms of the earth hath the Lord, the God of heaven, given me; and He hath charged me to build Him a house in Jerusalem, which is in Judah. Whosoever there is among you of all His people—his God be with him—let him go up to Jerusalem, which is in Judah, and build the house of the Lord, the God of Israel, He is the God who is in Jerusalem. . . .'

Then rose up the heads of fathers' houses of Judah and Benjamin, and the priests, and the Levites, even all whose spirit God had stirred to go up to build the house of the Lord . . .

Now these are the children of the province, that went up out of the captivity of those that had been carried away, whom Nebuchadnezzar the king of Babylon had carried away unto Babylon, and that returned unto Jerusalem and Judah, every one unto his city; who came with Zerubbabel, Jeshua, Nehemiah, Seraiah, Reelaiah, Mordecai, Bilshan, Mispar, Bigvai, Rehum, Baanah.

The number of the men of the people of Israel: . . .

Then stood up Jeshua the son of Jozadak, and his brethren the priests, and Zerubbabel the son of Shealtiel, and his brethren, and builded the altar of the God of Israel, to offer burnt-offerings thereon, as it is written in the Law of Moses the man of God. . . .

Now the prophets, Haggai the prophet, and Zechariah the son of Iddo, prophesied unto the Jews that were in Judah and Jerusalem; in the name of the God of Israel prophesied they unto them. Then rose up Zerubbabel the son of Shealtiel, and Jeshua the son of Jozadak, and began to build the house of God which is at Jerusalem; and with them were the prophets of God, helping them. —Ezra: 1:1-3, 5; 2:1-2; 3:2; 5:1, 2.

B.   Now after these things, in the reign of Artaxerxes king of Persia, Ezra the son of Seraiah, the son of Azariah, the son of Hilkiah, the son of Shallum, the son of Zadok, the son of Ahitub,

. . . this Ezra went up from Babylon; and he was a ready scribe in the Law of Moses, which the Lord, the God of Israel, had given; and the king granted him all his request, according to the hand of the Lord his God upon him. And there went up some of the children of Israel, and of the priests, and the Levites, and the singers, and the porters, and the Nethinim, unto Jerusalem, in the seventh year of Artaxerxes the king. . . .

Now this is the copy of the letter that the king Artaxerxes gave unto Ezra the priest, the scribe, even the scribe of the words of the commandments of the Lord, and of His statutes to Israel: . . . And thou, Ezra, after the wisdom of thy God, that is in thy hand, appoint magistrates and judges, who may judge all the people that are beyond the River, all such as know the laws of thy God; and teach ye him that knoweth them not. . . .

Then we departed from the river of Ahava on the twelfth day of the first month, to go unto Jerusalem; and the hand of our God was upon us, and He delivered us from the hand of the enemy and lier-in-wait by the way. And we came to Jerusalem, and abode there three days. . . .

Then all the men of Judah and Benjamin gathered themselves together unto Jerusalem within the three days; it was the ninth month, on the twentieth day of the month; and all the people sat in the broad place before the house of God, trembling because of this matter, and for the great rain. And Ezra the priest stood up, and said unto them: 'Ye have broken faith, and have married foreign women, to increase the guilt of Israel. Now therefore make confession unto the Lord, the God of your fathers, and do His pleasure; and separate yourselves from the peoples of the land, and from the foreign women.' Then all the congregation answered and said with a loud voice: 'As thou hast said, so it is for us to do. . . .'–Ezra 7:1, 2, 6, 7, 11, 25; 8:31, 32; 10:9-12.

C.   The words of Nehemiah the son of Hacaliah.

Now it came to pass in the month Chislev, in the twentieth year, as I was in Shushan the castle, that Hanani, one of my brethren, came out of Judah, he and certain men; and I asked them concerning the Jews that had escaped, that were left of the captivity, and concerning Jerusalem. And they said unto me: 'The remnant that are left of the captivity there in the province are in great affliction and reproach; the wall of Jerusalem also is broken down, and the gates thereof are burned with fire.' . . .

And it came to pass in the month Nisan, in the twentieth year of Artaxerxes the king, when wine was before him, that I took up the wine, and gave it unto the king. Now I had not been before time sad in his presence. And the king said unto me: 'Why is thy countenance sad, seeing thou art not sick? this is nothing else but sorrow of heart.' Then I was very sore afraid. . . . And I said unto the king: 'If it please the king, and if thy servant have found favour in thy sight, that thou wouldest send me unto Judah, unto the city of my fathers' sepulchres, that I may build it.' . . . And the king granted me, according to the good hand of my God upon me. . . .

So I came to Jerusalem, and was there three days. . . .

Then I said unto them: 'Ye see the evil case that we are in, how Jerusalem lieth waste, and the gates thereof are burned with fire; come and let us build up the wall of Jerusalem, that we be no more a reproach.' And I told them of the hand of my God which was good upon me; as also of the king's words that he had spoken unto me. And they said: 'Let us rise up and build.' So they strengthened their hands for the good work. – Nehemiah 1: 1-3; 2: 1, 2, 5, 8b, 11, 17, 18.

D.   And when the seventh month was come, and the children of Israel were in their cities, all the people gathered themselves together as one man into the broad place that was before the water gate; and they spoke unto Ezra the scribe to bring the book of the Law of Moses, which the Lord had commanded to Israel. And Ezra the priest brought the Law before the congregation, both men and women, and all that could hear with understanding, upon the first day of the seventh month. And he read therein before the broad place that was before the water gate from early morning until midday, in the presence of the men and the women, and of those that could understand; and the ears of all the people were attentive unto the book of the Law. . . . And Ezra blessed the Lord, the great God. And all the people answered: 'Amen, Amen,' with the lifting up of their hands, and they bowed their heads, and fell down before the Lord with their faces to the ground. . . .

Now in the twenty and fourth day of this month the children of Israel were assembled with fasting, and with sackcloth, and earth upon them. And the seed of Israel separated themselves from all foreigners, and stood and confessed their sins, and the iniquities of their fathers. And they stood up in their place, and read in the book of the Law of the Lord their God a fourth part of the day; and another fourth part they confessed, and prostrated themselves before the Lord their God. . . . Then the Levites said: 'Stand up and bless the Lord your God from everlasting to everlasting; and let them say: Blessed be Thy glorious Name, that is exalted above all blessing and praise. . . . Thou art the Lord the God, who didst choose Abram, and broughtest him forth out of Ur of the Chaldees, and gavest him the name of Abraham; and foundest his heart faithful before Thee, and madest a covenant with him to give the land of the Canaanite, the Hittite, the Amorite, and the Perizzite, and the Jebusite, and the Girgashite, even to give it unto his seed, and hast performed Thy words; for Thou art righteous. . . .

Nevertheless they were disobedient, and rebelled against Thee, and cast Thy law behind their back, and slew Thy prophets that did forewarn them to turn them back unto Thee, and they wrought great provocations. . . .

Now therefore, our God, the great, the mighty, and the awful God, who keepest covenant and mercy, let not all the travail seem little before Thee, . . .

Howbeit Thou art just in all that is come upon us; for Thou hast dealt truly, but we have done wickedly; . . .' And yet for all this we make a sure covenant, and subscribe it; and our princes, our Levites, and our priests, set their seal unto it.

Now those that set their seal were:

Nehemiah the Tirshatha, the son of Hacaliah, and Zedekiah; . . .
– Nehemiah 8: 1-3, 6; 9: 1-3, 5a, 7, 8, 26, 32a, 33; 10: 1-2.

COMMENTARY

A. The decree of the King of Persia, Cyrus, is given here in Hebrew. Later in the book it is quoted in Aramaic. This first part of the book reviews the history of the returned exiles who first came a century earlier and tells of their building of a Temple.

B. Then Ezra begins to tell his own story of the permission that he received to go to Palestine, his gathering of men of Judah and

Benjamin, his arrival in Jerusalem, and his exacting a pledge from the people there to separate from their heathen wives.

C.   These are the memoirs of Nehemiah. While performing his official duties in the Persian capital, he is informed of the depressing situation of the community in Palestine and he gets permission from the king to go there. He comes to Palestine and he persuades the people to build the walls of Jerusalem.

D.   This is the great meeting at which Ezra and Nehemiah read the Book of the Law to the people and they formally accept it.

CHRONICLES

The Hebrew name for this book, which is now divided into two parts, is *Divrei Ha-yomim*, which means the "words" or the "events of the days," in other words, "History," or "Chronicles," as the English name indicates. The Greek name is somewhat more descriptive. It signifies "the events which are left out" (*Paraleipomenon*), that is to say, it includes some events that are left out in the earlier historical books as, for example, events in the reign of the King Asa. While it is true that the Book of Chronicles does mention certain events which are omitted in the earlier historical books; it also omits a vast number of facts which are found in them. Actually it omits very much more than it adds. These omissions are significant. When the reader of the Book of Chronicles realizes precisely what the author has omitted, the purpose of the book becomes quite clear.

The book is supposed to cover the entire history given in the Bible from the creation of the world to the end of the Exile in Babylon, in other words the contents of all the Biblical books beginning with Genesis and ending with the Book of Kings. The author does all this in a comparatively small space, in spite of the fact that he gives a great amount of detail which is not found in the earlier books. In spite of the great additions which he makes, he covers this vast extent of history by means of systematic omissions.

The whole history of the world from Adam up to King David occupies only nine chapters. Then the history of King David occupies twenty chapters, the rest of Book One. Book Two contains the history of King Solomon and then, after the kingdom is divided, in the reign of Solomon's son Rehoboam, the author omits the entire history of the northern kingdom and gives only the history of the southern kingdom, the kingdom of Judah, whose capital was Jerusalem. The northern kingdom, Israel, is referred to only when its kings come into contact with the kings of Judah.

Even though the history of King David, which occupies the bulk of the first book, is so full, a great many of the events concerning David which are mentioned in the Book of Samuel are omitted here. The events omitted are those which show David in a poor light—the story of Bathsheba, the rebellions of his sons against him, the story of Amon and Tamar. But a great amount of space is given to David's extensive preparation for the building of the Temple by his son Solomon. We are told that David organized the Levites to serve and to sing in the Temple and a complete listing of the Levitical families is given as David had classified them.

All this makes it clear what the purpose of the book really is. The author was interested primarily in the Temple and its worship and in the idealized King David and his household. Anything to the discredit of David is therefore omitted. The history of the whole northern kingdom is considered irrelevant. The entire service of the Temple, the complete organization of its officialdom, is given in loving detail.

No one knows the author's name and therefore he is referred to as "The Chronicler." He was very likely a Levite. It is clear that the Chronicler lived during the Second Commonwealth. According to generally accepted modern opinion, he wrote about three hundred years before the present era. Some modern scholars consider that the books of Ezra-Nehemiah, in their final form, and the Book of Chronicles were written by one author. This opinion is based on the fact that the Book of Chronicles ends with the decree of Cyrus, permitting the exiles to return from Babylon, and the Book of Ezra begins with almost the identical words.

While the book cites many historical sources, the "History of the Kings of Judah" and that of the kings of Israel, works ascribed to Samuel the Seer, to Nathan the Prophet, etc., it is hardly to be considered an historical book. It is a detailed description of the building and the service of the Temple and an idealized picture of David and Solomon.

SYNOPSIS OF TEXT

A.   Adam, Seth, Enosh; Kenan, Mahalalel, Jared; Enoch, Methusaleh, Lamech; Noah, Shem, Ham, and Japheth.

The sons of Japheth: Gomer, and Magog, and Madai, and Javan, and Tubal, and Meshech, and Tiras. . . .

Now the Philistines fought against Israel; and the men of Israel fled from before the Philistines, and fell down slain in mount Gilboa. . . .

So Saul died for his transgression which he committed against the Lord, because of the word of the Lord, which he kept not; and also for that he asked counsel of a ghost, to inquire thereby. . . .

Then all Israel gathered themselves to David unto Hebron, saying: 'Behold, we are thy bone and thy flesh. In times past, even when Saul was king, it was thou that didst lead out and bring in Israel; and the Lord thy God said unto thee: Thou shalt feed My people Israel, and thou shalt be prince over My people Israel.' So all the elders of Israel came to the king to Hebron; and David made a covenant with them in Hebron before the Lord; and they anointed David king over Israel, according to the word of the Lord by the hand of Samuel. – I, 1: 1-5; 10: 1, 13; 11: 1-3.

B.   And David commanded to gather together the strangers that were in the land of Israel; and he set masons to hew wrought stones to build the house of God. And David prepared iron in abundance for the nails for the doors of the gates, and for the couplings; and brass in abundance without weight; and cedar-trees without number; for the Zidonians and they of Tyre brought cedar-trees in abundance to David. And David said: 'Solomon my son is young and tender, and the house that is to be builded for the Lord must be exceeding magnificent, of fame and of glory throughout all countries; I will therefore make preparations for him.' So David prepared abundantly before his death. . . .

Now David was old and full of days; and he made Solomon his son king over Israel. And he gathered together all the princes of Israel, with the priests and the Levites. And the Levites were numbered from thirty years old and upward; and their number by their polls, man by man, was thirty and eight thousand. Of these, twenty and four thousand were to oversee the work of the house of the Lord; and six thousand were officers and judges; and four thousand were doorkeepers; and four thousand praised the Lord 'with the instruments which I made to praise therewith.'–I, 22:2-5; 23:1-5.

C.   And Solomon the son of David was strengthened in his kingdom, and the Lord his God was with him, and magnified him exceedingly. . . .

Now Solomon purposed to build a house for the name of the Lord, and a house for his kingdom. . . .

And Solomon sent to Huram the king of Tyre, saying: 'As thou didst deal with David my father, and didst send him cedars to build him a house to dwell therein (even so deal with me). Behold, I am about to build a house for the name of the Lord my God, to dedicate it to Him, and to burn before Him incense of sweet spices, and for the continual showbread, and for the burnt-offerings morning and evening, on the sabbaths, and on the new moons, and on the appointed seasons of the Lord our God. This is an ordinance for ever to Israel. And the house which I build is great; for great is our God above all gods. . . .'–II, 1:1, 18; 2:2-4.

D.   Zedekiah was twenty and one years old when he began to reign; and he reigned eleven years in Jerusalem; and he did that which was evil in the sight of the Lord his God; he humbled not himself before Jeremiah the prophet speaking from the mouth of the Lord. . . .

Therefore He brought upon them the king of the Chaldeans, who slew their young men with the sword in the house of their sanctuary, . . . And they burnt the house of God, and broke down the wall of Jerusalem, and burnt all the palaces thereof with fire, and destroyed all the goodly vessels thereof. And them that had escaped from the sword carried he away to Babylon; and they were servants to him and his sons until the reign of the kingdom of Persia; . . .

Now in the first year of Cyrus king of Persia, that the word of the Lord by the mouth of Jeremiah might be accomplished, the Lord stirred up the spirit of Cyrus king of Persia, that he made a proclamation throughout all his kingdom, and put it also in writing, saying: 'Thus saith Cyrus king of Persia: All the kingdoms of the earth hath the Lord the God of heaven, given me; and He hath charged me to build Him a house in Jerusalem, which is in Judah. Whosoever there is among you of all His people—the Lord his God be with him—let him go up.'—II, 36: 11, 12, 17a, 19, 20, 22, 23.

COMMENTARY

A.   The author rushes through the early history in order to get to King David, who made preparations for the building of the Temple. The opening verses are not even complete sentences. They are simply lists of names of the early generations.

B.   The complete preparation which David made for the building of the Temple, his organization of the Levites to be doorkeepers and musicians is described.

C.   The Temple is built by Solomon with the help of the king of Tyre.

D.   The end of the kingdom of Judah, the Exile, and the end of the Exile with the decree of Cyrus permitting the exiles to return completes this selection.

Questions and Bibliography

QUESTIONS I

1. The author speaks of the Torah as having been the most influential book in the whole history of Judaism. Do you think the Torah has retained this preeminence in modern Liberal Judaism? Support your opinion.
2. The Book of Exodus contains the record of a covenant made between God and Israel. Discuss the idea of such a special covenant in the light of democratic concepts of the present day.
3. Discuss the problem of reconciling the positions of science and religion. Do you agree with the author's solution? Why or why not?
4. What is the primitive religious custom referred to in the story of Abraham's attempted sacrifice of Isaac? Why and how is it significant that Abraham's hand is stayed?
5. How would you interpret the doctrine of "an eye for an eye," etc., which first appears in the Bible in the Book of Exodus?
6. Many regard the story of Joseph as one of the finest narratives in the world. Point out some of the qualities of its excellence.

BIBLIOGRAPHY I

GRAY, G. B., *A Critical Introduction to the Old Testament*, 2nd ed., New York. 1919.

The Pentateuch and Haftorahs, edited by Dr. J. H. Hertz, Soncino Press. 1938. See particularly the commentary.

PETERS, J. P., *The Religion of the Hebrews*, chaps. 1-3, Harvard University Press. 1932.

QUESTIONS II

1. Some critics maintain that Moses was a legendary rather than an historical figure. Would the acceptance of such an assumption affect our interpretation or evaluation of the Bible?
2. Through the use of the following examples trace the development of laws found in Exodus and repeated in Deuteronomy. See: Exod. 21:12-14 and Deut. 19:1-13; Exod. 23:1 and Deut. 19:15-21; Exod. 22:21-24, 23:9 and Deut. 24:17f.; Exod. 22:21 and Deut. 10:19.
3. In your opinion, what should be the importance of home ceremonials in modern Judaism?
4. What is the meaning of the word "holy" as used by the Book of Leviticus? How does this compare with our use of the word today?
5. Do you think that the punishment of Moses and Aaron (not permitting them to enter the Promised Land) was justified?
6. What is the prime religious exhortation of the Deuteronomic editors?

BIBLIOGRAPHY II

See above, chap. 1.

AHAD HA-AM, Essay on Moses, in translation of his essays by Sir Leon Simon.

GREENSTONE, J. H., Numbers with Commentary (The Holy Scriptures), J.P.S. 1939.

REIDER, J., Deuteronomy (ibid.). 1937.

QUESTIONS III

1. According to the Book of Joshua, how much of the conquest of Canaan had actually been accomplished at the time of that leader's death? How does this compare with Judg. 1:29; II Sam. 5:6-9; I Kings 9:16?
2. Describe the general conditions of life and government among the Israelites during the period of the Judges. What was the function of the Judges, and whence did they derive their authority? Were they judges in the modern sense?

3. What were the conditions which seemed to necessitate a king in Israel?
4. What were the contributing factors which led to the division of the kingdom?
5. Discuss the strength and weaknesses of David's character.
6. Discuss the philosophy of history motivating the narrative of these four books. Do world events seem to have borne out such a philosophy?

BIBLIOGRAPHY III

FLEG, EDMOND, *The Life of Solomon.*

GARSTANG, J., *Foundations of Bible History: Joshua and Judges*, London. 1931.

SEGAL, M. H., "Studies in the Books of Samuel" (JQR N.S. 5-10, 1914–1920).

QUESTIONS IV

1. Discuss the origins and development of the prophetic movement in Israel, comparing the early prophets with the later ones. See Exod. 4:14-16; 7:1-2; 1 Sam. 10:5ff.; 9:9; 1 Sam. 19:19-24; Num. 24:2-4; Jer. 1:9.

BIBLIOGRAPHY IV

CORNILL, C. H., *The Prophets of Israel*, Chicago. 1897.

BUTTENWIESER, M., *The Prophets of Israel*, New York. 1914.

SMITH, J. M. P., *The Prophets and Their Times*, chap. I, University of Chicago Press. Revised 1941.

QUESTIONS V

1. Choose one important ethical concept for each of the major prophets and state it in your own words.
2. Describe the differences in the messages of Isaiah, Jeremiah, and Ezekiel.
3. How does Ezekiel differ from the earlier prophets in his feeling about ritual? Compare Amos.
4. What is the belief held by modern Liberal Judaism concerning the coming of the Messiah?

5. Many Christians believe that Jesus fulfilled the servant prophecies of Deutero-Isaiah. What is the traditional Jewish interpretation of these prophecies?

BIBLIOGRAPHY V

BLANK, SHELDON, Studies in Deutero-Isaiah, Hebrew Union College Annual, Vol. 15. 1940.

CALKINS, RAYMOND, Jeremiah the Prophet, Macmillan. 1930.

COHON, BERYL D., The Prophets, Scribner's. 1939.

DRIVER, S. R., Isaiah: His Life and Times (Men of the Bible), New York. 1888.

LOFTHOUSE, W. F., The Prophet of Reconstruction: A Patriot's Ideal for a New Age, London. 1920.

QUESTIONS VI

1. Discuss Amos' attitude towards ritual and sacrifice.
2. What is Hosea's great contribution to prophetic thought?
3. What is the significance of the story of the gourd in Jonah? See Jonah 4:6-11.
4. In what way did the humble background of the prophet Micah affect the tone of his prophecies? Compare with Amos; contrast with Isaiah.

BIBLIOGRAPHY VI

Refer to bibliographies for chapter IV and V above.

QUESTIONS VII

1. The Psalms are considered the greatest expression of the inner feelings of man. Select a few psalms which you feel express these feelings particularly well. Give reasons to support your choices.
2. Compare the idea of suffering as expressed in the Psalms with that expressed in Job. See Psalms, 6, 13, 22, 31, 38, 42, 69, 88, 102, 144; Job 3; 6:1-13; 12:4-6, 14; 16:6-16.
3. Why is the Book of Proverbs referred to as "Wisdom Literature"? Characterize the mood and message of the book.

4. Identify a number of proverbs which have become a part of our every-day language.
5. What answer does the Book of Job give to the question: "Why do the righteous suffer and the wicked prosper if God is just?"
6. What does the Book of Job tell us about our ability to understand God by means of reason alone?

BIBLIOGRAPHY VII

BUTTENWIESER, M., *The Psalms*, University of Chicago Press. 1938.
———, *The Book of Job*, Macmillan. 1922.
PFEIFFER, R. H., *Introduction to the Old Testament*, Part V, chapters I through III, Harper & Bros. 1941.
RANKIN, O. S., *Israel's Wisdom Literature* (Kerr Lectures), London. 1936.

QUESTIONS VIII

1. What is the traditional interpretation of the Song of Songs?
2. What seems to have been the purpose behind the Book of Ruth?
3. Of what event was the Book of Lamentations traditionally considered the expression?
4. What are some of the reasons given to justify the inclusion in the Bible of so pessimistic a book as Ecclesiastes?
5. In what ways do you disagree with the predominant philosophy of the Book of Ecclesiastes? Give reasons.
6. Can you find any religious significance in the Book of Esther? Where?

BIBLIOGRAPHY VIII

BETTAN, ISRAEL, *The Five Scrolls, a Commentary*, U.A.H.C. (In Press.)
DRIVER, S. R., *An Introduction to the Literature of the Old Testament*, chap. x, Scribner's. 1906.
The Five Megilloth, with commentary, Soncino Press.

QUESTIONS IX

1. Characterize apocalyptic literature using examples from the Book of Daniel. What is the purpose of such writings?
2. What two great events took place during the period of Ezra and Nehemiah? Discuss the importance of each.

3. On the basis of its omissions and its emphases, what would you say was the purpose of the Book of Chronicles?

GENERAL BIBLIOGRAPHY

The following general references will be found useful as supplementary material to the specialized bibliographies:

HASTINGS, JAMES, *A Dictionary of the Bible*, Scribner's.

The Jewish Encyclopedia, Funk and Wagnalls.

OESTERLY, W. O. E., & T. H. Robinson, *A History of Israel*, Oxford University Press. 1932.

RADIN, M., *The Life of the People in Biblical Times*, J.P.S.

The following translations of original texts will also prove helpful:

The Chumash, with commentary, Soncino Press.

The Book of Job, with commentary, Soncino Press.

The Old Testament: A New Translation, James Moffatt, New York. 1922.

The New-Century Bible, Oxford University Press.

The Cambridge Bible.